John Hardyng

CHRONICLE

EDITED FROM BRITISH LIBRARY MS LANSDOWNE 204

MIDDLE ENGLISH TEXTS SERIES

GENERAL EDITOR
Russell A. Peck, University of Rochester

ASSOCIATE EDITOR
Alan Lupack, University of Rochester

ASSISTANT EDITOR
Martha Johnson-Olin, University of Rochester

ADVISORY BOARD

The Middle English Texts Series is designed for classroom use. Its goal is to make available to teachers, scholars, and students texts that occupy an important place in the literary and cultural canon but have not been readily available in student editions. The series does not include those authors, such as Chaucer, Langland, or Malory, whose English works are normally in print in good student editions. The focus is, instead, upon Middle English literature adjacent to those authors that teachers need in compiling the syllabuses they wish to teach. The editions maintain the linguistic integrity of the original work but within the parameters of modern reading conventions. The texts are printed in the modern alphabet and follow the practices of modern capitalization, word formation, and punctuation. Manuscript abbreviations are silently expanded, and *u/v* and *j/i* spellings are regularized according to modern orthography. Yogh (ȝ) is transcribed as *g, gh, y,* or *s,* according to the sound in Modern English spelling to which it corresponds; thorn (þ) and eth (ð) are transcribed as *th.* Distinction between the second person pronoun and the definite article is made by spelling the one *thee* and the other *the,* and final *-e* that receives full syllabic value is accented (e.g., *charité*). Hard words, difficult phrases, and unusual idioms are glossed either in the right margin or at the foot of the page. Explanatory and textual notes appear at the end of the text, often along with a glossary. The editions include short introductions on the history of the work, its merits and points of topical interest, and brief working bibliographies.

This series is published in association with the University of Rochester.

Medieval Institute Publications is a program of
The Medieval Institute, College of Arts and Sciences

 WESTERN MICHIGAN UNIVERSITY

John Hardyng

CHRONICLE
EDITED FROM BRITISH LIBRARY MS LANSDOWNE 204

Volume 1

Edited by

James Simpson and Sarah Peverley

TEAMS • Middle English Texts Series • University of Rochester

MEDIEVAL INSTITUTE PUBLICATIONS
Western Michigan University
Kalamazoo

This book is printed by CPI Group (UK) Ltd, Croydon, CR0 4YY on acid-free paper.

Library of Congress Cataloging-in-Publication Data

Hardyng, John, 1378-1465?
  [Chronicle of Ihon Hardyng]
  John Hardyng chronicle : edited from British Library MS Lansdowne 204 / John Hardyng.
    <2> volumes cm. -- (Middle English texts series)
  Includes bibliographical references and index.
  Contents: "Volume 1 edited by James Simpson and Sarah Peverley."
  ISBN 978-1-58044-213-8 (pbk. : alk. paper) -- ISBN 978-1-58044-214-5 (pbk. : alk. paper)
  1. Great Britain--History–To 1485. 2. Great Britain--History--Tudors, 1485-1603. 3. British
Library. Manuscript. Lansdowne 204. I. Simpson, James, 1954- editor. II. Peverley, Sarah,
1976- editor. III. British Library. Manuscript. Lansdowne 204. IV. Title.
  DA130.H35 2015
  942--dc23
                                                                      2015007673

ISBN 978-1-58044-213-8

P 5 4 3 2 1

❦ CONTENTS

LIST OF ILLUSTRATIONS

🌿 ACKNOWLEDGMENTS

James Simpson

In 1983 I received a letter warning me that editing Hardyng required stamina: "Hardyng," the letter commented, "has burned out a great many would-be editors." Had I not been rescued by the co-operative energies of Sarah Peverley, I would myself have joined the club of exhausted Hardyng editors. I am extremely grateful to my co-editor. Tony Edwards first suggested this edition to me in the early 1980s. Clifford Peterson and Christina von Nolcken both generously supplied me with some materials early on, and Janet Cowen gave some sage advice as I set out. In later, though not now recent work, I warmly acknowledge the help of my research assistants Laura Kuruvilla and Julie Orlemanski. More recently, Nicole Miller put in many hours of arduous checking and indexing work that can only be described as heroic. In the final stages, Neil Wright clarified a passage of mangled Latin, for which I am deeply grateful. Above all, I offer thanks and pay homage to my co-editor, the indefatigable Sarah Peverley, with whom it has been a pleasure to work.

Sarah Peverley

My earliest debts are to Wendy Scase, who introduced me to Hardyng in 1998, and Veronica O'Mara, who encouraged me to edit part of his *Chronicle* for my Ph.D. thesis. James Simpson also assisted in those early years, equipping me with a microfilm of Lansdowne 204 and cautionary tales of Hardyng's ability to make the most resilient editors weep. We joined forces several years later, outrageously optimistic that the *Chronicle* could be finished in a couple of years. A decade on, my editorial odyssey has coincided with several life-changing events that James has graciously accepted and supported, despite the delays that they have brought to our project; I hereby thank him for his unfailing encouragement and good humor through what, at times, seemed like an impossible task.

My co-editor and I would like to acknowledge the staff at the University of Rochester for their unceasing energy and patience with this huge endeavor; special thanks go to Russell A. Peck, Martha M. Johnson-Olin, Jenny Boyar, Kara L. McShane, Pamela M. Yee, and former staff John H. Chandler and Ryan Harper, as well as the NEH for sponsoring METS and Medieval Institute Publications, especially Patricia Hollahan. Colleagues in the School of English at The University of Liverpool likewise merit thanks for the backing they have given this edition.

Over the years, many other scholars have provided advice and assistance, including Alan Crosby, Ian Doyle, Alfred Hiatt, Andy King, William Marx, Richard Moll, Laura Nuvoloni, Raluca Radulescu, Felicity Riddy, Lisa Ruch, Kathleen Scott, and Toshiyuki Takamiya. The continued support I've received from Don Kennedy and Erik Kooper merits recognition:

aside from their boundless enthusiasm for Hardyng-related questions, both commented on early drafts and offered perceptive advice.

In the last year, Godfried Croenen, Sean Cunningham, and Paul Dryburgh helped me untangle the Pipe Roll entries relating to Hardyng, Erik Kwakkel read a draft of the Manuscript Description, and staff at The British Library, particularly Sarah Biggs, facilitated the multispectral photography of Lansdowne 204; sincere thanks are due to Christina Duffy for capturing and processing the images and to The British library for their permission to use them.

Lastly, the greatest debt is to my family, who have furnished me with love and devotion throughout this venture. My late grandfather, Ramsey, was unfailingly supportive, helping me through financially bleak times as I pursued an academic career. Stephen, my husband, has lived with the ghost of Hardyng far longer than any sane human being should, but he has indulged my obsession with infinite patience and steadfastness, providing strength and common sense when most needed. Without him and my son, William, who arrived just after the desolation of Arthur's kingdom in Book Three, my 'erthly lyfe' would lack perspective and balance.

A Note on Division of Labor

This edition is profoundly collaborative; all the work has been read and passed by both editors. We were, however, primarily responsible for distinct areas of editorial activity: James Simpson transcribed and checked the text; he also produced the glossary. Sarah Peverley wrote the Introduction and Manuscript Description, the Explanatory Notes, and the Textual Notes.

Dedication

This edition is dedicated to the memory of Ron Simpson, who once told his son that now he'd started something, he'd better finish it. [JS]

and to

Ramsey, Stephen, and William: 'My soules ese and alle my hertes wele.' [SP]

Figure 1. Folio 196r. Pedigree of France. Photo courtesy of The British Library.

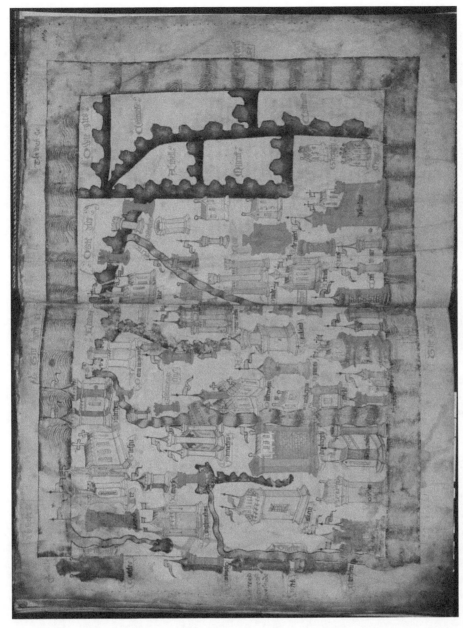

Figure 2. Folios 226v–227r. Map of Scotland. Photo courtesy of The British Library.

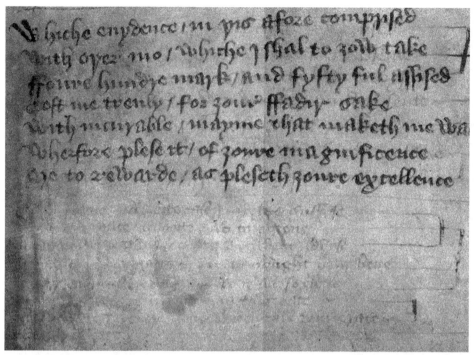

Figure 3. Folio 4r. Evidence of an additional stanza at the end of Hardyng's Prologue. Data captured at 420 nm on the electromagnetic spectrum in two datasets and images montaged in post-processing. Photo courtesy of Dr. Christina Duffy, Conservation Science Team, The British Library and The British Library.

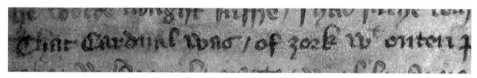

Figure 4. Folio 4r, stanza 2. The third line of the stanza shows evidence of some alteration to the text. The parchment has been scraped away, but partial letters are observed. Image captured at 420 nm on the electromagnetic spectrum. Photo courtesy of Dr. Christina Duffy, Conservation Science Team, The British Library and The British Library.

❧ INTRODUCTION

JOHN HARDYNG'S LIFE

Born *circa* 1378, John Hardyng appears to have been the son of a Northumbrian gentleman.[1] At the age of twelve he was placed in the household of Sir Henry Percy (1364–1403), son of Henry Percy, first earl of Northumberland (1342–1408), where he was brought up and educated as a squire.[2] For the thirteen years he was with Percy, Hardyng's activities were centered on the English Marches, defending the Anglo-Scottish border, and fighting in numerous campaigns against the Scots, most notably at Homildon Hill (1402) and the Siege of Cocklaws Tower (1403).[3] When his patron died rebelling against Henry IV at the Battle of Shrewsbury (1403), Hardyng, now twenty-five, was one of those lucky enough to survive and receive a pardon for fighting on the wrong side.[4]

Shortly after Percy's demise, Hardyng secured a place in the service of Sir Robert Umfraville, whom he would serve until 1437, first at Warkworth, Northumberland (c. 1406), as sub-constable of the castle, and later, after 1421, at South Kyme, Lincolnshire, presumably

---

[1] Notable accounts of Hardyng's life and work include Kingsford, "First Version of Hardyng's Chronicle"; Gransden, *Historical Writing in England II*; Kennedy, *Chronicles and Other Historical Writing*, pp. 2644–47; Peverley, "John Hardyng's *Chronicle*" and "Hardyng, John"; Summerson, "Hardyng, John (b. 1377/8, d. in or after 1464)." Hardyng is referred to as a Northumbrian esquire and soldier in 1416 (*Calendar of Close Rolls: Henry V, 1413–19*, pp. 321–22, m. 13, 16 September 1416). In The National Archives of the UK (hereafter TNA): Public Record Office (hereafter PRO) E 101/330/9, he is referred to as a "gentilman." Peverley discusses Hardyng's possible association with the Hardyngs of Beadnell, Northumberland, particularly Sampson Hardyng, a prominent Northumbrian gentleman and Member of Parliament who had long-standing connections with the Percy and Umfraville families (see "John Hardyng's *Chronicle*," pp. 10–12). King has also identified a "John son of John Hardyng" who held land in Trickley, near Chillingham, who may have been a relation ("'They Have the Hertes of the People by North,'" p. 148n50).

[2] Hardyng provides this information in the prose passages of the second version of his *Chronicle*. See Oxford, Bodleian Library MS Arch. Selden B. 10, fols. 190r and 192r (which is currently being edited by Peverley), and *Chronicle of Iohn Hardyng*, ed. Ellis, p. 353. For Henry Percy, nicknamed "Hotspur," see Walker, "Percy, Sir Henry (1364–1403)."

[3] Neville explores life on the Anglo-Scottish Marches in this period in *Violence, Custom and Law*. Hardyng provides information about the campaigns in the second version of the *Chronicle* (Arch. Selden B. 10 fol. 192r, and *Chronicle of Iohn Hardyng*, ed. Ellis, p. 351).

[4] An instruction from Westminster telling the sheriffs of Northumberland, Cumberland, Westmoreland, and Yorkshire to proclaim that all adherents of the Percies could sue for pardon before the Epiphany can be found in Thomas Rymer's *Foedera, conventiones, literæ*, (8:338, dated 22 November 1403).

as constable of Kyme Castle.[5] In addition to performing the administrative duties associated with his constableship(s), Hardyng continued to serve in a martial capacity, participating in further raids across the border, defending against Scottish incursions, and fighting abroad for Henry V's French inheritance.[6]

Sometime around 1418, Hardyng was commissioned to spy for Henry V. He spent "Thre yere and halfe amonge the enmyté" in Scotland (Prol.44), gathering topographical information in anticipation of an invasion and acquiring documents pertaining to English sovereignty over the smaller realm (the majority of which he forged himself).[7] By his own account, he presented the fruits of his labor to the treasurer at Bois de Vincennes, France, and the king promised him the Manor of Geddington in Northamptonshire as recompense for the "peryle" and "costages grete" that he had incurred (Prol.45–46).[8] Unfortunately, Henry V's premature death in August 1422 devastated Hardyng's prospects, and he received nothing.

Between 1421, when Umfraville inherited the estates of his nephew Gilbert Umfraville, and 1428, Hardyng left Northumberland to take charge of Umfraville's castle at Kyme in Lincolnshire, where he appears to have been based until his master's death in January 1437.[9] According to the *Chronicle*, Hardyng was actively pursuing his interest in history in 1424 when Henry Beaufort, bishop of Winchester, arranged for Julian Cesarini to instruct him in Justin's *Epitome* of Pompeius Trogus's *Philippic History*.[10] Several years later, on 22 June 1429, Hardyng was granted a portable altar, which may indicate that he was preparing

---

[5] Details of Umfraville's career can be found in Summerson, "Umfraville, Sir Robert (d. 1437)." For Hardyng's claim to have been constable of Warkworth, see Arch. Selden B. 10, fol. 158v, and *Chronicle of Iohn Hardyng*, ed. Ellis, p. 361.

[6] Hardyng claims to have fought with Umfraville at Harfleur (1415), Agincourt (1415), and on the Seine (1416); though plausible, extant muster rolls fail to verify his presence in the 1415 campaign. James Hamilton Wylie and William Templeton Waugh note that Hardyng's "name occurs among others not bound by indentures" in Hunter's study of Agincourt (*Reign of Henry the Fifth*, 2:192), and Robert Umfraville's retinue of twenty men-at-arms and forty archers is recorded in Nicolas, *History of the Battle of Agincourt*, p. 385. An indenture between the king and Umfraville for the relief of Harfleur survives in TNA: PRO E 101/69/8/540. The Close Rolls confirm that Umfraville and Hardyng were back in England by September 1416 following the battle on the Seine; Umfraville had to act as mainpernor for his esquires, Hardyng and Nicholas Rothdone, until he could prove that they had all returned with the sanction of John, duke of Bedford (see *Calendar of Close Rolls: Henry V, 1413–19*, pp. 321–22, m. 13, 16 September 1416).

[7] The most recent study of Hardyng's forgeries is Hiatt, *Medieval Forgeries*.

[8] Reference to the presentation at Bois Vincennes is made in the second version of the *Chronicle*, see Arch. Selden B. 10, fols. 129r, 129v, and 135r, and *Chronicle of Iohn Hardyng*, ed. Ellis, pp. 292, 293, 306.

[9] Hardyng is styled as "of Kyme," or associated with the county of Lincolnshire, in a number of documents dating between 1428 and 1467/68: see, for example, TNA: PRO C 241/225/6 (dated 14 November 1433, but referring to 22 January 1428); *Calendar of Entries in the Papal Registers: Papal Letters, 1427–47*, p. 131 (22 June 1429); and *Calendar of Patent Rolls: Henry VI, 1429–36*, p. 382, m. 25 (1434).

[10] Henry Ellis believes that Hardyng traveled to Rome for his instruction (*Chronicle of Iohn Hardyng*, p. vii), but Kingsford proposes that Cesarini tutored him during his visit to England as a papal envoy in 1426–27 ("First Version of Hardyng's *Chronicle*," p. 464).

to travel on military or other business,[11] and in the summer of 1434, pursuant to an act of the 1433 parliament, he was one of seventy-three members of the Lincolnshire gentry required to take an oath "not to maintain peacebreakers."[12]

In the years that followed, Hardyng sporadically delivered additional Scottish documents to Henry VI, petitioning him to honor the reward his father had pledged.[13] He claims to have visited Scotland again in 1435, offering the king a forged safe conduct from James I as evidence of his trip, but the new items that he deposited in the treasury in July 1440 and November 1457 were counterfeit and it is unlikely that he left England.[14] Hardyng was never gifted Geddington Manor, but after his submission of 1440 he secured an annuity of ten pounds from the Manor of Willoughton, Lincolnshire, which he appears to have received until the mid 1450s.[15]

---

[11] *Calendar of Entries in the Papal Registers: Papal Letters, 1427–47*, p. 131 (22 June 1429). Interestingly, the prior of the Augustinian priory at Kyme, Robert Ludburgh, and another John Hardyng, "donsel, of the diocese of Lincoln" were also granted portable altars in June 1429; though this may be a coincidence, the entries could indicate that all three men planned to travel together and that Hardyng's namesake was related to him in some way.

[12] *Rotuli Parliamentorum*, IV:421–22, and *Calendar of Patent Rolls: Henry VI, 1429–36*, p. 382, m. 25 (1434).

[13] Submissions mentioned in the first version of the *Chronicle* include a batch of documents presented to the king at Easthampstead Manor in 1440 (Prol.48–49), which is corroborated by *Calendar of Patent Rolls: Henry VI, 1436–1441*, p. 431, m. 15, (15 July 1440), and a petition made to the king in 1451, which was thwarted by Cardinal John Kemp (Prol.113–33); there are no governmental records relating to the alleged petition of 1451, but it coincides with the fact that Hardyng's annuity from Willoughton was resumed under the 1449 Resumption Act. The pending delivery of the documents Hardyng gave to the treasury in November 1457 is alluded to at Prol.149 and corroborated by TNA: PRO E 39/96/3 (15 November 1457) and *Calendar of Patent Rolls: Henry VI, 1452–61*, p. 393 m. 8, (18 Nov 1457).

[14] The forged safe conduct is extant in TNA: PRO E 39/2/9 (dated 10 March 1435). Summerson also agrees that Hardyng probably did not cross the border (see "Hardyng, John").

[15] The pipe rolls for the period 1440/1 to 1467/8 (TNA: PRO E 372/286 to E 372/313) contain detailed references to Hardyng's annuity and the administrative processes associated with it. Despite some confusion with the original grant — the manor had already been issued to John Middleton in 1438 at a rent of ten pounds and on 12 September 1449, it was granted again to Henry, archbishop of Canterbury, and others — Hardyng appears to have received the award without difficulty until the manor was resumed in 1449. On 31 July 1441 the reversion of the manor was granted to the provost and scholars of King's College, Cambridge, and the college was later granted exemption from the Resumption Acts of 1449 and 1450. Though investigations into the true value of Willoughton Manor were undertaken in the early 1450s, Hardyng appears to have continued claiming his annuity and paying his two-shilling rent until c. 1454, but annotations and additional entries in the pipe rolls concerning Richard Hansard and Richard Wenslow, escheators for Lincolnshire, suggest that he did not receive the income after that. The pipe rolls for the period 1454 to 1464 (TNA: PRO E 372/300 to E 372/309) and 1466 to 1468 (TNA: PRO E 372/312 to E 372/313) show an accrual of debt where Hardyng's annual two-shilling rent is in arrears, though the exchequer annotations suggest that the copying of the terms of Hardyng's grant up to 1468 had continued in error. On TNA: PRO E 372/309 the debt is paid off; on E 372/313 it is discharged. A petition from Hardyng to Henry VI (in French) and a grant under the sign manual relating to the annuity survive in TNA: PRO C 81/1432/53 and C 81/1432/54; see also *Calendar of Patent Rolls: Henry VI, 1436–1441*, p. 431, m. 15 (15 July 1440). For

By October 1440 Hardyng, now in his sixties, was ensconced at the Augustinian Priory of South Kyme as a corrodiary, paying twelve pence a week for his upkeep. As a long-term resident of Kyme, he was already familiar with the canons and regularly sat and ate with them in the frater, a liberty that gave Brother Thomas Durham, warden of the chapel of St. Thomas of Northolme (a cell of Kyme), grounds for complaint during Bishop Alnwick's visitation to the house.[16]

We do not know the precise year that Hardyng began composing the first version of his history of Britain, but at 18,782 lines of verse and seven folios of prose, he undoubtedly spent the much of the 1450s, perhaps even some of the 1440s, working on it.[17] The prologue indicates that it was completed in 1457, probably just before November, when it was apparently presented to Henry VI with six articles relating to English suzerainty in Scotland. Hardyng was rewarded with a yearly rent of twenty pounds out of the revenues of the county of Lincolnshire.[18] Yet, whether the new award enriched or frustrated Hardyng is difficult to determine; while the Willoughton annuity is recorded repeatedly on the pipe rolls (sometimes even in error), the extant accounts of the county farm from which the 1457 grant was to be paid are so poor that it is impossible to tell whether Hardyng received the new income. Like others with similar grants in this period, it is feasible that the chronicler

the problems associated with the original grant of Willoughton Manor, see *Calendar of Patent Rolls: Henry VI, 1436–1441*, p. 490, m. 14 (1 December 1440), p. 484, m. 19 (22 December 1440), and p. 557, m. 18 (31 July 1441); Cambridge University, King's College Archive Centre KCE/11 and KCE/136 (reversion of Willoughton, 1441); and TNA: PRO E 159/217 (King's Remembrancer Memoranda Rolls, Hilary Term "Brevia Directa Baronibus"). Additional documents relating to the resumption of the manor and its value can be found in TNA: PRO E 101/330/9 and Cambridge University, King's College Archive Centre KCE/20. Other documents relating to the manor in this period include Cambridge University, King's College Archive Centre WIL/47 (accounts from 1450–54); WIL/48 (account of John Kydwell, bailiff, 29 September 1455); KCE/106 (accounts 1459–60); KCE/110 (accounts 1460–61); WIL/34 (two indentures for the lease of Willoughton by King's College to Richard Langton, 1463).

[16] Thompson, ed., *Visitations in the Diocese of Lincoln*, 2:168–170.

[17] Kingsford suggests that parts of the text were written between 1447 and 1450, though the evidence he cites could also be interpreted in favor of a slightly later date, see "First Version of Hardyng's Chronicle," pp. 473–75. Riddy also speculates that Hardyng began writing in the mid 1440s, prompted by increased financial demands for his upkeep at the priory, but there is no evidence for this. Despite a complaint from Brother Durham about Hardyng only paying twelve pence a week for his corrody, there is no reference to Bishop Alnwick addressing the issue in the record of his visitation (see Riddy, "Wars of the Roses," pp. 94–95). At any rate, Hardyng probably had sufficient surplus from his Willoughton annuity to cover additional expenses. If financial instability compelled Hardyng to begin writing, or to finish a work he had already begun, the resumption of his annuity in 1449 seems to provide a more likely stimulus.

[18] See *Calendar of Patent Rolls: Henry VI, 1452–61*, p. 393, m. 8 (18 November 1457); *Calendar of Close Rolls: Henry VI, 1454–61*, p. 235, m. 28 (18 November 1457); and TNA: PRO E 159/234, the King's Remembrancer Memoranda Rolls for Michaelmas 1457 ("Recorda" and "Brevia directa baronibus" sections). An indenture bearing Hardyng's seal, dated 15 November 1457, records the delivery of several Scottish documents to the treasury (TNA: PRO E 39/96/3); see also Palgrave, *Documents and Records*, pp. 373–78 and Peverley, "John Hardyng's *Chronicle*," pp. 659–60 (with image). A transcript of a memorandum relating to the delivery occurs in Palgrave, *Antient Kalendars and Inventories*, II:234–35.

encountered difficulties because the annuity had been issued out of the overstretched Lincolnshire revenues.[19]

Equally opaque is the moment that Hardyng decided to rewrite the *Chronicle* for Richard, Duke of York. Having not long finished the first version, over which he had labored so long, he set about revising and condensing his history of Britain to promote York's claim to the throne. Parts of the new text could only have been written between York's election as Henry VI's heir on 8 November 1460 and his death at the battle of Wakefield on 31 December 1460, but it is impossible to tell whether Hardyng commenced work before this. It is likely that he only started his second text after York's election, yet anytime between November 1457 and December 1460 is feasible, especially when the *Chronicle* is considered alongside other items circulating in the late 1450s which explained and celebrated York's genealogy.[20]

Undeterred by York's death, and perhaps in hope of a new grant or the prolongation of his 1457 annuity (if he had been receiving it from the Lincolnshire revenues), Hardyng continued revising the work for York's son and heir, Edward IV.[21] Now in his eighties, he also submitted two Scottish documents to the king at Leicester.[22] Ever persistent in his literary endeavors, he came close to completing over 12,400 lines of the new *Chronicle* before he died, presumably sometime around 1465.[23]

It was the second, unfinished version of Hardyng's *Chronicle* that went on to enjoy a degree of popularity under the Yorkist and Tudor dynasties, surviving today in twelve

---

[19] Only three accounts for the county farm for Lincolnshire are extant for this period: TNA: PRO E 199/23/37 (covering 1454–56), E 199/24/3 (covering 1464–66), and E 199/24/4 (1465–67). Of these, the first is irrelevant because Hardyng's annuity had not been awarded. The second and third, dating from around the time of Hardyng's death, are similarly unhelpful and do not contain any information pertinent to Hardyng, but he may have already passed away, or lost his second annuity when Edward acceded to the throne. Two of the pipe rolls concerning Hardyng's 1440 annuity are, nevertheless, important to our understanding of the 1457 grant. The accounts for the sheriff's farm in TNA: PRO E 372/307 (1461–62) and E 372/308 (1462–63) are incomplete, but at the top of the relevant section of E 372/307, there is a memorandum noting that the sheriff, Thomas Blount, had been pardoned for not returning a complete account. Although the documents relate to the reign of Edward IV, they raise the question of how well the Lincolnshire accounts were being kept and recorded. Griffiths has commented on the problems facing sheriffs in the mid–1450s, noting that problems with revenues seem "to have been most serious in Lincs" (*Reign of Henry VI*, p. 769n195).

[20] The issue of Hardyng's revision for York is discussed in Peverley, "Genealogy and John Hardyng's Verse *Chronicle*" and "John Hardyng's *Chronicle*." For contemporary examples of Yorkist genealogical rolls see Allan, "Political Propaganda Employed by the House of York" and "Yorkist Propaganda."

[21] We have been unable to locate any records re-confirming Hardyng's grant under Edward IV.

[22] Arch. Selden B. 10, fol. 139v, and *Chronicle of Iohn Hardyng*, ed. Ellis, p. 317. The documents appear to be copies of items previously given to Henry VI.

[23] The last datable entry in the second version of the *Chronicle* — a reference to Edward IV's queen Elizabeth Woodville — could not have been added before September 1464. The pipe roll entries concerning Hardyng's Willoughton grant continue to mention the annuity until 1468, but they seem to have been copied in error and, unfortunately, cannot be taken as a reliable indicator that Hardyng was alive (or dead).

manuscripts, several fragments, and two printed editions of 1543.[24] The first version, arguably Hardyng's greater achievement, remained relatively unknown, despite the fact that the Tudor historiographer and antiquarian John Stow drew upon it for his own works. Extant only in London, British Library MS Lansdowne 204, almost certainly Hardyng's presentation copy, it is edited here in its entirety for the first time.

THE *CHRONICLE*: IMPORTANCE, THEMES, STYLE

As one of only a handful of texts written in the twilight years of Henry VI's reign, Hardyng's first *Chronicle* offers a compelling insight into the tastes, hopes, and anxieties of a late fifteenth-century gentleman who had witnessed, and all too often participated in, each of the key events that defined his era. Hardyng's interest in the kingdom's past is typical of the gentry's enthusiasm for works of an historical nature, while his ubiquitous concern with war, duty, and the restoration of "lawe and pese" (4.1676) reflects the importance of such matters to men of his rank, who served the nobility in martial and administrative roles and who were frequently relied upon to "dispense justice" for the crown.[25] In lamenting the disorder in "every shire" (7.1009), the problems arising from maintenance (7.1044–50), the widespread neglect of the "pore mennes cause" (7.1013), the loss of territories abroad, and the threat of invasion, Hardyng's work also captures the sense of exasperation at the aristocratic feuds and ineffectual governance that dominated the 1450s and that led, as the *Chronicle* forewarns, to Henry VI's deposition (7.1030–36, 7.1058–64).

Yet for all this, the political immediacy of the *Chronicle* and its relationship with other fifteenth-century literature has been largely overshadowed by Hardyng's decision to submit the work to his sovereign with six forged documents pertaining to Scotland's vassal status. Many critics have claimed that the text's association with the documents and its repeated engagement with the "Scottish issue" indicate that it was composed to provide a context for the forgeries and to strengthen Hardyng's plea for remuneration for the services rendered to Henry V across the border.[26] While there is no doubt that the *Chronicle* and the paratextual materials annexed to it, such as the map of Scotland, invasion plan, and Latin letters to Boniface VIII, are designed to justify England's sovereignty over Scotland and equip Henry VI with everything he needs to assert his title as overlord, diplomatically or militarily,

---

[24] For the manuscripts see Edwards, "Manuscripts and Texts"; and Peverley, "John Hardyng's *Chronicle*," pp. 47–118; and "Adapting to Readeption in 1470–1471."

[25] For recent studies of the gentry see Mercer, *Medieval Gentry*, p. 4; and Radulescu and Truelove, eds., *Gentry Culture in Late Medieval England*.

[26] Kingsford was the first to suggest this in "First Version of Hardyng's *Chronicle*," pp. 466, 468. Critics repeating Kingsford's opinion include Gransden, *Historical Writing in England II*, pp. 276–77 (though Gransden does acknowledge the other dimensions of Hardyng's work); Kennedy, "John Hardyng and the Holy Grail," p. 190; Riddy, "Wars of the Roses," p. 94; and MacDonald, "John Hardyng, Northumbrian Identity and the Scots," p. 30. For an alternative view see Peverley, "Anglo-Scottish Relations."

Hardyng's disquiet at the unrest in England is too prominent for the text to have been written solely to endorse the conquest of Scotland and elicit a reward.[27]

Throughout the history, Scotland is representative of a much larger inheritance, portions of which are portrayed as lost or endangered. Drawing on Geoffrey of Monmouth's *Historia Regum Britanniae*, Robert Mannyng's *Chronicle*, and a version of the Latin Prose *Brut* as his principal sources, Hardyng incorporates his knowledge of Scotland's history, geography, and people alongside material from romance, hagiography, instructional and chivalric literature, polemic, occasional poetry, and Boethian tragedy to tell the story of Britain's past and define the extent of the king's dominion and obligations.[28] Henry VI is heir to the thrones of England, Wales, Scotland, Ireland, France, and Jerusalem, heir to an ancient system of law that he is obliged to uphold, heir to a great nation of Christian souls that he is sworn to protect, and heir to a body of knights whose duty it is to help preserve peace and govern.

Each aspect of the king's birthright has its own history woven into the more familiar account of Britain's past or underlined in the marginalia accompanying the text. The basis of fifteenth-century law, for example, is said to date back to ancient Greece, the home of Albion's founder, Albine, who invokes "the law and consuetude" of Greece with regards to the inheritance of property when claiming the island as her own. By plotting the evolution of British and, later, English law through the enhancements made to it by Brutus (2.667m–678, 2.807–834), Dunwallo (2.1521m), Marcian (2.1850m–1858), Constantine I (3.526m), Aurilius Ambrosius (3.1857–70), Uther Pendragon (3.2045–49), Arthur (3.2477–78, 3.2601–10, 3.2730–33, 3.3290m–3324), Galahad (3.3115–26), Edwin (4.754–81), Elfride (4.2395–2406), Edgar (4.2880–2889), Edward the Martyr (4.2916–20), Edmund Ironside (4.3184–90), William the Conqueror (5.242–52), William Rufus (5.388–92), Edward I (6.99–112, 127–61, 546–52), Edward II (6.1372–85), and Henry V (7.589–651), Hardyng is able to emphasize the seriousness of Henry VI's role as "chefe justyse" of the realm (7.631) and encourage the king to prioritize a fair judicial system like his greatest ancestors did. Time and again, the *Chronicle* shows that rulers who fail to maintain "lawe and pese" (4.1676), like the last British king Cadwallader, court civil war, which ultimately results in the loss of their kingdom and invasion by foreign enemies.

Lest the immediacy of such episodes escapes his audience, Hardyng uses various rhetorical techniques, such as parallelism and exclamation, to highlight the similarities between episodes of lawlessness and accentuate the relevance of past losses to contemporary disturbances. The "compleynte and lamentacioun" of Cadwallader "at his departynge oute

---

[27] Hardyng's decision to include the Latin letters to Pope Boniface is in keeping with other chroniclers' use of, and response to, materials associated with Edward I's "Great Cause." *The Chronicon de Lanercost*, for example, uses Edward's correspondence "almost *verbatim*" to describe the destruction of Hexham in 1296; Pierre de Langtoft, likewise bases his *Political Letters* on the documents and later includes them in his Anglo-Norman verse *Chronicle*; and Scottish chroniclers, like John of Fordun, incorporate articles issued in defence of the Scottish cause in their works. See the following entries in Dunphy, ed., *Encyclopedia of the Medieval Chronicle*, Ruddick, "Chronicon de Lanercost," 1:357–58; Summerfield, "Pierre de Langtoft," 2:1216–17; and Kennedy, "John of Fordun," 2:931–32.

[28] Further discussion of, and information about, individual sources is provided in the Explanatory Notes. Peverley discusses the influence of late fifteenth-century polemic on the *Chronicle* in "Political Consciousness." Hardyng's use of Boethian works and occasional poetry is explored in her "Chronicling the Fortunes of Kings."

of Bretayne into his shyppe" (4.1657m), is a case in point. Hardyng alters his sources' account of the king's speech, allowing him to proclaim:

> O God, mercy, I am defaute of alle
> That chastysed not the friste rebellioun   *first*
> Thrugh whiche this wo importable ys befalle   *intolerable*
> That we ere putte oute from oure regioun.
> O lorde, seth I had keped unyoun   *if*
> The lawe and pese with alle my hole pusance   *power*
> Than had not falle on us this hiegh vengeance. (4.1671–77)

In blaming the ruin of Britain on Cadwallader's failure to chastise "the friste rebellioun" that arose during his reign, Hardyng creates a marked correspondence with periods of civil strife in other epochs. Looking backwards, we are reminded of Albine and her sisters, who are exiled in a ship by the "right excellent" king of Greece as punishment for their rebellion against their husbands (1.2); soon after, the sisters lose control of their new home, Albion, as a result of their failure to imitate their father's good rule and castigate the strife among their giant progeny. Looking forwards, Hardyng echoes Cadwallader's lament when he advises Henry VI to reprimand "the firste mysreule and violence" occurring in his realm, because the earliest, unpunished violations of a monarch's laws will develop into larger, unmanageable problems:

> **Principiis obsta ne deterius contingat**
> **[Resist the first encroachments, lest worse should befall you]**

> Bot thus I drede fulle sore, withouten gabbe,   *idle talk*
> Of suche riottes shalle ryse a more mescheve   *greater harm*
> And thrugh the sores unheled wylle brede a skabbe
> So grete that may noght bene restreynt in breve.   *quickly*
> Wharfore, gode lorde, iff ye wylle gyffe me leve,
> I wolde say thus unto youre excellence:
> Withstonde the firste mysreule and violence.

> **Nota**

> Wythstonde, gode lorde, begynnynge of debate
> And chastyse welle also the ryotours
> That in eche shire bene now consociate
> Agayn youre pese, and alle thaire maynetenours.
> For treuly els wylle falle the fayrest flours
> Of youre coroune and noble monarchy
> Whiche God defende and kepe thrugh his mercy. (7.1023m–1036)

While Hardyng takes care to emphasize the destructive nature of disobedience and conflict, he also tempers the miserable periods of British history with positive portrayals of concord, or "pese." Junctures where justice is privileged and administered impartially are depicted as supremely beneficial to the nation, for the peace that ensues from a contented people provides the foundation on which a monarch can build a more prosperous kingdom and expand his territories abroad. Cultivating stability at home, Hardyng suggests, will allow Henry VI to reclaim the lost parts of his territorial inheritance because, as is evidenced by Henry V's successes in France, "The pese at home and law so wele conserved" are "rote and hede of alle grete conqueste" (7.603–04). As the *Chronicle* draws to a close, it promises that if the king takes care of England — his principal charge — the realm will unite behind him in his pursuit of former vassals, like Scotland, and none will withstand his "noble monarchy" (7.1078).

Read in this context, the two petitions for reward that frame the *Chronicle*, and encourage Henry VI to honor Hardyng's outstanding remuneration, take on new meaning; Hardyng becomes an "Everyman" figure who has suffered great misfortune that only the king can assuage. Operating on a microcosmic and macrocosmic level, he represents both the individual plight of the loyal, long-suffering subject and all distressed Englishmen who desire justice. Just as it is in Henry VI's power to alleviate the chronicler's financial hardship by fulfilling his father's promise of a reward, so it is in his power to alleviate England's suffering by maintaining his father's legacy and restoring justice and peace to the realm.[29]

Though Hardyng outlines his grievances to the king in the Prologue and Book 7, he does not explicitly lay the blame for existing wrongs with him. Instead, he censures the "lordes that suffre the law and pese mysledde" (3.253) for abusing their power and failing to assist the king in maintaining the realm.[30] Communicating the rest of his grievances and advice to "prynces and lordes of hye estate" (2.1486) and "the lordes that have reule of kynges counsaylle" (5.505m), Hardyng underlines the importance of the nobility to the body politic and makes the aristocracy's customary role as protectors of the common weal one of the *Chronicle's* most prominent narrative threads.[31] The hopes of the realm depend not only on Henry asserting his royal prerogative and punishing those who shape the law to meet their own needs, but also on all those in positions of power who put duty before personal gain.

The concept of a symbiotic relationship between king and aristocracy is introduced at the start of the Prologue, when Hardyng claims to be writing so that Henry VI, his wife, Margaret of Anjou, and his son, Prince Edward, will know the extent of Henry's dominion and appreciate how the land has been "kept alway of greet pushance, / With baronage and lordes of dignyté" (Prol.10–11). From here in, readers can trace the illustrious history of the island's nobility and its service to successive kings, beginning with the Trojan exiles who help Brutus to build "New Troy," right down to the late fifteenth-century marcher lords protecting the Anglo-Scottish borders for Henry VI. Just as Hardyng uses historical exemplarity to highlight the best and worst characteristics of former sovereigns for his king, so he offers models of good and bad conduct for England's lords. Members of contemporary chivalric orders, such as the Order of the Garter, are encouraged to see their own fraternities as the natural successors of earlier organizations like King Arthur's Knights of the Round Table or Galahad's "ordour of Saynte Grale" (3.3038m), and all men of status

---

[29] For a more detailed discussion of Hardyng's petitionary stance see Peverley, "Dynasty and Division," and "Chronicling the Fortunes of Kings." However, Peverley herewith revises the comments made in these articles about the pipe rolls testifying to Hardyng's financial security; since the publication of these articles Peverley has identified additional entries in the rolls and located several other documents relating to the manor, which appear to indicate that Hardyng's annuity was affected by the Resumption Act of 1449, and that he was not receiving an income from Willoughton by the mid to late 1450s, when the *Chronicle* was nearing completion and the petitionary prologue was being composed.

[30] There are obvious connections with other writers' use of the "wicked advisers" trope; for more on this see Rosenthal, "King's 'Wicked Advisers,'" and Peverley, "Political Consciousness," p. 3.

[31] See, for example, 2.1486–1492, 3.246m–280, 3.3962–68, 5.505m–518, 5.2344–64, 6.1575–88.

are encouraged to imitate the chivalric conduct of Hardyng's late patron, Sir Robert Umfraville, whom the *Chronicle* depicts as the best of knights.

Although the *Chronicle* draws on traditional representations of kingship and nobility, and is particularly indebted to "Mirrors for Princes" literature, Hardyng's concern with the influence of overmighty magnates, his request that they refrain from avenging personal slights and cooperate peacefully, and his appeal to the king to take action against corruption reflect the unique circumstances of Henry VI's reign and the root of the social and political unrest in the 1450s. As Hardyng notes, members of the Privy Council had wielded unprecedented power during the king's long minority, but some council members were more dominant than others and friction had developed between them. When Henry began ruling independently, the authority of his councillors should have lessened, but he remained dependent on favorites, who retained immense power and often abused their influence for personal gain. Thrown into that mix was Richard, Duke of York, who, as the next in line for the throne until Henry produced an heir, became increasingly discontent with the roles assigned to him.[32] The situation was exacerbated when the king suffered a mental collapse and was unable to govern; rivalry amongst the governing elite deepened under York's protectorate and later erupted into open warfare at the battle of St. Albans (1455), the conflict commonly held to mark the start of The Wars of the Roses.

In reminding the Privy Council that the king has merely "lente" (5.514) the rule to them and that he has the power to bring them down if he discovers that they have abused their position, Hardyng appears to have penned at least part of Book 5 during such a moment of crisis, when the king was either too young or too sick to exercise his will unaided and the council had responsibility for the governance "everiche a dele," or in every particular (5.514). Though this precise interjection could have been composed any time before Henry's minority ended in 1437, its correspondence with other interjections bemoaning increased violence in the localities suggests that it was most likely written during one of Henry's bouts of illness in 1453–54, or 1455–56, when the council officially oversaw matters for the king once again under York's second protectorate.

The "historical mythology" that Hardyng creates for England's lords teaches that the best periods in the country's history occur when the body politic is healthy and harmonious: when the lower ranks are protected by those of higher status, and given fair recourse to justice, and when those of higher status work with the king for the greater good of the realm.[33] On occasions when the body politic sickens on account of a deficient king or a self-serving noble, Hardyng often introduces snippets of Boethian philosophy from the works of English poets, such as Chaucer's *Troilus and Criseyde*, to accentuate the tragic nature of the situation and offer

---

[32] An overview of the period can be found in Wolffe, *Henry VI*; Griffiths, *Reign of Henry VI*; and Watts, *Henry VI and the Politics of Kingship*. York's career is discussed in P. Johnson's *Duke Richard of York 1411–1460* and Watts, "Richard of York, third duke of York (1411–1460)."

[33] For the concept of an "historical mythology of chivalry" in medieval texts see Keen, *Chivalry*, pp. 102–24. Part of the value of Hardyng's *Chronicle* also lies in the insight it offers into the exploits of those Hardyng served. Offering information about fourteenth- and fifteenth-century affairs that is not available anywhere else, Hardyng presents the families of his former patrons as paragons of good conduct.

readers their own "Consolation of Philosophy."[34] Despite the fact that the *Chronicle* ends with England's fortunes at an all time low — invoking images of the "world-turned-upside down" with murderers roaming free in the localities, barons maintaining malefactors, justices of the peace acting neither justly or peacefully, and wars being fought between Englishmen rather than against enemies abroad — the pattern established by the history, whereupon disaster follows prosperity and prosperity follows disaster, offers hope for the future: it suggests that Fortune's wheel will turn upwards again once those in power champion the common weal. In reality, things only got worse for Henry VI, who was overthrown within a few years of Hardyng's poignant appeal for action, but the *Chronicle* stands as a testament to the hope entertained by men like Hardyng that, despite all of the difficulties of his rule, the king could still restore order and be the figurehead the nation needed.

We cannot know for certain how Henry VI reacted to the *Chronicle;* the fact that Hardyng was rewarded with a second annuity after submitting the text and forged documents does not, unfortunately, prove that the king was delighted with the work, or that he even read it, merely that Hardyng's earlier service to the crown in Scotland was acknowledged and compensated. Nevertheless, the timing of Hardyng's presentation is crucial to our understanding of how topical the text was and how it *might* have been received. In November 1457, the same month that Hardyng was in London to put his seal to the indenture recording the Treasury's receipt of his forgeries, the king's Great Council convened at Westminster "to tackle the pressing political problems of the kingdom," particularly, it seems, the on-going hostilities between the Yorkist lords and the heirs of those killed at St. Albans, and the threat of foreign invasion.[35] When discussions could not be "fully concluded," Henry VI arranged for the meeting to reconvene in January because the "wele" of the land and people remained "in greet juparte."[36] According to John Whethamstede, the king was inspired to seek peace between his magnates after reading several books of advice and Scripture. The theme of his address to the lords when the council assembled once again was based on the gospels' warning that "Every kingdom divided amongst itself shall be made desolate."[37] In his speech Henry aligned his own desire for peace with that of God, citing examples of historic and recent kingdoms ruined through civil division, and emphasizing the susceptibility of war-torn realms to invasion.[38] The reconciliation, or "Love Day" that followed on 25 March, once a settlement had been agreed

---

[34] On this topic see Peverley, "Chronicling the Fortunes of Kings," who discusses Hardyng's use of poetry by Geoffrey Chaucer, John Lydgate, and John Walton. Hardyng's borrowings from Chaucer were first identified by Edwards in "Hardyng's *Chronicle* and *Troilus and Criseyde*," p. 156, and "Troilus and Criseyde and the First Version of Hardyng's Chronicle," pp. 12–13. For Hardyng's use of Gower's *Cronica Tripertita* see Moll, "Gower's Cronica Tripertita and the Latin Glosses to Hardyng's Chronicle," and Peverley, "Dynasty and Division."

[35] Griffiths, *Reign of Henry VI*, p. 805.

[36] Nicolas, ed., *Proceedings and Ordinances of the Privy Council of England*, 6:290–91.

[37] Riley, ed., *Registrum Abbatiae Johannis Whethamstede*, 1:295–96 ["sacro Evangelio teste, haberet omne regnum in se divisum, si non statim susciperet unionem, in desolationem ire": "according to the sacred gospel, every kingdom divided against itself shall pass into desolation if it does not assume unity at once"]. Compare Matthew 12:25, Mark 3:25, and Luke 11:17.

[38] Riley, ed., *Registrum Abbatiae Johannis Whethamstede*, 1:296–97.

between the lords, saw the Yorkist magnates and the heirs of the Lancastrians slain at St. Albans process hand in hand around London in a public display of unity.

Though historians have noted the shallowness of York's reunion with the court faction, which, according to another English writer, "endured nat long,"[39] and though Whethamstede was no doubt indulging his poetic licence by claiming that the king was inspired to seek accord by books of advice and scripture, the events of November 1457 and the following four months highlight the social and political currency of Hardyng's *Chronicle* and the significance that Hardyng's contemporaries attached to the notion of supplying "good advice" to a sovereign. Embodying all of the topics touched upon in Henry VI's alleged speech to his council, Hardyng's first work, for all its reliance on traditional models of British history, could only have been borne out of the crises that troubled Henry's reign. It is precisely the sort of book that Whethamstede had in mind when he imagined Henry contemplating the troubles of his kingdom, and it is precisely the sort of book that Henry might have drawn examples from in his speech to reiterate the perils of civil war.

Instructional, inspiring, and anchored by the same rhetorical tropes, Boethian frame of reference, and rhyme-royal or "Chaucerian" stanza underpinning other fifteenth-century vernacular "public poetry," the *Chronicle* uses historical exemplarity to highlight the transience of divided nations and the susceptibility of kings and highborn men to the vicissitudes of Fortune.[40] Engaging with traditional, yet historically specific themes, such as war, lawlessness, justice, ineffectual leadership, and self-governance, it is far from being the product of a "self-serving" old man.[41] More accurately, the first version of the *Chronicle* is the invention of a remarkable individual, who had lived through the reigns of four very different kings, witnessed the rise and fall of England's fortunes at home and abroad, and felt the impact of peace degenerating into civil war. When he gifted the text to Henry, Hardyng could not have known that he would go on to revise his work for Henry VI's political rival; instead he must have believed that his legacy would be that he advised "prynces and lordes of hye estate" (2.1486) how to reinvigorate the country's "fayrest floures" of law and peace (7.1056).

MANUSCRIPT DESCRIPTION

London, British Library MS Lansdowne 204 is a mid-fifteenth-century manuscript consisting of 230 parchment folios, measuring 430 mm by 300 mm, and four unfoliated paper flyleaves (ii + 230 + ii).[42] It was produced in Lincolnshire or the East Midlands in the

---

[39] *An English Chronicle 1377–1461*, p. 77.

[40] Hardyng's use of autobiographical material is comparable with that of Hoccleve in *The Regiment of Princes*.

[41] Riddy, "Wars of the Roses," p. 94.

[42] Other descriptions of Lansdowne 204 have been published in Ellis and Douce, *Catalogue of the Lansdowne Manuscripts*, II:73; and the British Library's Online *Catalogue of Illuminated Manuscripts*. We are particularly grateful to the staff of the Manuscripts Reading Room at the British Library for their kind assistance during our visits and for allowing Lansdowne 204 to be photographed. Special thanks go to Sarah J. Biggs and Christina Duffy for their assistance with, and execution of, the multispectral imaging.

1450s and was probably commissioned by Hardyng as a presentation copy for Henry VI.[43] The text of John Hardyng's *Chronicle*, the only item in the manuscript, is written in single columns of verse with a height of approximately 320 mm; each column generally comprises six stanzas per folio, normally of seven lines each.[44]

Foliation occurs in the top right-hand corner of each leaf, written in ink by an early hand; it contains two leaves marked "25" in error. From folio 26 onwards a second, modern foliation occurs in pencil, correcting the earlier foliation. This edition follows the modern foliation. With the exception of folio 2v, each folio has frame ruling in red; prick marks can be seen on many leaves.

Collation

Two unfoliated paper flyleaves; one parchment leaf inserted in the seventeenth century containing the arms of Gerards, earls of Macclesfield (marked as fol. 1); quire 1^{4-1} (fols. 2–4, one leaf excised, probably iv);[45] quire 2^{12-1} (fols. 5–15, i excised);[46] quire 3^{8} (fols. 16–23); quire

---

[43] The belief that Lansdowne 204 is Hardyng's presentation copy is widely accepted among scholars; while we cannot be absolutely certain that Henry VI received, or even read, the manuscript, we are confident that it was made for the king and that Hardyng submitted it to him, or one of his officials, at the same time that he submitted his forgeries to the Treasury in 1457 (see "John Hardyng's Life" above). The wording used to describe Hardyng's activities in Scotland in the government records relating to the annuity granted to Hardyng in November 1457 appears to have been taken directly from the prologue and/or epilogue of the *Chronicle* (See *Calendar of Patent Rolls: Henry VI, 1452–61*, p. 393, m. 8, 18 November 1457; *Calendar of Close Rolls: Henry VI, 1454–61*, p. 235, m. 28, 18 November 1457); and TNA: PRO E 159/234, the King's Remembrancer Memoranda Rolls for Michaelmas 1457 ("Recorda" and "Brevia directa baronibus" sections).

[44] Hardyng occasionally produces six- and eight-line stanzas, with one stanza comprising nine lines; see Textual Notes 2.1–512, 2.513–21, 2.522–617, 3.883–90, 3.2004–09, and 3.2528–33. The six-line stanzas may indicate that Hardyng left several stanzas with blank lines, which he intended to complete later. Hand Two's insertion of a seventh line into several six-line stanzas written by Hand One shows that Hardyng provided the missing lines for some verses, but failed to complete others. This practice matches what we know of the methods he employed when composing the second version of the *Chronicle*. Extant manuscripts of this version include blank lines that are "not necessary for sense, but essential to stanza form" and "most tricky in terms of rhyme," suggesting that Hardyng left them for completion at a later stage (Edwards, "Manuscripts and Texts ," p. 83). The eight- and nine-line stanzas generally occur at the start of Book 2, with one occurring in Book 3, which could point to Hardyng's drawing on a source using eight-line stanzas for this section of the text; see the Explanatory Notes covering the start of Book 2 for further discussion of possible sources and influences.

[45] The current binding is too tight to confirm which leaf was excised, but iv seems likely. The parchment of this gathering is different from the parchment used for the rest of the manuscript; it is much thicker and coarser, but it is still a contemporary addition. The editors thank Dr. Laura Nuvoloni for her advice about the unusual construction of the first two quires and the binding of Lansdowne 204. It is our opinion that this quire was added to accommodate Hardyng's prologue after the main text had been written. The incomplete nature of the contents page on fol. 4v suggests that the missing folio was the final leaf of the gathering.

[46] The presence of quire signatures on fols. 6–9 (numbered iii–vi) and the sewing of the gathering between fol. 9 and fol. 10, with six leaves extant on the second half of the gathering (fols. 10–15) shows that this was once a quire of twelve leaves. Since there are no apparent gaps in the text of this

4^8 (fols. 24–31); quire 5^8 (fols. 32–39); quire 6^8 (fols. 40–47); quire 7^8 (fols. 48–55); quire 8^8 (fols. 56–63); quire 9^8 (fols. 64–71); quire 10^8 (fols. 72–79); quire 11^8 (fols. 80–87); quire 12^8 (fols. 88–95); quire 13^8 (fols. 96–103); quire 14^8 (fols. 104–111); quire 15^8 (fols. 112–119); quire 16^8 (fols. 120–127); quire 17^8 (fols. 128–135); quire 18^8 (fols. 136–143); quire 19^8 (fols. 144–151); quire 20^8 (fols. 152–159); quire 21^8 (fols. 160–167); quire 22^8 (fols. 168–175); quire 23^8 (fols. 176–183); quire 24^8 (fols. 184–191); quire 25^8 (fols. 192–199); quire 26^8 (fols. 200–207); quire 27^8 (fols. 208–215); quire 28^8 (fols. 216–223); quire 29^{8-1} (fols. 224–230, one leaf excised, probably viii).

Quires 2 to 29 are numbered on the first folio of each quire (i–xxviii respectively). In addition to this, quire 2 has quire signatures on folios 6–9 (numbered iii–vi). Signatures in the first half of each gathering from quires 3 to 25 comprise an Arabic latter (*a–i, k–t, w–z* respectively) and a Roman numeral (i–iv).[47] Signatures in quires 26 to 29 comprise *et, con,* yogh, and *est* respectively, and a Roman numeral (i–iv).[48] Regular catchwords occur at the end of each quire in decorative scrolls.

Binding

The manuscript is bound in restored eighteenth-century brown calf, decorated with a frame of thin gilt-roll.

Handwriting

Two distinct hands are responsible for the text. Hand One, perhaps a legal scrivener, writes in a professional Common Law anglicana script and Hand Two in anglicana formata, with the occasional secretary form. It is difficult to state with absolute certainty whether the two hands belong to one scribe writing with varying degrees of care, or to two scribes sharing some similarities of script. On balance, it seems more likely that two individuals were involved, but both hands are inconsistent enough in their use of specific letter forms to belong to the same scribe working at different times, using different scripts, pens, and ink.

If there are two hands present, the principal hand (Hand One) is responsible for fols. 5r–225v (Books 1.1 to 7.1358, the main body of the *Chronicle*) and many of the marginalia that accompany the verse in thicker, red ink.[49] This hand is distinguished by a preference for a two-compartment *a*, anglicana *w* (with ascenders curling towards the right), anglicana *d* (with looped ascender), and the reversed, ovoid form of *e* (both open and closed). Lowercase

---

gathering (or indeed any of the other quires), we conclude that the first leaf of the quire has been excised. It is not clear when the leaf was removed or what, if anything, it contained; if blank, it may have been removed when the previous quire was added to avoid having a blank folio between the contents page and main text.

[47] Quire three, for example, is labelled "ii" on the first folio and contains quire signatures ai–aiv on the first four folios.

[48] The form of the alphabet established by the late medieval period normally ended with the abbreviations for *et, con,* three tittles, and the words *est amen.* For forms and examples of medieval alphabets in manuscripts see Wolpe, "Florilegium Alphabeticum," pp. 69–74; Orme, *English Schools,* p. 61, and "Children and Literature in Medieval England," p. 226.

[49] We would like to thank Dr. Ian Doyle for his help with our analysis of the Lansdowne scribe(s).

graphs *b*, *h*, *k*, and *l* generally have looped ascenders; and lower case *h* has a limb that usually flicks to the right. However, the scribe intermittently uses a simpler secretary form of *w* (which leans to the left), secretary *e*, hooked, rather than looped, ascenders on *b*, *h*, *k*, and *l* (more common to anglicana formata script), and *h* with a limb that curls to the left. The size of the hand in question is similarly inconsistent, but always neater than Hand Two; at first it is very compact and formal, but as the work progresses it becomes more loose and cursive.

The copyist provides large calligraphic initials at the start of each of his folios, unless an illuminated initial occurs at the top of the page. The decorative initials have elaborate strap- and cadel-work and small, red guide letters included in the design for clarity. In addition, the scribe exaggerates the ascenders on the top line of each folio and extends them into the top margin; descenders on the bottom line similarly protrude deep into the lower margin and often end with an elaborate flourish and decorative pen-work.

Hand Two — if not Hand One writing at a later stage — appears to be responsible for those parts of the *Chronicle* that were added towards the end of production, possibly in haste, after Hand One had completed the main text.[50] His contribution includes: fol. 2v (Prol.1–28, Hardyng's dedication, with black rhyme bands and no discernible frame ruling); fols. 3r–4r (Prol.29–161, Hardyng's prologue, with red rhyme bands);[51] fol. 4v (an incomplete contents page in red ink); fols. 226r–230v (7.1359–1720, part of the itinerary, prose passages, and closing stanzas); the book and chapter divisions; the running heads at the top of each folio giving the name of the king(s) being discussed; and a considerable number of the marginalia (including some later additions to existing glosses by Hand One), all of which are written in red ink, some in red over black ink.[52] Throughout the manuscript, Hand Two also appears to add to, erase, and alter occasional stanzas, words, lines, and marginalia written by Hand One, perhaps indicating that Hardyng was working closely with the scribe(s), supplying additional material, corrections, and lines for unfinished stanzas as production was underway.[53] It looks as though aspects of the text, such as the prologue and book divisions had not been planned, or finalized, when Hand One commenced his contribution, which may explain why the first and final folios of the manuscript look less polished and more impromptu in terms of layout than the rest of the work and why some

---

[50] The absence of decorative ink initials on the folios copied by Hand Two, the lack of pen flourishes stemming from the first and last lines of his text, the ad hoc appearance of the prefatory matter, and the presence of ink smudges resulting from folios having been turned over before freshly written marginalia and chapter headings had dried, suggest that Hand Two took less care completing his contribution or that time or money for the project had expired and he finished in a hurry. The inferior appearance of the illuminated initial on folio 3r and the incomplete nature of several illuminated initials in the final quire may be indicative of the latter.

[51] The final stanza of the prologue, which is now only visible under ultraviolet light, was squeezed into the bottom margin of fol. 4r; like the incomplete contents page, this may indicate that the space this hand had available to write in was limited when the prologue was added.

[52] See, for example, Textual Notes 1.1m, 1.176m, and 2.1234m.

[53] See, for example, Textual Notes 1.1m, 2.639m, 7.421–22, 7.449–55, 7.1331–37, and 7.1352–1414. Distinctions between the two hands are less clear in the following examples: 4.1817–19, 6.3365–66, 6.3372, and 6.3373. Multispectral imaging similarly reveals that both hands made corrections to the text, erasing and rewriting occasional lines, stanzas, and marginalia; see, for example, Figures 4–7 and 11.

of the text written by Hand Two (including book and chapter divisions) had to be squeezed into the limited space available.[54]

At first glance, Hand Two prefers the simpler secretary forms of *e*, *d* (with unlooped ascender), and *w* (leaning to the left); in the dedication and prologue a preference for single-compartment *a* can also be seen. The scribe frequently uses thorns and the ascenders of his *b*, *h*, *k*, and *l* are regularly hooked rather than looped. The limb of lower case *h* often hooks round to the left. Nonetheless, closer inspection reveals that this hand also employs anglicana forms of *e* (reversed ovoid form), *d*, and *w*; two-compartment *a*; lowercase *b*, *h*, *k*, and *l* with looped ascenders; and *h* with a limb that flicks to the right.

Annotations, Graffiti, and Ownership Marks

There are numerous contemporary and post-medieval jottings present in the manuscript. The first flyleaf bears the following markings: "No. ~~200~~ 204," "$1510B," "~~2511c~~," "~~74i~~," and "LXXIV.I"; the first number, occurring at the top of the folio, relates to the manuscript's current shelfmark. On fol. 2r the hand of Sir Robert Cotton (1571–1631), a previous owner of Lansdowne 204, writes "A Chronicel of Britane gathered out of diuers auters the auter vnknown." Below this, his librarian, Richard James, provides a brief description of the manuscript's contents (in Latin) and names Hardyng as the author.[55]

Several other hands have added intermittent marginal notes beside the verse, usually consisting of a single word or phrase concerning a famous king, event, battle, or source.[56] The first of the hands belongs to the famous antiquarian John Stow (c. 1525–1605).[57] Stow makes notes about the sources of Hardyng's early history, religious artifacts, places, miracles, and events affecting the succession of the crown. His annotations demonstrate the nature of his interests and often emphasize the differences between the two versions of the *Chronicle*, which undoubtedly led to his criticism of Richard Grafton's edition of the second version.[58]

The second hand, writing in a large secretary script belonging to the late fifteenth or early sixteenth century, is responsible for five annotations on fols. 7r, 88v, 89r, 166v, 170r, and 170v.[59] The third hand, a late fifteenth-century secretary, smaller and narrower than

---

[54] The four-stanza dedication on fol. 2v was evidently an after-thought. Written by Hand Two on the reverse of the first leaf of quire one, no space has been left for a decorated or illuminated initial, which one would expect at the opening of a manuscript containing decorated initials at the start of every other section. Unlike the prologue that follows on fol. 3r, the dedication has black rhyme bands and no discernible frame ruling, indicating that it was added after the completion of the prologue. Several of the marginalia added by this hand also seem to have been inserted into the gutters of the inner margins after the manuscript had been bound.

[55] Tite has noted that it is logical to assume that James added his note after Cotton's because he names the "auter vnknown" as Hardyng. See "'Lost or Stolen or Strayed,'" p. 281.

[56] All of these are recorded in the Textual Notes beside the lines or stanzas against which they occur.

[57] For the identification of Stow's hand see Tite, "'Lost or Stolen or Strayed,'" p. 303n127.

[58] See Textual Notes 2.1128, 2.1185, 2.1689m, 2.2574, 3.39, 3.84, 3.86, 3.680–81, 3.2164, 3.2197, 3.3115m, 4.2651, 4.2670, 4.2702, 4.2755, 5.2312, and 6.1160–61. Other annotations that may belong to Stow include 4.3359–65, 6.2188–90, and 6.2325.

[59] See Textual Notes 1.197–203, 3.4004, 4.42, 6.1, 6.295, 6.332, and 6.346.

the previous hand, writes six notes on fols. 120r, 121r, 128v, 161v, 180r, and 192v.[60] On fol. 134r, a sixteenth-century hand makes a note on the foundation of Battle Abbey and later writes "Italia" on fol. 194v.[61] Another reader has drawn a manicule pointing to one of the stanzas on fol. 171r and added a note in the right-hand margin about the king's sovereignty over Wales and Scotland.[62] On fols. 203r and 223r an early hand, possibly of the sixteenth century, copies phrases from the text in an attempt to mimic the scribe.[63]

Several names occur in the manuscript: "John Clapsshan born the fourth day of [Januarie?] 1555," and "London" are mentioned on fol. 2r; the name William Bowyer 1566 ("Sum Guiliel Bowyer 1566") occurs at the top of fols. 3r and 5r, presumably added by William Bowyer (d. 1569/70), Keeper of the Records in the Tower;[64] and "Edward Colwell" appears on fol. 166v.[65] The first of the end flyleaves has "230 folios W. Lo Fran (?). G. C. T" written in pencil, doubtless added when the manuscript was acquired by the British Library.

Decoration

The illumination of Lansdowne 204 has been linked stylistically and decoratively to a group of fifteenth-century manuscripts originating from Eastern England, most likely Lincolnshire or East Anglia: New York Library MS Spencer 19;[66] London, British Library MSS Egerton 615;[67] London, Wellcome Medical Library MS 8004;[68] Oxford, Bodleian

---

[60] See Textual Notes 4.3359–65, 5.2312, 6.1160–61, and 6.2188–90.

[61] See Textual Notes 5.8 and 6.2345 respectively.

[62] See Textual Notes 6.386.

[63] See Textual Notes 6.3010m and 7.1107–1127.

[64] Bowyer owned a number of manuscripts, including British Library Cotton Faustina A. ix, Harley 3776, Harley 4565, Cambridge Trinity College R.5.33 (724), and eleven manuscripts in the College of Arms. Several contain notes of ownership similar to that in Lansdowne 204; see, for example, Wright, *Fontes Harleiani*, p. 79, and Campbell and Steer, *Catalogue of Manuscripts*, pp. 196–217, 417. For a succinct account of Bowyer's life and collection see Alsop, "Bowyer, William (*d.* 1569/70)."

[65] See Textual Note 5.2716. It is also possible that this "name" is in fact related to the text, as it occurs beside a stanza dealing with Prince Edward, son of Henry III, later Edward I.

[66] See Scott, *Later Gothic Manuscripts*, 2:217–19. Spencer 19 contains a copy of Guillaume Deguileville's *Pilgrimage of the Soul*, produced between 1413 and 1450, probably c. 1430. It was "in the hands of Sir Thomas Cumberworth of Somerby, Lincolnshire, sometime before February 1450" (Scott, *Later Gothic Manuscripts*, 2:218; see also McGerr, ed., *Pilgrimage of the Soul*, pp. lxxx–lxxxiv).

[67] Egerton 615 contains Guillaume Deguileville's *Pilgrimage of the Soul*. It was produced c. 1450, slightly later than Spencer 19, but, like Lansdowne 204, comes from the "same shop, or at least from the same geographical area" as Spencer 19 (Scott, *Later Gothic Manuscripts*, 2:218).

[68] Wellcome 8004 is a medical and astrological compendium produced c. 1454. It contains "borders and a miniature by the artist of Spencer 19" (Kathleen Scott, private communication, 8 September 2003). The manuscript also has "internal and linguistic evidence [suggesting] that the writer came from the East Midlands, possibly from Lincolnshire"; see the *Physician's Handbook*, a digital facsimile available online. The editors are grateful to Kathleen Scott for drawing our attention to Wellcome 8004 and for her comments about the Spencer group.

Library MS Laud Misc. 740;[69] London, British Library MS Harley 2885;[70] Arundel Castle, John Lydgate's *Lives of Saints Edmund and Fremund*;[71] and, less directly, Nottingham, University Library MS 250.[72] Decorative features distinguishing the group include: daisy flowers, green sprays, twisted acanthus leaves, and foliate columns.[73] The illuminations in Lansdowne 204, Spencer 19, Egerton 615, Wellcome 8004, and Laud Misc. 740 also feature

---

[69] Laud Misc. 740 is a mid-fifteenth-century copy of Deguileville's *Pilgrimage of the Life of Man*. According to Scott, the decoration in this manuscript is "distantly related to the preceding group," but may have been executed by a second "trainee or associate of the Spencer Master" (*Later Gothic Manuscripts*, 2:218). It has a linguistic profile belonging to north-west Lincolnshire or north-east Nottingham (McIntosh, Samuels, and Benskin, *Linguistic Atlas*, 1:150). Like Spencer 19, it may have belonged to Sir Thomas Cumberworth; see McGerr, ed., *Pilgrimage of the Soul*, p. xxiv, and Clark, *Lincoln Diocese Documents 1450–1544*, p. 48.

[70] Harley 2885, produced in the third quarter of the fifteenth century, contains a Breviary (York use). In 1996 Scott suggested that the border artist of Egerton 615 was responsible for "most of the borders (except fol. 27)" in this manuscript (*Later Gothic Manuscripts*, 2:218). However, in a private communication dated 8 September 2003, she revised her opinion, concluding that the decoration of Harley 2885 "appears to be from the same milieu or shop, if not precisely by the same limner." For images see The British Library's *Catalogue of Illuminated Manuscripts*, available online.

[71] This manuscript was probably produced in Suffolk after 1461; it contains a pasted–down border on fol. 56 (c. 1450), which Scott believes is evidence of "another book from the Egerton-Lansdowne shop" (*Later Gothic Manuscripts*, 2:218, and "Lydgate's Lives of Saints Edmund and Fremund," p. 347).

[72] More famously known as The Wollaton Antiphonal, the manuscript was compiled c. 1430 in eastern England and owned by Sir Thomas Chaworth; see Scott, *Later Gothic Manuscripts*, 2: 204–206; Cole and Turville–Petre, "Sir Thomas Chaworth's Books," pp. 26–27; and Hanna and Turville-Petre, "The Catalogue," p. 107a. Two other books owned by Chaworth — London, British Library MS Cotton Augustus A iv (John Lydgate's *Troy Book*, c. 1430) and New York, Columbia University Library, MS Plimpton 263 (John Trevisa's *On the Properties of Things*, c. 1425–50) — have been linked to the Wollaton Antiphonal through decoration, though neither manuscript is directly related to Lansdowne 204 (see Scott, *Later Gothic Manuscripts*, 2:205–06). In *Later Gothic Manuscripts* (2:218), Scott highlights the possibility that the *Myrror for Devote People*, once owned by William Foyle (now Notre Dame, IN, University of Notre Dame MS 67), might also be related to the Spencer 19 group. However, since the publication, Scott has examined the manuscript and revised her opinion. In a private correspondence dated 31 March 2013, she confirms that the manuscript "does not belong to that group." The manuscript, which also contains *O Intemerata* and *The Craft of Dying*, was originally owned by John Scrope (d. 1455), fourth baron of Masham, and his wife Elizabeth Chaworth. For more information see Edwards, "Contexts of Notre Dame 67."

[73] Borders with gold balls made into daisies have also been found in other East Anglian manuscripts: Harley 2278 (Lydgate's *Lives of Saints Edmund and Fremund*, c.1434, Suffolk; Scott, *Later Gothic Manuscripts*, 2:225–29); Oxford, Bodleian Library, MS Duke Humphrey b. 1 (John Capgrave's *Commentarius in Exodum*, compiled c. 1440–44, possibly at King's Lynn and presented to Humphrey, duke of Gloucester; Scott, *Dated and Datable English Manuscript Borders*, pp. 60–63); and San Marino, Huntingdon HM55 (Capgrave's *Life of St Norbert*, 1440, Norfolk; Scott, *Later Gothic Manuscripts*, 2:219). Hatfield House, Marquis of Salisbury, Cecil Papers 270 (Deguileville's *Pilgrimage of the Soul*, probably produced in London), also contains "gold balls made to resemble daisies," which suggests contact "possibly through the exemplar" with the Spencer group "or the geographical area in which the motif was used" (Scott, *Later Gothic Manuscripts*, 2:221).

the same child-like figures; and Egerton 615 and Lansdowne include gold filigree sprays in the background of their scenes (see below).[74]

On fol. 5r of Lansdowne 204, there is a fine champ initial of five lines in height, in gold, with a pink, burgundy, and white foliated leaf at the center, on a blue and white ground. The initial has extended feathered sprays that fill the top and left-hand margins to form a partial border around the text; the sprays consist of green ball motifs, daisies with gold centers, squiggles, and twisted acanthus leaves, outlined in black, and colored either blue and white, red and white, or burgundy, red, and white; a small line of white dots embellishes the inside of the stems.[75]

Elsewhere champ initials of three lines in height are used to mark the beginning of each new chapter and a change of sovereign. The initials consist of a gold letter on a burgundy and blue quartered ground with white filigree work; they are decorated with small feathered sprays and daisies, with gold ball motifs, circular lobes tinted green, and squiggles. Several folios at the end of the manuscript contain unfinished champ initials, where only the burgundy quarters have been completed or spaces for champ initials that have been filled with large ink letters.[76]

A spectacular full-page illuminated pedigree of Edward III occurs on fol. 196r detailing the king's entitlement to the French throne.[77] The pedigree comprises eleven seated figures, each having a gold crown and scepter (except "Charles of Valoys, erle," who has only a crown); they have simple faces, with eyes, noses, and lips highlighted in black, and other features, such as cheeks and hands, rendered in white and pink.[78] Three of the figures (labelled "Philippe," "Isabel," and "Iohn") have yellow curly hair; the rest have brown curly hair.[79] All the figures are clothed in either red and blue or gold and blue, with ermine trim on their robes. The figures in gold and blue highlight the pure line of descent from "Saynt

---

[74] For a discussion of motifs particular to the Lincolnshire and East Anglia region, and the production of manuscripts outside of the capital at this time, see Scott, *Later Gothic Manuscripts*, 1:33–34; and *Dated and Datable English Manuscript Borders*, p. 62. For an analysis of pigments used in this region and associated with the group see Porter, "Meaning of Colour and Why Analyse?" noted in Hanna and Turville-Petre, "The Catalogue," p. 107a. Digital images of Spencer 19, Egerton 615, Wellcome 8004 and Laud Misc. 740 are available online at *The New York Public Library Digital Gallery*, *The Digital Scriptorium*, The British Library's *Catalogue of Illuminated Manuscripts*, The Wellcome Library, and the Bodleian image collections.

[75] The daisy sprays in Lansdowne 204 are closer to those in Spencer 19 and Laud Misc. 740.

[76] The plain ink initials occur on fols. 223v, 225r, 225v, 226r, and 227v. The unfinished champs occur on fols. 227v and 230r. All occurrences of champ initials (finished or unfinished) are recorded in the Textual Notes.

[77] Scott believes that "The Egerton Master," the illustrator of Egerton 615, was "almost certainly" responsible for the seated monarchs in Lansdowne 204. The daisy borders were illuminated by a different individual, whose style is closer to the daisy sprays in Spencer 19 and Laud 740 rather than the "densely black, unattractive work in Egerton 615" (Scott, *Later Gothic Manuscripts*, 2:218).

[78] Images of the Pedigree taken at a wavelength of 420 nanometers (nm) on the electromagnetic spectrum reveal lines on the upper lip of the figures and white 'skeletal' detail on the hands. See Figures 8 and 9.

[79] Details of the curls are most evident in a false color image and at a wavelength of 860 nm on the electromagnetic spectrum. Guide letters are visible beneath most of the blue initial letters of the royal names. See Figure 9.

Lowys" through to his great-granddaughter "Isabel," or Isabella of France (1295–1348), mother of Edward III. The remaining figures are depicted in stripy red garments and blue robes.[80] Additional emphasis is given to the importance of Isabella, as she is the only figure to gaze directly forward; all of the other figures look towards her, with the exception of Edward III, who gestures towards King John of France, the usurper. Each figure is seated on a throne colored red, yellow, or purple; the thrones belonging to the "pure" line of descent have blue and/or gold ornamentation, and some seats are decorated with filigree sprays.[81] The backgrounds behind the figures alternate between red and black and are filled with long gold filigree sprays or gold cross-hatching. Twisted foliate columns of leaves, in blue and white or two-tone green, decorate the golden bar frames around the figures in the top half of the folio, and clusters of feathered sprays consisting of daisies made from gold balls, circular green lobes, and twisted colored acanthus leaves (in red, blue, pink, and green) adorn the space around the pedigree.

A unique colored map of Scotland — the earliest independent cartographic representation of the realm — occurs on fols. 226v–227r. Oriented with west at the top, it is illuminated in gold, blue, pink, yellow, green, red, purple, and white, and it depicts the main fortifications and towns with an intriguing array of castles, walled towns, gatehouses, churches, and bridges.[82] Forests and rivers are included and a blue and white ocean surrounds the land, giving Scotland an island-like appearance, separate from England.[83] Many of the castles and churches bear an odd but fascinating resemblance to the real buildings, particularly those representing Glasgow, Tantalloon, and Dunfermline.[84] Geographically speaking, the layout is compellingly accurate; it was clearly informed by someone with detailed knowledge of Scotland's topography, and there is no reason to doubt Hardyng's claim to have compiled it. It was drawn and illuminated by the same artist responsible for the Pedigree of France, and since there are no instructions to the limner beneath the painting, indicating where the toponyms, rivers, and forests should appear, the artist may have been working from a separate diagram provided by Hardyng.[85]

---

[80] Stripes in the red garments are faintly visible with the naked eye, but best observed at a wavelength of 560–580 nm on the electromagnetic spectrum. The elaborate folds on the robes are observed most clearly at a wavelength of 460 nm. See Figure 8.

[81] The filigree pattern is observed best at a wavelength of 420 nm on the electromagnetic spectrum.

[82] For scholarship on Hardyng's map and its political significance, see Harvey, *Medieval Maps*, pp. 71 and 73; Delano-Smith and Kain, *English Maps*, p. 23; Hiatt, *Medieval Forgeries*, pp. 119–21 and "Beyond a Border," pp. 87–88; and Peverley, "Anglo-Scottish Relations."

[83] This aspect of the map makes for an interesting comparison with the images of Scotland in Matthew Paris's maps.

[84] The buildings on the map are of the same design and coloring as those depicted in Spencer 19 and Laud Misc. 740. Multispectral imaging of the Lansdowne map reveals the original guidelines for the building structures. Viewing the map at a wavelength of 1000 nm reveals that the bottom of the towers at Stirling and Falkland were initially drawn straight; ridges and flared bases were added over the top (see Figure 12). The tower at Tantallon was originally drawn with a closed, rather than open, top, which was altered when the tower was painted.

[85] No limners' marks or instructions were observed during the multispectral imaging undertaken on Lansdowne 204.

Small colored coats of arms occur infrequently in the margins beside the main text: on fol. 46v, the arms of Constantine (incorrectly painted gules, a cross argent instead of argent, a cross gules); on fol. 67v, the arms of King Arthur (gules, three crowns or); on fol. 129v, the arms of Edward the Confessor (azure, a cross or, four martlets or); and, on fol. 220r, the arms of Sir Robert Umfraville (gules, a cinquefoil, an orle of crosslets or). On fol. 217v, the arms of Margaret of Anjou, entitled "The Quene," have been erased, but the outline can still be seen (quarterly of six: i barry of eight argent and gules; ii azure, semy fleurs-de-lis or, a label of three points gules; iii argent a cross potent between four crosses crosslet potent or; iv azure, semy fleurs-de-lis or, a bordure gules; v azure, semy of crosses crosslet fitchy, two barbels haurient addorsed or; vi or, on a bend gules, three alerions displayed argent). Quarters i, iv, v, and vi still have traces of the original design and colors (gules and azure).[86] A second coat of arms, presumably belonging to Henry VI, may also have existed on fol. 217v in the small section that has been cut away from the margin.

There is one final decoration in Lansdowne 204 which is much later than the medieval illumination. On fol. 1v, the emblazoned arms of one of the previous owners, the earl of Macclesfield, occur, quarterly of six: i argent, on a saltire gules an imperial crown or; ii or, a mullet sable, on a broad fesse-wise a bordure componée argent and azure, quarterly France modern (azure, three fleur de lys or) and England (gules, three lions passant guardant or); iii per pale azure and gules, three lions rampant or; iv per fesse gules and argent, a canton argent; v argent, on a bend azure, three garbs or, a canton gules; vi argent, two chevrons gules, a canton gules; supporters, sinister and dexter a lion rampant crowned.

Contents

1. fol. 1r: Blank.
2. fol. 1v: The arms of the Gerard family, earls of Macclesfield.
3. fol. 2r: Originally blank, now contains notes by Robert Cotton and Richard James.
4. fol. 2v: Hardyng's dedication to King Henry VI. Begins "O soverayne lord, be it to youre plesance" and ends "To byde forevere undir his hool proteccioun."
5. fols. 3r–4r: Prologue addressing Hardyng's grievance and the king's sovereignty over Scotland. Begins "Who hath an hurte and wille it nought diskure" and ends "Me to rewarde as pleseth youre excellence."[87]
6. fol. 4v: An incomplete table of contents. Begins "Of the sustirs of Grece how thai came to this londe and called it Albion" and ends "Of Seynt Edward Confessor and Harolde, son of Godwyn."
7. fols. 5r–230v: Books 1–7 of the *Chronicle*, from Albyne to Henry VI, including a commendation of Sir Robert Umfraville, an account of Hardyng's grievance, advice on conquering Scotland, and evidence of the king's entitlement to the Scottish throne. Begins "The while that Troy was regnyng in his myghte" and ends "Ne chaungen hew for thayre inequyté."
8. fol. 196r: A full page illuminated pedigree of Edward III's claim to France.
9. fols. 226v–227r: A double-page colored map of Scotland.

---

[86] Multispectral imaging enhances the faded design at an electromagnetic wavelength of 420 nm. See Figure 10.

[87] An erased stanza occurs after this. See Textual Note Prol.155–61. See Figure 3.

10. fols. 227v–230r: A Latin prose letter sent from Edward I to Pope Boniface VIII detailing his right to the sovereignty of Scotland. Begins "Sanctissimo in Christo patri domino Bonifacio" and ends "datur apud Westminster septimo die Maii anno domini MˡCCCI et regni nostri vicesimo nono."

11. fols. 230r–230v: A Latin prose letter from the lords and barons to Pope Boniface VIII regarding English sovereignty over Scotland. Begins "Sanctissimo in Christo Patri, domino Bonifacio" and ends "inquietudine pacifice possidere ac illibata percipere benignius permittatis."

Provenance

Aside from the few jottings mentioned above, there are no marks of medieval ownership. The quality of the volume, its lavish decoration, its association with Hardyng's locale, and its dedication suggest that Hardyng commissioned the manuscript as a presentation copy for Henry VI, but whether the king ever saw, read, or retained it is unclear.

The presence of William Bowyer's name on fols. 3r and 5r seems to indicate that he was in possession of Lansdowne 204 in 1566, while annotations by the antiquarian John Stow confirm that he read, and perhaps owned, it in the sixteenth century.[88] Later, the manuscript found its way into the collection of Sir Robert Cotton, whose hand, along with that of his librarian Richard James, occurs on fol. 2r.[89]

It is unclear when Lansdowne 204 left the Cotton collection, but by the late seventeenth century it was in the possession of the Gerards, earls of Macclesfield, whose arms occur on fol. 1v.[90] The manuscript was presumably owned by at least one other individual before it was acquired by William Petty, formerly Fitzmaurice (1737–1805), second earl of Shelburne and first marquess of Lansdowne. Petty was the last private owner of Lansdowne 204, and it is from his collection that the manuscript was purchased by the British Library (then the British Museum) in 1807.[91]

EDITORIAL PROCEDURES

The aim of this edition of the longer version of John Hardyng's *Chronicle* is twofold: (1) to reproduce the linguistic state of the text as accurately as we could; (2) to supply a text that is accessible to readers who might not have the highest level of expertise in Middle English.

The results of these two aims are by no means always consonant.

---

[88] Stow later cites Hardyng as a source for his own historical works. For an overview of his life and interests see Beer, "Stow, John (1524/5–1605)."

[89] Although there is "no record of the manuscript in any of the Cotton catalogues or loans lists to clinch the question of ownership or to indicate when it may have been lost," the summaries provided by Cotton and James on fol. 2r suggest that the manuscript was with Cotton sometime before 1625, or at least between 1625, when Richard James was appointed as Cotton's librarian, and 1631, when Cotton died (Tite, "'Lost or Stolen or Strayed,'" p. 281).

[90] Charles Gerard (c.1618–94) was promoted to the earldom of Macclesfield in 1679 by Charles II. Upon his death, his son, another Charles (c.1659–1701), became the second earl of Macclesfield.

[91] For notice of the purchase see Burke, *Annual Register*, p. 321.

The following decisions derive from the desire for accurate linguistic representation of the text.

The spelling of the text is almost entirely the spelling of the manuscript, with minor adjustments noted below.

Punctuation is minimal. Commas are not inserted following modern practice. The large majority of Hardyng's lines are end-stopped; we allow end-stopping to do the work of a comma. This seemed preferable to clogging up the text with punctuation marks when the meter is doing the work of visually supplying comma-level pauses in any case. Of course this occasionally means that an enjambed line needs to be understood differently, but that relatively rare inconsistency is preferable to consistency achieved at the cost of a clogged text. There is no need to punctuate this poetic text as if it were prose.

Hardyng's syntax is loose; he characteristically creates long sentences made up of line-length strings of relative or adverbial clauses. Often it is unclear where one sentence precisely stops and another begins. This is not to say that the overall sense is often unclear. Our practice has been to insert full stops either when a syntactic unit of a sentence has clearly been achieved, or when a sentence has done quite enough work as it is. The result of this practice is a lack of complete conformity with modern standards of syntactic punctuation, since we occasionally begin a sentence with a relative clause.

The interests of accessibility have been served by the following decisions.

Caesural virgules, found consistently across the entire text, have been removed. All contractions have been silently expanded. Whether or not a mark constitutes an expansion has been decided on philological and metrical grounds, as well as by reference to the scribe's standard practice. Capitalization conforms to modern usage. Speech markers have been introduced. Modern word division has been observed. The Tironian "and" has been expanded. Obsolete letter forms, just as letter forms for *u/v/j*, have been rendered by their modern equivalents. Where a final *e* is sounded as to rhyme with "hay," the letter is given an acute accent. In the very rare cases where emendation is necessary, the emended word is silently corrected and an explanation is provided in the Textual Notes. The rare instances of scribal correction have been silently followed in the main body of the text, but recorded in the Textual Notes. The text has been glossed. We have tried to address the reader whose familiarity with Middle English vocabulary may be relatively new. Complete consistency in glossing is impossible and undesirable: parts of the text would, for example, require constant and consistent repetition of a single gloss.

Prose marginalia are for the most part presented in bold, between stanzas, in the vertical run of the text. We have attempted to show which stanza the marginalia occur beside by presenting them in the text before the stanza they accompany; in instances where more than one gloss occurs beside a stanza, we have endeavored to present them in the order that will make the most sense to our readers. In a few instances where a marginal "Nota" is located within the bounds of a stanza, it is placed before the stanza it accompanies and a record of the line number it occurs beside is given in the Textual Notes. Marginalia have been lightly punctuated according to modern standards. All marginal notation has been registered except for the very rare instances of sixteenth-century or later notations, which are recorded in the Textual Notes.

Original book and chapter numbering is preserved; line numbers are editorial. At the top of each folio of the manuscript, the book number and name of the monarch under consideration are provided as page headers in inconsistent forms. We have omitted the medieval page headers, but provided the names of the kings in our own headers to aid navigation.

fol. 2v	O soverayne lord, be it to youre plesance	
	This book to take of my symplicité	
	Thus newly made for rememorance,	
	Whiche no man hath in worlde bot oonly ye.	
5	Whiche I compiled unto youre rialté	
	And to the quenes hertes consolacioun	
	To know the state of youre domynacioun.	

	And for the prynce to have playne conyshance	*understanding*
	Of this regioun, in what nobilité	
10	It hath been kept alway of greet pushance,	*power*
	With baronage and lordes of dignyté	
	The whiche alway God graunte that ye and he	
	May so kepe forth undir youre governance	*maintain*
	To Goddes plesire withouten variance.	

15	Thus to yow thre rials in unyté	*royals together*
	This book with hert and lowly obeishance	*deference*
	I present now with al benygnyté	*good will*
	To been everemore within youre governance	
	For soveraynté and youre inherytance	
20	Of Scotland hool, whiche shuld your reule obaye	
	As sovereyn lorde, fro whiche thay prowdly straye.	

	Wythin thre yere thaire grete rebellioun	
	Ye myght oppresse and uttirly restrayne	
	And have it alle in youre possessioun	
25	And to obeye youre myght make thaym ful fayne	*eager*
	As Kynge Edward the first with hungir and payne	
	Thaym conquerde hool to hys subjeccioun	*completely*
	To byde forevere undir his hool proteccioun.	*dwell; comprehensive (total)*

fol. 3r	Who hath an hurte and wille it nought diskure	*sickness; uncover*
30	And to his leche can nought his sore compleyne	*doctor*
	In wo evermore withouten any cure	
	Alle helples forth he muste comporte his peyne.	*endure*
	And who his own erande forgatte to seyne	*tell*

As alle thise wise men say alway and wote   *know*
35   Men calle a fool or elles an idyote.

Wherfore to yow, as prince moste excellent
I me compleyne, as resoun techeth me   *myself*
That youre fadir gafe me in commaundement
In Scotlonde ryde for his regalyté   *sovereignty*
40   To seke his ryght thare of hys sovereynté
And evydence to gette and to espy
Appurtenant unto hys monarchy.   *Pertaining*

Whiche evydence, by labour and processe   *passing of time*
Thre yere and halfe amonge the enmyté   *enemy*
45   On lyfes peryle, maymed in grete distresse   *injured*
With costages grete, as was necessité   *At great expense*
I boughte and gatte of grete autorité.
Of whiche I gafe unto youre excellence
At Esthamstede, parte of that evydence.   *Easthampstead*

50   I gafe yow there a lettre of rialté   *royal power*
By whiche ten men claymyng the croun
Of Scotlond than boonde thaym by thaire agré   *bound; agreement*
The juggement to bide and constitucioun
Of Kynge Edward, with Long Shankes by surnoun   *surname*
55   Whiche of thaym shulde of Scotlonde been the kynge
Undre thaire seels hys sovereynté expressynge.   *declaring*

I gafe yow als other two patents rial   *Letters Patent*
By whiche David and Robert the Scots kynges
Boonde thaym and al thaire haires in general   *heirs*
60   To holde Scotlond of Kyng Edward, expressynge   *declaring*
His soveraynté by clere and playn writynge
Undre thaire seels to bide perpetualy
As playnly is in thaym made memory.

I gafe yow als the relees that Edwarde   *document of release*
65   The thrid to Kyng Robert of Scotlond made
In tendre age, whiche whille it was in warde   *custody*
Of Umfrevile was dreynt in oyl and defade   *immersed; faded*
Sex woukes liggyng in it, as it abade.   *Six weeks remaining*
But noght forthy it may hurte yow right noght   *nevertheless*
70   For it is alle agayn youre hieghness wroght.

fol. 3v   In tho lettres is graunt Yorkes primacy
Thrugh alle Scotlonde, and to hys successours
To have and use above the prelacy   *authority of a prelate*
As dyd afore of olde hys predecessours

75	And also the hows of Durham of honours	
	And Cuthbertes ryght with alle the liberté	
	Thrugh all Scotlonde withoute difficulté.	
	Also that prynce of grete magnificence	
	Your fadir, so gafe me in commaundement	
80	Scotlond to espy with alkyns diligence	*all kinds of*
	How that it myght bene hostayde thurgh and brent	*plundered; burnt*
	[. . .] wele to hys wille and intent	
	What kyns passage were for ane hoste to ryde	*What kind of; army*
	What toures ande towns stode on the este see-syde	
85	Where that hys flete myght londe and with hym mete	
	With hys vitayle, gunnes and ordenance	*food; military supplies*
	Hys hoste to fresshe, and lygge in alle quyete	*army to restore; encamp*
	From stormes grete and wethyrs variance.	
	Whiche alle I dydde and putte in remembrance	
90	At hys biddynge and rialle commaundement	
	Bot was nought rewarded aftyr hys intent.	
	Whiche remembrance now to youre sapience	
	Upon the ende of this boke in figure	
	Illumynde is for youre intelligence	*Illuminated*
95	Declared hool by wrytynge and lettrure	*text*
	How lyghte were now unto your hiegh nature	*easy*
	For to conquere by rial assistence	
	And kepe it ever undir youre hiegh regence.	*sovereignty*
	Now seth that prynce is gone, of excellence	*since*
100	In whom my helpe and makynge shulde have bene	
	I vouche it sauf, wyth alle benyvolence	*bestow it*
	On yow, gode lorde, hys sonne and hayre that bene	*heir*
	For to none other my complaynte can I mene	*express*
	So lynyalle of hys generacioun	*in direct ancestral line*
105	Ye bene discent by verry demonstracioun.	*descended; proof*
	For other none wille favoure hys promyse	
	Ne none that wylle ought forther myne intente	
	Bot if it lyke unto youre owne avyse	*judgment*
	Alle oonly of youre rial regymente	*soverignty*
110	To comforte now withoute impedymente	
	Your pore subgite, maymed in hys servyse	
	Withoute rewarde or lyfelode any wyse.	*sustenance*
fol. 4r	Sex yere now go I pursewed to youre grace	*passed; made a formal plea (see note)*
	And undirnethe youre lettres secretary	
115	And pryvy seel that longeth in that cace	

Ye grauntled me to have perpetualy
The manere hool of Gedyngtoun treuly   *Geddington Manor*
To me and to myne hayres in heritage
With membres hool and other alle avauntage.   *all rights*

120   Bot so was sette youre noble chauncellere
He wolde nought suffre I had such warysoun   *reward*
That cardinalle was of York withouten pere
That wolde noght parte with londe ne yit with toun
Bot rather wolde, ere I had Gedyngtoun,
125   Ye shulde forgo youre ryalle soveraynté
Of Scotlonde, whiche longe to youre rialté.

Youre patent cowthe I have in nokyns wyse   *letter patent; by no means*
But if I sewed to alle youre grete counsayle   *pleaded*
To whiche my purs no lengar myght suffyse.   *purs*
130   So wente I home withoute any avayle.
Thus sette he me alle bakhalfe on the tayle   *he set me back*
And alle youre grace fro me he dyd repelle.   *revoke*
Youre lettres bothe fro me he dyd cancelle.

Bot undirnethe youre fadirs magnifence
135   He durste nought so have lette hys righte falle doun
Ne layde o syde so rialle evydence
Appurtenant unto hys rialle croun   *Appropriate*
Who sonner wolde suche thre as Gedyngtoun   *settlement*
Hafe yove than so forgone that evydence   *granted*
140   By whiche the Scottes obey shoulde hys regence.

For whiche Kynge James unto my warysoun   *reward*
A thowsond marke me highte of Englysshe golde   *promised*
Whiche I forsoke in myne oppynyoun
As natyfe birth and alkyns resoun wolde.   *every kind of*
145   Sex and thretty yere I have it kepte, and holde
In truste ye wolde of youre haboundant grace   *abounding*
Youre fadirs promyse so favoure in thys cace.

Whiche evydence in this afore comprised   *included earlier in this [book] (see note)*
With other mo whiche I shal to yow take   *evidence*
150   Foure hundre mark and fyfty ful assised
Cost me treuly for youre fadir sake
With incurable mayme that maketh me wake.   *injury; weak*
Wherfore plese it of youre magnificence
Me to rewarde as pleseth youre excellence.

155   O soverayne lorde sette case I myghte suffyse   *(see t-note)*
Myne evydence to get and to obtene.

How wold ye thenke that I should it advyse   *resolve*
[. . .] for your [. . .] it [. . .] nought bothe bene?
Your chaunsler doth revoke it alle so clene
160   That here me compleyne in this cace
Or els gette I never your intent, ne youre grace.

fol. 4v   **The First Book**

The Second Book

The .iii. Book

The iiii Book

[The contents page is incomplete.]

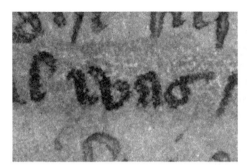

Figure 5. Folio 4r, stanza 2. Evidence of underwriting. Remnants of erased text observed, but main original is unrecoverable. Image captured at 420 nm on the electromagnetic spectrum and RGB. Photos courtesy of Dr. Christina Duffy, Conservation Science Team, The British Library and The British Library.

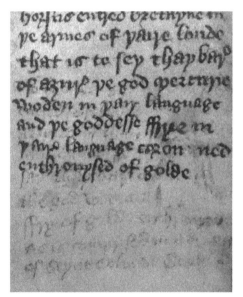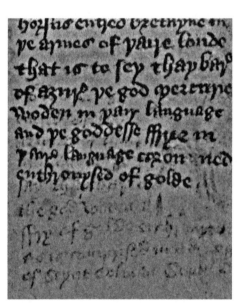

Figure 6. Folio 56r, marginalia. The bottom half of the first image shows the orginal, erased marginalia captured at 420 nm on the electromagnetic spectrum; the second image reflects enhanced brightness and contrast. Photos courtesy of Dr. Christina Duffy, Conservation Science Team, The British Library and The British Library.

 # BOOK ONE

fol. 5r   **The First Book**

The First Chapitle.

How thay came into this londe and named it Albion of Dame Albyne the eldest sustire (*sister*), as Seynt Colman, doctour Bisshop of Lyndisfarn, specifieth in hys *Dialoge*, and as the grete cronyclere, Trogus Pompeyus, in hys book of storyes of alle the worlde hath wryten; the whiche book hys disciple Justynus hathe drawe into xliiii books that bene at Rome in the kepynge of the pope, alle compiled agayn in til (*into*) oon, so that the stories of alle the worlde in it may be clierlyche sene; the whiche Julyus Cesaryne, auditour of the pope Martynes chaumbre, the fyfte, in hys sevent yer, gafe the maker of this book, John Hardyng, dayly inspection and discripcion at instance and wrytyng of the cardynal of Wynchester.

	The while that Troy was regnyng in his myghte	*its*
	There was in Grece a kinge right excellent	
	That doughtirs had thretty, right faire and brighte	*thirty; beautiful*
	Echone weddid to kinges of regyment.	*great power*
5	Whiche aftyr longe by ful avisement	*consideration*
	Right of thaym alle dyd mete by fulle acorde	*of their own initiative*
	For thaire gladnesse and susters fulle concorde.	*agreement*
	Whiche felle in pride and hiegh elacioun	*arrogance*
	Thinkynge to ben in no subjeccioun	
10	Of hosbonde more, ne domynacioun	
	But oonly by a foul conjeccioun	*conspiracy*
	Thay caste so than by alle inspeccioun	*planned; scrutiny*
	To sla anone thaire husbondes sodenly	*slay immediately*
	Sovereynes to bene and regne alle severaly.	*separately*
15	Bot what thay hight I can nought fynde ne se.	*were called*
	Bot Albyne hight the eldest of echone	
	That set thaym alle of that inyquyté	
	Whanne thaire hosbondes were slepynge by thaym one	
	To sla thaym alle and severally anone	*slay*

20   Save only than the yongest in hire mynde   *Except; her*
        Wolde nought assent, that was so trewe and kynde.

        Bot nought forthy she graunted with hire mouthe   *nonetheless*
        For drede of deth that elles thay had hire slayne.
        Bot whan she myght or first diskever it couthe   *reveal; could*
25   Unto hire lorde she telde and wolde noght layne.   *conceal*
        But for hire sistres she had alway grete payne
        Prayng hire lorde to staunche thaym of thaire thought   *assuage*
        Of thaire ymaginacioun that it were nought so wrought   *carried out*

        For pyté that she had of tho gode lordes
30   That sakelesly in perile stode to de   *without cause; die*
        Thurgh hire sisters covenaunts and concordes.   *agreements*
        Bot if it myght or couthe distourebed be   *Unless; stopped*
        She thought it shame to thayr paternyté
        So foule a werke be done thurgh trechery
35   Was nought semynge unto thaire auncetry.   *fitting*

        It was a poynt so of alligory   *deceit (oblique language)*
        Thaire husbondes so to plese in alle semblaunce   *appearance*
        Accordant als with pride and tirany   *also*
        And undyr it to do thaym suche meschaunce   *injury*
40   Of alle falshode it was a consonaunce   *in keeping*
        And to alle treuthe alway a fulle party   *wicked*
        To shew one thynge and do annother in hy.   *straight away*

fol. 5v   Thus in this muse for sorow and for thought   *this musing; anxiety; reflection*
        Thay rode bothe forthe thaire fadir forto se
45   To lete hym witte afore that it were wrought   *know before*
        It forto staunche by his paternyté   *stop*
        In alle suche wise as thaire fraternyté   *brotherhood*
        Might holpen be and saufe fro alle meschaunce
        Thaire sisters als be sette in governaunce.   *to be*

50   Thay tolde hym alle how as it was devysed
        Amonge his doughtirs by fulle and hool sentence   *judgment*
        And bot it were sone holpen and avysed   *unless; amended; recognized*
        Elles were thay like be slayne withoute offence.
        The kinge byhelde his doughtirs innocence
55   How that for care hire sorows multiplyed   *grief*
        That like she was afore hym to have dyed.   *likely*

        She quoke, she felle, she cried fulle ofte "allase"   *trembled*
        Forthought the tyme that she was bred or borne.   *Regretted*
        So mekel shame she had for thaire trespase   *much*
60   She liste nought leve, she thought hireselff forlorne.   *desired; to live; lost*

She scrat hire face, hire hede was alle fortorne   *scratched*
And fro that she myght speke hire fadir tille   *as soon as; to*
She seyde "Fadir I am here at youre wille

"I pray you lorde for mercy and for grace
65   And yow my lorde, my dere hosbonde also
That whiles I leve in worlde and may have space   *live*
I wille amende whare ever I ride or go.
My systirs alle have wrought me alle this wo
By thaym compelde to swere my husbonde dede.   *dead*
70   Allas what shalle I do, what is youre rede?   *counsel*

"For drede of dethe I durste it nought forsake   *dared; deny*
For thay there swore of thaires right so to do.
But nought forthy that thynge on honde to take   *therefore*
I thought it never indede to do hym to.
75   The tenthe day now comynge shulde it be do.
Thus were we alle accordet and consente
Bot in myn herte til it I never assente."

This mater sanke in tille hir fadirs witte   *mind*
So sore and depe he myght no lengar bere.
80   Bot forthe anone his lettres made by wrytte
Whiche to his sonnes he sende whereso thay were
And also to his doughtirs for that affere   *matter*
To come hym to withoute any dilay
And that in alle the godely haste thay may.

fol. 6r   With that thay came als sone as ever thay myghte
86   Forto fulfille what was his comaundemente.
And whan thay were alle come into his sighte
Anone he sayde to thaym alle his entente: *Straight away*
"O doughtirs myne whi did ye so consente
90   Youre husbondes deth so cruelly diffyne?   *plan*
O cursed be the day that ye were myne!

"What was youre cause to wyrke that felony   *perform*
Agayne my lawe and als my rialté
To shame youre blode by suche a vileny
95   That comen bene alle of hiegheste regalté
And maride wele unto youre egalté   *married; equals*
With kinges alle and grete of excellence?
Whi did ye thaym and me this grete offence?

Here is youre sistir that alle this case me tolde."
100   Thay couthe it nought by ordal than defende   *could; ordeal*
As was thaire lawe hote irne in honde to holde   *hot iron*

	And bere aboute in places that were kende	*known*
	Bot with thaire othe thay profred to defende	*oath; offered*
	The whiche he wolde in no wise lete thaym done	*permit*
105	Trowynge thay wolde of it forsworne thaym sone.	*Believing; forswear*

	The kinge than swore by alle his hiegh parayle	*character*
	So irouse was that thay hote irne shulde bere	*angry; iron*
	"And which of yow of it that doth so faile	
	Shalle de foule deth, or exilde for that feere."	*die; fearful action*
110	Thay saide echone "What so youre willes ere	*desires; are*
	Do with us than, for we wille never it done.	
	We swere yow here by sonne and als by mone."	*sun; moon*

	Thus were thay alle right dampned and attaynte	*judged; convicted*
	Sauf she that was the yongeste of thaym alle	*Except*
115	That tille hire fadir of it had made complaynte.	*to*
	So dyd she to hire lorde, fair mot hire falle	*may good fortune befall her*
	Whose fame therfore in no-wise may appalle	*diminish*
	For recomende she stode in alkyn grace	*praised; all manner of*
	Amonge the folke that herde ought of that case.	*anything*

120	Thensforthe hire lorde hire helde in grete noblesse	
	And love evermore above alle creature.	
	And she hym als in alkyns gentillesse	*also in all manner of kindness*
	With alle constance whils she on lyfe myght dure	*endure*
	Above alle thynge, as come hire of nature	
125	For his noblay and als his worthynesse	*nobility; also*
	She plesed hym ever with alle hire bisynesse.	*activity*

fol. 6v	Bot so the kinge anon gafe jugyment	
	Of his doughtirs that nyne and twenty were	
	Bycause thay cam doun of so hiegh descent	
130	Of blode rial and also maride ere	*married are*
	To kinges of myght that corons did alle bere,	
	No foule done deth he wolde nought lete thaym have	*allow*
	Bot in a ship be putte to spille or save.	*to be killed or saved*

	So in a ship he dyd thaym putte anone	*directly*
135	Withouten men to be thaire governoure	
	Bot with the flode whareas the ship wold gone	*current*
	Forthe in the se with tempest and with showre.	
	To se that sight it was ful grete doloure	*grief*
	Bot that no wight than had of thaym pité	
140	For thaire treson and thaire inyquyté.	

| | Within the se the flode so did thaym dryve | |
| | Ay forth right as the se his course had ronne. | |

	The wynde thaym drofe, now here, now thare, bylyve	*rapidly*
	That unnethe myght thay in thaire wittes wonne	*hardly; remain*
145	In grete perile thay were and litille konne	*knew*
	To helpe thaym self, so were thay superate	*overcome*
	And seke thurgh stormes, and als infortunate.	*ill; unlucky*
	Thus in sorow thay ere ful sore bystadde	*are; badly situated*
	Exilde forever away oute of thaire lande	
150	Whiche were alle quenes richely arayd and cladde	*dressed*
	With servants feel to knele at fote and hande	*many*
	That now in se and flodes ben wayfande.	*tossing*
	And to what parte that thay shalle draw or wynne	*arrive*
	Thay know nothynge bot hungre that thay were ynne.	
155	Thay wote no thinge if ever thay come to lande	*know*
	Ne whether the dethe or life that thay shalle have	
	So feble were thay, myght no fote on stande.	
	Thaire braynes febled, thaire mouthes did bot rave	*enfeebled*
	Thare was grete reuthe to se how that thay drave.	*pity; traveled*
160	Was never that wight that bare suche herte on lyve	*person; alive*
	Bot it wold rewe to se thaym sogates dryve	*grieve; thus journey*
	In stormes grete forhungred and forwake	*utterly sleepless*
	Thaire hertes sore with sekenesse closed aboute	
	Swownynge ful sore, suche wayknesse dyd thaym take.	*Fainting*
165	Lo thay that were byfore so proude and stoute	*strong*
	How thay ere tame for care within and oute	*are meek*
	And how afore thaire hosbondes wold have slayne	
	To whom subgets thay wold now bene right fayne.	*subjects; eagerly*
fol. 7r	So longe thay drofe and sailde upon the se	*travelled*
170	That at the laste thay cam unto a lande	
	And landed sone tharein as it myght be.	
	Bot Albyne first sette fote on grounde to stande	
	And seysyne firste she toke there with hire hande	*legal possession*
	As hire conqueste by ful possessioun	
175	As eldeste sister by trew successioun.	

**Nota that hir fadyr hight Dioclician and hyr modir Albyne payens (*pagans*).
And as some cronicle sayth he was Kynge of Syry, in qua sunt iste provincie:
Palestina, Judea, Chanaan, Idumya, Samaria, Galilea, Cichen, et Fenycia.**[1]

**Bot Martyne in his cronycle sayth thaire fadir was Danaus, Kyng of Argyves,
and thaire husbondes fadir was his brother Egistus that had fyfty sonnes wed
to .l. doughtirs, which thaire wifes slew alle but oone, fore whiche Danaus and
Egistus exiled thaym as Trogus Pompeius sayth in his cronicles of al stories
of the worlde, whiche Justyne his disciple abregid in xliiii bookes.**

	As in Grece than from whyne that thay were sente	*whence*
	The rite so was the law and consuetude	*custom*
	Whare brether failde theldeste sistir by jugement	*the eldest*
	Shuld have the londe by right and rectitude.	*justice*
180	So thinke me wele I may right wele conclude	
	Of hire conqueste she shulde have regency	*governance*
	By alle reson and alle gode policy.	
	But hir sistirs come aftir as thay myght	
	Unnethe thay myght ought gone for febillesse.	*Hardly; at all*
185	Thay felle to grounde with deth as thay were dight	*agony; doomed*
	Forhungred sore and sette in suche distresse.	
	Thay had foryette fro whyne thay come I gesse	*forgotten; whence*
	And also alle the tempests of the se	
	In whiche thay felte ful grete adversité.	
190	Thaire hungre was so grete withoute mesure	
	Thay had foryette alle harme thay felte afore.	
	Save oonly mete thay had non othyr cure	*Except; food; restorative*
	Of whiche thay brought with thaym but lytille store.	
	Yit thay ne wiste whither to go therfore	*did not know*
195	Bot erbes thay founde whiche of necessité	*herbs*
	Thay ete, of whiche thay fonde gude quantité.	

---

[1] *And as some chronicles say he was King of Syria, in which these provinces are to be found: Palestine, Judea, Canaan, Idumea, Samaria, Galilee, Shechem, and Phoenicia*

The .ii. chapitle

Nota whan Dame Albyne and hir systers cam into thys ile whiche thay named than Albyon, for Albynes name, how they bicame hire sugits of whom she had sovereynté aftyr the lawe of Grece, fro whyne thay came, so that the eldest sister had the sovereynté that dwells in that party that now is called Englonde, as Seint Colman sayth in his sayde (*aforesaid*) *Dialoge*.

	This was the yere afore the incarnacioun	*incarnation of Christ*
	A thousand and foure hundre als and fyve	
	Whan thay come in this londe by al relacioun	*accounts*
200	Ful sore anoyed and dredinge of thaire lyve	*distressed; fearing for*
	Oute of the se whan that thay dyd arryve	
	As Omer whiche was poet sapient	*Homer; wise*
	To Agrippe wrote from Grece by his entent.	

	Bot of these systirs now forther forto say	
205	How that thay dyd I wille me now enforse	*direct my energies*
	That wente aboute this londe forto assay	*find out*
	Who dwelte therein, bot thay no mannysshe corse	*male body*
	In it couthe fynde, so nede thaym no dyvorse	
	Ne women none, bot right thaymselff allone.	
210	So sovereyns were thay of thys londe anone.	

fol. 7v   **Nota how Fortune foloweth a mannes devyse**

	Thus Fortune than folowed aftir thaire devise	*plan*
	As thay afore desired soveraynté	
	The whiche thay had so thus at thaire avise	*according to their wish*
	Thurgh Fortunes stroke and mutabilité	
215	That brought were thus from thaire priorité	
	The sovereynté to have and governance	
	Of alle this londe withoute disobeyshance.	

	Bot Albyne than sayde to hire sistirs bright	
	"This lande shalle hatte Albyon after me	*be called*
220	It awe to bere the name of me by right	*ought*
	I am first borne to have the sovereynté	
	And first toke lande by my fortuyté	*chance*
	Wherfore ye alle owe me obedience	
	And service als by right and consequence.	

225	"Fortune it gafe to us by desteny	
	Seynge afore oure cruelle aventure	
	At natife birthe sette oure predesteny	
	This londe to have whils we may leve and dure	*live; endure*
	To us and to alle oure hool engendrure	*lineage*

230   Wherfore sethe we have it so sovereynly
    Lete us go bigge and dwelle here fynaly."   *build*

The .iii. chapitle

How the ladise felle in syn and lychery had geants (*giants*) to sonne that leved agayne (*against*) the law of God and kepte no pese amonge thaymselfe, bot grete stryfe and wronge sustened, for whiche God toke vengeance on thaym whan Brute destroyed hem.

    The ladise so with mete and drinke replete   *satisfied*
    And of nature revigourde corporaly
    And alle thaire care foryete and undrefet   *forgot; subdued*
235   Thay felte desire to play thaym womanly
    As women yit wille do fulle lovyngly
    To have fulfilde the werke of womanhede
    And frute to have the londe to reule and lede.   *offspring; govern*

    So were thay tempte and felle in vaynglory   *imbued with*
240   That nyght and day thaire hertes were implyde   *intent*
    To have at do with men in lichory   *lechery*
    And how thay myght of men bene beste provyde
    So inwardly in it thay glorifyde   *obsessed*
    That spirits than on thaym toke mannysshe fourme
245   Liggynge by thaym thaire lustes to refourme.   *Lying; satisfy*

    So dwellynge forthe in that luste and delyte
    With nature of thaymself and semynacioun   *production of semen*
    Tho spirits gat childre that were geants tyte   *soon*
    On thaym and thurgh thaire owne ymagynacioun
250   By fervent hete moved with temptacioun.
    Thus gat thay than grete geants fulle of myght
    Within short tyme that were bothe hieghe and wight.   *powerful*

fol. 8r   So usualy echone by other lay
    Modir ne sistir agayn it nought replyde.   *objected*
255   Of children feel sonnes and doughtirs ay   *many*
    Thay gate eche day and strongly multiplyde.   *begot*
    Of peple so this londe was fortyfyde
    That in it was so grete generacioun
    Non durste it noye for drede of supplantacioun.   *trouble; usurpation*

260   Thay were so stronge by thaire fortunacioun   *chance*
    Bothe myche and large and of thaire persones wight   *great; powerful*
    Men were adred of thaire malignacioun   *malignancy*
    There was no wight durste come in to thaire sight   *person; dared*
    Ought thaym to greve so were thay prest to fyght   *In any way; ready*

265 Cruel and stern and hideuse onto se
  So that oon of thaym a thousond wold nought fle.   *flee from*

  Thay dwelte on heghtes on helles and hiegh montayns   *hills*
  In whiche thay made grete edificaciouns   *dwellings*
  And wondirfulle, withoute water or fountayns
270 Bot castels grete whare were thaire habitaciouns.
  Yit men may se in crags thaire operaciouns   *works*
  Of holes and house and kaves alle destitute
  Bot whan werre is, yit do thay grete refute. *still; serve as; refuge*

  Comons for feere of enmyse and of were   *Commoners; war*
275 Yit bere thaire gudes this day into suche kaves
  With strengh of men ful seure abyde thay there   *protected*
  Fro spoylinge of ennemyse, boyes and knaves *Against plundering by; ruffians*
  In whiche ful ofte the peple thaire godes saves.
  Bot alle tho werkes that were on hilles mast   *highest hills*
280 Bene now alle doun by tempest and by waste.

  Thise geants thus this londe did so obtene *take possession of*
  Thay no wight durste ourwhare thaym ought offend *person; dared; anywhere*
  From Dame Albyne cam to this londe I mene *From [the time]*
  Whils that tho wightes it had and comprehende. *possessed*
285 So regned thay and strongly it defende
  Two hundre yere fully also and fyve
  To tyme that Brute with thaym dyd aftir stryve. *Until; fight*

  Thaire custome eke and thaire consuetude *also; usage*
  Thaire glory and mesgoverned appetyte
290 So curste were ay in yowthe and senectude *old age*
  That longe thay myght not dure in thaire delyte. *endure*
  Of alle levynge thay were so inperfyte *corrupt*
  That God right by his reule and regyment
  Of thayre regnynge wolde putte impediment. *wished to*

fol. 8v As God it wolde of his hiegh provydence
296 At laste dyd sette amonge thaym grete dissencioun *civil strife*
  That who maistry myght gete by violence *control*
  Distroed othyr by batayle and contencioun. *fighting*
  Amonge thaym felle thanne so grete succensioun *violence*
300 Of ire and wrathe thrugh thaire mesgovernaunce *anger*
  That eche of thaym of other toke vengeance.

  For echone other slew and brought to nought
  Within few yeres, sauf thretty bode in alle *except; remained*
  Of thousandes twelfe so were thay dede forfought *dead through battle*
305 Thaire mysreulde pride and boste so doun was falle.

Than were thay few, thaire power did appalle,   *diminish*
Whose regne thus felle afore the incarnacioun
Twelfe hundre yere by very computacioun.   *true*

Of these now wille I cese and speke no more
310   Til tyme come efte that Brutus have thaym slayne   *afterwards*
       Of whom I wille telle forthe how he was bore   *born*
       And of what kynde and blode he came sertayne
       And how he wan and named it Bretayne
       This londe mysled thurgh cruelle tyrany   *destroyed*
315   Of geants felle that leved cursidly.   *fierce; lived*

       And whare he firste arryved in this ile
       Of Albyon that hight afore that day   *was called*
       And as my tonge can langage it and file   *express; record*
       At Adam nowe I wille bygynne and say
320   Of whom he came and clerly doun I may
       Convay his blode as I fynde it writen.
       In olde storise it is wele know and wytyn.   *understood*

BOOK TWO

Secundus Liber

.i. capitulum
How Brutus discomfyte (*defeated*) the Kynge of Grece and Albion had, and called it than Bretayne after hym and of his auncetry and his successours, the genology as is comprised in the grete Brute and in the cronicles of Itaylle, as Pli(?) saith in his book *De Gestis Enee Regis Latinorum*.[1]

Cronica Bruti per Galfridum Monmentensem extracta de quodam libro britannico sibi tradito per Walterum Oxoniensem archdiaconum et translata in latinum ad rogatum Roberti ducis Gloucestrie filii Regis Henrici primi Anglie.[2]

	As cronycles say and make notificacioun	
	Who loke thaym wele schal know and undirstonde	
	Of watkyns blode and generacioun	*what kind*
	Brutus first came that conquerde alle this londe.	
5	It to remembre I shal now take on honde	
	Thurgh olde storise by philofres compiled	*learned men*
	In olde bokes as I have sene and fonde	
	In Englisshe tonge it shal be made and fyled.	*recorded*
	At the Bible therfore I wille begynne	
10	At Adam whiche was so firste creature	
	Convaynge doun lynyaly in kynne	
	As thay descent in birth and engendrure	
	Next unto Brute as mencionde hath scripture	
	I shalle reporte as God wille deyne to lede	
fol. 9r	My symple goste unkunnynge in lettrure	*spirit; unskillful*
16	As liketh hym with language me to fede.	*it pleases him; provide*
	To whom I pray for spede unto the ende	*success*
	My wytte enforce in myght and sapience.	*strengthen*

---

[1] *Concerning the Deeds of Aeneas, the King of the Latins*

[2] *The Chronicle concerning Brute, extracted by Geoffrey of Monmouth from a certain British book given to him by Walter Archdeacon of Oxford and translated into Latin at the request of Robert Duke of Gloucester, the son of King Henry I of England*

	Of other goddis whiche poetes used and kende	*knew*
20	In olde poeses I lak intelligence	*poems; knowledge*
	Ne nought I wille so hurte my conscience	
	On thaym to muse whiche God defendeth me	*prohibits*
	And als for sothe for any eloquence	
	I tasted never the welles of Caliope.	

25	Yit wille I nought pray helpe of Saturnus
	Of Jubiter, ne Mars or Mercury
	Venus, Ceres, Phebus or Seneus
	Of Pallas, ne Alecte or Megary
	Of Genyus or yit Thesiphony
30	Of Cupido ne of Ymeneus
	Mynerve, Diane, Bachus or Cerbery
	Manes, Glaucus, Vulcane or Protheus.

	Tho goddis olde and fals I alle refuse	*Those*
	And pray to God that sitte in Trynyté	
35	My goste to guy on thaym that it nought muse	*spirit; guide; become lost*
	Enspirynge it in alle sufficienté	
	Of suche language as is necessité	
	This boke to ende in balade and translate	*poetry*
	Thus newe bygunne of my symplicité	
40	Amonges makers it be unreprobate.	*poets; unreproved*

	For wele I wote withoute his supportacion	*know; help*
	For to reporte alle his genology	
	How he descent by alkyn generacion	*all kinds*
	From Adam doun to Troiane auncetry	
45	Goten and borne certayne in Italy	*Begotten*
	Who Grece conquerde, Guyen, Fraunce and Spayne	
	Makers can I none counterfete ne revy	*imitate; rival*
	So symple ere my spirits and my brayne.	*are my mental faculties*

	Bot to thaym alle this boke forto corecte	
50	Whare as thay thynke my wytte in ought hath merred	*gone astray*
	Mekely I wylle submytte now and directe	
	Bysekinge thaym amende whare I have erred.	
	Allethoughe I am unworthy be preferred	*to be raised up*
	Amonges makers, yit I wolde I fayne bene one	*poets; desire; to be*
55	Of thaire servants accounted and referred	*reckoned; numbered*
	Thurgh thaire mercy, that thay were noght my fone.	*foes*

fol. 9v **The genlogie fro Adam to Brutus**

	Bot of Adam that was firste creature	
	That ever had life and alther wisest man	*of all*

Cam Seth his son so holy clene and pure.
60 And Seth for sothe Enos his son gatte than *truly; begot*
And of Enos cam his son Caynaan
Of whom cam doun his son Malaleel
Of whom so forthe descended Jareth than
Of whom Enoch that gatte Matussaleel.

65 Of whom Lameke, noght he was weddid twyse *the one who*
Whiche was that tyme agayn the law of man *against*
Bot he of whom Noe cam so gude and wise
Of whom Japhet cam the whiche gatte so Javan *begot*
Of whom so doun descended Cythym than
70 Who Cypre gatte that Cypres first dyd name
Of whom cam Crete that the Ile of Grece bygan
And dyd it name ay forth after hym the same. *forever*

Of Crete than cam his son hight Celi *called*
Of whom Saturne that taught men firste to bygge *build*
75 Nerwhare that Rome now ys in Italy *Near*
And edyfy thaire houses into lygg *build; dwell*
Vynes to plante the londe to tele and dygg *till*
So with thaire swynke and bodily laboure *work*
For than was thare nayther hen, gose, ne pygge *goose*
80 Ne other flesshe for thaire lyves socoure. *sustenance*

Of whom cam than Jubyter of Frygy *Phrygia*
Whiche Turky hight in whiche Troy cyté *is called*
In honoure stode and in grete victory
That chief cyté was so of alle Turké.
85 Dardanus cam of his paternyté
His sonne he was and gretly magnifyed
That regned firste as kinge of alle Frygé
And as a god amonges thaym glorified.

Of whom cam than his son Eryctonius
90 Who gatte a son that Troy first edifyde *begot; built*
Who Troyus hight of whom came Kynge Ilus *was called*
That Ilyon made a palays of grete pryde
Whiche forpassinge other was longe and wyde *surpassed*
Rychely within wrought with stones precyus.
95 Whiche Ilus gatte Leamedon that tyde *begot; time*
That aftyr was kinge of Troy so gloryus.

Whom Ercules at Troys firste eversion *destruction*
In bataylle slew whan Jason with his hoste
fol. 10r Destroyed Troy and wasted by subversioun
100 The rialle blode and led away with boste

In dyverse parte within the Grekesshe coste   *lands*
Thaym holdynge thare in bondship and in servytude
Perpetualy to byde thare leest and moste   *endure*
Thus into peyne thay felle fro altitude.   *height*

Conceyte of the maker how Troy for litil myght hafe bene undistroyed, by whiche is to consider favoure, whare none hurte may be, whan aliens com in to a reme by distresse of tempest or wynde.

105   Whiche sorowes so for lytille thynge dyd falle
      Bycause thay lette Jason whan that he wolde   *hindered*
      Have vytayld hym thare and his navy alle   *provisioned*
      Whom nayther for money ne for golde
      Thay wolde refresshe, bot whether he wolde or nolde   *wished to or not*
110   Thay bad hym voyde on payne of forfeture   *leave*
      The londe anone, in story as it is tolde
      And iff he bode upon hys aventure.   *remained; chance*

      O thou gude lorde that was Leamedoun
      What fortune drofe thee do thaym unkyndenesse
115   Whare thay to pay for it were redy boun   *prepared*
      Considerynge how he cam in by distresse
      Whiche aftyr was cause of thy hevynesse
      Whan he thee slew distroynge Troys cyté
      And caste doun alle thy myght and grete noblesse
120   Withouten hurte that saved myght have be?

      Leamedon gat than Kinge Priamus   *begot*
      And Anchises that worthy duke and wyse.
      Whiche Priamus gat Ector and Troylus
      And Dephebus, Helenus, and Paryse
125   Whiche were alle dukes in Troy of grete empryse   *grandeur*
      Of ryalle blode and of most excellence.
      And alle were slayne thurgh Fortunes excercyse
      At sege of Troy knyghtly in thaire defence

      Sauf Helenus and his sistir Exiona   *Except*
130   Were holde in Grece in thraldom and servage
      Unsemyngly for Priams childer and Eccuba   *Unfittingly; children*
      Whiche kinge and quene so were of heritage
      And made Troy new agayn in his yonge age
      Aftyr the firste sege and subversioun   *destruction*
135   And Ilion als rialle to his parage   *heritage*
      That wasted was by that same eversioun.   *destruction*

The largesse of Troye cyté

So brode he made Troy and in longitude
Thre days jornays it was on horse to ryde
With walles stronge and toures grete multitude
140   And yates therto ful strongly fortyfyde.   *gates*
fol. 10v   Never cyté was so gretly edyfiede   *constructed*
Of marbre clere, fresshe of dyverse coloure   *marble; bright*
Of whiche the walles were murifyde   *encased*
Two hundre cubits with many rial toure.   *splendid tower*

145   This longeth nought I say to my matere   *pertains*
It is so ferre and longe degrecioun   *digression*
Wherfore fro it I wille agayn refere   *return*
To Anchises, fro whom I made egrecioun   *divagation*
That fadyr was by alle repetycioun
150   To Eneas as cronyclers expreme   *express*
Who gat Ascanyus by disposicioun   *begot*
Of God above by ought that men can deme.   *judge*

How Eneas regned in Itayly and was Kynge of Latyne and of Tuskayne by hys wife Lavynyane.

Whiche thre cam doun playnly by discent
Of rialle blode of Troy next Priamus
155   And worthi dukes were in werres and excellent
Tyl Troy was take, in bokes I fynde it thus   *taken*
The Grekes exilde Eneas and Ascanyus
And Anchises by se that dyd forth passe
Thurgh many stoure and tempest aventrus   *battle; dangerous*
160   Tylle in Sisilé thaire ship arryven wasse   *Sicily*

Whare Anchises dyd dye and was dispent.   *exhausted by death*
Eneas and his son toke than the se
With alle thaire shippes to Itaylle had thay ment   *intended*
Bot wynde thaym drofe in Aufrike withoute lee   *Africa; shelter*
165   From whyne thay myght so nayther sayle ne fle   *whence*
Bot welcome were for Duke Eneas sake
For Quene Didone hym had in specialté   *special favor*
And thought of hym hire husbonde forto make.

He stale fro hire and toke the see agayne
170   And rofe on londe whare now is Italy   *arrived*
In Tyber mouthe with travaylle and with payne   *Tiber; difficulty*
Whare Ostia the porte ys fynaly.
Whare hym was tolde in vision pryvaly
That he shuld helpe Kynge Evandre that reyned

175 In seven mountaynes whare Rome is now oonly
     Whiche londe on hym he vouched sauf and deyned   *granted*

     For by thaire god it was so prophecyde
     That he shuld have grete parte of Italy
     And regne tharein of peple magnyfyde   *exalted*
180 Thurgh his wisdome and dedes of chyvalry.
     Wharefore he cam to hym fulle worthyly
     To do hym bothe his servyce and plesance
     Bryngand a braunche of olyfe pesibly   *Bringing; olive*
     In honde for signe of pese and concordance.

fol. 11r Of whom the kynge Evandre gan glorify
186 And of his come was wele rejoysed and gladde   *coming*
     For his worshyp and for his auncetry
     And gaffe hym londe and reule of alle he hadde.
     And for he was so exilde and bystadde   *ill-situated*
190 He gaffe hym thare bothe castels and rychesse
     To leve upon, and rialy hym cladde   *live*
     And golde ynewgh, right of his worthynesse.   *plentiful*

     This kinge Evandre made werre on Kynge Latyne
     In whose socoure Turnus kinge of Tuskayne   *support*
195 Cam with his hoste of Tuskalayns so fyne
     Agayn Evandre and faught til he was slayne.
     Eneas dyd that dede and that derayne   *combat*
     With myghty strokes and corage chyvalrouse
     Of whiche so was Evandre glad and fayne   *delighted*
200 Whan that he saw hym so victoriouse.

     Bytuyx Evandre than so and Kynge Latyne   *Between*
     The pese he made, reste and ful concordance
     And Kynge Latyns doughtir that hight Lavyne   *was called*
     Weddyd to wyfe by trew and gode accordance
205 Bytwyx thaym forthe was no more discordance.
     Bot ful posseste kynge was of alle Tuscayne   *Tuscany*
     Syr Eneas, and had the governance
     And Lavyne quene in grete plesance certayne.

     Sone after that dyed the kynge Latyne
210 So Eneas had bothe remes in pese   *realms*
     And reuled thaym by reson wele and fyne   *fine*
     Tyl he dyd dye withouten werre or prese   *external pressure*
     Of enmyse ought. By lawe it was no lese   *lie*
     So rightewysly he kepte the regymente   *rule*
215 That fame of hym went wyde at his decese
     Of honoure hiegh deserved in hys entente.

	This Eneas dyd byg and edify	*build; construct*
	Within his reame a castel passynge fayre	*exceptionally*
	Lavynyon by name specialy	
220	Aftir his wife Lavyne thareof was hayre	*heir*
	Of whom he gat a son, bot in despayre	*begot*
	Therof he dyed wenynge have had son none	*thinking*
	Who borne so was of beuté nought unfayre	
	Aftyr he was dede, to hayre his londes echone.	*inherit*

225	The fourth yere after that Troy was desolate	
	Whiche was afore that Rome was edifyde	*constructed*
	Or had the name of Rome denomynate	
	Thre hundre yere and thretty specifyde	*thirty*
fol. 11v	Whan Abdon was in Isrelle magnyfyde	
230	And reuled alle thynge aftyr his jugyment	
	As Omer sayde and hath it notyfyde	*told*
	That poete was, and wyse of sentement.	

	This worthy prynce Kynge Eneas mortaly	
	Endyd his lyfe that was of hyegh prowesse	
235	Whare that God wylle to regne eternaly	
	Withyn the House of Fame, whare as I gesse	
	Ere knyghtes fele of grete worthyness	*Are; many*
	That more desire had ay to bere grete fame	
	Of doughty dedes alle of thare own prowesse	
240	Than beste knyght be and bere therof no name.	

	Bot than his sonne Sylvyus Postumus	
	New borne was than and yonge of tendre age.	
	Kynge of his londes was made Ascanyus	
	His brothur dere that reuled his heritage	
245	Ful pesybly kepte oute of alle servage	*subjection*
	Twenty wynter and eght corporaly	*(see note)*
	Wythin whiche tyme he gate a sonne so sage	*begot*
	Hight Sylvyus and Julus nomynaly.	*Called*

	Whiche Sylvyus dyd gette and generate	*beget*
250	His sonne Brutus on Creusa, Lavynes nese	*neice*
	Alle pryvely by hym devirgynate	*deflowered*
	And sore bisoughte with his subtilitese	*fervently entreated; trickery*
	And nought forthy some parte by hire pitese	
	That tendred hym of hire femynyté	*grew compassionate towards*
255	As womanhode wolde of gode humylitese	
	Have reuthe on alle men in adversité.	*pity*

| | Askanyus whan he knew that it was so | |
| | Amonge hys clerkys he dyd anone enquere | |

260	What shuld become of Brutus, welle or wo	
	Alle answerde hym as ye shalle after here	
	That he shuld sla Creusa his moder dere	*slay*
	His fadir als thurgh grete fortuyté	*ill chance*
	And afterwardes to grete estate affere	*befit*
	And reames wyn thurgh his humanyté.	*courtesy*
265	So after sone the fate of dethe wolde so	
	That passe away shuld than Ascanyus	
	He gaffe his brother Silvyus Postumus tho	*then*
	His heritage of richesse plentyuus	
	In whiche he made a cyté merveylus	
270	On Tyber, so hight Aube and yit hatte so.	*called; named*
	A dignyté it is to Rome famus	
	A cardynalle it hath ay and no mo.	*always*
fol. 12r	Dame Creusa than that tyme lay in gisée	*preparation for delivery*
	Afore hire tyme by right disposicioun	
275	Of Brute hire sonne in whose natyvyté	
	She dyed right thurgh thayr dyvysioun.	
	Thus was he cause of hire occisioun	*death*
	Fro his modir whan he was seperate	
	As clerkes seyde by thaire prevysioun	*foresight*
280	It felle right so and lyke predestinate.	
	His fadir than that hight Syr Sylvyus	
	Dyd brynge hym up as he up grew in age	
	In alle nurture that myght be fructuus	*edifying*
	And vertu als semynge for his parage.	*lineage*
285	So was he grounde and taught in alle language	
	Within fewe yeres and in his juventude	*youth*
	That by the tyme he was fiftene yere age	
	In eloquence he had the plenytude.	

How lordes sonnes shuld bene lerned in tendre age, aftyr the consayte of the makere of this boke, to induce hem to take vertu and eschewe vices.

Nota	And as lordes sonnes bene sette at foure yere age	
290	To scole at lerne the doctryne of lettrur	*to*
	And after at sex to have thaym in language	
	And sitte at mete semely in alle nurture.	*good breeding*
	At ten ande twelve to revelle is thaire cure	*engage in merrymaking*
	To daunse and synge and speke of gentelnesse.	
295	At fourtene yere thay shalle to felde isure	*sally forth*
	At hunte the dere and catche an hardynesse	*To; master a fearless boldness*

Nota	For dere to hunte and sla and se thaym blede	
	Ane hardyment gyffith to his corage	*courage; heart*
	And also in his wytte he takyth hede	
300	Ymagynynge to take thaym at avauntage.	
	At sextene yere to werray and to wage,	*do battle; fight*
	To juste and ryde and castels to assayle,	
	To scarmyse als and make sykyr scurage[1]	
	And sette his wache for perile nocturnayle.	

Nota	And every day his armure to assay	*assault*
306	In fete of armes with some of his meyné	*household*
	His might to preve and what that he do may	
	Iff that he were in suche a juparteé	*danger*
	Of werre byfalle that by necessité	
310	He muste algates with wapyns hym defend.	*in any case*
	Thus shuld he lerne in his priorité	
	His wapyns alle in armes to dispende.	*use*

	So was Brutus after other lessons hadde	
	Upon a day at age of fiftene yere	
315	Nurtured fully right faire, wyse and gladde,	
	Gentile and god and of right humble chere	*good*
fol. 12v	And of his age that tyme he had no pere.	
	So was he sette in alle nobilité	
	And trew in alle by ought that couthe appere,	
320	Stedfast also withoute mutabilité.	

	His fadir so for joy he of hym hadde	
	As Fortune wolde, executrice of weerdes	*mistress of fate*
	Led hym to wode apon a day fulle gladde	
	Of hertes and hyndes to hunte right at the heerdes.	
325	Thay slew thaym doun with houndes and som with swerdes	
	With that Brutus as he an herte dyd shete	*shoot*
	His fadyr slew as was afore his weerdes	*destiny*
	Wharefore his herte was oute of alle quyete.	

	Thus were his werdes at that tyme execute	
330	By Fortunes fals and fallible execucioun	*untrustworthy*
	By clerkes aforne spoken and prelocute.	*predicted*
	How myght it be bot verry constitucioun	
	Of God above and by his institucioun	
	Whiche myght noght be in no wise dissolute	*relaxed*
335	Withouten hym to whom alle retribucioun	
	Fully longeth and may alle retribute?	*repay*

---

[1] *To fight in small parties and become a careful scout*

How Brute, after the dethe of his fadir, fled fro Itaylle into Grece whare that he discomfid (*defeated*) the kynge and his Grekes.

Brutus seand thys fals fortunyté   *wicked destiny*
The sorows grete in hym so multiplyde
That thare for shame of that fortuyté   *accident*
340   In no wyse wolde he lengar dwelle ne byde
Bot into Grece his sorows forto hyde
He wente anone whare exils were of Troy
Of whom thay were right glad and medifyd   *cured*
Thaire double sorowe he leched alle with joy.   *healed*

345   Syr Helenus was Priams son of Troy
And Anchises an olde worthy knyght
And sex thousond that of hym had gret joy
Of gentilmen fro Troy exiled ryght
Hym thare besought with instance day and nyght
350   To helpe thaym oute right of thare heped sorow
In whiche thay lay opressed agayns myght
In servytute and thraldome even and morow.   *evening; morning*

For pyté of thaym he made than his avowe
What whils that he myght armes bere and ryde
355   He shuld never lete no Troyan to Greke bowe
Ne in servage thare langer to abyde.
For whiche he wrote his letture in that tyde
To Pandrase that the kynge was of that londe
Requyrynge hym to late thaym passe and ryde
360   With fredom whare thaym lyste to sytte or stonde.

fol. 13r   **How the Grekes segid Brute, and by a wile of werre he putte the Grekes to flyght and toke the kynge.**

For whiche the kynge had scorne and grete derisioun
Sendinge aboute for alle his barons stoute
Tellynge thaym alle of Brutus disposicioun
How he was sette the Troyans to have oute
365   Of Grece alle fre, right in a rialle route
Whiche was grete harme unto his regioun
Iff thay shuld fre with myght departen oute
And to his lawe a foul abbregioun.   *illegality*

With that the Grekes cam on with alle thaire hoste
370   Thaym purposynge with Brutus forto fight.
So dyd also Brutus withouten boste
And sodenly he felle on thaym that nyght
And slew thaym doun the tyme while he had light.

	The Grekes gafe bak and fled to Askalone	*turned and ran*
375	The kynge also thare fled at alle his myght	
	In whiche water ware drowned mony one.	

	And in that chase were take Antigonus	
	The kynges brothur and Syr Anacletoun	
	That pryvy was with Kynge Pandrasius	
380	Whiche Brutus had and sette in his prisoun.	
	For whiche the kynge agayn dyd make hym boun	*ready*
	And sought Brutus whare he in castel lay	
	Makynge a dyke aboute it up and doun	*trench*
	So stronge he myght nought owt bot by o way.	*one way*

	Wherefore Brutus seynge alle this meschefe	
385	That seged was his castel in suche wyse	*besieged*
	He sente so than Anacletus in briefe	
	Unto the hoste to say thaym on this gyse	*manner*
	How he had stolne fro Brute Antigonyse	
390	And in the wode hym hyd withouten fayle	
	From whyne withoute grete helpe he durste not ryse	*whence*
	And byd thaym helpe "ere eny you assayle."	

	To whiche disceyte graunted Anacletus	
	So he alle fre delyverd myght so be	
395	Withoute raunson fully consentynge thus	
	And to the Grekes he made this propre le	*lie*
	Ledynge thaym forthe unto the wod he se	*until he saw the forest*
	Levynge thaire warde open withouten wache	*gate; guard*
	By whiche way Brute wente forthe with his meyné	*company*
400	Embusshynge hym in it the Grekes to cache.	*ambushing*

fol. 13v	The Grekes ful glad came to that wode anone	
	Trustynge in alle his wordes that he were trewe	
	Bot Brute brake oute and slew thaym everychone	
	At sprynge of day whan nyght had chaunged hewe	
405	From whyne he wente that Grekes aftir knewe	*whence*
	Forth whare the kinge of Grece in tente dyd lye	
	Undiskevred with alle his Troians newe	
	So had he slayne thaire scurage sutylye.	*scouts skillfully*

	And toke the kynge and slew his men right faste	
410	So that thay fled forbeten on every syde	*severely beaten*
	And some were drownde ere thay the water paste	
	Som in tentes slayne, som fled and wold not byde	
	And Troians ever after thaym chace and ryde	
	And wan the feeld with honoure and victory	

| 415 | Rejoysed gretly of alle thaire dedes that tyde | *time* |
| | As wryten is and put in memory. | |

How Brute wedde the kynges doughter of Grece and came to Leogice with his flete whare Diane sayde he shuld have Albion.

	Brutus thynkynge no langar thare abyde	
	So that he myght have Innogene to wyfe	
	And shippes ynew fulle vytailde in to ryde	*aplenty stocked; travel*
420	By se to seke hym londe upon to thryfe	*thrive*
	His purpose was with Troians to arrife	
	Thaym forto holde in alle fulle liberté	
	As natife byrthe of his prerogatife	*(royal) prerogative*
	Had ordaynde thaym of olde antiquité.	

425	The kynge he sette in alle fulle liberté	
	Anacletus also and Antigone	
	And lordes alle with alle tranquylité	
	With thy he myght alle fre with Troyans gone	*these [men]*
	Saufly to passe oute of the londe anone	
430	With alle suche thynge as longe to thaire dispense	
	To whiche the kynge with gode wille graunte anone	
	Sendynge for shippes that were of grete defence	

	Thre hundreth shyppes wel stuffed of vytaylle	*provisioned with*
	With alle tresoure and golde grete quantyté	
435	And riche aray for thaire two apparaylle	
	Accordant wele unto thaire parenté	*lineage*
	And armours als in oportunyté	
	Thaym to socoure from alkyns violence	*protect*
	And wedded thaym with grete felycyté	
440	And gaffe thaym gyftes of his magnyficence.	

	So saylynge forthe by two days and two nyghtes	
	With sex thousand of Troyans in his flete	
	Right welle arayed for werre on alkyn rightes	*in all manner*
	His wyfe swownynge he comforte and rehet	*comforted; cheered*
fol. 14r	Hyre kyssynge ofte with wordes kynde and swete	
446	Tyl at the laste in Leogice thay cam	
	An ile it was forwasted and forlete	*abandoned*
	By outlawde men that it conquerde and nam.	*seized*

	So on thrid day thare in a cyté fayre	
450	Alle waste, no man ne woman dyd thay se	
	Bot o goddesse to whom right grete repayre	*one; dwelling place*
	Of olde had bene and of priorité	
	Dyane she hight and couth of destené	

        And telle the werdes of men what shulde byfalle.
455   Bothe hert and hynde grete sufficienté
        Within that ile were spred and sene overalle.

        His men thaym slew and to the shippes dyd lede
        For thaire vitayle and for thaire sustynance
        To leve upon if that thay stode in nede.   *live*
460   But Brutus went Dyane to do plesance   *propitiate*
        Made his prayers to hyre with exspectaunce   *(see note)*
        Offrynge bothe blude and mylke of a white hynde
        And wyne also for his observaunce
        Whiche was the use of Troyans as I fynde.   *custom*

465   He lay alle nyght upon a hynde skyn white
        Bysekynge hire to lete hym wytte what place   *know*
        He shuld byde in with his Troyans grete and lyte
        And slepynge so Dyane hym shewed hire grace
        And sayde "Byyonde alle Gaule a se grete space
470   Ane ile thou shalt fynde gode and fructuouse   *fruitful*
        Toward the weste which se doth alle enbrace
        That geants now holden ful maliciouse

        "That londe shalbe to thee and thy posterité
        Evermore lastynge whare thou shalt edyfy   *build*
475   New Troy forsoth with grete felicité
        A cyté grete thy name to magnify.
        Thou and thyne heyres thare shalle so multiply
        That alle the worlde shalle drede and doute youre name
        So shalle ye growe in welthe and vyctory
480   That over alle londes wyde whare shalle sprede youre fame."

        And whan he woke of slepe he tolde his dreme
        Unto his men for whiche thay were ful fayne   *eager*
        That thay shuld wyn and have so gude a reme   *realm*
        Unto thaire shippis thay went ful faste agayne
485   Saylynge so forthe by se in storme and payne.
        In thretty days into Aufrike thay cam
        And so forthe sayled towardes the se of Spayne
        And richesse grete he gette aywhare and nam.   *everywhere; seized*

fol. 14v So saylynge by the Columpnes of Ercules
490   That men do calle in oure Englisshe language
        Ercules Pylers of Bras it is no les   *lie*
        Who wan alle theder and had therof truage   *tribute*
        And sette thaym so to stonde by that ryvag   *shore*
        In signe that he was thedir conqueroure   *thither*

495   And wan it alle only of his corage
       Evermore to dure in signe of his honoure.   *remain*

**How Brute bylaste (*bound*) Coryneus to ben with hym, and how thay faughte with
Kynge Goffore of Aquytayne and discomfyd.**

       Fro thens thay came in tille the se of Spayne
       Whare that thay founde Troianes of thare lynage
       That fled fro Troy with sorow grete and payne
500   Whan Troy was loste that was thaire heritage   *necessities*
       Whiche wan by se thare lifelode thurgh outrage   *piracy*
       Robbynge also and takyng what thay fonde
       Of grete rychesse thay made alle thayre lastage   *ballast*
       Thare shippes so to charge thay toke on honde.   *load*

505   Coryneus than hight thaire capitayne   *was called*
       A mykylle man and thereto ful of myghte   *great*
       A geant like of Brute he was ful fayne
       Bycause thay were of Troy and Troyans hight.
       Wherfore with Brute he dyd passe forth ful right
510   Bycam his men he and his company
       Whare so he wolde in any place to fight
       Sayand it was thayre werdes of desteny.

       Thay sayled so forthe by se to Aquitayne
       That Guyen now is, whare thay rofe to londe   *Guyenne; landed*
515   And thare thay slew of whiche thay were ful fayne
       Both buk and do, bothe herte and hynde thay fande
       Of no wight had thay leve ne yit warrande.
       Wharfore Goffore and alle his meyny felle   *fierce band*
       That thare was kynge faught with thaym hande by hande
520   So at that tyme Coryneus bare the belle   *won the field*
       Discomfyte thaym thai durste not byde ne stande.   *Routed*

       With that Goffore wente into Gaule agaste
       That now is Fraunce and so denomynate   *named*
       Prayande ful fayre the Dusze Piers right faste   *Entreating; Twelve Peers*
525   To socoure hym that was extermynate   *driven out*
       And putte out of his londe and superate   *overcome*
       With enmyse felle and of grete multitude
       As he that oon of thaym was ordynate   *appointed*
       To reule the londe oute of alle servitude.

530   In this mene tyme whils he gatte his socoure
       For Turnus sake that was his cosyn dere
       Was slayn so thare, Brutus dyd make a toure
       Whiche yit thys day hatte Toures who wille enquere   *is called*

fol. 15r	For cause Turnus was layde thare in his bere	*bier*
535	And byried thare for whose rememorance	
	Aftir his name Turnus as myght affere	*be suitable*
	Brutus so made in signe and conyshance.	*recognition*

That castelle made and fully edifyde
The Dusze Piers alle with thare power rialle
540 Faught with Brutus and Coryneus defyde.
Yit never the les the Dusze Piers had a falle
The Troyans dyd that tyme so welle over alle
And so dyd Brute and als Coryneus.
Gret multitude of thaym that were of Galle
545 Was slayne and fled — Ovyde hath wryten thus.

At Toures thay helde after that gret bataylle
Thaire counselle wyse to se what governance
Were to thaym beste and moste myght thaym avaylle
And to thaym als that myght be leste hyndrance.

550	In whiche by oon assent and concordance	
	Thay toke to rede whare that thay were assigned	*considered*
	By the goddesse to passe with alle plesance	
	Lesse she be wrothe thurgh which it be repigned	*angry; denied*

How Brute londed at Tottenes and conquerde Albyon upon the geantes.

Nota how Brutus entred at Totnesse in Grete Bretayne in the armes of Troye as heire to Eneas; he bare of goules (*red*) two lyouns golde rawmpants, a contrarie (*opposite each other*), also he bare a banere of vert (*green*) a Diane of golde dischevely (*with hair hanging loose*) corouned and enthronysed, that were Eneas armes whan he entryed the reme of Latyne that now is Romanye, as it is specifyed in the cronycles of Romanye, as Giraldus Cambrensis wryteth in his Topographie of Brutes armes of Troye aforsayde, and as Trogus Pompeyus wryteth in his book of al storyes touchant (*concerning*) the forsaide armes of Eneas.

	Wharefore thay wente anone to shyp and sayle	
555	Restynge no thynge tille that thay were anente	*facing*
	The coste thay sought, and myght nought of it faile.	
	Enhabite so with geants of defence	*warlike giants*
	Albyon it hight by alkyns evydence	*was called; every kind of*
	As ye have herde in this before expreste	
560	Whiche by malyce and grete malyvolence	
	The poraylle ever devourde sore and oppreste	*poor*

	At Totteneys so this Brutus dyd arrive	
	Coryneus als and alle thayre company	
	Whiche name no wight that tyme that bare the lyve	*was alive*
565	Couthe telle of it or say specialy.	

Bot alle this londe that tyme hight certanly
Albyon as ye have herde afore
Only protecte and kepte by tyrany
Of geants whiche mysgoten were and bore.   *misbegotten; born*

570   Into this londe he came so fortunate
       A thousond fulle right and two hundre yere
       Afore Cryste was of Mary incarnate
       In whiche he thought to make his dwellynge here
       By alle wrytyngs that I can ought enquere.
575   Thus Brutus wan thys londe and it conquerde
       And slew alle way whare as thay durste appere
       The geants alle that were of hym ful ferde.   *afraid*

fol. 15v   So felle it than a geant of grete myght
           That Gogmagog was callyd by his name
580   With other geants right grete and longe of highte
           Nynetene thay were that with hym came fro hame   *home*
           Assaylynge sore the Troyans with grete grame   *anger*
           Whan thay were beste at ese and gode quyete
           Affrayand thaym of whiche thay felte no game   *Startling*
585   With strokes stronge at mete thay dyd rehete.   *attack*

How Brute slew alle the geantes excepte Gogmagog that wrastylde with Coryneus

Bot aftyr thys Brutus with his Troyans
Sought tho geants that hiegh upon the hilles
Were dwellynge than sothely for the nanes   *truly at that moment*
For drede of Brute, for thay knew noght his wylles.   *stratagem*
590   He slew thaym doun with axe swerde and bylles   *pikes*
       And made of thaym a felle occisioun   *fierce slaughter*
       And lefte bot oon levynge than by his willes   *deliberately*
       Was Gogmagog by his previsioun   *foresight*

Who sesed was for alle his resistence
595   To wrastille with the duke Coryneus
       That Brute myght se who was of moste defence   *most skillful in fighting*
       And strongar als in case aventerus.   *perilous*
       Twelf cubit longe he was I say you thus
       Bothe royde and brode and uggly forto se.   *boorish*
600   On the se banke thay mette afore Brutus
       Whare thaire wrastlynge was ordeynde forto be.

This Gogmagog so thraste Coryneus   *crushed*
That ribbes thre he brake than in his syde
Bot than for shame he luked on Brutus   *rushed*
605   And thought he wold revengen hym that tyde.

With that he stode and sette his legges wyde
And gatte hym up bytwene his armes faste
And to the roche hym bare that was besyde   *rock*
And with alle myght he had thare doun hym caste.

610   And yit this day alle men that place do calle
       In oure language for his derisioun   *ridicule*
       The saute I say of Gogmagoges falle   *battle place (assault); leap*
       In remembrance of his occisioun.   *slaying*
       Thus was thare made a faire divisioun.   *description*
615   Gladnesse to Brute it was and acceptable
       That thay departe so by previsioun   *parted company; providence*
       In alle thaire play that was so jocundable.   *fight; pleasurable*

fol. 16r   **Brute Kynge of Bretayne inhabyte it and called it Bretayne and his men named
            Bretons**

       Thus Brutus than was kynge in regalté
       And after his name he called this londe Bretayne
620   And alle his men by that same egalté   *equanimity*
       He called Bretouns of Brutus noght to layne.   *in truth*
       So were thay alle of that name glad and fayne.
       Than rode he forthe departynge as he wolde   *distributing*
       Thurghoute the reme the londe to yonge and olde   *realm*

625   Rewardynge ever his men so juste and trewe
       In dyverse londes that with hym had grete payne.
       Gafe thaym londes upon to dygge and plewe   *plow*
       Of whiche for sothe thay were right glad and fayne.
       And to Coryneus he gafe the sothe to sayne
630   The londe that nowe is called so Cornewayle
       Coryneus named withouten fayle.

       So was the name right of Albyon
       Alle sette besyde in kalendes of a chaunge   *as the beginning*
       And putte away with grete confusion   *shame*
635   And Bretayne hight it than by new eschaunge   *substitution*
       Right after Brute that slew thise geants straunge
       And wan this londe by his magnificence
       In whiche he dwelte longe tyme in excellence.

How the maker of this sayth his conceyte of evyl levynge and wrongful governance of peple, as of thise geants that cursidly were goten and wrongfully and tirantly levyd for the whiche God sette Brute to distroye thaym as Salamon sayth: "In malicia sua expelletur impius et adversio parvulorum enim interficiet et prosperitas stultorum perdet eos."[1]

Nota	O ye yonge fresshe and lusty creatures	
640	In whiche the pride upgroweth with youre age	
	Take hede of thise unsely aventures	*ill-favored*
	Of thise ladise and of alle thaire lynage	
	And thynke on God that after his ymage	
	Yow made and thynke this world shalle passe away	
645	As sone as done the floures fresshe and gay.	
Nota	Suche fyne lo hath Dame Albyne and hir sisters	*end*
	That groundyd were to sla thaire husbondes alle	
	Suche fyne lo hath thaire cursed werkes and mysters	*projects*
	Suche fyne lo hath upon thaire isshue falle	*progeny*
650	Such fyne lo hath thaire generacion alle	
	That bene dystroyde so sone and slayne away	
	For pryde and synne and for thaire fals array.	*behavior*
Nota	Thus after pryde thare commeth alleway grete shame	
	And after synne so commeth grete vengeance	
655	Aftyr wyke lyfe commeth a wykyd name	
	And after wronge lawes come shorte perseveraunce	
	After olde synnes come new shames and meschaunce.	
	Thus may ye se right by the ende and fate	
	Thare cometh no gode of lyfe inordynate.	*ill-governed*
fol. 16v	Of this matere now ys sufficienté	
661	Reported here through my symplicyté	
	That lytille have of konnynge or sapience	
	To ende this boke of my synglarité	
	So farre passith it myne abilité	
665	But thus of Brute I wylle now forth procede	
	As lyketh God with language me to fede.	*[it] pleases; provide*

How Kynge Brute bygged (*established*) Trynovant that now is Londoun and made Troian law in Bretayn.

	Thus Kynge Brutus of whom I spake afore	
	Fully provysed in wytte and sapience	*endowed*

---

[1] *The evil doer is overthrown by his malice* (Proverbs 14:32), *for the turning away of the children shall slay them, and the prosperity of fools shall destroy them* (Proverbs 1:32)

	His reame thurghoute in contrese lesse and more	*regions*
670	Departed so that by his diligence	*distinguished*
	Eche shire was know from other by difference	
	And every town also thurgh alle Bretayne	
	Whiche Englond now Wales and Scotlond ere certayne.	

	Whiche with the se ere closed alle aboute	
675	And Albyon was called so afore	
	In whiche he made his rytes and lawes thurghoute	
	Grounded after lawe Troyane lesse and more	
	Of whiche he was descended doun and bore.	
	The pese he made saufly to go and ryde	
680	And thurgh the londe the townes edifyde.	*founded*

	He made men tele the londe and sawe with sede	*till; sow*
	Of cornes whiche that myght be gette ourewhare	*grain; everywhere*
	Controvynge so with hosbondry to brede	*Devising; cultivation*
	And brynge forthe corne whare before none ware	
685	The feldes that were barayne and alle bare	
	With muk he dyd becomposte and bespred	*manure*
	Thurgh whiche the londe with corne ynewth was bred.	*plenty*

	He sought a place thurghoute his regioun	
	Whare he myght have a wonnynge delytable	*dwelling*
690	Of alle dysporte and for dygestyoun	
	And for his helthe were moste comfortable	
	Moste plentyuouse and als moste profytable	
	Thare to abyde and have his habitacioun	
	Right after his own hertes delectacioun.	

695	So came he by a ryver fresshe and fayre	
	Rennynge his course ay fresshe unto the se	
	On whiche he chese to bygge and to repayre	*build*
	For love of Troy was his priorité	
	A cyté fayre and of grete dygnyté	
700	Above alle othyr to ben incomperable	
	Within Brytayne and als moste profytable.	

fol. 17r	Thamyse he gafe that ryver so to name	*Thames*
	On his language hym liked to do so	
	On whiche he sette his cyté of grete fame	
705	Of Novel Troy to kepe in wele and wo	*New Troy*
	In remembrance of Troy his kyn cam fro.	
	Som say to name he gaffe it Trynovaunt	
	Of his language natyfe so consonaunt	

	Bot Troynovant som boke sayth so it hight	
710	Of Troyane speche to sounde it oute alle playne	
	Whiche language yit the Turkes speke ful right	
	Alle Turky thurgh of modre tonge certayne.	
	For Troy ys yit in Turky sothe to sayne	
	Thof it be waste yit ys the grounde thare stille	*Although*
715	The language als upholde that longe there tylle.	*remains; pertains*

	So thynke me wele it shuld hight Troynovaunte	*be called*
	Or els I say that Trynovaunt itte hight	
	Of Troys language as Turkes yit use and haunte	*speak*
	Rather than to calle it Novel Troy by right.	
720	That Frenshe language was nought to thaym so light	*comprehensible*
	Whare Brute and his no tendyrnesse couthe fynde	
	Bot emnyté, grete bataylle, and unkynde.	

	Whan Brute his werke had made and brought til ende	
	Of Troynovant that now ys London named	
725	He led his lyfe, his reame to kepe and mende	
	In every londe his name so wele was famed.	
	Of pese and reste alle wykednesse he blamed	*rebuked*
	Levynge so forthe in myrth and rialté	*Living*
	With Innogen his wyfe ful of beuté.	

Nota quod quidam Hely iudicavit in Iudea; Silvyus Postumus filius Enee et Lavyne regnavit in Ytalia, et Brutus filius Silvii Iuli in Britania nunc Anglia regnavit.[1]

	That tyme Hely so regned in Judé	*Eli; Judea*
730	The Arke of God eke take by Philistiens	
	Than regned als in Troy of novelté	
	The sonne of Ector with helpe of Trogyens	
	And put away Anthenores Posterieus	
735	And Sylvius as Gildas seyth in story.	
	Eneas sonne regned in Italy	

	Grete justes he helde with grete felicyté	*(i.e., Brutus)*
	In gyftes also he was right liberalle	
	Glad and mery festes with grete solempnyté	
740	He made fulle ofte to his peple and lordes alle	
	Huntynge hawkynge and revelynge in halle	
	And by his wyfe he gat so sonnes thre	
	Benygne of porte and godely onto se.	*conduct*

---

[1] *Note that a certain Eli judged in Judea; Silvius Posthumous the son of Aeneas and Lavinia ruled in Italy, and Brute, the son of Silvius Juilius ruled in Britain (now England)*

fol. 17v	And at his ende he made by his previsioun
745	Of alle Bretayne certayne until the se
	After his decese a playne dyvysioun — *clear*
	To bene departe amonge his sonnes thre
	The quene hire thrid of ful sufficienté
	That worthy was of alkyn womanhede
750	In so ferre forthe she passed other and excede.

But Giraldus Cambrensis sayth in his Topographie of Wales and Cornwail that he regned in Bretayne lx yere, that is more lyke to bene for he might have made Londoun in xxiiii yere, as it is specifyed in this balade.

	Whan he had so in fulle prosperité
	Fully regned by foure and twenty yere
	In his cyté of Troynovant dyd de — *die*
	And byried thare with alle that myght affere — *pertain*
755	To suche a prynce who that tyme had no pere
	That knowen was in any reame aboute
	So was he dred that every londe hym doute. — *feared*

	And in the yere afore the incarnacioun
	A thousond hole eght score and sextene
760	Aproved welle by calculacioun
	Amonges these clerkes as wele it may ben sene
	Whan deth his soule refte fro his body clene
	And led away withoute impedyment
	Whare God ordeyned right by his jugyment

765	In the temple that tyme of Appolyne — *Apollo*
	Whiche now ys Paules in vulgar tunge so hight — *St. Paul's*
	Before Diane that was his goddes fyne — *pure*
	Whiche thare he made in name of Dyane right
	In Leogyce that Albyon hym hight — *promised*
770	He byred was and layde in sepulture
	In rialle wyse as come hym of nature. — *was becoming*

Lamentacioun of the makere why God suffred so rightwis a prynce to bene dampned

	O gude lorde God what dole it ys to here — *grief*
	Of suche a prynce so rialle and benygne
	Ful of vertu by sight as dyd appere
775	Nothynge wyllynge to mysdone ne maligne
	Why was so gode a person and so dygne — *worthy*
	In godenesse sette and alle humylité
	To dye and noght his soule to saved be?

Bot thus thou myght whan that thou heried helle   *harrowed*
780   Knowynge his trouthe and rightwis governaunce
Of thy mercy from peyne perpetuelle
His soule within some restfulle place avaunce
Consideringe welle unto the olde creaunce   *belief*
Whiche only was that in grete God above
785   How myght thou Lorde foryette that hym dyd love?   *forget*

fol. 18r   **.ii. capitulum of Kynge Locryne and hys two brether**

Nota for homage of Scotlond. How Kynge Brute devydyd Bretayne in thre remes: Logres, Cambre and Albany.

Of Brutus sonnes now wille I thus bygynne
Locryne than hight the eldest sonne of alle   *was called*
Whiche Loegres had that Englond is with wynne   *possessions*
Unto his parte men did it Loegres calle
790   The beste it was also moste pryncipalle.
Locryne Loegres dyd calle after his name
Whiche was that tyme as yit ys of grete fame.

Kynge Camber

The seconde sonne Syr Camber so he hight
Who Camber had that cald is now Wales
795   So after his name it hight Camber right
And now in Frensshe so is it calde Gales.
Ful ofte it hath sen that tyme done us bales   *since; tribulations*
For servyce dew we claymed of it to have
Whiche ys now sure us nede no more to crave.

Kynge Albanacte

800   Syr Albanacte the thrid sonne than so hight
Had to his parte the londe of Albanye
After his name so cald he it be right
Whiche Scotlond now ys named sertanly
The whiche he helde of Locryne soveraynly
805   As Camber dyd than for his parte the same
Yit sen that tyme for it hath risen grame.   *strife*

Nota how Kynge Locryne had the sovereynté and servyce of Camber and Albanacte for thaire londes that now ere called Wales and Scotland.

Thus Locryne had, as come hym welle of right
Of Troyans lawe of grete antiquyté
In Troy so made whan thay were in thaire myght

810 The eldest sonne shuld have the soveraynté
His brether alle of his pryorité
Shuld hold thaire londe withouten variance
So was that tyme thaire lawe and ordynance.

Nota And alle resorte so shuld ever apperteyne
815 To the elder by superyoryté
If the yongar non issu have to reyne
The elder shuld by alle priorité
Have alle his parte to his posteriorité.
Thus Brute by lawe of Troy and consuetude *custom*
820 Thurgh Bretayne made the same by rectitude.

Nota At Mewytryne some tyme a place of fame *Glastonbury*
In Bretons tyme in whiche was oon Mewyne
So wyse poete that tyme was non of name
That florisht so ful longe afore Merlyne
825 Who in his boke so wrote for dissiplyne
The lawes of Troy to this day unreversed
Amonges the whiche is that I have rehersed

fol. 18v
Nota How Brutus made in Bretayne Troyans lawe
Thaire sacrifyce, thayre customes and thayre rytes
830 And in his boke he sette thaym hye and lawe *low*
Whiche tretise so was called Infynytes
Evermore to dure and byde as fulle perfytes
As poyntes whiche longe to the monarchy
Of Bretayne so and to his successory.

835 Bot as these brether sette beste in pese and reste
Thaire servyce done that dewe was of thayre londe
The kynge Humber of Hunneslonde fulle preste *ready*
Wyth shyppes arrofe whare now ys Humbre sonde *landed; water*
In Albany was than I undyrstonde
840 With whom the kynge was than of Albany
Syr Albanacte dyd fyghten manfully.

In whiche bataylle was Albanactus slayne
His men that fled, fro he was dede away, *after*
To Locryne came thare sores to complayne
845 Tellynge hym of Humbre and his aray
And prayd hym fayre to helpe iff that he may
Thayre londe to voyde of ennemyse and to clenge *purify*
His brothyr dethe also for to revenge.

How aftir the decese of Albanacte, Kynge Locrine dyd seyse Albany in his honde by eschete (*escheat*) and resort (*right*) as soverayne lord and hayre.

	The kynge Locryne to Cambre than forthe sente	
850	His lettres sone, fulle wofully endyte	
	Hym chargynge sore with alle his hole entente	
	To come anone his brothyr deth to quyte.	*avenge*
	Who come anone and taryde bot a lyte	*tarried*
	With bothe thayre hostes with Humbre forto fyght	
855	Besyde a water agayne hym dyd thay lyght.	*come*

	And wyth hym faught amoved in thare herte	
	For thayr brothyr dethe whiche sette thaym wondir sore	
	Thay slew thaym sore with strokes grete and smerte.	*strong*
	Bot Humber fled in that ryver therefore	
860	Whare he was draynte, that sene he was no more,	*drowned*
	For whiche Locryne so dyd that ryver calle	
	Humbre of hym that dyd so in it falle.	

	Wythin tho shyppes Locryne had mekyl gode	*great*
	That made hym stronge so forth of alle rychesse.	
865	His brother als thaire men that with thaym stode	
	In bataylle sore bysette in grete dystresse	*beset*
	He delte it welle and with grete bysynesse	
	Amonge thaym alle as ferre as myght sustene	
	Thayre pore estates to menden and to meyntene.	

fol. 19r	Whan seysed he Albany sothe to sayne	
871	Into his honde to byde for evermore	
	As itte that owe of right resorte agayne	
	To hym that was sovereyne eldeste bore	
	Who kepte itte wele fro ennemyse and alle sore	
875	As longe as he dyd leve and bare the crowne	
	His men thay were and at his byddynge bowne.	*obedient*

	Bot in tho shippes thre maydens there he fonde	
	Of beuté faire and of gode auncetry	
	Of whiche oon was on whom his love he bonde	
880	The doughter of a kynge of Germany	
	Estrilde that hight wham he thought womanly	
	And for his wyfe hire helde at his plesaunce	
	The whiche he thought to wed by ordynaunce.	

	Coryneus than for that with hym was wrothe	
885	And to hym sayde "Why art thou so untrewe	
	My doughter so to falsen and to lothe	*deceive*
	Thy wyfe shulde ben if that thou were ought trewe	

For whiche I shalle thy bales bake and brewe.   *troubles*
Bot thou hire wed I shalle now be thy dethe   *Unless*
890   Testment othur shalt thou never make ne quethe."[1]

Wyth that for fere and som dele by avyse   *partly; judgment*
Of alle his lordes that were to it acorde
He wed his doughter that was bothe gode and wyse
Anone forthwith by trety and concorde.   *agreement*
895   Bot ever he thought Estrilde shuld bene restorde.   *regained*
Bot with his wyfe that hight Quene Guendolyne
A son he gatte by wedlayke and right lyne.

Whiche Maddan hight right by his propre name
And in mene while this Estrylde was with childe   *meanwhile*
900   Kepte undir erthe for drede of speche and blame
And whan he wold ought gon to this Estrilde
He sayd his wyfe with tonge as he couth fylde   *deceive*
He yede sogates to do his sacryfise   *in this way*
Unto his god in his moste pryvy wyse.

905   And undyr this this lady Dame Estrylde
So kepte in mewe with alle grete pryvyté   *kept concealed; secrecy*
Whan tyme so cam delyverd was of chylde.
A doughter it was of ful femynyté
Of womanhede and alle abilité
910   Whiche Sabren hight as cronycles done recorde,
I can se non that fro itte dothe discorde.

fol. 19v   Coryneus as whan the day of deth
Was come hym to and nedes muste he de   *die*
Passed so forthe to Jubyter bequethe
915   His woful goste to sitte with hym and be
Perpetualy so undur his deyté.   *power*
Than Guendolene Maddan sente to Cornewayle
Thare to be kepte within hire londe and baylé.   *protection*

.iii. capitulum of the Quene Guendelyne that regned aftyr Locryne

After the deth of Coryneus so
920   Locryne toke Dame Estrilde and hire wedde
And put away the quene with mekyl wo.   *great*
And she anone so in tille Cornewayle fledde
And raysed thare the power that she hedde

---

[1] *You will never make, or promise, another declaration of marriage*

925 And in the felde she faught with Kyng Locryne
Whare he was slayne: he had none other fyne.   *end*

Anone she toke that lady Dame Estrilde
And Sabren als hire doughter fayre and dere
And drowned thaym bothe two, hire and hire childe,
In a ryver grete rennynge faire and clere
930 Whiche Severne now is cald ferre and nere.
For Sabren sake she dyd it so forth calle
After hire name and quene she was overalle.

Nota For ten yere than had regnyd Kynge Locryne
And fiftene yere after she regned quene
935 And had the reule and governd wele and fyne.
Than Maddan so that was hire sonne I mene
She made than kynge and crouned hym I wene
And to Cornewayle she went agayn so este   *pleasant*
To kepe that londe the whiche hire fadyr lefte.

Nota This tyme than was the prophete Samuel
941 Of grete wysdome and of high sapience
Governynge than the childer of Israelle
From alkyns evel thurgh his intelligence
That was so wyse in al experience
945 To lerne the folke to love God over alle thynge   *teach*
Thus dyd he longe afore his laste endynge.

Nota And Sylvyus the son of Eneas
Yit regnyng than and kynge in Italy
Of Tuskayne hole and of Latyne so was   *Tuscany; Rome*
950 By heritage and right of auncetry
As Omer sayth that florissht in poetry   *Homer; who was famous*
In rethoryke forpassyng other famouse
That philosofre was clere and curiouse.   *skillful*

fol. 20r **.iiii. capitulum of the Kynge Maddan**

Nota of gude reule in this kynges tyme and therfor he regned .xl. yeres

This Maddan so was kynge of Loegres than
955 And also of the londe of Albany
Ful fourty yere he regned as a man
And kepte his landes in pese fro tyrany.
In wisdome was he grete to magnyfy,
Manly and wise, of knyghthode corageouse,
960 Hardy and stronge like to Coryneus.

In pese he was his tyme and so he ende
Bot sonnes two he gat right of his wyfe,
Manlyn also and Membrice, to defende
His remes bothe from alkyn werre and strife
965   And dyed so and byried by his wife
With grete praysynge and ful comendacioun
Of alle his reames thurgh his dominacioun.

Fulle of vertu he regned fourty yere
That no man durste his neyghbur oughte displese
970   So wele the lawe he kepte while he myght stere
That every wight was glad hym forto plese
And every man eche othur for to ese
So dred thay hym alle for his rightwysnesse
Kepynge his lawe and pese in sykyrnesse.   *security*

.v. capitulum of the Kynge Manlyn and Membrice

975   Manlyn his sonne whiche of priorité
Have regned shuld and fully have bene crounde
With treson fals and grete iniquyté
By his brother Membrice falsly founde
A day was sette to se who shuld that stounde   *time*
980   Bene kynge and regne in pese by ful concorde
To cese alle strife amonge thaym and discorde.

Upon whiche day Membrice his brothyr wounde
And slew hym thare by his imagynacioun   *devising*
For he wold regne oonly and be crounde
985   And upon that he made his coronacioun
Thurgh falshode foule and hiegh conspiracioun.   *conspiracy*
Kynge was he made and had the londes two
And led thaym so in wykednesse and wo.

Kynge Membrice

Membrice this kynge distroyed his men thurghoute
990   Thaire londes, thaire godes or els thaire life sertayne
He toke fro thaym and held thaym ever in doute   *fear*
So wyk he was and fulle of grete dedayne.   *wicked; arrogance*
His comons sore dyd vexen and distrayne   *distress*
To plese and pay in alle that he wold have
995   Or dye he shule foule deth so God me save.

fol. 20v   His wedded wife he dyd falsly forsake
Hauntynge the synne so foule of sodomyte   *Practicing; sodomy*
With bestes ofte instede right of his make   *partner*

1000

To thaym he had suche luste and appetyte
And of his wife havynge right no delyte
Bot hire avoyde out of his companye
Withouten cause bot of his trechary.

How this cursed kynge was dede thurgh vengens

Whan he had so fulle regned twenty yere
As God wold he shuld have he had deserved   *wished*
To wod he went folowynge upon a dere
Right by hym oon with wolfes feel overswerved   *alone; savage overcome*
He was anone thare slayne and alle forterved   *thrown down*
That lym fro lym was fro hym draw and rente   *limb; torn*
He myght never have gode ende that falsly mente.

1005

He had a sonne, Syr Ebrauke was his name,
To have hys reames aftyr his cursed ende.
Thus was Membryce than dede and made fulle tame
His body eten with wolfes and alle torende   *torn apart*
Whose soule Mynerve with bales al tobrende.   *Minerva; torments; burned*
And in his tyme Saul regned in Judea
Eristens in Lacedemonya.   *Lacedaemon (Sparta)*

1010

1015

.vi. capitulum of the Kynge Ebrauke

Ebrauke his sonne crowned so was anone
Whiche made grete shippes upon the se to saile
With helde his knyghtes with hym so forth to gone
And als his men than waged of Cornewayle
And into Gaule he sayled withouten fayle
In whiche he wan richesse innumerable
To holde estate rialle and honorable.

1020

And twenty wyfes had, as cronycle sayth,
And alle wedded by maner as was than
Trouthed fully right with his honde and fayth
With other rytes the whiche that I ne kan
At this tyme telle, ne say unto no man,
Bot twenty sonnes had by generacioun
Thretty doughters als by alle relacioun.   *accounts*

1025

1030

**How Ebrauke (*York*), Maiden Castel, Mounte Dolorous and Alclude this Kinge
Ebrauke did make**.

A cyté than he made that hight Ebrauke   *was called*
After his name whiche now that Yorke so highte.   *is called*
A castelle stronge sette on the north se banke

		strong

Whiche he dyd calle Mounte Dolorouse so wighte   *strong*
1035   That now Bamburgh ys castelle of grete myght
In which there ys a toure hatte Dolorouse Garde
Bot by what cause I can nought wele awarde.   *discern*

fol. 21r   Bot thus I have in olde bokes red and sene
That Ebrauke whan he was put to the flight
1040   For his socoure than thydyr came I mene.
By other bokes I have eke sene be sight
For Launcelot love a lady dyed fulle bright
Whiche in a bote enchaunted for the nones
Arofe up thare: so named he tho wones.   *Arrived; dwellings*

1045   And in the londe for sothe of Albany
The Mayden Castelle strongly than dyd he make
Callynge it so on his language forthy
That he had thare his luste with maydens take
In yowth whan that hym lyste with thaym to wake
1050   Whiche now so hatte Edynburgh ryghte by name.
Alle Scotlond thurgh it hath now alle the fame.

High on the Mounte Agneth so was it sette
A castelle stronge and of grete altitude
To whiche thare were thre score maydens sette
1055   By a geant for his solycitude   *special attention*
Agayn thaire wille for thaire grete pulcritude   *fairness*
And bewté als that hym liste with thaym play   *it pleased him*
Whom for thaire sake Syr Ewayn slew men say.

And thaym he dyd delyver of that servage
1060   And put that place so fulle in obeyssance   *obedience*
Of Kynge Arthure, it was his heritage
As sovereyn lorde. And so for that myschaunce,   *wrongdoing*
That maydens were there kepte to ther grevaunce,
So was it calde Mayden Castelle aftirwarde
1065   Many a day ful longe by that awarde.

Nota quod Policronica dicit Alclude esse iuxta Caerleyle prope Sulwath tunc in Albania et nunc in Anglia, vastata per Danos ita quod nichil inde videtur hiis diebus sed omnis apud omnes incognita. Tamen Scoti dicent Alclude esse illam villam quae nunc vocatur Dunbretayne.[1]

	The cyté als he made than of Alclude	
	Whiche bare that tyme the fame of Albany.	
	A castelle by was of grete fortitude	
	Whiche Dunbretayne now hight ful notably	*is called*
1070	Whare Seynt Patrike bycame man natifly	*born*
	For whiche in itte never seth was sene vermyn	*afterwards*
	Ne yit non horse that ought myght donge therein.	*void excrement*

Nota how Ebrauk maryed alle his daughters in Itaylle and alle his sonnes saufe his hayre he sent in Germany

Nota	He sent his doughters so unto Italy	
	Thare to be wedde to lordes of Troyans kynde	
1075	At grete requeste of Brutus cosyn Silvy	
	Who kynge was than of Latyn as I fynde.	*Rome*
	For ladise thare had neyther wylle ne mynde	
	To Troyans blode be wed ne yit maryde	
	So lothe thay were with thaym to ben allyde.	

fol. 21v	Whare thay were wed echon to thaire degré	
1081	To Trojans grete and of the beste estate	
	Thurgh Kynge Sylvy of whose consanguynyté	*kinship*
	Thay were echone descende and generate.	
	And alle his sonnes that were so procreate	*(Ebrauke's)*
1085	To Germany he send thaym forth anone	
	Savande only his eldeste sonne alone.	

Nota how wisely this gode Kynge Ebrauke reuled his londe

	Thus was his wytte and als his policy	
	That thay shuld wyn in other cuntré lande	
	To leve upon oute of alle mysery	
1090	With navy grete by se and eke by sande	*shore*
	For he nolde payre ne harme no lorde he fande	*damage*
	For love of thaym, ne in no wyse wold spille	*slay*
	So was he trew his lordes alle to stylle.	*pacify*

---

[1] *Note that the Polychronicon says that Alclude is next to Carlisle, near to Sulwath, then in Albany and now in England, destroyed by the Danes. For which reason nothing is seen in these days, but is entirely, by everyone's account, unknown. The Scots, however, say that Alclude is that town that is now called Dumbarton*

Undyr the reule and by the regyment
1095 Of thaire brother that hight Syr Assarak
Alle Germany thay had at thaire entente   *desire*
And lordes were thare ay forth withouten lak.   *deficiency*
Thus were thay lordes and holpen alle the pak   *army*
Outwarde fro home by wytte and governaunce
1100 Tylle his barons and reme fulle grete plesaunce.   *Unto; realm*

Than Kynge Davyd so regned in Judé
Undyr whom than prophecyed in Israelle
Gad, Nathan and Asaph of the deyté.   *power of God*
And Sylvyus also regned fulle welle
1105 In Italy as dyverse cronycles telle
Who was the sonne right of Kynge Eneas
That Brutus cosyn and nere of blode than was.   *kindred*

And sexty yere Kynge Ebrauc bare the croune
Regnynge fully with alle prosperyté
1110 With honoures high and myghty of renoune
Redouted bothe in age and juventé   *youth*
Of alle ennemyse for his humanyté   *courtesy*
And at Ebrauke was made his byrialle
Whiche was so than his cyté pryncipalle.

.vii. capitulum of the Kynge Brute Grenesheelde

1115 Hys sonne Brutus Grenesheeld by name so hight   *was called*
Bothe gode and trew and esy of alle porte   *manner*
Wyse and manly and feyre to alle mennys sight.
In alle desese he wold his men comforte   *tribulation*
To ryde his londe thurghout was his dysporte   *custom*
Nota Alle wronge to mende and fully to redresse
1121 Thus was his life as bokes done expresse.

fol. 22r He regned fulle in pese and reste twelve yere
And dyed than and by his fadyr syde
Beryed was right as I can enquere
1125 With grete honoure aboute hym in that tyde.
Of alle Bretayne the barons dyd hym guyde   *guide*
Tylle tyme he was layd in his sepulture
As Gyldas sayth for sothe in his scripture.

.viii. capitulum of Kynge Leyle

So Leyl his sonne was kynge than after so
1130 That made anents the londe of Albany   *near to*
A cyté fayre whiche that Caerleyl highte tho

That now Carlele men callen fynaly.
In whose tyme so regned than corporaly
Kynge Salomon so wyse in alle Judé
1135   Begynnynge thurgh his noble dygnyté

To bygge and make the temple of Jerusaleme   *build*
And Saba quene that same tyme came to here   *Sheba*
His hiegh wysdome spoken of mony reme.
And in the tyme of Leyl were prophetes sere   *various*
1140   Prechynge of God the peple forto lere   *teach*
Amos, Aggeos, Joel, Azarias also
With othur als bot I canne telle no mo.

He in his tyme held welle the londe in pese
Bot in his age it was sette alle on stryve.   *maturity; strife*
1145   Whan he had bene so kynge withouten lese   *lie*
And regned had fulle twenty yere and fyve
The deth his goste oute of his corse gan dryve
And unbody so fro his erthely place
That tylle another he yede withouten grace.   *went*

.ix. capitulum of the Kynge Rudhudibrace

1150   At his cyté of Caerleyl there he lythe   *lies*
Buryed right fayre and of grete honesté.
That he was gone the barons alle were blythe.
Hys son anone of grete nobilité
So regned than with alle habilité   *worthiness*
1155   Rudhudibrace by propre name that hyghte
His barons alle he sette in pese fulle ryghte.

Caerkent he made that now ys Cauntyrbyry
Caergwent also that now hatte Wynchestre
Caerpaladoure whiche hatte Shafftesbyry
1160   He made amonge his werkes terrestre   *terrestrial*
Whare that tyme sette an egle on the cestre   *eagle*
Whiche in Englisshe we calle a castelle right
And spake bot what I saw it never in sight.

fol. 22v   So regned he oute thretty yere and nyne
1165   And buried is besyde his fadir Leyle.
In whose tyme so Amos, Joelle prophetes fyne
Azarias als prophecyed wythouten faile
Ful treuly so thay taught and toke no vayle   *profit*
Bot only dyd of gode perfeccioun
1170   The folke to lerne by gode affeccioun.   *teach*

.x. capitulum of the Kynge Bladud

Bladud his sonne so aftyr hym succede
And regned so fully than twenty yere   *ruled*
Caerbladon that now ys Bathe I rede.
He made anone the hote bathes alle in fere   *together*
1175 Whiche to thys day in that place yit appere
Made so by crafte that ever thay have grete hete
In whiche men have grete ese and grete quyete.   *rest*

Helyas than so prayd it shuld not rayne
At whose prayer it rayned noght thre yere
1180 And sex monethes upon the erthe sertayne.
And in his tyme Amos, Hien, Joel in fere
Azarias as prophetes to God fulle dere
Preched and taught and also prophetysed
As the Byble it hath autorysed.

1185 Thys Bladud was, as Gyldas seyth the clerke,
Fully instructe and lerned in nygromancy   *necromancy*
And by his crafte he dyd devyse a werke   *object*
A fedyr-hame with whiche that he wold fly   *plumage*
And so he dyd, as Waltier sykyrly   *certainly*
1190 The archedeken of Oxenford ful graythe   *fully in possession of (the story)*
In story whiche he drewe sogates saythe.   *thus*

He flaw on high to temple Appolyne
Whiche now ys Poulys with worschip eedifyde
Whare on he felle and made his ende and fyne
1195 So was he cause of his own homysyde.
Thus slayne he was I say and mortyfyde
Thurgh his own wytte and thurgh his fals atyre   *equipment*
He whom he served so quyte hym than his hire.   *repaid; reward*

.xi. capitulum of the Kynge Leyre

Aftyr hym than regned Leyre his sonne
1200 Who that dyd make a cyté upon Sore   *(the River) Soar*
Caerleyre in whiche he dyd most dwelle and wonne
Leycestre ys now callyd but wherefore
I wote not why but Leyrecestre afore
I trow it hight. We leve out R this lettre
1205 For lyghter speche to make the language swettre.

How this Leyre proved his doughters which of hem loved hym moste and beste

This Leyre had to his heyres bot doughters thre
So aftyr tyme that he had regned longe
In alle honoure and high prosperyté
And falle in age, he sette hym thaym amonge.
1210   To the eldeste with voys he spake and ronge   *proclaimed*
Imagynynge how that they myght be proved
Whiche of thaym thre that best and moste hym loved.

He asked so the eldeste Goneryle
How welle she dyd hym love he prayd hyr say
1215   She aunswerde hym agayne than with a wyle   *deceptive strategy*
Wele better than hir own lyfe in gode fay   *faith*
Off whiche he was so plesed to his pay   *satisfaction*
That he hyre graunte fully forto avaunce
With suffysaunt parte of his enheritaunce.   *full portion*

1220   The secunde than that cald was Ragawe
He askyd so, to whom she sayd anone
"Fadyr I love yow right so as I awe   *ought*
More than al thys hole erthly world alone."
"Doughter" he sayd "as trewe as eny stone
1225   The thyrde parte of my reame so shalt thou have
Thou sayste so welle I may no more thee crave."

To Cordele than the yongeste of thaym thre
He asked than right on that same avyse.
Who answerde hym with alle benygnyté
1230   Right in thys fourme and as she couthe devise
"Yow as my fadyr I love withoute queyntise   *trickery*
And as myche as ye bene worthe of rychesse
So myche I love yow fadyr and shalle doutlesse."

Nota, for homage of Scotland. How Maglane Duke of Albany and Ewayn Duke of Cornwail did homage to Kyng Leyre for Cornwail and Albany, and afterward thay wed his doughtirs and put hym out of the reme by unkyndenes.

To hyre he sayd "Why lovest me no more?
1235   Now treuly thou shalt never have gode of me
Bot helpe thyselff fro thys day forth therefore."
With that the duke of Albany wete ye   *know*
Wed Goneryle his wyfe for to be
Syr Maglayne than hight withouten fayle   *was called*
1240   And Ragawe had Ewayne duke of Cornewayle.

Aftyr alle this the kynge of Fraunce Aganypé
For gode love wed withoute any rychesse
Cordeyle to whom hyre fadyr no quantyté
Of godes gaffe that I can ought expresse
1245   Bot alle his londes departed by processe
Betwyx Maglayne and Ewayne so in fere   *together*
With his doughters two that to hym were ful dere.

fol. 23v   And in his age the prynces two toke governaunce
Of alle his londe and lete hym have no myghte
1250   For whiche thay graunte hym than by ordynaunce
To fynde hym so with fourety knyghtes right   *provide for himself*
Whils he myght leve, so layde thay doune his hight,   *honorable position*
For whiche he wente to his doughter Gonerile
Of whom certayne she irked in shorte while.   *(i.e., Leyre); wearied*

1255   Than wente he forthe unto his doughter Ragawe.
She dyd right as hyre syster with hym had done.
Wythin a yere she wolde have made hym lawe   *low*
His knyghtes voyde and halden bot a whone   *discharge; while*
So wente he thens he wyste nought what to done
1260   For sorow he wold have liggen on his bere   *lain on his bier*
Suche thought he had and made right hevy chere.

Than toke he fulle to counsaylle and to rede   *advice*
By frendes he had tille Cordeyle forto gone   *to*
To fele hyre helpe thedyr thay dyd hym lede.   *obtain*
1265   He sent to hyr his messengere anone
For whom she was anoyed and made grete mone.   *troubled*
Both golde and gode she sente hym and array
Right sufficient and ryche unto his pay.

Thay brought hym so to hyre with grete honoure
1270   Whare he had chere ful fayre and alle dysporte   *pleasure*
And welcome was and hight him hool socoure   *promised*
To wyn agayne his londe with grete comforte.
The kynge of Fraunce, his hoste assembled and resorte   *recalled*
To passe with hym to wyn his londe agayne,
1275   Dyd sende his wyfe to helpe hym in his payne.

So wan he than his londe with myght agayne   *won*
In whiche he stode the sovereyne kynge thre yere
And than he dyed and byried is nought to layne   *lie*
At his cyté of Caerleyre as dyd affere   *was appropriate*
1280   With alle worshyp within a temple clere
Of Janus god, and than Aganypé
Hyre lorde at home dyd passe away and de.   *(i.e., Cordele's)*

So stode she forthe wydew regnynge fyve yere
Wythoute issu and helde the monarchy
1285   Of alle Bretayne after hyre fadyr dere.
The quene she was and helde the regency
Tylle on a day hire syster sonnes forthy
That thay were come and also generate   *begotten*
Of hyre elder systers and procreate.

fol. 24r   **.xii. capitulum of Kynge Margan and Kynge Condage**

Nota for servyse of Scotland.

**How Margan regned from Humbre north and Albany, for whiche he did homage
to Cundage and helde of hym.**

1290   Margan that was than duke of Albany
Condage that was so duke of Cornewayle
With hostes grete thurgh right of auncetry
Forto be kynges and have the governayle
Than faught with hire and gafe hire stronge batayle.
1295   So atte the laste overcome she was and take
Emprisounde sore hire own deth sought to make.

She slew hireself for wo she loste the reme
And buried was besyde hire fadyr right
Within a tombe undyr the water streme
1300   Of Sore, that she had wrought for hym and dyght
Within Caerleyre that now Leycester hight.
Hyre soule so wente to Janus whom she served
And to Mynerve whose love she had deserved.

Syr Margan than the eldest syster sonne
1305   From Humbre northe alle oute had regency
Condage that was so borne by south to wonne   *dwell*
From Humbre south had to his persenary.   *portion*
Bot after that thurgh falshed and envy
The northen folke sente Margan so on strife
1310   With hoste to ryde on Condage than ful ryfe.   *mighty*

He brente he slew and toke alle that he fande
As he that claymed alle Bretayn hole aboute
For his modyr was eldeste sister in lande
To have the chefe he thought withouten doute.   *priority*
1315   Syr Condage than with hoste hym mette ful stoute
And made hym flye whare now is so Glamorgan
In whiche Margan was slayne and dede was than.

Nota for resort of Scotland.

How Kynge Condage seysed Albany by deth of Margan by resort (*right*) **and eschete** (*escheat*), **in defaut of heire of his body**.

	And for his name it hight so Glamargan	
	Whiche now men calle Glamorgan uttyrly	
1320	In Wales it stant, thurgh whiche Syr Condage than	
	Sesed alle his londe and helde it sykyrly	*securely*
	In pese and reste out of alle mysery.	
	Ful gloriously by thre and thretty yere	
	The monarchy of Bretayne kepte he clere.	

1325	In whose tyme was the prophete Isaye	*Isaiah*
	Ful of wysdome enformed and instructe	
	So was also the prophete Osee	*Hosea*
	In sapience gloriously inducte.	*endowed*
	And Rome byggid was than and fulle constructe	*built*
1330	By Remus and his brother Romulus	
	Whiche cyté was above alle other moste famus.	

fol. 24v	By ought that I can undurstonde and know	
	Kynge Brutus had so conquerde alle this londe	
	Afore that Rome was byggyd as I trow	*believe*
1335	Fyve hundre yere who wille it undurstande	
	Foure score and als nynetene I darre warrande.	*dare say*
	Thus had this lande of longe grete soveraynté	
	Afore that Rome ought was of dignyté.	

.xiii. capitulum of Kynge Ryval and other kynges folowynge

	Ryval his sonne whiche was pacificalle	
1340	And esy in alle thynge of governaylle	
	After his fadyr succede in specialle	
	Havynge the croune in pese withouten faylle	
	Undestourbed durynge with grete avaylle	*prosperity*
	In pese and reste and alle fulle charité	
1345	So was he sette in alle tranquylité.	

In his tyme it rayned blode and men venymde (*infected*) **with flyes to the dethe**

	In whose tyme so thre days it reyned blode	
	And flyes als thare were suche multitude	
	That peple were so venymde as they stode	
	Thurgh that tempest and foule amaritude	*bitterness*
1350	Dyed right doun so in thaire juventude	*youth*

As alle shuld waste with fulle paralité   *paralysis*
Suche pestelence was and mortalyté.

Kynge Gurgustius

Nota of drunkenes

Gurgustius his son so regned than
With mykyl joy and wordly celynesse   *great; blessedness*
1355   That kepte his londe right strongly as a man
In mekyl welthe and ful of worthynesse.   *great*
Bot oon defaute he had yit neverthelesse
As writen ys that he wolde drounken be
Unacordant with his hie dignyté.   *Inappropriate to*

1360   To drounkenesse succedyth every vyce
Wherfore it is for to eschew alway   *avoid*
Namely in grete estate iff he be wyse   *Especially*
That regneth overe his peple every day
That other vyce thurgh it make none aray   *showing*
1365   Agayne His wylle that made alle thinge of nought
Or yit his reame to noye in dede or thought.

Kynge Sisilius

Nota how he was overe paciente, for law and pese was unexecute.

Sisilius his son so dyd succede
And bare the croune so wele many a day
Savynge his men that grete wronge wrought in dede
1370   He punyshte nought but suffred his barons ay   *ever*
To sustene wronges and quareles as I say.
Thay dred hym nought so was he meke of porte   *manner*
Whiche was more vyce than vertu to reporte.

fol. 25r   Thurgh whiche thay toke on thaym so grete boldnesse
1375   That thay distroyd his pore comonalté   *populace*
Thurghoute the londe and thaym dyd sore opresse
That every man of myght in his contré
Dyd other over renne with grete crudelité   *cruelty*
So that oure Lorde for his mysreuled regence
1380   In litargy hym smote and epilence.   *lethargy; epilepsy*

Kynge Iago

Iago than was kynge in londe certayne
As it is so writen and notified.

Newfangle was at alle tyme sothe to sayne   *Fond of novelty*
Now this, now that, to do he glorified
1385   For of his wille he wold nought be replyed   *resisted*
Ful lyte he dyd that was to autorise
Bot mekylle wronge withouten gode advise.

How he wolde noght be replied of his wylle thurgh whiche the reme was gretely noyed

For whiche God toke on hym so hiegh vengeance
That he hym smote in suche a frenesy   *fit of madness*
1390   Growynge dayly with fervent affluence
Of color rede as made ys memory
Descendynge in his braynes so myghtyly
That slepe he myght none have ne yit ought reste
Tyl he was dede so sore it hym oppreste.

Kynge Kymar

1395   Kymar his son had than the diademe   *sovereignty*
And crouned was with alkyn rialté
He kepte his londe right pesibly and queme   *pleasingly*
Also his law as was necessité
Withoute favoure or mutabilité
1400   Unto alle men ever in unyversalle
Whiche to a prynce ys vertu pryncipalle.

Conceyte of the makere of this in defaute of conservacioun of pese and lawe

For iff he kepe no pese, no lawe certayne
Amonge his folke in every shire aboute
In moste perile he stonte forto be slayne
1405   Or els put doun right by his undirloute.   *subordinates*
For unrestreynte by law, it ys no doute
The porest man of alle his reame to fight
Durste hym supprise conffedred with grete myght.   *allied*

Kynge Gorbodian

Gorbodyan that was his sonne and hayre   *heir*
1410   So regned than the whiles his sonnes grewe
Tylle age hym made to feble and appayre   *decline*
That he was dede for whiche this reame dyd rewe.
In whose tyme so was reule and alle vertewe
Bot sonnes two he had couth never acorde
1415   Ferrex and als Porrex that ever discorde.

fol. 25v	Thaire fadyr levyng Ferrex the elder brother	*living*
	For his discorde to Sywarde kynge of Fraunce	
	Wente so and dwelte with hym and with non other	
	For borne he was of his kyn and aliaunce.	
1420	And whan he knew of his fadyr deth the chaunse	
	With power grete so came he than agayne	
	And with his brother faught whare that he was slayne.	

Thayre modyr than Quene Judon was fulle wrothe
And in hire mynde she thought to take vengeaunce.
1425   The next nyght after she dyd a thynge ful lothe   *terrible*
       That Porrex throte she cutte for that distaunce   *strife*
       While that he slepte and trusted no grevaunce.
       The whiche vengeaunce was after many yere
       So spoken of that wounder was to here.   *hear*

1430   She cutte hym alle in peces smalle for ire   *anger*
       Whiche forpassynge was modyrs cruelté
       So fervently with rancoure sette on fyre
       She couthe nought cese of hire maliciousté
       Byfore she had fulfild so hire decré.
1435   Whiche vengeance was over felly arbytrate   *too severely judged*
       For oon lese bothe hire sonnes so generate.   *loss*

Cloten, Pynhere, Ruddan, Scatere: kynges of Bretayne devyded by barons werres in defaute of lawe and pese.

       Cloten the duke that than was of Cornewayle
       Right haire he was by alle successioun   *heir*
       And next of blode by lyne withouten faile
1440   To have the reame hool in his possessioun
       Whiche Pynher than had gote by wronge ingressioun   *usurpation*
       Ruddan also that tyme dyd Cambre holde
       And Albany had Scater that was bolde.

       Thus was Bretayne to kynges foure devyded
1445   Echone of thaym werrynge so upon other
       And undur thaym the barons were provyded   *intent*
       To dystroy other alle, were thay kyn or brother.
       The yonger brother dyd than overrenne the tother
       The sonne his fadyr dyd often tymes dyssese   *deprive*
1450   Of his lyfelode and put hym fro his ese.   *livelihood*

Nota Every cyté and walled toune and toure
       Other werrayde and brought thaym unto nought.
       Every tirant than was a conqueroure
       And lordes fayne subgyts bycome forfought   *utterly defeated*

1455	So were thay lowe unto meschefe than brought.	
	Thus worthy blude of honoure and estate	
	Was brought to nought and fouly alterate.	*changed*
fol. 26r		
Nota	The pore men that afore were desolate	
	Of none honoure ne yit of worthynesse	
1460	Thurgh thayre manhode with peple congregate	*assembled*
	Lordships conquerde and rose to hie noblesse	
	And ladyse wedde that were of grete rychesse.	
	Thayre kynne afore had neyther londe ne house	
	Defaute of pese made thaym victoriouse.	*Lack*

Nota	Fourty wyntyr durynge the barons werre	
1466	The londe so stode in sorow and in strife	
	In fawte of myght the waykere had the werre	*lack; weaker; worse*
	And suffryde wronge that wo was thaym the lyfe	
	For who that myght ought wyn with spere or knyfe	*anything*
1470	He helde it forthe as for his heritage	
	And grew a lorde byfore that was a page.	

How the makere of this moveth his conceyte for the gode sureté of the kynge and of hys reme of Englond for to kepe and conserve law and pees in his lond amonge his peple.

Nota	Defaute of lawe was cause of this myschefe	*Lack*
	Wronges sustened by maystry and by myght	*violence; force*
	And pese layde doun that shuld have be the chefe	
1475	For whiche debate folowed alle unright.	*strife*
	Wharefore unto a prynce acordyth right	
	To kepe the pese with alle tranquilyté	
	Within his reame to save his dygnyté.	

Nota	What is a kynge withouten lawe or pese	
1480	Within his reame suffyciently conserved?	
	The porest of his reame may so increse	
	By injury and force to bene preserved	
	Tylle he his kynge with strenght have so overterved	*overturned*
	And sette hymself in rialle magesté	
1485	If that it be in suche a juparté.	*turmoil*

Nota	O ye prynces and lordes of hye estate	
	Kepe welle the lawe and pese with governance	
	Lesse youre sugettes you foule and deprecyate	*mistreat; devalue*
	Whiche bene as able with wrongfulle ordenaunce	
1490	To regne as ye and have als grete pussaunce.	*power*
	Iff pese and lawe be layde and unyté,	*put aside; public order*
	The floures ere loste of alle youre sovereynté.	

.xiiii. capitulum of Kynge Dunwallo

	And whils thise foure so chefly in thayre floures	
	Regned so moste, and had the soveraynté	
1495	Of alle Bretayne as verry conquerous,	
	As God it wold, that nede it muste so be	
	Of alkyns right and oportunyté,	
	Cloten was dede oute of this world expyred.	
	Dunwallo than right with his men conspyred	

fol. 26v	As son and heyre to Kynge Cloten discrete	*intelligent*
1501	His heritage to wynnen and conquerre	
	Of alle Loegres that stode fulle unquyete	
	In neygburres stryfe and also barons werre	*war*
	That longe had laste and of it spokyn ferre.	*far*
1505	His name was than Dunwallo Molmucyus	
	A lusty knyght in armes and corageus.	*energetic*

	Whiche Dunwallo grete hoste assembled right.	
	On Kynge Pynhere he came fulle vygrously	
	And in batayle hym slow throw strokes wight.	*powerful*
1510	This Scater herde and Ruddan for envy	
	Thaire hostes brought upon hym spytuysly	*cruelly*
	And faught with hym ful sore withoute fayntyse	*faint-heartedness*
	Tylle Dunwallo bethought of his quantyse	*cunning*

	He made his men to arme thaym efte anone	
1515	In armure of his ennemyse that were slayne —	
	Thaire armes and sygnes and clothynges everychone	*heraldic badges*
	Lyke as thay were thayre frendes cam new agayne —	
	Thurgh whiche coloure thay donge thaym doun with mayne.[1]	
	The kynges thay toke bothe two, the whiche thay slew,	
1520	Dunwallo thus in conqueste wexe and grew.	*prospered*

How this Dunwallo made his lawes called Lawes Molmutynes and graunted pese and fraunchise (*privilege*) to alle temples, plowes (*plowland*), markets and comon wayes that was the seconde lawe.

	So whan he had overcome alle his ennemyse	
	With trihumphe and with joy and victory	
	He sette his lawes and pese at his avyse	*judgement*
	And ordeyned than and graunted fraunchesy	*liberties*
1525	And also gyrth for alkyns felony	*protection against*

---

[1] *With which stratagem they overcame them with strength*

In temple, market and alle comon wayse
And at the plewgh, so loved he it his dayse.   *plow; during his reign*

At plough who yede, or to the marketwarde,   *went*
Or in hieghway that was the comyn strete
1530   Iff any dyd hym harme or hym forbarde   *blocked*
He shulde be dede and hanged by the fete.
In temple als who so dyd harme or lete   *hindrance*
The deth shuld bene his fulle punyssioun   *punishment*
Of whiche peyne so he shuld have no remyssioun.

1535   He was friste kynge that ever bare croune of golde   *first*
In alle Bretayne afore that day I fynde
And kepte the pese evermore tille yonge and olde.   *towards*
What so a wyght, as cronycle makyth mynde,   *Whatever; person; recalls*
Had done, iff he the plough in hande myght wynde,   *manage*
1540   Hieghway, or yit market myght gete for fere,
Suche gyrthe shulde have as he in temple were.   *protection; as if*

fol. 27r   He made a temple of pese and of concorde
In his cyté so grete of Trynovaunte
Whare he was layde in grave as is recorde.
1545   Aftyre that he this londe had kepte and haunte   *inhabited*
Fourty wynter as Gyldas dothe avaunte   *declare*
In alle honoure myght and prosperyté
Wythoute supprise or any adversyté.   *oppression*

Nota   O noble prynce take hede how that this kynge
1550   In lawes made called Molmutynes
How rightwysly he kepte thaym in alle thynge
And sette his pese fro whiche none durste declyne   *dared divagate*
Ne thaym attempte in ought or countremyne.   *challenge; undermine*
And if thay dyd he wolde thaym seke at home
1555   Bot iff that thay the sonner to hym come.   *Unless*

.xv. capitulum of Kynge Belyn

Than felle discorde betwyx his sonnes two
Whiche of thaym than shuld have alle hole Bretayne
Bot happely thay were acordyd so   *by good chance*
By frendes helpe of whiche men were fulle fayne   *glad*
1560   That Belyne so that elder was shuld rayne
In Loegres fulle and Cambre als eche dele   *part*
As Trojan lawe and custome wold it wele.

Nota for homage of Scotland

Nota how Belyn graunted to Brenny his brother Albany to holde of hym and dyd homage for it to Kynge Belyne

Nota	And Brenny so, who was the latter borne,	
	Shuld have in pese the reame of Albany	
1565	And also alle Northumbreland aforne	
	From Humbre north to mende his parte forthy	*regulate*
	That he shuld holde of Belyne alle his parcenry	*portion*
	As Troyans lawe and fulle consuetude	*custom*
	Afore was ever by subgitts servytude.	*subjects'*

Nota	Homage he made therefore unto Belyn	
1571	His man to be and to his parlemente	
	By semons made to come and be therein	*summons*
	Olesse that he had cause of gode entente	*Unless*
	Escuse hym, by that he were so absente.	*if*
1575	And fyve yere so thay regned wele in pese	
	With honoure grete and vertu dyd encrese.	

The conceyte of the makere compleynynge of Fortune for dissencioun bituix the two brether Belyn and Brenne

Nota	Bot O Fortune with alle thy feyned chere	*feigned*
	So fayre showynge afore in alle semblance	
	And undyrnethe thou can right welle refere	*place*
1580	Thaym that he truste to do contrariance.	*the contrary*
	Whare is thy fayth that maketh suche distaunce	*strife*
	Amonges prynces to sette impedyment	
	Whan thay truste beste to bene in stablysement?	*stability*
fol. 27v		
Nota	Thurgh thy faynte chere and fals felycité	
1585	Thou deceveste that trusteth on the wele	*prosperity*
	So chaungeable ys evermore thy sertaynté	
	The sweigh also so light ys of thy whele	*motion*
	It casteth doun from alkyn welth and sele	*happiness*
	Whiche now with thee above alle men is chefe	
1590	Als faste with thee shalle undyr bene unlefe.[1]	

---

[1] *All associated with you shall be brought down unwillingly*

How Brenny went into Norway for helpe again his brother and wed the kynges doughter

Nota	The forgers so of lese and mendacyté	*lies; falsity*
	Thou sette above so fully fortunate	
	Upon thy whele thurgh mutabilité	
	Betwex tho brether that made a grete debate	
1595	Whiche made Brenny to breke and alterate	*change*
	His covenaunts alle anents his brother dere	*with regard to*
	Who trusted hym in alle that myght affere.	*was pertinent*

	Thay counsayld hym tille passe into Northway	*to*
	Kynge Alsynges doughter to have unto his wyfe	
1600	Thurgh helpe of whom he shuld conquere som day	
	Alle Loegres hool whiche was his grounde natyfe.	*native country*
	For better it was to make with Belyne stryfe	
	Than holde thay sayde of hym by suche servage	
	The londe whiche that shulde bene his heritage.	

1605	So ful counsaylde he wente into Norway	
	Declarynge to the kynge alle his entent	
	To whom he gaffe his doughter gent and gay	*noble*
	To bene his wyffe with fulle and hoel assente	*whole*
	And hight hym helpe to conquere Loegres gente	*promised; noble*
1610	And as he came homward with hyre anone	*her*
	Upon the se he mette than with his fone.	*foes*

How Kynge Guthlake of Danmarke toke Brennys wife on the se fro hym and were brought to the Kynge Belyn, wharfore Brenny faught with Kynge Belyn and, discomfyte, he fled to Burgoyne.

	Guthlake that kynge of Denmarke was so stronge	
	Who had hyre loved in alle his wytte and myght	
	Ful many day so had she hym of longe	
1615	Upon the se for hire dyd with hym fight	
	Toke hyre fro hym and put hym to the flighte	
	And that same nyght was Guthlake than and she	
	By tempeste dryve within Loegres cuntré.	

	He was so brought and she to Kynge Belyne	
1620	To whom he hight his kyngdome of hym holde	*promised*
	And eche yere pay truage to hym and fyne	*tribute; payment*
	With-thy hym and his wife he fre then wolde	*As long as*
	Whiche to fulfylle he bonde hym monyfolde	
	Whom Kynge Belyne lete passe than home agayne	
1625	With hyre in fere of whiche thay were ful fayne.	*together; happy*

fol. 28r	With that Brenny with hoste and grete envy	*hatred*
	Agayne Belyne came than in grete aray	*battle formation*
	And bade hym sende his wife to hym in hye	*quickly*
	Iff that he wolde so cese alle tene and tray	*grief; affliction*
1630	Or els he shuld hym make many affray	*attack*
	And waste his londe with mekylle werre and strife	*much*
	That he shulde irke fulle gretly of his life.	*be grieved*

	Of whiche manace Kynge Belyn nothynge rought	*threat; cared*
	Bot sende hym worde and bade hym do his beste	
1635	For at his wille so wold he do right nought	
	He shuld it fele and fynde whan so hym leste.	*wanted*
	For whiche anone and that withouten reste	
	Right in the wod of Calathere thay mette	
	In Albany with strokes sore thay bette.	*struck*

1640	At whiche batayle Kynge Brenny had the werre	*worse*
	And putte to flight unneth myght gon away	*hardly*
	For bought he never afore no bargayne derre.	*more dearly*
	Out of his own was bette in foule aray	*state*
	And fayne to fle the londe forever and ay	
1645	Bot unto Fraunce he wan to Duke Segwyne	*came*
	Of Burgoyne so was lorde by verry lyne.	*inheritance*

	To whom he was so plesand to his pay	*satisfaction*
	So manly als and in his wytte so wyse	
	That every wight hym loved nyght and day.	*person*
1650	And what was done it was by his avyse	*counsel*
	In so ferre forthe the duke dyd so devyse	
	To hym anone his doughter in spousage	*marriage*
	With alle Burgoyne to holde in heritage.	

How Kynge Brenny was made Duke of Burgoyne by the dukes doughter that he wed to his wife, and brought grete hoste on Belyn, whare thaire modir made thaym accorded and kysse.

	Sone after whiche the duke than dyd decese	*die*
1655	And Brenny duke was of that grete duché	
	A myghty prynce that tyme withouten lese.	*lie*
	Bythought hym off his grete adversyté	
	How Belyn putte hym fro his ryalté	
	And drove hym oute from alle his hye puissaunce	*power*
1660	For whiche he thought on hym to take vengeaunce.	

	Wyth that anone grete hoste upon hym brought
	Of whom Belyne fulle knowlage had and wytte
	And redy was to do that he had sought

	In felde with hym to fyght his way to dytte	*rule*
1665	Thynkynge to make hym so a sory fytte	*episode*
	For whiche than came thayre modyr Quene Conwen	
	To cese thayre strife displayd hire pappes then.	*breasts*

fol. 28v	Tylle oon she wente and seth unto the tother	*To; afterwards*
	Saynge right thus "Lo here the pappes thou soke	*sucked*
1670	I bought thee son fulle dere, I am thy modyr.	*dearly*
	Whan that thy fete lay to, my herte fast stroke.	*kicked; beat fast*
	For love of me lete alle this stryfe be broke	
	And cesed so that pese and charité	
	Betwyx you forthe alway may dure and be.	*endure*

1675	"Lo here the wombe that to this world yow brought	
	In erthe to regne and conquerours to bene	*be*
	Of other londes by menes that may be wrought	*means*
	And lete me nought this sorow betwyx you sene.	
	Do of thyne armes and come with me I mene."	*Put off*
1680	To Brenny sayde she "Thus for love of me	
	Elles treuly son anone right wille I de."	*die*

	For pyté so he cam forth with his modyr dere	
	Unto Belyne and saughtylde with mekylle blysse	*made peace; happiness*
	And thus was than so staunched alle thaire stere	*ceased; strife*
1685	In love and pese togedyr bounde iwysse	*certainly*
	For evermore and thareto dyd thay kysse	
	And so to Fraunce thay purposed forto gone	
	To wyn that londe and conquer it anone.	

How Kynge Belyn and Duke Brenny conquerd Fraunce, Almayne and Itaylle, with Rome and the hool empire secundum Alfridum Beverlaicensem et Galfridum Monemutensem.[1]

	Whiche after so by processe thay conquerde	
1690	And so forth in the londe of hiegh Almayne	
	Whare alle the folke were of thaym dred and ferde	*afraid*
	Obeyssynge thaym with servyce wondir fayne	*Obeying; ready*
	Of whiche thay chese oute men, is nought to layne,	*lie*
	Right of the beste and that grete multitude	
1695	And Almayne so thay wan with fortitude.	*Germany*

	Alle Savoy thurgh thay rode and Lumbardy	*Savoy; Lombardy*
	And had it hole in thare subjeccioun	
	And so forthe over mountayns of Italy	

[1] *According to Alfred of Beverley and Geoffrey of Monmouth*

	Thay had it alle withoute objeccioun.	*resistance*
1700	Alle Tuskayne so at thayre eleccioun	*Tuscany; will*
	The londe of Gene and also Romany	*Genoa; Rome*
	Calabre and Puyle and also Campany.	*Calabria; Apulia; Campania*
	To Rome thay came with hoste besegyng ytte	
	In whiche were so that tyme two counsellours	
1705	Syr Gabas and Porcenna fulle of wytte	*skill*
	And of manhode appreved in many stours	*conflicts*
	By whose counsaylle and of the senatours	
	The Romayns so to Belyne and Syr Bren	
	Sende oute hostage and heght to ben thayre men.	*promised*
fol. 29r	The whiche hostage because Romayns were false	
1711	And lefte thaire hight and promyse that thay made	*oath*
	Afore Rome yates were honged by the halse	*gates; neck*
	Whan Belyn and Brenne thaym new aseged hade	*besieged*
	To thayre falshode that knowyn was fulle brade	*widely*
1715	As Romayns ere ay perilouse with to dele	*are; dangerous*
	What so thay hight thay wille ful sone repele.	*promise; repudiate*
	The Romayns sente unto thaire councellours	
	And ofte to reyse the cyté to reskowe	*lift (the siege)*
	With whiche so came the forsayde governours	
1720	Syr Gabas and Persenna I trowe	*believe*
	To breke the sege so made thay there avowe	*promise*
	Upon Awbe flode with Belyne and Syr Brenne	*River Allia*
	Thay faughte ful sore as men myght after kenne.	*know*
	Suche multitude of folke was never are sene	*before*
1725	As thare dyd fight with strokes sore and felle	*fierce*
	On ayther parte were slayne that wold not flene.	*flee*
	Bot at the laste the Bretons bare the belle	*had the victory*
	And wan the felde thare was no more to telle.	
	Syr Gabas was slayn in that batayle	
1730	And Porsenna was take withouten fayle.	
	The cyté so was wonne with strengh and take	*taken*
	Whare Belyn had and Brenny alle thaire wylle	
	Of grete rychesse whare with here men to make	*their*
	Thurgh alle the londe thayre byddynge to fulfylle.	
1735	So Itaylle alle obeyd thaym untylle	*with respect to*
	Of whiche thay had fulle domynacioun	
	Withoute more stryfe or yit malignacioun.	*foul play*

Secundum computacionem Orosii ad Augustinum[1]

This was after that Adam was create
Foure thousand yere seve hundre foure score and eghte   *seven*
1740 And als byfore Criste was associate
To mankynde, so whan that thay dyd so feght   *fight*
Thre hundre yere and oon that tyme it neght   *approached*
Whan Rome was reuled hool by two councelours
Whiche stode for juges and were the governours.

1745 And after Rome was fully edyfyed   *built*
Thre hundre yere, as Martyne cronyclere
In his cronycles hath clerly specifyed,
In whiche tyme so regned Kynge Assuere
In Perse alle hool. Socrates with gode chere
1750 The venym dranke in prison whare he lay   *poison*
And pusound was by his own wille that day.   *poisoned*

fol. 29v **How Kynge Belyn gafe to Brenny the empire and cam into Bretayne and made
the cité called Caeruske, now Caerlioun, and seysed Albany in his hande by resort
and by eschete, in defaute of heire of Brenny after his deeth.**

Kynge Belyn thare so graunted to Brenny than
That londe alle hole and wold thare byde nomore   *remain*
And to Bretayne agayne remove bygan.
1755 And Brenne his lyfe alle Itale held evermore
Holdyng alleway Romayns in awe ful sore
Thay durste not route for fere of hym ne stere   *assemble; resist*
So was he dred in Itayl fere and nere.   *far and near*

Nota of resort and eschete of Albany

So in mene while Kynge Belyn was come home   *meanwhile*
1760 With mekyl joy to alle his baronage
And Albany he seysid at his come   *took possession of; arrival*
From thens forthe as for his heritage
Kepynge the pese and put away outrage.   *illegality*
The lawes whiche his fadyr dyd so make
1765 Were kepte so welle that none that tyme thaym brake.

Than made he up his castels that were doun
And thare with made a cyté of grete myghte
On Uske water that now ys Carlyoun
That called than was Caeruske fulle righte

---

[1] *According to the computation of Orosius to Augustine*

1770   In Glamorgan bycause of Uske it highte.   *was called*
        In Breton tonge a cyté men calle "Cayre"
        Caeruske so called on Uske for it stode fayre.   *beautifully*

How he made Bilyngate in London, than callede Belyngate, and sette a barelle of golde in whiche he was biryed at his deth.

        Than made he so a toure at Troynovaunte
        Stronge and rialle and of grete worthynesse
1775   Upon Thamyse whare shippes most dyd haunte   *remain*
        In signe of his trihumphe and hyegh prowesse
        That straungers alle of outen londes I gesse   *foreign*
        His victory myght thare remembre wele
        His honoure als and knowe it every dele.   *part*

1780   Upon the heght above upon that toure
        He sette right than a barelle made of golde
        His batayls alle and trihumphes wrought there oure   *over*
        That every man myght se thaym and byholde
        In what honoure he stode and never dyd folde   *give in*
1785   For whose name so than hight it Belyngate   *it was called*
        Whiche at London is knowen arely and late.   *early*

        In whiche barelle was fully his entente
        Oute of this worlde whan he were dede and paste   *past*
        Hys body alle to poudre shuld be brente   *powder; burned*
1790   Faste loken in evermore to dure and laste.   *locked; endure*
        Thus was his wylle and als his grete forcaste   *plan*
        Bycause he wolde nevermore foryeten be   *forgotten*
        And rayse his fame ever upward in degré.

fol. 30r So ende he than, his body sogates brente   *thus; burned*
1795   In poudere alle and putte tharein to kepe.
        The peple alle of sorow couthe not stynte   *cease*
        For hym so faste thay gan to crye and wepe.
        Thare sorows grete with teres did thay stepe   *soak*
        Whiche from thaire eyen in stremes ran ful faste   *eyes*
1800   Thaire heped sorow so multiplyed and laste.

.xvi. capitulum of Kynge Gurguyn

Nota that this kynge had homage of Danmark and gafe Irelonde to certeyn folke of Spayne to holde it of hym and his heyres as it is contened in Policronica Radulphi Cestrensis.

        Gurguyn his son so crouned after hym
        Of Bretayne bare so than the diademe

Semely and faire rightwyse and large of lym

Right meke and juste what so that he shuld deme.   *judge*

1805   By gode avyse he dyd alle thynge me seme.   *it seems to me*

Gode pese and reste with alle tranquylité

He loved welle and no malignyté.

Who dyd agayne hym any rebellioun

He wolde hym brynge unto his friste degré   *first warrant of decree*

1810   And make hym know in his opynyoun

That wronge he dyd agayn his dygnyté.

That poynte so come of his paternyté

Of nature so he muste do so algates   *in any case*

For so his fadyr dyd ever to alle estates.

1815   So felle it than the kynge of Denmarke nolde   *did not wish*

His tribute pay bot yt withhelde by force

Whiche to his fadyr was graunted many folde

And payd alway unto his rialle corse.   *person*

To Dannemarke wente to menden that deforce   *default*

1820   Whare he the Danes than slew in grete batayle

Thare kynge also withouten eny fayle.

He made the londe to bowe and to enclyne

To his lordshyppe and to his soveraynté

In paynge of tribute and thayre fyne   *fine*

1825   As it dyd friste to his paternyté   *first*

Thus sette he it agayn in friste degré.   *condition*

And as he came by Iles of Orkenay

Homwarde he founde whare thretty shippes lay.   *thirty*

Alle were thay fulle of men and women fayre

1830   Besekynge hym of mercy and of grace

To have some grounde whither thay myght repayre   *take refuge*

To dwelle upon and make there wonyng place.   *dwelling*

Thaire governoure that was so in that case

Partholoym hight that came of gode lynage   *was called*

1835   From Spayne exilde of youthe and tendre age.   *young*

fol. 30v   To whom Gurguyne graunted and gafe Irelande

And sente two shippes to gyde and brynge thaym thare   *guide*

Whiche was alle waste, nor houses non thay fande,

Than gan thay tele and howses made aywhare   *till; everywhere*

1840   The londe to holde of Bretayn everemare

By homage so and servyce sovereyne

And to Bretayne perpetualy obeyne.   *pay homage*

	Gurguyne Batrus this kynge hight of Bretayne	*was called*
	Come home agayne after his vyage sore	
1845	And sone thereafter he felte suche sore and payne	
	That fro his corse his goste departed thore	*body; spirit; there*
	Regnynge fully thretty wynter afore	*thirty*
	In Caerlyoun so after his hiegh estate	
	Was buried than as usage was Gode wate.	*custom; knows*

.xvii. capitulum of Kynge Guytelyn and iii kynges next aftir hym.

How Quene Marcyan made the lawes called Lawes Marciane that was the thrid lawe.

1850	Guytelyn than his son dyd regne as hayre	
	Of alle Bretayne thurghout unto the se	
	Who wedded was and had a wyfe ful fayre	
	That Marcian hight so was hyre name pardé	*was called; indeed*
	Bothe wyse and gode whiche of hyre synglerté	*uniqueness*
1855	So lerned was made the lawes Marcyane	
	In Bretoun tonge of hyre own wytte alane.	*alone*

	Whiche Kinge Alverede in Saxon tonge translate	*Alfred*
	And Marchen lage did calle in his language.	*laws*
	This Guytelyne was gode of his estate	
1860	And meke also and manly of corage	
	Right juste and wyse and fayre of his vysage	
	And regned fulle and pesebly ten yere	
	And to his wyfe he lafte his reame ful clere.	

Kynge Sisilyus

	Sysilius his sonn so than of seven yere age	
1865	Undre the reule and wytty governaunce	*intelligent*
	Of Marcian his modyr so gode and sage	
	She was so wyse in alle hyre ordynaunce	*management*
	Who kepte the londe from alle mysgovernaunce.	
	At hyre decese she crouned Sisilius	
1870	That was hyre soune as cronycles tellen us.	

	He dyed yonge and als in tendre age	
	And yit he gatte a son to bene his hayre	
	Upon his wyfe in wedloke and in spousage	
	Afore his deth, and byried was ful fayre.	
1875	To whose son so the barons dyd repayre	*come*
	And brought hym than with grete and hyegh reverence	
	To Caerlyoun with alle obedyence.	

fol. 31r **Kyng Kymar**

Nota how he was wyse piteuse for ther is grete difference bituix wise piteuse and fool piteuse. That first is vertu, the seconde is vice and foly.

	Kymar his sonne the barons dyd corowne	
	With honoure suche as felle for his degré	*befitted*
1880	Who twenty yere and oon so bare the corowne	
	And kepte the londe in alle tranquylité.	
	Pyteuse he was right as a kynge shulde be	
	In rightfulnesse accordant with his lawe	
	Agayn his pese that dyd, he made thaym lawe.[1]	

Kynge Danyus

1885	Danyus than his brother so succede	
	Durynge ten yere in werre and als in payne	*war*
	Withouten reste in cronycles as I rede.	
	Bot how it was or why cronycles layne	*remain silent*
	And of his dedes me liste nought forto fayne	*I did not wish; lie*
1890	Bot as myne autor seyth and doth expreme	*express*
	Now in my wytte I can non othur deme.	*judge*

.xviii. capitulum off Kynge Morvyde

How this kynge was so immoderately irouse (*wrathful*) that nayther he ne none other myght staunche it. Who was slayne feghtynge with a monstre that cam oute of the se and stroyed (*destroyed*) men.

	Morvyde his sonne whom that he gatte of baste	*bastardy*
	On oon that hight Tanguste his paramoure	
	Stronge and myghty and irouse ful of haste	*wrathful; violence (impatience)*
1895	Hardy and kynde and fre as conqueroure	*generous*
	Of alle largesse forpassynge emperoure	*generosity; surpassing*
	Or any kynge that in his tyme dyd reyne	
	So was he kynde whan ire was paste and deyne.	*wrath; anger*

	Bot in hys ire there myght none with hym speke	*anger*
1900	He was so hote and fulle of cruelté.	
	He rought nothynge of whom he dyd hym wreke	*cared; violence*
	Hys yre excede his wytte in alle degré	
	In so ferre forthe his sensybilité	
	Couth nought in wrath his cruelté restrayne	
1905	So fulle he was of fury and disdayne.	

---

[1] *He dishonored those who went against the peace*

Nota for sovereynté of Scotlond and resort of it

In whose tyme so the kynge than of Murreve   *Moray (Scotland)*
With hoste fulle grete distroyd Northumbrelonde   *army*
Bothe brente and slew and alle the lande dyd reve.   *rob*
With hys lege lorde that werre he toke on honde
1910   Whom Kynge Morvyde with hoste mette to withstonde
And slew hym than for his rebellyoun
And sette the londe in pese and unyoun.

Nota of vengeance immoderate without mesure which is vice and no vertu

Bot so irouse and fulle of wrath was he
He myght not cese afore the dede were brente   *burned*
1915   That thare ware slayne of his grete cruelté
The bodyse alle, afore that he couth stente,   *cease*
In fyre be caste and into poudre spente.   *to be reduced to ash*
To it was done his ire myght not appese   *until*
His vengeaunce than thus sette his herte in ese.

fol. 31v   Sone after that cam fro the Irisshe se
1921   A wonder beste or fysshe, whiche men do calle
A monstre grete, of whiche the comonté   *community*
Were alle affrayed thurghoute the londe over alle
For it dovourde the folke bothe grete and smalle.   *devoured*
1925   For whiche thay fled the londe as exulate   *exiles*
That waste it stode and also desolate.

The kynge seynge his londe in poynte bewaste
His corage was so stronge and cruelté
Hym thought he wold alone fight with that gaste   *wicked creature*
1930   And destroy hym so than in pryvyté
Trustynge oonly in his synglarité.   *singular ability*
He faughte with hym that no man wiste ne knewe   *understood*
Whiche hym deuourde right sodenly and slewe.

Nota how the maker sayth by this cruelle kynge

1935   So were bothe dede withoute any delay
With cruelté of thaymselff inordynate   *excessive*
By rightfulle dome of God seand alway   *judgment; seeing*
His cruelté so foule intemporate   *intemperate*
To fyghte with suche a monstre and debate.   *oppose*
I can nought se bot of his rightfulnesse
1940   That reuleth alle it came right as I gesse.

.xix. capitulum of Kynge Gorbonyan first and iiii kynges next

Nota how this kynge helde pees and lawe in hys tyme

Gorbonyan his eldest sonne of fyve
Was after kynge and helde the magesté
Rightfulle and trew to every man of lyve
His reame in pese and fulle prosperité.
1945 And to his peple he helde fulle equyté   *upheld; justice*
Tele men of londe with godes he dyd comforte   *To*
Sowdyours als from wronge hym to supporte.   *soldiers*

Ten yere he stode so kynge in pese an reste
With moste plenté that any reame myght have
1950 And as nature of lyfe may noght ay leste   *forever*
The deth his soule oute fro his body drave.   *drove*
So byried was he than and layde in grave
At Trynovaunt that was his grete cyté
With alle honoure and alle regalité.

Kynge Argalle

Nota of this kynge how he was put doun for wronge sustened by hym

1955 Argalle his brothyr sygned with dyademe   *appointed; crown*
The kynge was tho with alle solempnyté   *then*
By natyff byrthe next brother he was men deme.   *agree*
Alle gode men ever he hate at his powsté   *hated under his power*
Oppressynge thaym by his subtilité   *guile*
1960 And alle fals folke fulle ofte he dyd avaunse   *advance*
The baronnage hym putte doun for that chaunse.   *situation*

fol. 32r   **Kynge Elydoure**

This kynge deposed hymself and made his brother Argalle kynge efte sone agayne

Elydoure who brother thrid ful generate
Was than the nexte by alle successioun
And bare the croune with alle rialle estate
1965 By lordes wille and thaire concessioun.
Who regned wele withoute oppressioun
Unto his folke ought done in any wise
So reuled he wele his own dyd hym suffise.   *own (income)*

Whan he had fulle regned so by fyve yere
1970 As he was gone a day for his disporte   *pleasure*

Tille a foreste the wode of Calathere   *To*
He mette Argalle his brothyr of symple porte   *manner*
Fully despayrde and oute of alle comforte   *lacking hope*
Besekynge hym that he wolde hym socoure   *aid*
1975   For his brothir and bene his govenoure.

Kynge Elidoure for pité that he se
Toke hym so than betwyxe his armes two
And comforte hym so in his poverté.
And to Alclude his cyté gan he go
1980   Of Albany moste famouse cyté tho   *then*
Whiche now but fewe wote in what place it is   *know*
So is it now that name unknowe iwys.   *certainly*

And made hym seke and for his barons alle   *seek*
So sende he than in haste to come hym tylle.   *to*
1985   Whiche came anone in haste so at hys calle
His comaundement in allethynge to fullfylle.
He toke thaym in and told thaym alle his wille
Ever on by on and made thaym swere the othe   *one by one*
To Argalle so whether thay were lefe or lothe.   *desirous; loathe*

1990   And after this anone right so he yede   *went*
To Ebrauke than and helde his parlement   *York*
Whare he right than of tendre brotherhede
Toke of his croune right by his own intente   *off*
And on his brothers heved it sette and spente   *head; gave*
1995   By fulle decré and jugement of his mouthe
And made hym kynge agayn by northe and southe.

Kynge Argalle the second tyme

Argalle so kynge crouned new agayne
Fulle welle his lordes dyd after love and plese
And lefte his vyce and toke vertu to sayne.
2000   So sette he alle his peple in gode pese
Regnynge ten yere and then felle hym diseese
Thurgh malady and dyverse grete sekenesse
He dyed and lyeth at Carlele as I gesse.

fol. 32v   **Kynge Elydoure twyse made kynge and ever mercyfulle**

The barons alle than made Syr Elidoure
2005   The kynge agayne with alle the rialté
So wele thaym payed to have hym governoure   *it pleased them*
For his godenesse and his benygnyté.
And for he was so fulle of alle pyté

	That in alle thynge mercy he dyd preserve	
2010	To every man beter than thay couthe deserve.	*did*

Ingen and Perydoure kynges

	But Ingen than and als Syr Peridoure	
	His brether two rose thurgh grete trechery	
	And hym put doun oute of his hiegh honoure	
	Emprisounynge hym than corporally	
2015	Within the Toure of Trynovaunt forthy	
	That thay departe the reams amonge thaym two	*Such that; divided; realms*
	Bot nought forthy it dured nought longe so	*nevertheless; endured*

	For Ingen tho so leved bot seven yere	*lived*
	Whan deth hym toke and ravyshit hym away	
2020	His issu yonge of his own body here.	
	And byried was as usage was that day	*custom*
	With alle honoure that the barons may	
	For wele he dyd his parte alway governe	
	As ferre as men couthe knowe or yit discerne.	

Kynge Perydoure

2025	Peridoure had than alle the londe fulle clere
	Who kynge was than as alle cronycles telle.
	Fulle pesybly the reaume he reuled here
	Tylle sudeyn deth hym toke, so it byfelle
	And byried was as kynge bothe fayre and welle
2030	After thaire rytes and als thaire olde usage
	With hiegh honoure by alle his baronage.

Kynge Elydoure thryse made kynge

	Elydoure whiche in prison so foryette	*forgotten*
	Alle this mene while so lay in hevynesse	*sorrow*
	The barons alle oute of the Toure dyd fette	*fetch*
2035	And crouned hym with alkyn worthynesse	*all kind of*
	Thus was he thryse so crouned as I gesse	
	And every tyme he kepte his olde condiciouns	
	Withouten wronge or any evelle addiciouns.	

	And whan the tyme that deth hym had exspyred
2040	Oute of this world that dede he was away
	Thay layd hym than as he had theym requyred
	In Alclude whiche his cité was that day.
	Bot neverthelesse som cronycles otherwyse say

	That he was layd at Elud so and buryed
2045	That now Aldburgh is called and specyfyed.

.xx. capitulum of the Kynge Gorbonyan, the sone of Gorbonyan, the second of that name, and xxxii other kynges next folowynge.

	Gorbonyan whiche was Gorbonyan sonne	
	The croune had so and after his eme alle thynge	*uncle*
	Dyd kepe and reule in alle as he was wonne	*accustomed*
	And welle was loved with olde and als wyth yynge.	*by old; by young*
2050	And at his dethe was byried lyke a kynge	
	In alle honoure and worship hool entered	*interred*
	As to suche prynce of right shulde be requered.	

Kynge Margan the son of Argalle

	Margan that was the sonne of Kynge Argalle	
	Was corouned than and helde the ryalté	
2055	With mekylle blys his reame he rewled alle	
	And kepte it ever in alle tranquylité.	
	He ended wele with alle benygnyté	*kindness*
	For whiche he was fulle gretely magnyfyde	
	Thurghoute his reame and highly lawdyfyde.	*praised*

Kynge Enniaunus son of Argalle

Nota how this kynge was ended sone for his cursed lyfe and his tirantrye

2060	Enniaunus his brother so was kynge	
	Seven yere than in tyrantry he bare	
	The croune alway in cursidnesse regnynge.	
	For whiche he was put doun with sorow and care	
	The sexte yere so that no man knew ourwhare	*where*
2065	That he become; so secretly his ende	
	Was kepte counsaylle that never man after kende.	*secret; knew*

Ivalle kynge son of Ingen.

Nota of the gudenes of this kynge and of his vertue

	Ivalle the sonne of Kynge Ingen dyd rayne	*reign*
	Who loved ever to kepe alle rightwisnesse	
	And hated vyce the sothe of hym to sayne.	
2070	Amonge his men he loved ever alle clennesse	
	Pore men to helpe fallyn in febylnesse	
	Was his desyre and shrewes forto chastyse	*evil-doers*
	And sone he dyed and biried as myght suffyse.	

Kynge Rymo the sone of Perydoure

Nota of the gudenes of this kynge and of his vertue

Rymo the sonne than of Kynge Peridoure
2075 Corounde was than and loved alle gentyllesse
None evelle wold here bot vertu and honoure
Of lyfe fulle clene and lovynge alle clennesse.
In his tyme was alle plenté and largesse   *generosity*
Pese and reste and hool felycyté
2080 Of worldly welthe and grete prosperyté.

Kynge Geyennes the son of Elydoure

Nota of this kynges gode reule and governance

Geyennes than the son of Elydoure
To regne began and reuled welle his day
In grete vertu as noble governoure
And kepte his reame unto the peples pay   *satisfaction*
2085 And dyed sone and biried on gode aray   *state*
As noble prynce of deuté ought to be   *duty*
In ryalle wyse as men couthe for hym se.

fol. 33v   **Kynge Katellus**

Nota of punysement of trespassours

Katellus so his sonne dyd than succede
And regned welle and helde up lawe and right
2090 Oppressours alle that pore men dyd overlede   *oppress*
He hanged ever on trese fulle hiegh to sight.   *trees*
He spared thaym nought forsothe by day ne nyght
Bot ever forthwith he gaffe thaym jugyment
Whiche execute was aftyr his entent.   *was carried out*

Kynge Coyle

2095 Coyle his sonne than aftyr hym dyd succede
Corownde for kynge regnynge mony a day
In grete welfare withouten eny drede
And lefte the londe in riche and gode aray.   *state*
Whan he dyd de and passed hens away   *die; hence*
2100 Byried and layd as came hym of degré   *befitted*
Right ryally and of grete honesté.   *splendor*

Kynge Porrex

Porrex was than his sonne ful generate
Made kynge and had than forthe the rialté
And reuled welle by law preordynate
2105   His reme thurghoute and alle his comynté   *citizenry*
In grete quyete and gode stabilité
Withouten grevaunce or noy of any wight   *molestation; person*
So gode he was and plesand to mennes sight.

Kynge Cheryn

Nota of drunkenes

Cheryn was kynge replete of drunkenesse
2110   In whiche vyce so he wox a fole unwyse   *became; fool*
And couthe discerne no reson doutlesse
Bot bete his men and fouly thaym dyspyse
And voyde thaym ofte so oute of his servyse   *exiled*
Whiche in a prynce was nothynge to comende
2115   For in vertu he shulde al folke transcende.

Kynge Fulgyn, Kynge Eldrade, Kynge Andragius.

His sonnes thre, Fulgyn was eldest bore   *born*
The secunde hight Eldrade, the thrid Andragyus.   *was called*
But Fulgyn was so crouned than byfore
And dyed sone and Eldrade crouned thus
2120   And dyed anone as bokes tellen us.
After whom so Andragyus was kynge
Who in shorte tyme after made his endynge.

Nota how the maker off this moveth his resoun touchant drunknesse

Thof thay dyed sone no mervelle soth to say   *although*
That so were gote in drunkenesse and generate   *begotten*
2125   For drunkenesse cometh of fume of drynke alleway   *vapor*
That undygeste ascendyth the brayne algate   *undigested; in any case*
With quantité taken untemperate   *intemperate*
And coverth it as clowde above the sonne   *cloud; sun*
Whare thurgh his wytte and mynde away is ronne.   *fled*

fol. 34r   Wharfore I truste right by myne estymate
2131   Thay myght not dure so wayke was thayre nature.   *weak*
For whan the hede is seke and intemporate
Alle other membres in wyrkynge fayle thayre cure   *care*
And febled ere and wayke withoute mesure.   *are; debilitated*

| 2135 | How shuld thay than that were so procreate | |
| | Endure ought longe, by reson approbate? | *approved* |

Kynge Urian

Nota how viciouse this kynge was of lyfe

	Urian his sonne was kynge in magesté	
	And kepte his londe bot he was licherouse	*lecherousness*
	Eche woman so that was of grete bewté	
2140	He wolde thaym have, he was so vyciouse.	
	Bot neverthelese he was right bountynouse	*generous*
	To every wyght that had necessité	
	He gafe grete gode and richesse of suffishenté.	*sufficiency*

Kynge Elyud

Nota of gode reule of thise two kynges

	Elyud was kynge and than dyd bere the croune	
2145	And dyed sone that wyse was in alle thynge.	
	Detonus than who ever to werre was boune	*intent*
	Was crounede than in tendre age and yynge.	
	Thayre ennemyse ever to deth thay dyd doun dynge	*beat*
	And gode reule helde thurgh alle the reame fulle wele	
2150	So happy were thay and so fulle of sele.	*bliss*

Kynge Detonus, Kynge Gurgucius, Kynge Meryan, Kynge Bledudo, Kynge Cappe, Kynge Oenus, Kynge Sisilius, Kynge Bledud Gabred.

	Detonus than was kynge of alle Bretayne	
	And aftyr hym Gurgucyus bare the croune	
	And Meryan than aftyr hym sertayne.	
	Bledudo than after hym was redy boune	*set*
2155	To regne in londe as kynge of grete renoune.	
	Aftyr hym Kynge Cappe and than Kynge Oenus	
	Eche after other regned and Sisilyus.	

	Bledud Gabred, who in alle note and songe	
	Forpassynge was and in alle instruments	
2160	Of musyke so excede alle other amonge	
	In whiche he had for passynge sentements	
	That for a god in alle the folkes intents	
	Of myrthe and joy and als in alle musyke	
	Above alle other holden and none hym lyke.	

Kynge Archyvalle, Kynge Eldolle, Kynge Redyon, Kynge Redryke, Kynge Samuel, Kynge Pyrre, Kynge Penyssel, Kynge Capoyre.

2165 Than regned so his brother Archyvalle
And than his sonne Syr Eldolle wytterly.   *certainly*
To whom his sonne whom Redyon men calle
After whom his sonne Redrike was kynge in hy.   *haste*
Samuel than was kynge made sykyrly   *surely*
2170 So than succede Kynge Pyrre and Penysselle
After hym Capoyre and than Kynge Elyguelle.

fol. 34v **Kynge Elyguelle**

Nota how this kynge ded punysshe trespasours

Bot Eliguelle, the whiche was Capoyres sonne,
Bothe wyse and sad and in his reame helde righte   *solemn; steady*
To alle his folke that in his reame dyd wonne   *dwell*
2175 Fulle stedfastly certayne at alle his myght.
And thaym that dyd eny wronge or unright
Nota He prisounde thaym with sore and grete duresse
And helde thaym longe so after in greteste distresse.

Kynge Ely

Hely his son aftyr this Elyguelle
2180 Right debonayre in alle thynge gode and wyse   *even-tempered*
So dyd succede as cronycles us do telle
Who made so firste by his wytte and devyse   *planning*
The Ile of Ely that ys of grete empryse.   *renown*
And whan he had regned fully sexty yere
2185 Thare biried was by ought I can enquere.

Some sayth he lyeth at Castre nought forthy   *nonetheless*
The whiche I can nought trusten was aforne   *prior*
Nayther byggid, ne gun to edyfy.   *constructed; begun to be built*
For Hengest who it made was than unborne
2190 And Horsus als that some men callen Horne.
Wharefore me thynke it was to hym condygne   *fitting*
At Ely lygge how shuld men it repygne.   *to lie; however; deny*

.xxi. capitulum of Kynge Lud that chaunged the name of Trynovant and called it Carlud after whom it was called after (*afterwards*) Londoun

Than Lud his sonne his heyre was so of myght
For wysdome so and als grete worthynesse
2195 With honoure hole as came hym wele of right

Was crouned kynge by hole and dewe processe.   *due*
His citese alle and castels dyd redresse
Of mete and drynke alleway right plentyuouse
Rightwyse manly and also chyvalrouse.

How he called Trynovaunt Caerlud and made Ludgate

2200   With walles fayre and toures fresshe aboute
        His cyté grete of Trynovaunt so fayre
        Fulle wele he made and bataylde alle thurghoute   *fortified*
        And palays fele for lordes and grete repayre   *many; spaces*
        And mended fresshe alle places that were unfayre.
2205   He made a yate that now men calle Ludgate   *gate*
        Whareby he made hys palays of estate

        For love of whom Caerlud men dyd it calle
        In Bretoun tonge fulle longe and many a day
        Tylle Saxons came with language chaunged alle.
2210   Thys gode Kynge Lud whan he shuld passe away
        Byrid so was right in a temple gay
        Besyde Ludgate nere whare his palays stode   *near*
        In tombe rialle accordant to his blode.

fol. 35r Two sonnes he had whiche were of tendre age
2215   The reame to reule by gode discrecioun.
        Thay were to yonge to kepe thayre heritage
        Bot hayres thay were by alle successioun.
        Wharfore thare eme toke fulle possessioun   *uncle*
        In alle the reame by northe and als by southe
2220   And helde it wele in honoure as he couthe.   *knew how to*

.xxii. capitulum offe Kynge Cassibalan

        Cassibalan thaire uncle than was kynge
        And foonde thaym bothe right honestly and wele   *tended*
        Dyd nurture thaym whils thay were childre yynge.
        And whan thay came to age that thay couthe fele   *manage*
2225   To reule thaymselff the duché every dele   *part*
        Of Trynovaunt and Kent gafe Androgyus
        And of Cornewayle to Tenvancyus.

        Andragyus the elder brothyr wase
        The yonger was so Tenvancyus
2230   Whiche were bothe two manly in every case
        And wyse and tylle thaire eme fulle bounteuus.   *uncle*
        So felle a day that Cesar Julyus

After whan he alle londes had conquerde
At Boloyne of this londe he faste enquerde

How Julius Cesar came into Bretayne firste pretendynge title to conquere Grete Bretayne

2235   That it dyd hight and what folke were tharein   *what; called*
Thay tolde hym how that Bretayne was the name.
"O" sayde he than "me thynke it light to wyn.   *easy*
Belyne and Brenne it aught of noble fame   *possessed*
Whiche Rome so wan and helde it for thayre hame   *home*
2240   Whose successoure I am in dignyté
Wharefore I wylle of it have soveraynté.

"Brutus also that friste it had in walde   *control*
Come of Troyans and so was Romulus
Whose successoure I am now fully calde.
2245   Bot for as muche as bastard was Brutus
The right to me of it shuld longen thus
As we that cam of Eneas so gode
Descended doun by verry lyne of blode."

By thys tytle he came into this lande   *due right*
2250   And it claymed as for his heritage
And faught with Kynge Cassibalan with honde
With hostes grete of thaire bothers lynage
Bot Bretons yit fully had avauntage
And put Romayns alle utterly to flyght
2255   That thay were glad to sayle agayn forth ryght.

fol. 35v   ### How Julius Cesar came to Bretayne the seconde tyme

The Frensshe were prowde off that discomfyture   *defeat*
By whiche thay thought right so to do the same
Oute of thaire londe to chase thaym in some ure.   *propitious moment*
For drede of whiche Julyus fulle of fame
2260   In Flaunders was with mekyl tene and grame   *much difficulty; suffering*
And sente for Frenshe, Normayns and als Gascoyns
Flemyngs, Brabans, Henaldes, Gellers and Burgoyns.

The pore that were of corage and manhede
He gaffe lordshyp and landes sufficiaunte.
2265   The grete he gafe fraunchise off worthyhede.   *dominions*
The exilde men that ferre were conversaunte   *far; in touch*
He gaffe thaym grace evermore of ful covenaunte   *agreement*
Come home agayn and have thaire heritage
Fully restored agayn with alle damage.   *damages*

2270	The bonde he made alle fre out of servage	
	For joy of whiche the peple came so faste	
	That men inow he had withouten wage	*enough*
	To fyghten with the Bretons to the laste.	
	To conquer thaym he was nothynge agaste	*afraid*
2275	With alle his shippes and many under sayle	
	In Thamyse came certayn withouten fayle.	

Upon grete piles with irne poynted wele   *spikes*
Agayne thayre come were sette by ordynaunce   *coming; in preparedness*
Of Bretouns wyse to droune the flete eche dele   *part*
2280   And perse thayre shippes to sette thaym in balance.   *pierce*
Thus were thaire shippes dystroyd by that chaunce.
Thaymselff on londe fulle fayne were forto ryve   *eager; land*
And to the felde in bataylle gan to dryve.   *move*

Cassibalan so wyse and reuled wele
2285   By alkyns wytte and knyghtly provydence   *all manner of*
With his neveus so kynde and naturele   *nephews*
That manly were and fulle of alle prudence
In wham there wante nought of benyvolence   *was lacking*
To helpe thaire eme thay were fulle corageus   *uncle*
2290   With barons alle fulle bolde and batailous.   *martial*

And so thay mette with Romayns fresshe and stronge
And faught ful sore with corage odiouse   *full of hatred*
And mony one thare slayne were thaym amonge
With strokes grete and woundes tediouse.   *grievous*
2295   So aither parte on othur were dispytouse   *pitiless*
That alle the felde was colourde of the blode
Suche quantité of it there was and flode.   *abundance*

fol. 36r   Julyus thare so myghtly hym bare
That whom he stroke to deth he muste enclyne   *cede*
2300   His sworde was of suche myght and ege ware   *edge; prepared*
That Crocea Mors it hight so was it fyne.   *Yellow Death; called*
Syr Nemynus thought longe to undyrmyne
The batayle, so that he Julyus myghte
In batayle mete and with so worthy fighte.

2305   Tylle at the laste thay mette togedyr same
With strokes sore ayther on othyre layde   *attacked*
Thof Nemynus were hurte he thought gode game   *even though*
To dele with hym that never yit was afrayde.
Julyus sworde within his shelde men sayde
2310   He brought away and als his dethes wounde
So manly wele he bare hym in that stounde.   *encounter*

His neveus two with Kent and Trynovaunt
And Cornyssh folke so chyftenly thaym beere
That thurgh thayre myght and power habundaunt   *great*
2315   Put the Romayns in perele and in grete feere.   *peril*
With that Bretons cam fresshly on thaym there
And slew thaym sore and putte thaym to the flyght
To Normandy thay fled agayn fulle right.

Thare in a place Odnea that so hight   *was called*
2320   Julyus than for grete mystruste of Fraunce
Dyd make a toure right grete and stronge of myght
Hym and his godes to kepe in alle suraunce   *safety*
Thydyr to brynge his rentes by ordynaunce   *There*
And trewage als of diverse regiouns   *tribute*
2325   Agayne Bretayne to wage his legiouns.   *pay*

**How Kynge Cassibalan somonde all lordes of Bretayn to his feste whare grete
wrath and werre arose bituix the kynge and Andragius**

So than the kynge Cassibalan rialle   *majestic*
Admynystred so fulle in alle plesance
With alle honoure and glory trihumphalle
For joy dyd make his rite and observaunce
2330   His goddes only with alle his suffisaunce
For to honoure and do thaym sacryfyse
As that tyme was the manere and the gyse.   *custom*

His feste dyd crye thurghoute alle hole Bretayne   *(he) had announced*
In Cambre, Loegres and als in Albany
2335   And in Ireland with iles alle that pertayne
To his lorshyp and noble monarchy
That servyce dyd untyl his auncetry   *ancestry*
Praynge thaym alle that were of gode estate
Wyth hym to be at his feste ordynate.   *appointed*

fol. 36v   And forto drawe the knyghtes chyvalrouse
2341   To it he sette grete justes and turnement.   *jousts*
And forto make the knyghtes more corageuse
He ordeyned than at that feste excellente
Afore eche knyght ben sette a lady gente
2345   Fulle of beuté and alle fresshe juventé   *youthfulness*
To chere thaym wele as wold femynyté.   *womankind*

How the makere commendes the joysement of the peple for his triumphe and victory agayns Julius Cesar

	Suche joy was nought I say in Romany	
	Made for tryhumphe and the gloriousté	
	Whan Julyus came home with victory	
2350	Ne for conqueste of Sipions pousté	*Scipio Africanus's power*
	Whan he so at Cartage had alle degré	
	As was than at Cassibalaynes feste	
	Amonge the folke assembled moste and leste.	

Bot than Erle Andragius sent after Julius Cesar to helpe hym agayn the kynge

	Bot ever as nexte the valey ys the hill	
2355	So after joy comyth ay adversité.	
	So thare byfelle thurgh strife and evelle wille	
	Debate fulle foule of grete dyversité	*Quarrel; differences*
	Bytwene Syr Irelglas of hyegh degré	
	That cosyn was unto the kynge so nere	
2360	And Syr Hewlyn, Erle Andrage neven dere.	*nephew*

	Thurgh whiche debate Hewlyn slew Syr Irelglasse	
	For whiche the kynge Syr Hewlyn wold have slayne	
	Whom Androgyus withdrew right for that case	
	For drede right of his eme Cassibalayne.	*uncle*
2365	Wherefore the kinge to venge it dyd his payne	
	And hastily he thought hym to anoye	*harass*
	Hym to werray utterly and dystroye.	*attack*

	Wharefore Androge had in his wytte provyde	*foreseen*
	That he nede muste of alle necessité	
2370	Bene slayne hymselff and wrongely mortyfyde	*killed*
	Or his neveu withouten equyté	*justice*
	Slayne shulde be so only by cruelté	
	Or els to fle the londe as exilate	*exile*
	And leve his frendes hevy and desolate.	

	For grace and pese whan he the kynge had prayde	
2375	And none couthe gette, bot fully trusted warre,	*expected the worst*
	He wrote than to Julyus alle affrayde	
	Who cald hymselff in his writynge Cesarre	
	Besekynge hym to come agayn so farre	
2380	With alle his hoste to helpe hym in his right	
	Agayn the kynge in bataylle forto fight.	

fol. 37r	And hool trewage he of the reame shuld have	*tribute*
	For he of right therof the kynge shuld bene	

	As verrey heyre he myght it clayme and crave	*true; desire*
2385	Unto Kynge Lud as alle the reame may mene.	*realm; direct*
	Wharfore hym thought the more he myght hym tene	*trouble*
	And of the londe to graunte hym ful truage	*tribute*
	And wele the more it was his heritage.	

Than, at instance of Andragius, Julius cam into Bretayne thryd tyme whare, after sore bataile, the kynge graunted truage tille Rome and tribute.

	Syr Julyus than so humbely requerde	*petitioned*
2390	By Androgyus to whom he gaff credence	
	As doughty prynce that was nothing aferde	
	With alle his myght and his magnificence.	
	To have his wille dyd alle his diligence	
	Arrifynge up at Dovere certanly	
2395	Whither the kynge than came fulle spedely.	

	And thare thay faught so with Cassibalan.	
	The kynge was fayne to fle unto an hille	
	Whare Julyus with warde dyd sege hym than	*guard; besiege*
	By counsaylle of Androgyus and his wille	*determination*
2400	His hoste to hurte to famysshe and to spille.	*starve; destroy*
	Whare he for hungre sente to Androgyus	*(i.e., Cassibalan)*
	Besekynge hym of helpe and socoure thus.	

	And alle defaute shuld ben amended wele	
	And alle rancoure utturly appesed	*resolved*
2405	At his owne wille as he wole have eche dele	*part*
	So shuld his herte in alle thynge bene wele esed.	
	A man, he sayde, to se his kyn disesed	*harmed*
	It shuld his herte agrege and greve fulle sore.	*weigh down*
	Thus sende he worde to Androgyus thore.	*there*

2410	Who for pyté myght than no lenger byde	*continue*
	Bot to Cesare he wente anone forth right	
	Tretynge hym so that pese was made that tyde	*time*
	Betwyx thaym and trewage redy dight	*tribute; prepared*
	To pay by yere to Rome so hath he hight	*promised*
2415	Thre thousond pounde of sylver fyne in plate	*pure*
	Thus endyd was thaire werre and grete debate.	

	Thys was the yere afore thyncarnacioun	*incarnation*
	As Seynt Bede in his *Gestes of Englonde*	
	Affermed hath right in his compylacioun	
2420	Fulle sexty yere as he had red and fonde	*read*
	Who can his boke wele se and undyrstonde.	

Bot Martyne sayth nothynge of this matere
In his cronicle that Cesare ought was here   *at all*

fol. 37v   Who Romayne was and borne in Romany
2425   For honoure of his londe an reverence   *and*
           If it so were shuld it in memory
           Have made me thynke for Romayns excellence
           Seth he Romayne was borne of grete science   *Since; learning*
           And in cronycle alle Romes worthynesse
2430   Remembred hath how lefte he that prowesse.

           Bot as a *Boke of Brute* it hath comprised
           He wyntred here in Bretayne for grete love
           Tylle somer came as he afore devysed   *Until*
           At whiche tyme so he wente for his byhove.   *necessity*
2435   To Fraunce agayne he gan forto remove
           Upon Pompey to werray at his myght   *Pompey (the Great); make war*
           Of every londe he had men with hym right.

           With hym wente than Androgyus and his sonne
           For love and truste betwyxe thaym was so fyxte
2440   That none of thaym than couthe from othur wonne   *apart from; dwell*
           So were thaire hertes lovynge and entermyxte.
           And Tenvaunce his brother that heyre was nyxte   *next*
           He lefte at home the coroune forto bere
           After the tyme thayre uncle so dede were.

2445   Cassibalan so kynge stode forth seven yere
           Paynge tribute with alle humylité
           To Rome alway and was thayre truagere   *subject king*
           Unto the day of his mortalité
           That deth hym toke oute of his dignyté
2450   And biried was with laude and reverence   *praise*
           At Ebrauke than unto his excelence.

.xxiii. capitulum of the Kynge Tenvancius

           Tenvancius that duke was of Cornewayle
           Unto the heghte of alle the regymence
           Was raysed up and had the governaile
2455   Of Bretayne hole, who with fulle hiegh prudence
           Governed right wele with alle his diligence.
           Bot longe he stode nought kynge to deth hym toke   *until*
           As cronyclers have writton in thare boke.

.xxiiii capitulum ofe Kymbelyn Kynge of Bretayne in whose tyme Criste was borne

	Kymbelyne so that was his sonne and hayre	
2460	Noryssht at Rome instructe of chyvallry	*Brought up*
	And knyght was made with honoure grete and fayre	
	By Cesare Auguste regned than enterly	
	Thurghoute the world that helde the monarchy.	
	In whose tyme so was pese and alle concorde	
2465	And every reme to Rome was wele acorde.	

fol. 38r	Whiche Cesare so was called Octovian	
	By propre name who dyed the fiftene yere	
	Aftyr that Criste was so incarnate than	
	To whom succede Tyberyus in the emperé	
2470	Fro that tyme forth as clerly doth appere	
	Unto the yere after Cristes natyvyté	
	Eght and thretty in whiche that he dyd de.	*thirty; die*

Nota how Criste was borne the tenth yere of this kynge

	Ten yere forth this Kymbelyn was kynge	
	And dyed so the same yere Criste was bore.	*born*
2475	And aftyr Brute had made his arryvynge	
	In Albyon a thousond yere there wore	*were*
	Two hundreth als I say so mykylle more	
	Unto the tyme Kynge Kymbelyn dyd de	
	Whiche was the ferste yere of Cristes natyvyté.	

2480	The tyme whan Criste was so of Mary borne	
	In Bretayne was a clerke hight Thelofyne	*was called*
	Who prophecied and preched even and morne.	
	Of Cristes byrthe thus gan he to devyne	
	And sayde thaym than he fioound by his doctryne	
2485	How that a mayde had borne that tyme a childe	
	Hyre maydenhede preserved and unfylde.	*undefiled*

.xxv. capitulum of Kynge Guydere

Nota how this Kynge Guydere gan to regne in the first yere of the incarnacioun of Criste

	Guydere his sonne and hayre fulle corageus
	Up raysed sone and crouned with excelence
	The tribute whiche the Romayns had of us
2490	Denyed fully and made grete resistence
	And none wold pay but thought by fulle defence

	To voyde Romayns and alle thaire seyniory	*expel; authority*
	Who nought had here bot of thaire tyrany.	*had business*
	This kynge Guydere to regne friste bygan	*first*
2495	In the friste yere of Cristes natyvyté	
	Right after his fadyr so dede was than	
	Withoute delay or more prolyxité	*verbosity*
	Crouned than was with alle solempnyté	
	And Romayns wolde he nought obeye ne loute	*bow to*
2500	Bot thaym withstode with bataylle grete and stoute.	*valiant*
	For whiche cam than Claudyus themperoure	
	To Caerperis that Porchestere now hight	*is called*
	Whyche hym withstode and helde it with honoure.	
	And Claudyus made a walle afore it right	
2505	To famysshe thaym tharein so hath he hight.	*starve; promised*
	Bot Kynge Guydere and Syr Arvyragere	
	It reskowed than, that was his brother dere.	
fol. 38v	Thay faught thare with the emperoure of myght	
	And slew his men on every syde aboute	
2510	That he was fayne to ship and take his flight	*embark*
	Kynge Guydere and his Bretons were so stoute.	
	And so byfelle a Romayn spied whare oute	
	A Breton dyed bysyde lay in a slake	*ditch*
	Whos armes he toke and caste upon his bake.	*back*
2515	As Guyders man he rode with hym fulle nere	
	Waytynge his tyme and with his swerde hym slew.	*Looking out for*
	Whom Arvyragus that was his brother dere	
	Espyed friste and caste on hym alle new	*first*
	His brother armes, and fresshly dyd hym sew,	*follow*
2520	And hym ovretoke whare now ys Southamptoun	
	Whare he hym slew and in the haven dyd droun.	*harbor*

.xxvi. capitulum of Kynge Arviragus

	This Romayne hight by propre name Hamoun	
	For whom the toune whan it was edifyde	*built*
	First Hamon Haven and after Hamontoun	
2525	Men dyd it calle wyde whare on every syde.	*far and wide*
	Arviragus to Wynchestre than gan ryde	
	And Claudius aftir the towne to wynne	
	Bot he it had he wold not cese ne blynne.	*Until; stop*
	Wyth that foresoth Arvyragus with hoste	
2530	Right in the felde withoute the toun hym mette	

	In bataylle hole to fight and felle the boste	*destroy*
	Of Romayns alle hym thought it was his dette.	*duty*
	And as thay shuld eyther on other have sette	
	Thurgh counsaylle of there bothers councellours	*of each of their*
2535	Thay were acorde of pese with grete honours.	

	And to this fyne that Syr Arviragus	*end*
	Shuld reigne and wed his doughter Genvyse	*(i.e., Claudius's)*
	And bere the croune of Bretayne so famus	
	And pay tribute unto Romayns wyse.	
2540	For whiche accorde he sente as dyd suffyse	
	To brynge hyre to his noble hiegh presence	
	Thare to be wed with joy and sufficence.	*contentment*

How Claudius sent for his doughtir and wed hir to this kynge

	Whan Claudyus sente for his doughter dere	
	So after was that Criste was incarnate	
2545	As cronycle sayth the sexte and fourty yere	
	Oute of Latyne as I can hit translate	
	In balade thus and sense nought alterate	*distorted*
	Iff myne auctore ought wronge hath sayde of ytte	*author*
	To correccioun fully I me submytte.	

| fol. 39r | **Coronacion of Arviragus and his wife Genvyse** | |

2550	At certayne day accordyd and assygned	
	She was brought in a valey fresshe and fayre	
	On Severne syde by merkes and boundes signed	*boundary markers identified*
	Whare Gloucestere is now of grete repayre	*well-situated*
	Whare bot a mede was than of floures fayre	*meadow*
2555	Whan thay were wed with grete solempnyté	
	And crouned bothe with alkyns rialté.	*every kind of*

How Claudius Emperour made Gloucestre

	The emperoure thare callyd Syr Claudyus	
	A cyté made Caerglou he called it right	
	After his name some cronycles sayen thus.	
2560	Bot othur cronycles sayne Caergloy it hight	*was called*
	Bycause he gate a sonne tharein fulle wight	*energetic*
	Whiche Gloy so hight and lorde thereof was made	
	Whare alle his tyme he dwelled and abade.	*remained*

	After the weddynge so wente he home agayne.	
2565	Arviragus in Bretayne dyd abyde	
	And lorde he was thurghoute alle hole Bretayne	

With alle the iles aboute on every syde
Who felle in suche presumpsioun and grete pride
To Rome he wolde no trewage forward pay   *tribute; in advance*
2570   So was he stronge he dred thaym nought that day.

How Vaspasyan cam to Bretayne and had trewage, in whose tyme Seynt Petir preched at Antioche.

Than sente thay hyder worthy Vaspasien   *here*
To sette this londe in humble obeyshance
To Rome agayne, as sayth the historien
Gyldas in his storyese and remembrance,
2575   Or els dystroy his dyssobeyssance
Thurgh his worthy conqueste and chyvalry
By whiche Bretons shuld falle in mysery.

In his tyme was Seynte Petre than prechynge
Att Antyoche and came so forth to Rome
2580   The peple hool to Crysten fayth techynge
That was his werke whan he so thyder come   *there*
On whiche stode alle his sentence and his dome   *determination; judgment*
With benygne chere and verry humble herte
The folke aywhare to prechen and converte.   *everywhere*

2585   To Dovere than, that called was Rutupewe,
Vaspasien came there forto arryve.
On whom the kynge so fersely gan to shewe   *appear*
That to Totneys he gan with sayle to dryve
Whare he founde none with sworde, ne yit with knyve,
2590   His londynge ought to letten or to conturbe   *hinder; disturb*
Whare he arrove and no wight hym disturbe.

fol. 39v   So went he forth to Excestere his way
Caerpenelgorte so hight and hit assayled.   *was called*
On whom the kynge came than the sevent day   *seventh*
2595   With bataylle stronge that ayther party wayled   *suffered*
So wery were that bothe here hostes fayled.
For whiche by hyre tretyse Quene Genvyse   *treaty*
Acordyd thaym by gode concorde and wyse

Quia mulier desiderat nisi superioritatem[1]

To pay to Rome so forthwarde his tribute
2600   With love and pese as was afore conquerde

---

[1] *Because a woman desires nothing but governance*

	And nayther parte to suffere more rebute.	*repulse*
	Thus hath she thaym fully counsailde and sterde.	*managed*
	Vaspasian als tendyrly she requyred	
	To wynter here and byde unto the somyr	
2605	And graunte hyre alle; he myght no better ourcom hyr.	*overrule; here*

	From thens forwarde he worshipt eche Romayne	
	Paynge treuly eche yere his hoel truage	*entire; tribute*
	With wisdome so reduced was agayne	*guided*
	That welle he kepte his lond and heritage	
2610	Oute of alle werre and stryfe and alle outrage	*illegality*
	In whose tyme so, as some cronycle expresse,	
	Josep Aramathy in Bretayn came I gesse.	

Nota how Joseph of Arymathy cam into Bretayn, to whom Kynge Arvyragus gafe the Ile of Avalon and gafe hym leve to teche the Cristen fayth, whare he converte grete peple and made the rode of the north dore, whiche Agrestes caste in the west se bisyde Caerlyoun, for vengeance of whiche he brent hymself in an oven, as it is contened in the book of Joseph of Arymathi lyfe and of his governance.

Unde in Jeromia: "Et factus est sudor eius sicut gutte sanguinis decurrentes in terram."[1]

	The yere of Cryste so was syxty and thre	
	Whan he came with his frendes in Grete Bretayne	*(Joseph of Arimathea)*
2615	Whare he byred is withouten le.	*lie*
	And two fyols fulle of the swete to sayne	*vials; sweat*
	Of Jhesu Cryste as rede as blode of vayne	*vein*
	Whiche he gadered and brought with hym away	
	And layd in erth with hym at his laste day.	

2620	By lycense of the kynge, Josep gan teche	
	Within Bretayn the fayth in dyverse place	
	And parte converte whare so that he dyd preche	
	Thurgh wille of God graunted to hym by grace.	
	To whom the kynge than gaffe a dwellyng place	
2625	Mewytryne than it hight and had to name	*was called*
	Of Breton tonge that tyme it had no fame.	

	Twelve hydes of londe to hym he gaffe therewyth	
	To leve upon and gete his sustynaunce	
	Whiche byggyd ys and wele reparailde syth	*built; equipped since*
2630	To Goddes worshyp and his holy plesaunce.	
	Whiche is a place of worthi suffishaunce	*abundance*

[1] *Whence in Jerome: "And his sweat was as drops of blood falling to the ground"* (Luke 22:44)

That men calle nowe the house of Glassynbyry   *Glastonbury*
Whare that he lyeth men say and hath his byry.   *burial place*

fol. 40r   At Caerlegion, the whiche he had converte,
2635   Of Cambre hool that had the dignyté   *esteem*
             A crucifyxe he made thrilde thurgh the herte   *pierced*
             Fulle lyke to Cryste as whan he saw hym de   *die*
             In alle fygure to hys symylité
             Whiche in the chyrche was metropolitane
2640   He sette thare up to worshyp for Cryste alane.

             Whyche by processe and turnynge of the fayth
             Agrestes fals dyd caste therein the se
             That no wyght knew aftyr of it no graythe   *protection (sanctuary)*
             So was it loste thurgh his iniquyté.
2645   For whiche, and for his instabilité,
             Thare felle on hym suche fury and vengeance
             That in an oven he brente was thurgh meschaunce.   *burned*

             Kynge Advyragus in sekenesse grete dyd falle
             Whose worthyhed alle Europe gretely dredde
2650   Who in the pese was ever pacificalle   *peaceful*
             And in the werres alle vyctory he hedde.
             And at his dethe to Gloucester was ledde
             And buried thare in a temple edifyed
             In honoure of Claudyus and deyfyed.

Nota how our lady died, or was assumed, in the tyme of Kynge Arviragus.

2655   In whose tyme so of Kynge Advyragus
             Our lady dyed or els she was assumed   *taken up*
             In body hole and soule fulle gloriouse.
             Lesse clerkes sayne I have to myche presumed   *Lest*
             To thaym I wylle that matere be transumed   *entrusted*
2660   To argew on unto the Day of Dome   *Judgment*
             For it assoyle my braynes bene fulle tome.   *resolve; dull*

.xxvii. capitulum of Kynge Marius and Coile secund

**How Roderyke and the Peightes (*Picts*) faught with the kynge and, fro thay were
discomfyte, he gafe thaym Cattenesse to dwel in and inhabyte.**

             Maryus his sonne goten and propagate   *begotten*
             Right of his wyfe that was Quene Genvyse
             Was crouned kynge of Bretayne and create
2665   By alle his lordes in thaire moste solempne wyse.
             Who was at Rome so noryshed on thaire gyse   *brought up; manner*

Wyth his modyr kyn, the beste of that empyre,
With Claudyus als, who was his own graunsyre.   *grandfather*

      And in his tyme a Peght that hyght Rodryke   *Pict*
2670 With powere grete by se cam fro Sythy   *Scythia*
      Als proude and breme as lyoun Marmoryke   *fierce*
      Arryued up so than in Albany
      Dystroynge hool the londe alle sodenly.
      For whiche the kynge hym mette with hole bataylle
2675 And slew hym thare that day withouten faylle.

fol. 40v   In signe of his honoure and victory
      In that same place he sette a stone up right
      On whiche was sette and tytled that same story
      A bounde it ys of Westmerland by sight   *frontier marker*
2680 Whiche the Rerecrosse of Staynemore now so hight.   *is called*
      And Westmerlond the contré he dyd calle
      Than after his name and boundyd it over alle.

      To alle the Peghtes that bode he gaffe Cattenesse   *remained*
      In Albany to have in heritage
2685 Whiche toke thaym wyfes in Irelonde more and lesse
      For Bretons nolde mary in thaire lynage.   *did not wish to*
      Thay were of suche mysreule and grete outrage   *immoderation*
      That he thaym putte so ferre away I gesse
      From his Bretons for drede of thayre wyldenesse.

2690 Kynge Maryus so dyed than anone
      And buried was at Salysbyry cyté
      Who regned nyne and fourty yere echone
      Paynge tribute as dyd his parenté   *ancestors*
      Levynge the londe in richesse and plenté
2695 With lawes wele kepte in pese and fulle concorde
      As cronyclers bere wyttenesse and recorde.

Kynge Coule the secunde

      Coyle than his sonne was kynge right corounde so
      Who nurtured was at Rome with grete vertewe
      Helde welle his lawes egalle to frende and fo   *impartial*
2700 And in his domes constant he was and trewe.   *judgments*
      Amonge alle men his reule in werke up grewe
      So vertuouse that he had grete honours
      Welle more than other of his antecessours.   *ancestors*

      And at Norwyche as cronycles do telle
2705 He buryd was with grete solempnyté

After that he ten yere had regned welle
In alle gode reule and fulle felicyté.
Alle other kynges nere his extremyté   *frontier*
Aboute ourewhare he suffred to sytte in pese   *In each direction*
2710   Or els gafe thaym of his withouten lese.   *his [goods]; lie*

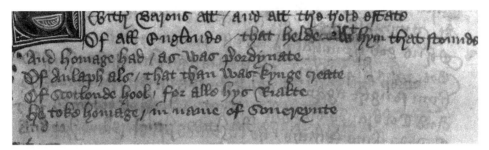

Figure 7. Folio 121v, stanza 3. This stanza was checked for possible underwriting. The background ink could be burn from previous iron gall ink, or the remnants of ink that has been scraped away. There appears to be some underwriting of this stanza, but it is unrecoverable and obscured by ink from the folio overleaf. Image captured at 420 nm on the electromagnetic spectrum. Photo courtesy of Dr. Christina Duffy, Conservation Science Team, The British Library and The British Library.

Figure 8. Folio 196r. The illumination was checked for any instructions or changes beneath the image. A single character inscription was observed behind the initial letters on the border titles. Elaborate folds and robe detail were observed at 460 nm on the electromagnetic spectrum (left). At 420 nm skeletal hand detail is observed (center). Striped detail in the central garment of the King is evident at 580 nm (right). Photos courtesy of Dr. Christina Duffy, Conservation Science Team, The British Library and The British Library.

BOOK THREE

Here bigynneth the thryd book

Primum capitulum (*First Chapter*) of Kynge Lucius, fyrst Cristen kynge of alle Bretayne.

Aftyr Kynge Coyle his sonne Syr Lucyus
So crouned was with rialle dyademe
In alle vertu pursewed his fadyr Coylus   *followed*
Hym to bene lyke in al that myght beseme.   *be fitting*
5 He dyd his myght to shew it and expreme   *express*
In so fer forth that of the Crysten fayth
He herde welle telle and of thayre werkes grayth.   *provided for*

fol. 41r **Nota how Kynge Lucyus sent to Pape (*Pope*) Eleuthery to have baptyme, who sent him Faggan and Duvian, that converte all Bretayne that Josep of Arymathy dyd noght, as Martyn in his cronicle hath wele remembred.**

In the yere so aftyr the incarnacioun
An hundre fulle foure score and foure also
10 He crouned was by verry computacioun   *true reckoning*
Desiringe sore baptysed to bene tho.   *then*
Suche appetyte his herte had taken so
He myght not staunche, ne cese, his gredy wille   *stop*
Tylle he had sente therfore the pope untylle.   *unto*

15 For whiche he sente to Pope Eleuthery
Bysekynge hym to sende hym clerkes wyse
To techyn hym the lawes faythfully
Of Criste Goddes sonne, and aftyr hym baptyse.
For whiche the pape by alle his hool avyse   *judgment*
20 Thankynge so God than of his grete godenesse
That Bretayne so converte withoute dystresse.   *obstruction*

And sente than forthe two doctors fulle approved   *teachers*
In law dyvyne rightwyse and fulle discrete.   *righteous*
Oon hight Faggan with God fulle welle beloved   *was called; by*
25 Another Duvyan with Goddes lawe fulle implete. *imbued*

121

Whiche were fulle fayne with Lucyus forto mete   *eager*
And so thay dyd and sone dyd hym baptyse
And alle his reame aftyr hym by hole avyse.   *realm*

Nota of the date when Lucius and his londe were baptized; he bare of sylver a crosse of goules (*red*) in fourme of Seynt Georges armes in tokne of clennesse by silver, and in tokne of Cristes blode and passioun by the crosse of goules.

Than was the date of Criste a hundre yere
30   Foure score and ten whan he was so baptysed
As written hath Martyn the cronyclere
In his cronycle, as he couth, devysed.   *wrote*
Of whiche I trow he was so wel avysed   *believe; informed*
So as he was doctore in theology
35   Approved welle thurghoute alle Romany.   *Rome*

By processe so thay taught the lawe right thare   *orderly manner*
That thousandes than on Criste so dyd beleve
And so to faith converted fully ware
Baptysed fully as Gildas doth it breve.   *compile*
40   Idolatry so than thay dyd repreve   *reprove*
And payens rytes and alle thaire consuetude   *pagans; former practice*
Up raysynge ever Crystes beatitude.

Nota how the Bretons payens had xxviii temples of flamyns (*pagan temples*) of dignité in thair lawe, the whiche Lucius made cathedral mynstirs halowed for bisshops and thre archebissops at Londoun, Yorke and Carlyoun.

Eght and tweynty temples of priorité   *Eight; honor*
In Bretayn were of old and grete estate.
45   Temple Flamyus that were of dygnyté
Of payen lawe above other exaltate   *pagan; given priority*
By thaym halowed and fully confyrmate
For bysshop sees, and bysshops in thaym sette   *dioceses*
To kepe Goddes law and fals lawe to oversette.   *repulse*

fol. 41v   To every bysshop thay sette his diocyse
51   Of parisshe kyrkes by countrese and by towns   *churches*
To reule thaire parisshe by gode and hool avyse
And thare bysshops to have correcciouns.
And thre other temples of hight renouns   *especial fame*
55   Above alle other that had the dygnyté
Whiche archefflames hight of antiquyté   *were called*

Thay halowed als, and made archebishoprikes.
And archebysshops in thaym thay sette so wyse
For to distroy and waste alle heritykes   *expel*

60	And over alle other to holden alle justyse	
	And thaym correcte as nede by excercyse	
	The faith to kepe and fully to mayntene	
	That errysy none holde, ne yit sustene.	*heresy*

Nota of iii archebisshops of Trynovaunte, of Ebrauk and of Carlyoun.

	Ooon was that tyme at Trynovaunt	
65	Undyr whiche than were Loegres and Cornewayle.	
	And at Ebrauke, that was fulle avenaunt,	*well-favored*
	The tother was then sette withouten fayle	
	Whiche had that tyme assigned to his bayle	*jurisdiction*
	From Humbre north and also Albany.	
70	And at Caerlegioun the thrid whiche had Cambry.	

	And whan this londe was thus to Criste converte	
	Kynge Lucyus rejoysed with alle his myghte	
	Thankynge Jhesu of it with alle his herte.	
	Than wente tho two legates to Rome fulle righte	
75	Thaire actes to bene confermed to folkes sight	
	The whiche thay dyd and with thaym came agayne	
	With other mo to preche the folke fulle fayne.	

	Wyth mo thay cam from Rome acompanyde	*more*
	Of worthy clerkes and techers of the lawe	
80	Of Cristes byrthe so fully glorifyde	
	To teche Bretons in herte thay were fulle fawe	*eager*
	His lyfe, his dethe in bokes as thay sawe.	
	Whose names alle also and alle thaire werkes	
	Gyldas dyd wryte as knowen wele these clerkes.	

85	Ryght in his boke titled and so hight	*was called*
	De Victoria Aurelii Ambrosii	
	In whiche men may se alle thare werkes right	
	Thare names als in scripture for memory.	
	And Mewytryne a place fulle solitary	
90	The kynge thaym gafe thay thought it sufficience	
	The lyfelode whiche Josep had to his dyspence.	*sustenance; expenditure*

fol. 42r	And to tho kyrkes and mynstirs cathedralle	*churches; monasteries*
	Alle that the temples flamynes had afore	
	Lucyus gaffe and fully confermed alle	
95	And of his own dyd gyff thaym mykylle more.	*much*
	Bot now to speke of Josep forthermore	
	Remembred now by open evydence.	
	The case felle so while Lucyus had regence	

How the rode (*cross*) at north dore, which Agrestes caste in the se in Wales, came up fletynge in Themse at Caerlud, now called Londoun in Lucius tyme Kynge of Bretayne, as is comprised in a table afore the rode at north dore and in a story in a wyndow byhynde the sayd rode.

	The crucyfyxe that was at Caerlegyoun	
100	By Agrestes a lorde was thare aboute	
	Caste in the se for that he wolde it droun	
	As mencyon ys afore withouten doute	
	In Lucyus tyme thurgh grace so came it oute	
	Right of the see in Themmys Ryvere righte	
105	To Poules Querfe fletynge so than on highte.	*Wharf floating; at the surface*

	Of whiche the kynge Lucyus so be name	*by*
	Rejoysed was and with solempnyté	
	Of Trynovaunt, his cyté of grete fame,	
	With alle the Kyrke thurgh grete humylité	*Church*
110	From thens it sette in université	
	With songe fulle swete by hool processioun	
	And prayers als in fulle devocyoun.	

	Whiche at Poules thay sette with reverence	
	At Northedore thurgh inspiracion	
115	That I can fynde by any evydence.	
	It was so after the incarnacioun	
	As cronicles make notificacioun	
	An hundred fulle foure score and sextene yere	
	That rode was founde and sogate dyd apere.	*cross; thus*

Nota of the date what Kynge Lucyus decesed and dyed

120	And after so this gode Kynge Lucyus	
	So regned than with mekylle joy and grace	*much*
	Of levynge ever holy and religious	*living*
	The Cristen fayth uphelde in every place.	
	In his tyme stode Bretayne in grete solace	
125	Tylle tyme that deth of hym had made an ende	
	And fro his corse his soule to heven had sende.	*body*

	Whiche than so was after the incarnacioun	
	Two hundreth ful also and eghtene yere	
	As written ys by alkyn informacioun	*all kinds of*
130	Of thaym that were so wyse and syngulere	*exceptional*
	Ful farre above my wytte can now appere.	
	Whose wrytyng so by me that was not fayred	*embellished*
	By my symplesse I wolde nough were appayred.	*not damaged*

fol. 42v	So in Caerglou that now Gloucestere highte	*is called*
135	Right in the chefe mynstere of dignyté	
	That firste was founde in that same cyté righte	
	Buried he was with hiegh solempnyté	
	And mournynge grete for his mortalité	
	For Bretons knew nought who shuld bene his heyre	
140	Who shuld be kynge thay had fulle grete dyspayre.	

.ii. capitulum of the Kynge Severe, Emperour of Rome and Kynge of Bretayne, but Scottes, Peghtes and som Bretons chese Fulgen to thaire kynge of Albanye.

	The Bretons than amonge theymselff dyd stryve	
	Thurghoute the londe and couthe nothynge acorde	*were able*
	Tylle worde thereof came than to Rome ful ryve.	*quickly*
	For whiche so than the senate by concorde	
145	Sent Severe forth to pesen that dyscorde	*settle*
	In Bretayne forth that alle the soveraynté	
	Might saved be to Romes dygnyté.	

	Whiche senator that hight so Syr Severe	*was called*
	With legyons two than londed in Bretayne	
150	With whom oon parte of Bretons halde fulle clere	
	Another parte sore werrayd hym agayne.	*fought against him*
	Bot with batayle to Albany and payne	
	He drofe thaym than whare thay a kynge thaym chese	
	Who Fulgen hight that was fulle proude in prese.	*brave in battle*

How Kynge Severe made a dyke (*wall*) bituix Bretons and Peghtes of soddes and turfes to kepe thaym from Bretayne

155	Wyth whom the Peghtes and some Bretons also	*Picts*
	That were futyfes and men unresounable	*fugitives*
	Ever rode Bretayne and dyd it mekylle wo	*much*
	Whiche to Severe than was ful lamentable	
	And forto kepe it wele inviolable	
160	A dyke he made ful high from se to se	*sea*
	The enmyse oute to holde fro his contré.	

	The whiche longe tyme from thayre iniquité	
	Dyd save thaym welle in mykylle reste and pese	
	Bot only whan thay myght be grete pousté	*Except when; by; force*
165	Breke it and so override it ere thay cese.	*before*
	So was it longe betwyx thaym is no lese	*lie*
	Ever as thay myght do any harme or werre	
	Thay bode no while, so cursed ay thay werre.	*were*

How Severe in reskows of the cité of Yorke in batayl was slayne and Fulgen, Kynge of Peghtes, had his dethes wounde.

	Bot after that to Ebrauke yit thay sought	
170	Assegynge there the cyté alle aboute	*besieging*
	Whiche to reskowe Severe powere brought	
	And faught with thaym in bataylle stronge and stoute	
	Whare he was slayne and dede withouten doute	*dead*
	And Fulgen als thare had his dethes wounde	
175	Thus in that warre so were thay bothe confounde.	*destroyed*

fol. 43r **Nota the date of this kynges deth after Saynt Bede**

	Whan he had bene so kynge by seventene yere	
	And sogate slayne as I have sayde afore	*thus*
	As Seynte Bede sayth and wrote as dothe appere	
	The yere of Criste was than fully nyne score	
180	So shalle I wryte at this tyme and no more	
	And nyne thereto by his calculacioun	
	As his story sayth and compylacioun.	

Nota the date of this same kynge aftir Martyne cronyclere of Romany

	Bot Martyne sayth, the Romayne cronyclere,	
	It was the yere after Cristes natyvyté	
185	Two hundreth hole and fyve and thretty clere	
	Whiche ys more lyke the verrey treuth to be.	
	For he knew more of Romes dygnyté	
	That alle his lyfe thare helde his resydence	
	Than Bede myght know by seldome affluence.	*frequenting*

190	Whiche Severe so his Romayns layde in grave	
	At Ebrauke than with sorowe multyplyed	
	With alle honoure right as a kynge shuld have	
	With gloriousté as myght bene artyfyed	*crafted*
	Abowte his tombe so was he magnyfyed	
195	For his honours and als his vyctoryse	
	So rially thay made his exequyse.	*funeral*

.iii. capitulum of Getan, Bassian and Carauce.

	Getan his sonne, whiche Romayne procreate	*descended*
	Of alle syde was and goten in Romany,	*begotten*
	Romayns hym made thare kynge in alle estate	
200	And helde hym up to kepe the regency.	
	Bot Bretons than Bassyan chese in hy	*chose rapidly*

Hys brother borne of the femynyté
Of Bretayne blode withoute diffyculté.

Bassyan kynge

This Bassian faught with Getan myghtyly
205   In bataylle stronge whare Getan was than slayne.
So Bassyan had the reme alle plenerly   *entirely*
Of whom forsoth the Bretons were fulle fayne
And crounede hym anone so than agayne
And welle he helde the reame longe while in pese
210   Tyl oon Karause fulle began his wo increse.

How this Carause robbour on the se, of pouer (*poor*) blode and kyn distroyed the Kynge Bassian in defaute of law and pese and coronde hymselfe, wharfor is moste necessary to a kynge to kepe lawe and pese in hys reme.

This Karauce fulle of covetyse alle blente   *blinded*
Ymagynynge the kynge forto consume   *destroy*
To have Bretayne by Bretons hole consente
And Peghtes als that evermore dyd presume
215   This londe to have, to spoyle and to deplume   *waste; rob*
Of alle rychesse and alle prosperyté
For olde hatred of thare maliciousté.

fol. 43v

Nota   He drew to hym the Peghtes fulle wyse of werre
And Bretons fele he hight grete waryson.   *promised; reward*
220   Outlondysshe men was nothynge to hym derre   *Foreign; dear*
And outelawed men withoute comparison
Thurghoute the reame he stuffed every garisoun
With mysdoers and mysreuled meyny   *bands*
Robbers, revers that had done felony.   *thieves*

Nota   For he was longe a robber on the se
226   Spoylyng marchantes of every londe aboute
Thurgh whiche he was more ryche in quantyté
Than any prynce and for his myghte more doute.   *feared*
Yit was he come of kyn both in and oute
Nota   Of pore degré and als of lawe estate   *low*
231   Thus sette on high thurgh robry and debate.   *strife*

Nota   To whom for giftes Bretons and Peghtes than highte   *promised*
The kynge Bassyan in batayle to betrayse   *betray*
To brynge hym to the felde at alle there myght
235   And turne agayne hym whan his banere rayse.
Tho traytours fals thus thought thaire kynge to trayse   *Those; betray*

And plese in worde and in the felde to holde
With his ennemy for lyfelode grete and golde.   *goods*

Nota   So on a day Karauce made hym to stryve
240   With Kynge Bassyan right for the comonté
Thurgh whiche he gan the kynge dispyse bilyve   *rapidly*
Departynge so thurgh that subtylité
That sone thereafter his hoste with cruelté
He brought on hym, and with hym so dyd fight
245   Thay slew the kynge and turned as thay hight.   *promised*

**How the maker of this moveth the lordes to kepe lawe and pese, lesse thay
bene depryved and unworthy blode in thair stede regne.**

Nota of kepyng of pese and of lawe

Bot o ye lordes consydre what myschefe
Rose in defaute of gode conservacioun
Of law and pese and what harme and reprefe   *shame*
Thurgh mayntenaunce of foly and instigacioun
250   That trespasours had no castigacioun   *punishment*
But sustende wele, whare thurgh the kynge was slayne
And beggars blode made kynge of alle Bretayne.

Nota   Ye lordes that suffre the law and pese mysledde   *misgoverned*
In every shire whare so ye dwellynge bene
255   Whare ye pore men oversette se or mysbedde   *you see; oppressed or mistreated*
Ye shuld thaym helpe and socoure and sustene
Nota   And chastyse thaym that trespasours so bene.   *are*
Why ys a lorde sette in so hiegh degré
Bot to mayntene undyr hym the comonté?   *common people*
fol. 44r
Nota   Bot o ye lordes fro this ful foule ye erre   *grievously; go astray*
261   From youre ordyre in tille apostacy   *into*
Whan ryotours punysshe ye ne derre   *dare*
For mayntenaunce of gretter seigniory.   *(see note)*
The pore men may seke law in Lumbardy
265   As welle as right of a riotouse man   *lawless*
Whose mayntenours the comons may sore ban.   *curse*

Nota   Than sewyth this of whiche ye take non hede   *follows; heed*
That who may gete moste myght and sovereynté
Wylle eche of yow supprisen and overlede   *take by surprise; overpower*
270   By that same way of lawe and equyté.   *justice*
And who of men may make moste assemblé   *gathering (of people)*
His lower to overrenne and oversette   *take control of and subdue*
By alle reson wylle thynke it is his dette.

Principio obsta et qui stas videas ne cadas[1]

Nota	Than seweth more, thus ryseth barons were	*follows; war*
275	That ofte hath bene in grete defaute of lawe.	
	He that noght hath acounteth nothynge derre	*considers; precious*
	For havelesse than the prynces wold overthrawe.	*the propertyless; overthrow*
	The ryalle blode above thay wolde make lawe.	
	Wharefore ye lordes the pryncyple ay withstonde	
280	Lesse beggars blode dryve you out of youre londe.	*Lest*

Carause kynge

	Thurgh treson of this Karause and the Peghtes	
	Assented so by grete confederacy	
	Thurgh his gyftes and his subtyle sleghtes	*deceptions*
	Betwyx thaym wrought with grete falsode whareby	
285	He was made kynge of alle the monarchy.	
	For whiche the Peghtes in Albany he sette	
	With grete lyfelode as he afore them hette.	*sustenance; promised*

Nota de alienigenis non receptandis in regno quia semper optant super indigenas regnare et eos expellere[2]

Nota	A prynce wote nought what harme he doth his londe	*knows*
	Whan alyens in it he doth resette	*welcome*
290	Whose blode by alle nature shalle ay withstonde	*resist*
	Comon profyte of alle his reme and lette	*hinder*
	As to the kyng Maryus now may be rette	*referred*
	Who sette the Peghtes in Albany afore	
	Whiche seth that tyme have batayld Bretayn sore.	*since*

Nota	Thus now bene Peghtes and Bretons playnly	
296	In Albany with blode so intermyxte	
	That now in alle that londe of Albany	
	Whiche Scotlond nowe knowen ys in tyxte	*text*
	Can no wight knowe a Peghte fro Bretoun fyxte.	*person; firmly*
300	So hool thay bene now alle of Peghtes kynde	
	That thay shalle never love Breton in thaire mynde.	

fol. 44v	The Bretons blode ys now thare waste alway	
	With Scottes and Peghtes so ys it devolute	*mixed*
	Whiche have the reule and governans this day	

---

[1] *You who rule, resist at the beginning and you may be certain that you do not fall*

[2] *Note this point concerning foreigners in a realm, since they always wish to rule over the indigenous and to expel them*

305   Of alle that londe so fully execute

            With Irisshe blode so myxte and involute   *entangled*

            That Bretons blode ys waste and consumate   *wasted and transformed*

            So thurgh thise other now is it alterate.

.iiii. capitulum of Kynge Allecte

            But whan to Rome was know the foule consayte   *plan*

310   Of Karauce that had made intrusioun

            In Bretayne so by covyne and dissayte   *conspiracy; deceit*

            And wonne that reme by grete colusioun

            And slayne the kynge by suche delusioun   *deception*

            His peple als had slayne for covetyse

315   To have the reme and holde by suche quantyse   *trickery*

How this Kynge Allecte slew that fals Carause

            For to dystroy his cursed tyrany

            The senate sente to Bretayne Syr Allecte

            With legions thre with hym in company   *three*

            Who in bataylle slew Karause and correcte

320   For his falshode that playnly was detecte.   *punished*

            Who crouned was with croune and dyademe   *royal authority*

            And Bretayne helde as dyd hym wele byseme   *befit*

            And alle that helde with Karause than he slewe

            That he myght take or reche in any wyse   *reach*

325   To venge the kynge Bassian was so trewe

            Whom thay betrayed falsly for covetyse

            Agayn comon profyte and alle justyse

            Whiche was oonly by Goddes own ordynaunce

            For thaire tresoun to have so foule meschaunce.

How the maker moveth of the ende and fyne of tresoun and falshode

Nota   Suche fyne comyth evermore of foule tresoun   *end*

331   It hath foule ende alle if it regne a while   *even if*

            And at the laste it is dystroyed by reson

            And shamed foule for his dyssayte and gyle   *deceit*

            Whan God chastyse thare helpeth than no wyle.

335   And after olde synne so commyth ay new shame

            And wronge lawes make lordes forsake thayre hame.   *home*

.v. capitulum of Kynge Asclepiadote

            The Bretons than dyd sette a parlement

            At whiche for ire to Romayns that thay hadde   *anger*

	Dyd chese a kynge by alle thaire hole consent	
340	Wham thay corounde with hertes blythe and gladde	*happy*
	Who duke than was of Cornewayle wyse and sadde	*stable*
	Asclepiadote so hight he by his name	*was called*
	Whiche that tyme was a worthy lorde of fame.	

fol. 45r	With Cambre hool and also Albany	
345	With alle Loegres holy at his devyse	*under his control*
	To Trynovant he came ful openly	
	Whils Romayns were thare at thare sacrifise	
	Of whiche thay harde grete crye and noyse arise	
	And to the felde thay wente anone forth right	
350	And with Bretons right manly dyd thay fighte.	

How the kynge was slayne and how Gallus Romayn helde London and was slayne at Walbroke in the cyté of Londoun

	Whare Allecte syde was nere so slayne away	
	Hymselff was dede right in the felde and slayne.	
	Wharefore Gallus that was his felow ay	
	Drew alle Romayns in the cyté agayne	
355	Kepynge the walles with mykylle care and payne.	*much*
	For whiche so than Syr Asclepiadote	
	Assege gan lay aboute the town God wote	*Siege; knows*

	Assaylynge ever aboute with feel assautes	*many*
	With engynes als and magnels grete thay caste	*military engines*
360	Thurgh whiche thay made so mony grete defautes	*damage*
	The walles aboute thay myghtt nought longe so laste.	
	Wharfore Gallus and Romayns were agaste	*afraid*
	And putte thaym hool in mercy and in grace	
	Right of the kynge to stonden in that case.	

365	Wyth that Walshemen so pryvely went yn	
	And Gallus slewe upon a lytil broke	*stream*
	In the cyté that in to Themse dyd ryn.	
	And Romayns alle thay slew so faste and toke	*captured*
	Whiche broke after longe was called Galbroke	
370	For Gallus that was slayne so in that place	
	And Walbroke now it hight; thus ys the case.	*is called*

How justfully this kynge helde his lawes and pese to tyme Maximyan the payen tirant transverte (*overturned*) the Cristen fayth therin.

Nota	The kynge so was than crouned new agayn	
	In ryalle wyse with ful solempnyté	
	The lawes alle he helde and putte grete payn	

375   On trespasours for thaire iniquyté
        Thefes and robbours with sworde he dyd thaym dye.   *made*
        Bot in his tyme was grete persecucioun
        Of Cristen fayth and sore prosecucioun.

**How Dioclican the Emperoure sente Maxymyan into Bretayne, who slew Seint
Albane and made grete persecucioun of Cristen fayth in Bretayne.**

        For Dioclycian than beyng emperoure
380   Maxymyan that hight Herculyus
        By his surname that was the governoure
        Of alle his werres sente into Bretayn thus
        The Cristen to distroy so malicyus.
        That tyme was so that he put alle to dede   *death*
385   Thurgh alle Bretayne that truste on Cristes Godhede.

fol. 45v Who than undyr this Dioclicyen
        Seynt Albane slewe, Julyus and Aarone
        With mony other this idoladrien   *idolater*
        Maliciouse so in his werkes echone
390   Thousandes of seyntes in Bretayne so anone
        Fulle cruely thare martyred to the dethe
        Whose soules were safe bypassed was the brethe.   *when life had ended*

        Seynt Amphybale the whiche was confessoure
        To Seynt Albane ascaped nought that tyde   *time*
395   Bot wylfully to that curst turmentoure
        Offred hymselff the martyrdome to byde   *endure*
        For Cristes love he wolde hym nothynge hyde
        With thousondes fele so slayne withouten grave   *many*
        Whose soules with God ere sette his blisse to have.   *are*

400   He brente chyrches and bokes of holy writte   *burned*
        The lawes also that were ought temporele   *in any way*
        Alle scriptures als of seyntes lyfes comytte   *he put*
        Unto the fyre and brente thaym every dele   *part*
        In playne markett alle openly I fele   *understand*
405   So that whare seyntes of Bretons were honoured
        Unnethe this day is oon of thaym adoured.   *Hardly*

        He reygned so in Bretayne cursydly
        Thurgh suffraunce of Kynge Asclepiadote
        Who wold nothynge withstonde his tyrany
410   Whils he distroyed the Cristen fayth God wote.   *knows*
        Were never mo seyntes undyr a prynce men lote   *believe*
        Martyrde as thare were than by alkyn wytte   *knowledge*
        That men can fynde in romans or in wrytte   *historical record; treatise*

Of every kynde bothe of men and women
415 Of chyldre als of eche estate and age
That pyté was and reuthe to se and ken.   *know*
Chyldre sowkynge whose mylke thare blode dyd swage   *mix with*
So ware thay slayne in alle thare tendre age
Cripils and blynde the dum als and the defe   *Handicapped*
420 The prestes and clerkes the lyfe he fro them refe.   *reft*

Nota the date whan Maximyan made this persecucioun of Cristen fayth

Two hundre yere foure score fro Criste was borne   *after*
Of his modyr and fully incarnate
Persecucioun, whiche I have seyde aforne,
Of Cristen fayth was than the verry date
425 By cruelté of thise two adonate.   *united*
Whiche Cristen soules in blisse forever remayne
The tyrant soules in evermore lastynge payne.

fol. 46r Kynge Asclepiadote regned fully bot ten yere
After cronycles, who suffride alle this payne   *According to; allowed*
430 And nothynge durste agayn that tyrant stere   *dared; move*
And hym withdrawe in hydils was fulle fayne.   *hiding places; eager*
And some cronycles otherwyse speke and sayne
That he was hool consent to thare malyse   *malice*
The whiche I can nought trusten in no wyse.

.vi. capitulum of Coyle fadir of Seynte Elene Kynge of Bretayne

435 Than rose on hym the duke with grete powere
Of Caercolim that Colchester hath to name
Who hight Syr Coyle by wrytynge as I here   *was called*
With strenght of lordes in hoste that with hym came   *strength*
A worthy lorde in Bretayn of grete fame
440 Fro Maxymyan was homward gon agayne
Hym werrayde sore to tyme he had hym slayne.

Who crouned was and sette in magesté
Of whiche Bretons and Romayns were fulle fayne   *eager*
And specyaly of that fortuyté   *good chance*
445 That Asclepiadote was dede and slayne
Bycause he was the comon wele agayne
Of Rome and of Bretayne whiche were anoyed   *troubled*
Thurgh his suffrance and Cristen fayth distroyed.   *affliction*

Bot this kynge Coyle than reuled this londe so wele
450 That for his wytte and vyrtuosyté
In alle thynge that I can ought se or fele   *understand*

Of rightwysnesse and gode moralité
Comende he was thurgh alle his regalté
Forpassyngly alle other in his day
455   So trew he was and vertuouse always.

Whose hayre was than his doughter hight Eleyne   *heir; was called*
Who lerned was in kunnynge and science   *doctrine*
Forpassynge other that tyme of alle Breteyne   *surpassing*
To reule a reme thurgh wytte and sapience   *wisdom*
460   Endowed so in alle intelligence
That hens to Rome knew no man hyre pere   *equal*
So was she wyse of wytte and syngulere.   *exceptional*

The Romayns sente Constance to reule Bretayne fro Rome

Bot Romayns so som parte at his requeste   *in part*
And sumwhat of thaire own desyre and wylle
465   Constance than sente, who Spayne hadde by conqueste
Subjecte to Rome obeyand evere it tylle
Paynge tribute everemore for gude or ille
Who over alle thynge ay the comon publyke
For Rome labourde that Romayns did hym lyke.

fol. 46v   Whom Romayns sente to werre upon Bretayne
471   To whom Kynge Coyle anone his message sente
Offrynge trewage to Rome so forto payne   *tribute*
Of whiche Constans was glad in his entent
So forto have the pese he was contente.
475   Within fyve woukes after Kynge Coyle dyd de   *weeks; die*
And none to heyre save Elyne than had he.

.vii. capitulum of Kynge Constance Emperour of Rome, Kyng of Bretayne.

Constance so than hymself dyd signyfy
With dyademe and wed Elyne to wyfe
And made hyre quene of Bretayne so forthy   *accordingly*
480   That Bretons shuld love hym and cese alle stryfe
And for grete love he wold not hyre deprife.
Hyre bewté so alle other dyd excelle
Within Bretayne that borne was or dyd dwelle.

Who in musyke instruments was so wyse
485   And in dyverse science so fulle instructe
That eny reme to reule she dyd suffyse
So fulle she was with sapience producte   *endowed*
Whiche from hyre myght nought refte bene, ne deducte,

| | So was she sad and constant in alle degree | *steady; sober* |
| 490 | That none in hyre newfangilnesse couthe se. | *fickleness* |

	On hyre he gatte a sonne hight Constantyne	
	Regnynge after fully elleven yere	
	And than to deth anone he gan inclyne	
	And at Ebrauke than was he leyd on bere.	
495	And certanly as seyth the cronyclere	
	He byried was with worthy exequyse	*noble funeral*
	And other servyce right at his own devyse.	*plan*

	The yere of Criste thre hundre was and sexe	
	Whan Constance dyed who with Galeryus	
500	The Empyre hool dyd governe and amplexe	*embrace*
	Agayne Maxcence of porte malicyus	*conduct*
	And alle the weste myne authore writeth thus	
	Thys Constans had and with grete manhode helde	
	Whiche to hym evere were subjetts in the felde.	

.viii. capitulum of Constantyne kynge and aftir emperoure

Constantynes armes whiche he bare aftir he had sene the crosse in the aire

505	Constantyne that was his sonne and hayre	
	So crouned was by alle the baronage	
	Who lykely was, semely als and fayre,	*handsome*
	In chyldissh yeres and in his tendre age	
	Grete manhode had to reule his heritage	
510	In wysdome als grete profe of sapience	*wisdom*
	To reule alle thynge by gode intelligence.	

fol. 47r	He had so thanne a lambysshe pacyence	*gentle*
	To here alle thynge softely with sobrenesse	
	A lyons chere and loke in alle regence	*sovereignty*
515	Amonge his folke to chastyse wykednesse	
	The welefare of his reme with bysynesse	*diligence*
	Preserved ever and kepte in regyment	
	And in alle nede he sette suppowailement.	*support*

	He helde his lawes withouten violence	
520	His pese also in grete establisement	*steadiness*
	And on his owne by alle experience	*on his own resources*
	He leved ever and thereof was content	*lived*
	As lawfulle prynce fully in his intent.	
	Whiche poynte untylle a prynce shuld ay appende	*with regard to; pertain*
Nota	Upon hys owne to leve and nought transcende.	

How the Romayns sente to Constantyne to bene Emperour of Rome relesyng alle truage aughte (*owed*) to Rome, the whiche he admytte and was made Emperour, by whiche the tribute and service and truage was extyncte in lawe for it is inconvenyent that he shulde bene bothe lorde and tenant or lorde and subgyte togedir at oons by Grekes law, Troian law, or any other lawe that now is.

526	And so byfelle that tyme there was at Rome	
	An emperoure that called was Maxence	
	Whiche was so fals maliciouse in his dome	*judgment*
	That Cristen folke with alle his diligence	*energy*
530	Distroyed sore thurgh his malivolence	
	Whome to distroy the Senate sente forth right	
	To Constantyne to come at alle his myght.	

Thay hight to stonde with hym at alle thare myght   *promised*
With strengh of men and alle sufficianté
535   That tyrant so maliciouse and so wight   *strong*
To waste and sla for his fals cruelté   *slay*
And for they herde of his abilité
Thay graunted hym to be thayre emperoure
Thaym to delyvere of that turmentoure.

540   Thay graunte hym als the trewage to aquyte   *tribute; free from*
Of Bretayne ever and never to aske tribute
Saynge these wordes to hym withoute respyte   *delay*
"O Constantyne, O Romayns hool refute   *refuge*
Byholde the right of Rome so foule rebute   *rejected*
545   Whiche thou may helpe and fully restitewe
Oure natyfe grounde to us that ys fulle dewe.

"Thy fadyr was a Romayne of grete myght
Bothe gote and borne so was in Romany   *begotten*
For kyndely were to thee by alkyns right   *all manner of*
550   The empyre holde and hool the monarchy
Of alle the worlde as dyd thyne auncetry.
Lete no sleuthe nowe thy corage so desteyne   *sloth; defile*
That what we lese alle thyne elders wan fulle pleyne."   *release*

fol. 47v   So purposed fulle this noble Constantyne   *resolved*
555   Of Rome to helpe the wytty senatours.   *intelligent*
He wente anone and to thaym dyd enclyne   *immediately*
With powere grete and als gode governours
Of his Bretons to make hym strong socours   *support*
And with hym toke his modyrs uncles thre
560   In whom he truste for consanguynyté.   *kinship*

Loeline was oon, the seconde was Traherne
The thirde Maryn thus were thare names right.
He had his modyr with hym who dyd hym lerne   *teach*
Fulle perfytly to reule hym lyke a knyght   *govern himself*
565   By whose counsaylle he wrought bothe day and nyght
And emperoure was made in dignyté
Of alle the worlde to have imperialté.   *imperial power*

To his moders eme Loeline he gaff a wyfe   *uncle*
A lady was in Rome of grete estate
570   On wham he gatte a sonne and that bylyfe   *rapidly*
Maxymyan that hight in the Senate   *was called*
A myghty man and als a fortunate
So after was in werre fulle wele approved
And with Romans evermore right wele biloved.

**How Kynge Constantyne fyrste bare the armes that men calle Seynt George
armes, after whom Breton kynges used to bere thaym for his sake many yeres
afore Seynt George was ayther goten or borne.**

575   The yere of Criste thre hundre hole and ten
This Constantyne to batayle as he went
To fyghten so with Dioclycien
Maximyan and Maxcence of assent
Assembled stronge agayne hym felonment.   *maliciously*
580   Whan he thaym sawe, he loked to the heven
In whiche he sawe a crosse than marked even

As in the legende of Seinte Elene is contened and Constantine "in hoc vinces."[1]

Wyth letters bright as golde thusgates wryten   *thus*
"O Constantyne in thys thou shalt overcome."
Who thurgh comforte as after welle was wyten   *known*
585   Of that devyne vysioun victore bycome
The signe of whiche afore hym made he come
Thurgh whiche his fose he putte unto the flight   *foes*
Grete multitude also he slew in fight.

Thensforthe the crosse he bare in his banere
590   Afore his hoste whare he to batayle went.
In his right hande a crosse agold he bere
Praynge to God with alle his hole entente
That never that hande shuld fouled be ne shente   *defiled; destroyed*

---

[1] *As in the legend of Saint Helen and Constantine (it) occurs and "in this [sign] you will gain victory"*

| | Of Romayns blode by none effusioun | *bloodshed* |
| 595 | Bot of tyrants for thare abusioun. | *abuse of power* |

fol. 48r	From that tyme forth in Criste he fully trewed	*believed*
	Bot noght forthy unbaptysed wold he be	*nonetheless*
	Wharfore he was in lepre so endowed	*leprosy*
	Deserved wele right by his owne decré	
600	His soule to putte so longe in juparté.	
	Bot neverthelesse thof he baptym dyd delay	*although*
	His werkes were gode and als his menynge ay.	*intention always*

	This Constantyne as bokes specyfyed	
	Uncristen was his baptyme so deferred	
605	Unto his days were wele forth ocupied	
	Bycause he thought it shuld have bene preferred	*postponed*
	In Flum Jordan after he had conquerred	*River*
	The Jewry hool and wonne the crosse rialle	
	On whiche Cryste dyed in manhode corperalle.	

610	At whiche tyme so sore leprous squames he hadde	*scabs*
	Hys leches counsaylde in blode of innocents	*doctors*
	Bene bathed ofte whiche shulde hym moste so gladde.	*ease*
	Bot Petyre and Poule that knew his gode ententes	
	To hym appered that nyght fulle excellentes	
615	And bade hym go to Sylvestre the pape	*pope*
	Who shuld hym hele withouten gyle or jape.	*cure; deception*

How leches counsailde Constantyne to bene wasshen in blode of innocents for his lepre, of whom whan he herd the cry he had suche pité that he had lever dye a lepre than bene heled with innocent blode.

	And on the morow he herde a pyteuse noyse	
	Of men women and childre alle at ones	
	So pytusly that thrugh his herte thare voyse	*piteously*
620	Dyd perse and thrille so sore thay made there mones	*pierce; penetrate; cries*
	To se thaire chyldre be slayne so in tho wones.	*those; dwellings*
	The chyldre als for colde dyd wepe and crye	
	Naked alle bare forto be slayne in hy.	*very soon*

	Bot fro he wyste how thay for hym shuld dye	*once*
625	He bade thaym alle "Take home youre chyldre quyte.	*freely*
	In werre whare oure imperialle dygnyté	
	Hath constytute no chyldre sla ne smyte	*prescribed; slay*
	It were to foule a werke and inperfyte	
	To sla oure owne that we in werre forbade	*forbid*
630	To alyens be done for any nede.	

And better is to me with pyté de   *die*
Than thurgh the deth of alle thise innocents
My cruelle lyfe recovere withoute pyté.
For who that hath pyté in his entents
635   Approveth hymselff a prynce in regiments."   *proves; governance*
Therefore ye lordes in alle youre sovereynté
Whare is dystresse loke that ye have pyté.

fol. 48v   **Nota of fole (*foolish*) pité whiche is a vice and no vertue**

I say not this that lordes in generalle
To fole pyté the rather shulde inclyne   *foolish*
640   Whiche ys a vyce and coloure idialle   *pretext false*
Destenynge foule the pyté so devyne.   *Defiling*
Therfor ye lordes in herte this enterlyne   *write*
To do pyté whare ys necessité
Of whiche friste grew imperialle dygnyté.

How Seynt Silvestre heled hym by baptyme of hys leprouse squames, whiche watir is yit kepte incorrupte and swete of savour as I haue sene it and savourede, secundum cronicas Martini.[1]

645   Than sente he for Sylvestre so anone
Hym forto hele with alle expedience.   *heal*
Who baptysed hym in watere than alone
In whiche grete light dyd shyne of excelence
And clene wente out in alle experience
650   Of his leprouse squames white and rede   *scabs*
Sayinge he sawe thare Criste in his manhode.

Thus was he than to Cristene fayth converte
His modyr als and all the comonté
And bysshops als that were afore perverte   *misguided*
655   To Cristen fayth in all tranquilyté.
And to the Chyrche with alle the soveraynté
Hys paleys grete and se imperialle
He gafe anone in almouse eternalle.   *almsdeed*

How this Constantyne and Seint Silvestre holde a seyne (*synod*) of ccc bisshops agayne the Arriens erresyes (*Arian heresy*), in whiche counsele and seyne Seynt Nicholas was present with Constantyne, secundum cronicas Martini.

Who helde a seyne of bysshops fully counted   *synod*
660   Thre hundre and eghtene, as Martyn sayth

---

[1] *according to the chronicles of Martin*

For to dystroy Arriens that surmounted
With herisyes agayne the Cristen fayth.
In whiche counsayl Seynt Nicholas ful grayth   *prepared*
Was oon present the Arrians to condempne
665   By Constantynes wisdome that was solempne.   *sound*

He sent his modyr unto Jerusaleme
The holy crosse to gete on which Criste dyed
With powere grete of every londe and reme   *realm*
And for his ese Besaunse edyfyed   *built Byzantium*
670   Whiche Constantyne to name he notified   *in name; he called*
Aftir his name whare throne imperialle
Thensforth he helde and se judicialle.   *seat*

How Seynt Elene his modir brought home the holy crosse secundum cronicas Martini.[1]

Whose modyr than the crosse of Criste home brought
With relykes fele whiche I cannot telle   *many*
675   And dyed at Rome fulle holy in werke and thought
Levynge the crosse of Criste that heried helle   *harrowed*
In sure kepynge for payens that were felle.   *safe keeping from; fierce*
She dyed in Rome byried at Ara Cely   *Ara Coeli (Rome)*
Whose soule to God fulle happy is and sely.   *blessed*

fol. 49r   But now to speke more of this Constantyne
681   Of whom Gyldas, ne Henry Huntyngdoun,
In thaire cronycles lyste not to inclyne
His lyfe fully to putte in mencioun.
I wote not what was thaire intencioun   *know*
685   Seth he and thay were alle of Bretons kynde   *race*
To hyde his actes me thynke thay were unkynde.

How this Constantyne gafe to Silvestre and to the cherche his palays and temporalté of Romany and made the cherche of his chambre atte Seint John Laterense secundum cronicas Martini[2]

Whan he had graunte the Chyrche his regaly   *dominion*
And his palays chief and pryncipalle
Of his chambre the Chyrche dyd edyfy   *build*
690   To whiche he bare on his shuldres corporalle
Bothe erthe and stones with herte fulle spyrtualle

---

[1] *How Saint Helen his mother brought home the holy cross according to the chronicles of Martin*

[2] *How this Constantine gave to Silvester and the church his palace and temporality of Rome and made the church of his chamber at Saint John Lateran according to the chronicles of Martin*

And with grete golde the chyrches dyd renewe
With tempraltese he dyd it welle endewe.   *worldly goods; endow*

**And than aftir his baptisme he bare of silver in tokne of clennesse, white as the
ayre is, a crosse of goules in tokne of the blode of Cristes passioun in fourme
of Seynt Georges armes.**

            And als this noble manly conqueroure
695   Unto the Chyrche gafe many dignytese
            And to it was defense and protectoure
            Conservynge it in alle hool libertese
            By his godenesse and grete benygnytese
            With relikes grete and hiegh adournements
700   Of Romany also hole regyments.   *full power*

            Bot Martyne sayth, the Romayne cronyclere
            That in the yere thre hundred thretty and nyne   *thirty*
            After that Criste was borne of Mary clere   *pure*
            The famouse sonne fulle bright bigan to shyne
705   And spred his bemes upon this Constantyne
            That thurgh the worlde alle odyr he dyd excelle   *others*
            Whan his leprouse squames felle of in the welle.   *scabs*

            Wyth wasshyng than of the holy baptymme
            With whiche his lepre was than purifyed   *leprosy*
710   Of squames white and rede in every lymme.   *scabs*
            With mercy than so was he magnifyed
            That levere he had hymselff be mortifyed   *rather; dead*
            Than Cristen blode have spylte by his regence
            Of any folke that stode in innocence.

**How this Constantyne is a seynte whose day is halowed the xxi day of May
yerely amonge the Grekes, as is specifyd in the cronycles of Martyne Romayn.**

715   Who after he had regned fulle thretty yere   *thirty*
            In the Empire dyed at Nychomede.   *Nicomedia*
            A saynt he ys anombred hool and clere
            Amonge the Grekes in cronycle as I rede.
            Isydorus and Martyn, who takyth hede
720   In cronycles sayn that Grekes hym have nombred
            In cathologe of sayntes and obombred.   *catalogue; (?)numbered*

fol. 49v   Whose day and feste with grete solempnyté
            Thay holde eche yere in the moneth of May
            Fulle certanly with grete humylité
725   And alle honoure the oon and twenty day.
            No wondre ys if he be worshypte ay

Seth he was fyrste that made devocyoun
Of emperours and gaff the Chyrche promocioun.   *advancement*

.ix. capitulum of Kynge Octave and Traherne

But in his tyme came on Octavyus
730   Upon wardayns whiche Constantyne dyd make   *guardians*
And slew thaym alle as cronycle telleth us.
Of whiche whan worde to Constantyne was take
So moved he was for ire began to qwake   *anger*
And Traherne sent who was his modyr eme   *uncle*
735   Bretayne to kepe and seurly to hym yeme.   *guard*

Whiche Octavyus crouned was than for kynge
And had this reame to Traherne cam fro Rome   *realm; until*
With grete powere with hym that he dyd brynge.
Who worthy was and rightwyse in his dome   *judgment*
740   Thurgh Italy was neyther yoman ne grome   *yeoman; groom*
Of alle his hoste dyd any violence
So myche thay dred his noble excellence.

Wyth legyons thre Traherne in Bretayne londe
At Kaereperis that Porchestere now hight   *is called*
745   And wan the toune it myght hym not withstonde.
And forth he wente to Caergwent than so right
Whare in the felde with bataylle dyd thay fight
Besyde Caergwent that Wynchestere now so hatte   *is called*
Whare Traherne fled and to his shippes gatte.   *arrived*

Kynge Traherne of Bretayne

750   So saylynge forth and londe in Albany
And Octave than anone agayne hym went   *against*
On Staynesmore thay mette and faught in hy.   *directly*
Wham Traherne thare chased and alle to shente   *destroyed*
Fro day to day tylle he the coroun hente   *seized*
755   And crouned was for kynge in dignyté
Of Bretayne so had he the sovereynté.

And reulde hys reme with grete nobilité   *realm*
His lawes and pese fulle welle he dyd conserve.
And welle was loved for his gode parenté   *ancestors*
760   Whiche so afore this londe dyd ofte preserve
From tyrants felle that cam it to overterve.   *fierce; overturn*
He regned so that alle his reme hym loved   *realm*
And honourde hym so wyse his wytte was proved.

fol. 50r	For whiche Octave than saylde into Norway	
765	For to have helpe alle of the kynge Gunberte	
	Who counsaylde hym to gete a frende som day	
	Within Bretayne to sla hym in a sterte	*slay; rush*
	Thurgh whiche he myght hym sonneste so subverte.	
	By whose counsayle and imagynacioun	
770	Thraerne was slayne so through his procuracioun.	*instigation*

How the makere of this moveth, touchant princes, to bene in company of heere men that love hem for drede of tresoun.

Unde Seneca dicit principis potestas numquam sine periculo est.[1]

Nota	O gode lorde God what peryle a prynce ys yn	*danger*
	Regnynge in his moste rialle magesté	
	And welle beloved with fremmyd and with kyn	*strangers*
	And eche day stonte his lyfe in juparté	*jeopardy*
775	Of suche traytours thurgh fals iniquyté	
	As ofte ys sene in remes mony one	*realms*
	Whare kynges were slayne thurgh tresoun alle allone.	

Nota	Wharfore a prynce shuld never bene hym allone	
	In any place for drede of felonye	
780	For falshode ay wylle wyrke upon his fone.	*foes*
	In pryvyté withouten company	
	To imagyne is alle his victory	
	How that he may his purpose brynge aboute	
	And save hymselff to stonden oute of doute.	

Kynge Octave

785	This Octave so than came into Bretayne	
	And sesed alle agayne into his honde	
	And sone thereafter for age he woxe unbayne	*incapacitated*
	And hayre had non that mayntene myght his londe	*heir*
	Saufe a doughter that couth nothynge withstonde	
790	The grete malice of cruelle conquerrours.	
	Wharefore he toke rede at his councellours.	*counsel*

	Som counsayld hym to Conan hire to geve	*give*
	Hys own cosyn a man of hyegh corage	
	By surname that hight Mariadoch, I leve.	*believe*
795	And som counsayld to graunte hyre mariage	
	Unto som lorde of Rome of hiegh parage	*noble family*

---

[1] *Whence Seneca says that the power of the prince is never without danger*

To cesen werre and dwelle in fulle quyete
With Romayns; so this counsayld som discrete.   *wise*

Bot Carodoch that duke was of Cornewayle
800   Counselde the kynge to sende to Rome message
Maximyan to brynge for grete avayle   *advantage*
His doughter to have in mariage.
For bothe he was right heyre by alle lynage   *heir*
To Constantyne and als a senatoure
805   Forpassynge other a lorde of grete honoure.

fol. 50v   Whiche counsaylle so was holden for the beste
And fulle exployte was done and execute   *speedily*
In so fere forthe Maximyane hym adreste   *prepared*
To Bretayne come welle sped withoute rebute.   *prospering; resistance*
810   To whom the kynge than offred grete refute   *succor*
Hys heyre to wedde and after hym prevayle   *heir; rule*
The coroune hool to have withouten fayle.   *entirely*

.x. capitulum of Maxymyan kynge, and Gracyan kyng, and Emperours of Rome.

The kynge Octave decesed than anone
After whom Maximyan succede
815   And corounde was maugré of alle his fone   *despite; foes*
For ire of whiche Conan departe indede   *anger*
And spoylede the londe to Humbre as I rede.
Wharfore this kynge Maxymyan so wyse
Encountred hym with hoste of grete assyse.   *magnitude*

820   And ofte tymes so thay faught in grete batayle.
Some tyme the kynge by batayl had his wylle
Some tyme Conan at bataylle dyd prevayle
And thus it felle tyl both thay had thaire fylle.
Thus was the londe thurgh thaym fulle lyke to spylle   *be destroyed*
825   Wharefore thare frendes by fulle and hole assente   *their*
Accorded thaym and trete incontynent.   *Reconciled; mediated immediately*

So stode he than fyve yere in reste and pese
That of rychesse he was so multyplyde.
He irked sore he was so longe in ese   *was displeased*
830   Thus in his herte bygan to ryse a pryde
And longe hym thought in Bretayne more to byde   *remain*
Wharfore his hoste of feghters ferre and nere
Assembled faste and gatte hym grete powere.

How Maxymyan conquerde Armoryke and named it Litel Bretayne and than he conquerde Fraunce, Almayne, and Romany and was than Emperoure of Rome.

	He londed than I say in Armoryke	
835	Whiche now so hight by name Lesse Bretayne	*is called*
	He wan it alle so welle he gan it lyke	
	So fulle it was of gode he was fulle fayne.	
	And to Conan than gan he thus to sayne	
	"For love of me Grete Bretayne thou foryede.	*surrendered*
840	This londe I geve thee now and graunte by dede."	

	He sente so than anone to Grete Bretayne	
	For ten thousondes hosbandes wyse and gode	*farmers*
	To tele the londe with carte, plowgh and wayne	*till; wagon*
	And knyghtes feel and squyers of hygh blode	*many; noble*
845	Yomen also myghty of mayne and mode	*Yeomen; strength; spirit*
	That londe to kepe and to defende fro shame.	
	Lytylle Bretayne he gaff it than to name.	

Kynge Conan of Lesse Bretayne

fol. 51r	Conan than kynge of Lesse Bretayn so bolde	
	Graunted forever it of his sovereyne lorde	
850	Kynge of Bretayne the more than forto holde	
	And bene his man withoute eny discorde	
	And plenysht it with Bretons by concorde	*replenished*
	Of alle estates with joy and grete plesance	
	Avoydynge Frensshe for drede of more distance.	*discord*

How Kynge Conan of Litille Bretayne sent into Grete Bretayne for Ursula and xi maydens of lordes doughters with xi thousand virgyns with hem, to bene maryed to hym and to his men.

855	And than Conan into Grete Bretayne sente	
	To Dyonote that duke was of Cornewayle	
	A noble prynce who heyre to Cradocke gente	*heir; noble*
	And brother was withouten any fayle,	
	To whom sertayne Maximyan the governayle	
860	Of Bretayne hole at his partynge gave	
	To his gayne come, to kepen and to save,	*Until; return*

	To sende hym than his doughter Ursula	
	That floure was than of alle the Grete Bretayne	
	His wyfe to bene evermore in wele and in wo	*prosperity*
865	On whom his herte was sette nothynge to layne	*hide the truth*
	Elleve thousand maydyns that wylle obayne	

With hyre to come to ben hys mennes wyfes
For Frenshe thay wolde none wedde in alle thare lyfes.

This Dyonote by gode deliberacioun
870   His doughter so to mary in that place
Elleve thousond vyrgyns of hire nacioun
He sente also to passe with hyre that race   *sea*
For hyre comforte to serve hyre in that cace
The kynge Conan to gladden and to plese
875   And for to sette hym and his londe in ese.

How Melga and Gwayns martired the xi thousand virgyns with Seint Ursula

In Themse that tyme, at Trynovant cyté
Thay shypped were to passe by governayle   *good management*
Towarde Bretayne the Lesse to maried be
With grete worshyp and to thare grete avayle.   *advantage*
880   Bot tempeste sore stroke than so in thare sayle
That thay dyd londe in iles of Germany
Whom Gwaynes kynge of Hunlonde gan espy

And Melga kynge of Peghtes in company.
Tho two tyraunts togedyre associate
885   Fulfylled hole of cursed tyrany.
For thare bewté that was so fayre create
Desyred thaym by way of lechery
And for thay wold nought graunte to suche foly
Seand thay were endowed in Cristen fayth   *Seeing*
890   And of Bretayne whiche was to thaym ful layth   *hateful*

fol. 51v   Thay gan thaym hate and had in odiousté   *regarded with animosity*
For whiche the folke thaym slew on every syde
And martred thaym by grete crudelité.   *cruelty*
For Cristes lawe in which thay glorifyde
895   So hieghly than in God thay dyd confyde
That thay had lever the Sarsens cruelté   *rather*
Suffre and dye, than lese thare chastyté.   *their*

So were thay alle ended by martyrment
Whose bones lyge at Colayn cyté fayre   *lie; Cologne*
900   In a mynstere of nunnes convenyent.   *monastery; appropriately*
Men may theym se that thydere wille repayre.   *go*
Wharein the quere Ursula hath hyre layre   *choir; protected place*
To hyde hyre corse in erthe thare fynaly   *body*
Whose soule in blisse shalle byde eternaly.   *remain*

905	Whiche ere alle seyntes and fully canonysed	*are*
	Ellen thousond vyrgyns undeflorate	*pure*
	In dede or wylle so wele they were avysed	*deed; thought; determined*
	So trew thare hertes to God were fortunate.	
	Thay had levere dye thanne bene devyrgynate	*rather; raped*
910	Or God dysplese or yit his law offende	
	In anythynge thare wyttes couth comprehende.	

	In this mene while the kynge Maximyan	
	Alle Fraunce had wonne and Almayne hole conquerde	*entirely*
	Itaille and Rome fully he had wonne than.	
915	Alle the Senate of his manhode were ferde	*afraid*
	For in batayle had he than slayne with swerde	
	Valentynyan the emperoure of myght	
	And Gracyane his brother put to flyght	

	And emperoure was than in dignyté	
920	To Cristen folke havynge fulle grete envy.	*malice*
	Who slayne was after thurgh grete maliciousté	
	By Gracyans frendes that hated hym forthy	*on account of the fact*
	That he afore had made hym forto flye	
	From the empyre of whiche he had estate	
925	With Valentynyan fully assocyate.	

Kynge Gracyan

	Gracyan, whan Maximyan was slayne	
	To Bretayne sente than by the senatours	
	In whose tyme so Kynge Melga and Kynge Gwayne	
	This londe overrode fulfylled of alle errours	
930	Whiche mortalle fone and cruelle tormentours	*foes*
	To Cristes fayth were and malicyus	
	Alle mercyles and passynge rigorus.	*exceedingly; severe*

fol. 52r	Whiche kynges two, rote of alle cruelté	*root*
	And payens fals fulle of grete felonye,	*pagans*
935	Afore had made thurgh martyrdome to de	*die*
	Elleven thousond vyrgyns right cursydly	
	For envy that thay had alle utterly	
	To Cristes fayth and to Maximyan	
	For the rebute he dyd to Gracyan.	*repulse*

940	Wenynge fully Maximyan had be kynge	*Thinking*
	Of Bretayne than thay spoylde the londe and brent	*burned*
	The peple slewe an every syde and hynge	*hanged*
	The chyrches als ay robbed as thay went	*also*
	Wyfes and chyldre and clerkes or thay stent	*before; stopped*

945   Thay slew doun right and harmelesse home agayne
          Thrughout the Northe thay wrought fulle mekylle payne.   *much*

How whan Melga and Gwayns had distroyed the londe, how Kynge Gracian was slayne with his comons for grete outrage of talliage (*tax*) that he had take of thaym withoute mercy.

          Bot Gracyan kynge of this londe was than
          Crouned fully by alle the baronage
          Who in his domes injuste was to every man   *judgments*
950   Right dispytouse, and toke grete talliage   *pitiless; tax*
          Of lordes and folke to passynge grete outrage   *excessive*
          So mercylesse and voyde of alle pyté
          He was that none hym loved that hym se.   *saw*

          For whiche anone the hool comonalté   *populace*
955   Of alle Bretayne by lordes hool assent
          Upon hym rose to cese his cruelté
          Thay slew hym so adnullynge his entent.   *quashing*
          Thus that tyrant fro his estate was rente   *torn*
          And plukked doun fro dygnyté rialle   *royal*
960   As mensioun ys in cronycle historialle.

Gwaynes and Melga payens the seconde tyme distroyed this londe of Bretayne

          Gwayns and als Melga tho kynges two   *those*
          Herynge welle how Bretayne was undemeyned   *without a ruler*
          And Gracyan so slayne with mekylle wo   *much*
          Bretayne lafte bare withoute kynge unchifteynde   *without a ruler*
965   And Maximyan with deth so felle desteynde   *extinguished*
          Who grete powere led into Romany
          And Lesse Bretayne to strengh and multiplye

          Than came agayne with mekel greter hoste   *[Gwayns and Melga]; much*
          Wastynge the londe with fyre fro se to se
970   And slew the folke aboute in every coste   *place*
          That pyté was with swerde so sore thay de.   *died*
          Thus Bretayne was thrugh thare crudelyté
          Subverte and brente by tho cursed tyrantes
          That payens were and cruelle mescreantes.   *pagans; misbelievers*

fol. 52v   **How Bretons sente to Rome for helpe to whom thai sente a legyon of knyghtes that made the Bretons to make a wall of lyme and stone bituix thaym and Peghtes, whare Severe afore had made a dyke, whiche wall Melga and Gwayns wan and rode all Bretayne londe secundum Bedam** *De Gestis Anglorum.*[1]

975	Than Bretons sent to Rome message agayne	
	Praynge Romayns to sende thaym more socours	*help*
	Promysynge thaym alway for to be bayne	*prompt*
	At thare byddynge and alle thare successours	
	And tribute pay unto the senatours	
980	Withoute dylay or eny excusacioun	
	For everemore withoute derogacioun.	*exception*

	For whose socoure the Senate sente a legioun	*help*
	Of noble knyghtes that were fulle corageus	
	So chosen oute of every regioun	
985	For moste worthy and als vyctoriouse	
	Whiche Gwaynes and Melga so noyouse	*troublesome*
	Out of this londe drofe into Albany	
	Whare thay dyd ship than into Germany.	

	These Romayns than and Bretons fulle assembled	
990	By thaire hole wyttes and also fulle advyse	
	Dyd make a walle of lyme and stones sembled	*gathered*
	Fro the este se unto the weste that lyse	*lies*
	The Peghtes to withstonde and alle ennemyse	
	With castels hyegh and toures at every myle	
995	Endlonge that walle with many other pyle	*Along; support*

	Whare Severe so afore had made a dyke	
	Of turfe and sodde that tyme of grete defence	*earth*
	To kepe out Peghtes from Loegres in case lyke	
	That noyouse were and of felle insolence.	*troublesome*
1000	Bot Romayns than no lengere residence	
	Wolde holden here in Bretayne more to byde	*remain*
	Bot with alle haste than homward dyd thay ryde.	

	Thay went thare way to Rome so than agayne	
	Forsakynge ever alle tribute and trewage	*taxation*
1005	After whose gate Kinge Melga and Kynge Gwayne	*departure*
	Had gode awayte and sekyre gode message	*watchfulness; secure*
	Whan Romayns wente and after thare passage	
	Came sone agayne with mekylle grettere hoste	*much*
	Rydynge Bretayne unto the south se coste.	

---

[1] *Concerning the Deeds of the English*

1010	Whiche tyme the kinges Melga and Gwaynus	
	Cursed tyrants and paynyms notyfyde	*notorious pagans*
	The walle betwyx thaym made and Loegres thus	
	The Peghtes walle to name was signifyde	
	Dyd bete alle doun with hostes tripartyde	*divided in three*
1015	In sondry place thay it so undyrmyned	*destroyed*
	That lyke the way alle playne it was declyned.	*level*

fol. 53r	And thanne thay slew the Bretons manyfolde	
	In so ferre forthe thay lay on hepes dede	*heaps*
	So myghtily the Bretons knyghtes bolde	
1020	Thare faught with Pyghtes and bare them in that sted.	*place*
	But Peghtes what with wyle and what manhede	*cunning strategy*
	The walle overe wan and slew suche multitude	
	That Bretons were overcome by fortitude.	

How Bretons sent to Egicio senatour of Rome for more helpe, who sente none bot refused thaire tribute for evere more secundum Bedam *De Gestis Anglorum*.[1]

	Wherfore to Rome the Bretons sente anone	
1025	To Egicyo the senatoure so wise	
	For socoure more as thay that strengh had none	*support*
	Thare enmyse to withstonde that myght suffise	
	Offrynge trewage forever withowte fayntyse	*tribute; slacking*
	To pay with thy that fro the enmyté	*as long as*
1030	Thay wolde thaym kepe in constabilité.	*security*

	Whiche trewage so the Romayns than forsoke	
	Relesynge it forever, I say yow why	
	Thay were so stad with werres that thaym woke	*preoccupied; arose*
	Aboute thaymselff right nere to Romany	
1035	And Bretayne was so ferre fro that party	
	And als a se betwyxe fulle daungerouse	
	And myght not passe for wyndes contrariouse.	

	Thay wold no more thaym socoure in thare nede	
	Bot bade hem helpe thaymself for evermore.	
1040	For thay no more wolde hostes thydere lede	*there*
	So were thare men mescheved there afore	*undone*
	Thurgh chaunse of werre and som by treson sore	
	Of Bretons fals thurgh thayre imagynacioun	
	At thayre above and domynacioun.	*On account of their superiority*

---

[1] *according to Bede in his book* Concerning the Deeds of the English

1045	The tyme Romayns the tribute so forsoke	
	Was in the yere of Cristes incarnacioun	
	Foure hundre ful and nyne as Bede gan loke	
	In his cronycles and compilacioun	
	This londe distroyed als by paynym nacioun	*pagan*
1050	For whiche Bretons dyd sette a parlement	
	At Trynovant that tyme by hole assent.	

How the Archebisshope of Londoun went than to Litil Bretayne for socoure, and brought home Constantyne brother of the Kynge of Lasse Bretayne to bene kynge of this londe.

	At whiche thay dyd conclude by hole assent	
	Brevely to sende forth Bysshop Gunthelyne	*quickly*
	Who Archebysshop of Trynovant present	
1055	Was redy thare that message to enclyne	
	And doctore was approved in law dyvyne	*teacher*
	With thaire intent to Lasse Bretayne instructe	
	Thaire socoure home to brynge with hym reducte.	*support; brought back*

fol. 53v **Nota how bissop Gunthelyne made compleynt of the grete distresse in whiche Bretayn stode**

	So forthe he wente and sayled undyr sayle	
1060	To Bretayne Lesse unto the Kynge Aldroene	
	Who kynge was thare and had the governayle	
	The fourth after Kynge Conan, so I wene,	*believe*
	Whom he admytte with honoure, as was sene,	
	Askynge the cause of his thydyre come	*coming there*
1065	And why it was he came so ferre fro home.	*far*

	To whom thus sayde the bysshop Gunthelyne	
	"Enewgh apperth to yowre nobilité	*Manifestly*
	Oure heped wo and endelesse lastynge pyne	*piled; pain*
	Whiche shuld yow move by alle gode parenté	*familial relation*
1070	Youre con-Bretons of consanguynyté	*fellow Bretons; kinship*
	To socoure now stondynge in grete dystresse	
	Thurgh paynyms werre the whiche ye may redresse.	*pagans*

	"The whiche distresse and heigh adversité	
	Of longe we have now susteynde and comporte	*endured*
1075	Seth Kynge Maximyane of his rialté	
	Thys londe dyd stuffe with men as is reporte	
	And thousondes feel to Rome for his comforte	*many*
	Dyd lede with hym so bare he made oure londe	
	We had no men oure enmyse to gaynestonde.	*withstand*

1080	"Wharethurgh paynyms cruelle as ye have herde	*pagans*
	Have us overronne and done fro day to day.	
	The Cristen fayth grete parte thay have conquerde	
	And lyke ere to dystroy it alle away.	*are*
	Wharefore of helpe we humblely yow pray	
1085	That ye oure reme and us wille now defende	*realm*
	Seth ye and we of oon blode bene descende."	

	Kynge Aldroene hym thankyd with hole herte	
	Refusynge than that noble dygnyté.	
	It for to have he lyste noght to adverte	*desired; accede*
1090	Suche drede he had of mutabilité	*changefulness*
	Thurgh Romayns myght and grete subtylité	*power*
	That levere he were his own in pese to have	*he preferred*
	Than More Bretayne iff Romayns trewage crave.	*tribute; should require*

.xi. capitulum. How the Kynge of Lasse Bretayne sent Constantyne his brother to bene of Grete Bretayne the kynge and governoure

	Bot Constantyne his brother fresshe and fayre	
1095	He than bytoke to Bysshop Guntelyne	*entrusted*
	To ben thare kynge with hym home to repayre	*go*
	With power suche right as he couth diffyne.	*control*
	To Tottenesse so the se thay dyd thurgh myne	*travel*
	Arrifynge thare with mekylle joy and blysse	*much*
1100	Of whom the reme was glad and blythe iwysse.	*realm; happy certainly*

fol. 54r	To whom anone assembled alle the floure	
	Of juventé and of the lusty eelde	*youth; energetic; aged*
	And toke hym for thare kinge and governoure	*accepted; as*
	Agayne thare fose to feghten in the felde	*foes*
1105	Whoso wele dyd with bowe, spere, and shelde	
	That of Melga and Gwayns the victory	
	Thay had forthwith, as made is memory.	*immediately*

Constantine of Litil Bretayne Kynge of Grete Bretayne

	This Constantyne by Bretons hole advyse	*agreement*
	Was crouned than with rialle dyademe	
1110	At Cyrcester, Caersyry on thayre wyse	
	In Breton tonge hight as thay couthe expreme,	*called; were able to express*
	In se rialle than sette whiche hym byseme	*seat; befitted*
	As prynce pierlesse thurghout the Occydent	*peerless; West*
	On every syde unto the Orient.	*East*

| 1115 | This archebyssop this gode man Guntelyne | |
| | The croune upon his hede on hegh he sette | *high* |

With alle honoure as he couthe determine   *could*

He dyd to hym, for nothynge wold he lette.   *obstruct*

A lady fayre and fresshe he dyd forth sette

1120   And wedded thaym with grete solempnyté

Of Gunthelyns and Romayns blode was she.

How this kynge had thre sonnes of whyche he made the eldest a munke for he was noght wyse to governe

Of whom he gatte thre sonnes that were echone

Kynges crouned of Bretayne to the se:

Oon Constance hight the eldest of echone;   *was called; them all*

1125   The seconde was Aurilyus hight he

Whose surname was Ambrosius wete ye;   *you know*

The thrid Utere Pendragon was his name

Of whom after in honoure rose grete fame.

This kynge so than his eldeste sonne Constance

1130   In Wynchestere dyd put a monke to be.

The other two he putte by ordynaunce

To Gunthelyne of thaire consanguynyté   *kinship*

To nurture thaym in alle nobilité

As he that was rightwyse and ful dyscrete   *righteous; wise*

1135   Of alle nurture als was he fulle implete.   *good training; informed*

How a Peghte (*Pict*) of this kynges hows (*house*) slewe hym by counsail of the Duke Vortygere

Whan he had bene the kynge so ful ten yere

Upon a day as he in gardyn wase

A Peghte that in his house was hym ful nere

In that gardyne hym slew, so felle the case.

1140   Thurgh counsaylle of oon Vortygerne it wase

To have the croune, whiche longe he had desyred,

For whiche his dethe men sayd he had conspyred.

fol. 54v   **.xii. capitulum Kynge Constance, the monke of Wynchestre, son of Constantyne.**

Constans than so that monke was in Caergwent

That Wynchestere hatte now so this day   *is called*

1145   In the mynstere of Seynte Amphibale spent   *monastery*

In cloyster thare that shulde have ben for ay   *permanently*

This Vortigerne toke oute and led away

And sette the croune upon his hede fulle he   *high*

With alle honoure and als regalyté.

1150	For love of whiche that he hym so preferred	*raised up*
	He made hym than alle hole his governoure.	
	Fro alle wysdome the kynge was so deferred	*From; distant*
	He knew not what appent to his honoure	*pertained*
	So symple was his wytte in alle laboure	
1155	He toke no hede of reule, ne governaunce,	*heed*
	So he were kepte in joy and hiegh plesaunce.	

How Vortiger by grete subtilité made the Peghtes to sla Kynge Constance and after he slew thaym for to excuse hym selfe

	This Vortygerne fulle sette in sapience	*cleverness*
	Of Kambre kynde that now so Wales hight	*is called*
	A duke was than of high grete excelence.	
1160	Of rethorike wytte, forpassynge every wyght	*elegant*
	In eloquence excedynge alle men right	
	Whare myght avayle he couthe of adulacioun	*[it]; gain an advantage; flattery*
	To fage and plese thurgh softe dissymylacioun.	*flatter*
	So castynge yn his mynde and alle his wytte	
1165	How to the croune he myght moste sone aspyre	*rise*
	To kepe the kynge, whethyre he wente or sytte	
	An hundreth knychtes he dyd withholde and hyre	*knights; retain; hire*
	Of Peghtes alle with whom he dyd conspyre	
	The kynges dethe by processe after so	
1170	In subtyle wyse that no wyght knew it mo.	
	Thare wage he payd thaym welle fro day to day	
	Doynge the kynge to know and to consayve	*Making; think*
	That Peghtes wolde ryse and distroy hym away.	
	Wharefore the Pyghtes thare londe forto dyssayve	*deceive*
1175	And thare consaylle to spy and to persayve	
	He waged had to warne hym of alle drede	*hired*
	Thrugh whiche he myght withstande thayre grete falshede.	
	So after that upon a day he sayde	
	Unto hys Peghtes that so were with hym holde	
1180	"For youre wages the kynge hath me upbrayde	*taken me to task*
	And blamed me, right for that I ne wolde	
	Yow voyde oute of his servyce and howseholde.	*expel*
	Bot not forthy iff I were kynge indede:	*nevertheless*
	Youre wages shuld ben payed fulle well in nede."	

fol. 55r	Thus sayde he than by grete subtilité	
1186	To make thaym truste his gode domynacioun	
	For welle he knew thare mutabilité	
	Or thay were voyde so fro thare prosperacioun	*Before; expelled; prosperity*

	Wold sla the kynge for his contemplacioun	*slay; thoughts*
1190	To croune hym kynge with alle the helpe thay may	*(i.e., Vortigern)*
	Thaire lyvelode forthe to have of hym alway.	*wages*

Thurgh whiche comforte and subtylle intisement — *temptation*
Thay trustynge in his domynacioun
Iff he were kynge and had the regyment
1195 He wold thaym pay withoute refreynacioun — *obstacle*
Thaire wages hole withoute defalcacioun — *withholding*
Seynge the kynge was bot an idiote — *seeing*
And couth not kepe his heghte that he behote — *promise; promised*

By oon advyse thay slew hym than anone
1200 And gaff his hede unto Syr Vortygere
Of whiche his herte was glad, but stylle as stone
He stode mornynge and hevy of his chere.
To blynde the folke he dyd crye fere and nere — *deceive*
That none shulde spare the Pightes by day ne nyght
1205 Bot sla thaym doune whare thay mete with hem myght. — *slay*

So were thay slayne thurgh his subtyle quantyse — *trickery*
The kynge also, of whiche his herte rejoysed.
And knowynge wele amonge the lordes fayntyse — *cowardice*
And how he was with comons welle anoysed — *considered*
1210 The Peghtes hym had afore so wele avoysed — *reputed him*
Consydrynge als the kynges castels alle
Were in his honde thurghoute bothe grete and smalle

And of grete gode he was so stronge of myght
The peple hole obeyant to his wille — *obedient*
1215 The olde lordes dede, thare hayres bot yonge to fight, — *dead; heirs*
The kynges brether fled Bretayne Lasse untylle — *to*
For fere of hym lesse that he wolde hem kylle — *lest*
To Kynge Budyce who nurrissht thaym fulle clene — *raised; faultlessly*
Who sybbe thaym was, as may in bokes bene sene. — *kin*

.xiii. capitulum of Kynge Vortigere and Vortymere his son

1220 This Vortygere thus seynge wele he myght
Unto the croune ben lyste at alle his wille — *chosen*
He dyd the croune upon his hede forth right
And helde estate rialle for gode or ille. — *royal*
The Peghtes and Scottes put sklaundire than hym tille — *slander; on him*
1225 Of thare frendes dethe and also of the kynges
Whiche thurgh hys wille was wrought in alkyn thynges. — *all manner of*

fol. 55v   For whiche thay thought on hym to be revenged
            For his falshode and his subtylle tresoun
            Of whiche he myght in nowyse ben ought clenged   *cleansed*
1230   So know it was that it was by enchesoun   *cause*
            He wolde ben kynge and for non other resoun.   *wished to be*
            Wharfore with alle the myght thay can or may
            Thay thought revenge that deth ful sore aday.   *each day*

How Engiste and Horne of Saxonye londed in Kente and bicame Kynge Vortygers men, which inhabite first in Lyndsay.

            In this mene while the kynge as he dyd ly   *stay*
1235   At Caunterbyry, whiche than so hight Caerkent   *was called*
            And as som say it hight Doroberny,
            But than arrofe thre shyppes fulle in Kent   *arrived*
            Of men of werre, at Sandwyche were they lent,   *came to land*
            For whom the kynge sente after sone anone
1240   To whom thay came as faste as thay myght gone.

            He asked what thay were and whyne thay came   *whence*
            And what was cause thay came upon his londe.
            To whom Engeste answerde, as meke as lame,   *lamb*
            And sayde "Gode lorde ye shalle wele undyrstonde
1245   Saxons we bene and Saxonay oure londe
            Whiche stondeth so ful fayre in Germany
            And hydyr come for servyce onaly.   *here; only*

            "The case was thus: oure prynce by his regence
            Fonde that oure londe gretly was overcharged   *crowded*
1250   With habundance of folke and affluence   *abundance*
            By generacioun excedyngly enlarged.
            As custome was the londe muste be dyscharged   *relieved*
            For whiche he sette amonge the juventé   *youth*
            A lotte who shulde passe forth over the see.

1255   "With oure manhode to gete us som lyvelode   *livelihood*
            The sorte on us felle, so we muste departe   *lot*
            Oute of the londe as of his hye godhode
            Mercury hath us brought into this arte.   *district*
            Thay vytaylde us and shypped for thare parte.   *supplied*
1260   On us thay made thensforth no more dyspence.
            Thus ere we voyde to seke oure residence.   *expelled*

            "My brother here hatte Horse and I Engiste   *is called*
            Of dukes blode we bene so procreate
            Leders to bene right by oure prynces liste.   *desire*
1265   Of this meyne we bene now ordynate   *band; in charge*

And dukes bene so called in oure estate.
Oure prynce us gaffe of armoure suffycence
To helpe us wyth atte alle oure indygence.   *need*

fol. 56r   "Wharfore we muste to youre servyce intende
1270   To wynne us londe with laboure and manhede
            Or to som other prynce we muste attende
            Of oure servyce that mystere hath and nede.   *requirement*
            Now have I tolde yow alle why thus indede
            We come upon youre londe by youre suffrance   *permission*
1275   To do servyce unto youre hye plesance."   *utmost satisfaction*

            The kynge saw wele of suche men he had nede
            That lykely were and also corageuse   *impressive*
            In armes proved as longeth to knyghthede.   *pertains; knighthood*
            Withhelde thaym alle at wages plentyuouse
1280   For to wythstonde the Peghtes perilouse   *dangerous*
            And als the hayres and brether of Constance   *heirs*
            Of whom he truste ay grete contrariance.   *resistance*

**And how this Engiste and Horne were payens levynge (*believing*) on Mercury
and Venus, and how Wednesday and Fryday had thaire names first of Mercury
and of Venus.**

            The kynge hym askte what was that Mercury
            That sente hym hydyr, to whom he answerd than   *here*
1285   "A god he ys that oure olde auncetry   *ancestors*
            Worshipt evermore in world whan thay began.
            And we also do so, right as we can.
            This Mercury we calle a god of fame
            The fourth day ever we honoure in his name.

**Nota also how Engist and Horsus entred Bretayne in the armes of thaire londe,
that is to sey thay bare of azure (*blue*) the god Mercure, Woden in thair language,
and the goddesse Frye in thaire language, corouned, enthronysed of golde.**

1290   "His name with us Woden so is called
            On oure language whom we honoure moste
            For every woke alway it so be falled   *week*
            The fourth day so we halowed alle oure coste   *sanctified; country*
            That Wodensday we calle and worshyp moste
1295   For love of hym. And so ys oure usage
            And ever hath bene amonge alle oure lynage.

            "A goddesse als we have of grete powere
            Venus men calle in whose name we adoure
            The sexte day ever of every woke ay sere   *sixth; week; different*

1300   Wham in oure tonge Fry we calle and honoure
        For wham the sexte day in laboure and sorore   *sorrow*
        We worshyp nexte, whiche we calle so Friday
        The sonne, the mone, with other of oure lay."   *belief*

        Sone after that the Scottes and Peghtes hoste   *army*
1305   In Bretayne brent and mekylle peple slewe   *burned; many*
        For whiche the kynge came northe to felle thare boste   *diminish their pride*
        With Engyste als and Horsus soudyours newe   *soldiers*
        That manly faught and on the fose dyd hewe   *foes; cut*
        In so ferre forthe thay made the vyctory
1310   And drofe thaym out agayne in Albany.

fol. 56v Off whose manhode and worthy vyctory
          The kynge was glad and gaffe thaym londes fele   *many*
          And als thare wages he dyd thaym multyplye
          And loved wele with thaym to speke and dele   *deal*
1315   And comforte thaym in sekenesse and in hele   *health*
          Above alle other with myrthes that myght be made
          Thare commynge so dyd comforte hym and glade.

How Engiste bigged (*built*) Thwongcastre

          Bot on day Engiste the kynge dyd plese
          And sayde "My lorde ye stonde in juparté   *danger*
1320   Bothe of youre lyfe and of alle hertes ese
          And lyke to falle in grete adversité
          Unto myschefe and alle paralité   *disease*
          For wele I here by worde and by language
          Es non yow loveth of alle youre baronage.

1325   "Thay say there bene of Constance brether two
          Thare lege lordes of right that aw to be   *ought*
          With whiche thay shalle hereafter ryde and go
          And venged bene that tyme of yow and me.
          Thay love us nought by ought that I can se
1330   Wharfore I wolde sende into Germany
          To wage yonge men and strengh youre chyvalry.   *hire; reinforce*

          "And of a thynge, my lorde, I wolde you pray
          A walled town or castelle I may have
          Or som cyté for seurté nyght and day   *security*
1335   In whiche I may my body kepe and save
          For I am hate for yow with knyght and knave   *hated on account of; by*
          Whiche may by nyght dystroy me as they wylle
          And whan thaym lyste to sla me and to kylle."   *want; slay*

	To whom the kynge than sodenly answerde	
1340	"That thynge to graunte I dare not so forthy	
	That ye so ben alieyens I am aferde.	*foreigners*
	My barons wolde it sone gaynesay in hy	*contradict immediately*
	And als ye ben paynyms so openly	*pagans*
	Thay wolde the more with me greve and gregge	*annoy; aggravate*
1345	Agayne my fayth it were thay myghte allegge."	*against*

	"Now seth ye darre nought graunte me so for drede	*since*
	Yit may ye graunte me than als mekylle grounde	*much*
	As with a thwange I may overlay and sprede	*thong (strip of leather)*
	In brede and length or els in cyrcuyte rounde	
1350	More than I have now so with in my bounde	
	Seand there was thareby a stony place	*seeing*
	Whiche nomore was bot even a castelle space."	

fol. 57r	The whiche the kynge hym gaff fully and graunte	
	Wharefore he kutte a boles skyn so grete	*bull's*
1355	Alle in a thwonge so rounde and hole curraunte	*strip; running*
	With whiche that grounde so stony he dyd mete	*measure*
	Of length and brede he toke his castelle sete.	*foundation*
	And thereupon dyd proppe his mete and bounde	*set; limit*
	Whare that he thought his castelle sette and founde.	

How Engiste sent for his doughter, who came to hym with xviii shippes full of Saxons and Englysshe men.

1360	So than he sente anone to Germany	
	To brynge his doughter that was bothe fresshe and fayre	
	And soudyours als to strengh hyre company.	*soldiers; reinforce*
	In whiche mene tyme his castelle to repayre	
	He labourde so that it was for his hayre.	*heir*
1365	So stronge it was and myghty for to wynne	*defeat*
	None enmyse myght it wynne, ne hym over rynne.	

1370	Sone after than his doughter Dame Rowen	
	With eghtene shyppes came out of Saxony	
	Alle fulle of knyghtes that were alle myghty men	
	Chosen for beste thurghout alle Germany	
	For whiche he thanke his god so Mercury	
	Woden that hight in his moder language	*was called*
	Dame Frie also, Venus called by clerkes sage.	

1375	He prayed the kynge to se his castelle then	
	And dyne with hym right at his owne devyse	*planning*
	His doughter als to welcome and his men	
	That knyghtes were fulle fayre, manly and wyse	

	Out of his londe that came by hole advyse	
	To helpe the kynge in his necessité	
1380	His enmyse to distroy by thare powsté.	*power*

	Of whiche the kynge was glad and graunted so	
	And ete with hym and made gode chere and gladde	
	Bot for tho knyghtes his herte was wondere wo	
	That thay so than the paynyms creance hadde	*pagans' belief*
1385	Whiche stode agayne his herte fulle sore and sadde.	*steadily*
	Bot neverthelesse his enmyse to dystroye	
	He plesed thaym foryetynge alle his noye.	*forgetting; anxiety*

	Of the castelle in herte he was ful fayne	*pleased*
	And of Rowene to wham there was none lyke	
1390	In bewté so perlesse she was sertayne	
	Hym lyked beste and gan therewith to syke	*sigh*
	With that she brought a coupe of golde fulle ryke	*when; splendid*
	Unto the kynge and sayde to hym "Wassayle"	*Good Health*
	To whom the kynge so lerned sayd "Drynke hayle."	

fol. 57v   How Vortygere wed Engyste doughtir

	With that hire kiste as he was taught by men	*kissed*
1395	That knew the gyse and manere of thare londe	*custom*
	Thurgh whiche he sette his herte so on hyre then	
	He wolde hyre wed anone and made hyre bonde	
	And quene she was right as I endyrstonde	
1400	Of Bretayne hole by fulle and hole sentence.	*authority*
	He gaff hyre Kent to dowere and dispence.	*as a dowry; source of income*

Now called Castre on the Walde in Lincolneshire

Sapiencia attingit a fine ad finem et disponit omnia suaviter[1]

	Bot Engiste than his castelle named and calde	
	Thwongcastre forth bycause so of that thwonge.	*thong*
	For it shuld bene in memory, he walde	*wished*
1405	How he it gatte and by what wyle it fonge.	*stratagem; took*
	So had he joy, his wytte be mynded longe,	*astuteness; remembered*
	For wysdome so he thought shulde ben comende	*commended*
	Whiche reuleth alle thynge mekely unto the ende.	

	The reme so hate the kynge by alle thare wytte	*realm; hated*
1410	Bycause he wedde in payens law and ryte	*pagans'*

---

[1] *Wisdom reaches from one end (of the earth) to the other, and disposes everything peacefully* (Wisdom 8:1)

	And favourde more payenis for love of ytte	
	Than Cristen men, for whiche thay had dyspyte.	*resentment*
	To hym his frendes and other more and lite	*greater and less powerful*
	His sonnes moste of alle hym dyd dispyse	
1415	For his weddynge so on the payenis wyse.	

	His eldeste sonne that hight Syr Vortymere	
	The seconde als was callyd Categerne	
	The thyrde Passhent whiche that fulle manly were	
	Of his friste wyfe by bokes who can dyscerne	*first*
1420	The sothe he may of it wele se and lerne.	*truth*
	Thare fadyr thay lafte by alle the lordes assent	
	Who thurgh his wyfe to payenis was consent.	*pagans; in league*

How the Bretons were infecte in diverse cuntreys with payens and errisyes Pelagien (*Pelagian heresy*), wharfore the lordes sent for Seynt Germayn and Seint Lupe bishops, who with thaire precchynge brought the peple out fro thaire errour and errisyes.

	Whare thurgh the reme fulle of idolatry	*on account of which*
	Was so, what with the payenis cursed usage	*pagans'*
1425	And what so with Pelagiens errysy	*Pelagian heresy*
	Whiche regned than in londes fele and lynage	*many*
	The Cristene were so myxt with mariage	
	Of payenis blode that neigh the Cristynté	*almost*
	Was brought unto payenis credulyté.	*belief*

1430	In this tyme came two doctours approbate	*teachers; approved*
	In law dyvyne of whiche on Seynt Germayne	*one*
	Lupus also the tother that consecrate	*the other*
	Were bothe bysshops, and sent by Seynt Romayne	
	To preche the folke thurghout this More Bretayne	*Great Britain*
1435	At the prayer of alle the baronage	
	By Vortymers assente and his message.	

fol. 58r	By whose prechynge the peple were converte	
	And came unto the fayth ay more and more	
	That were afore oute of the fayth perverte	
1440	Thurgh comonynge instructe of paynyms lore	*verbal instruction; teaching*
	By this Engyste and thay that his folke wore	*were*
	Who Kent had so in domynacioun	
	By kynges strength and quenes supportacioun.	

	This Engiste so for plesaunce of the kynge	
1445	By hole assent bytwyx thaym two agrede	*between*
	Sent after his sonne Octa, a knyght fulle yynge,	*young*
	His cosyn als Ebissa, gode in nede,	*also*

And Cherdyke with thre hundre shyppes dyd lede
Als many men as tho shyppes myght contene
1450   Thay brought with thaym of armed men ful clene.

The barons than distracte were and afrayde   *distressed*
Of hethen folke so grete in multytude
For whiche unto the kynge thay playnde and sayde   *complained*
And no redresse couth have it to exclude   *remedy; stop*
1455   Bot ever thay dyd encrese of fortitude
In so ferre forthe the barons were consente
Vortymere to corown by hole assent.

Kynge Vortymere of Bretayne, son of Vortygere.

Syr Vortymere thay crounde anone forth ryght
With rialle honoure that myght to hym appende   *pertain*
1460   Who was fulle wyse aproved lyke a knyght
In alle corage that to a knyght extende   *suited*
Forto assayle or els forto defende
Who hated sore his fadyrs governance
And by hys wytte distroyed the mescreance.   *paganism*

1465   He faught with thaym anone upon Derwent   *straight away*
And other tyme at Abyrford dyd mete
Whare he on thaym with batayle strongly went
The felde he had and caste thaym undyrfete.
Whare Katygerne his brothur, wylle ye wete,   *if you should wish to know*
1470   And Horsus als, eyther other on the playne
So felly stroke that bothe thay were there slayne.   *cruelly*

Upon a felde bysyde the north se banke
He faught eft sones and put thaym to the flight   *again soon*
Unto the Ile Tenette thaire unthanke   *Isle of Thanet; unwillingly*
1475   In truste of Engystes powere and his myght.
Whither he wente than with his powere ryght.
The barons als fulle hole with hym assembled   *also*
For whiche Saxons for fere quoke and trembled.

fol. 58v   He helde thaym there by se right many a day
1480   With shyppes and botes thaym every day assayled
With batayle stronge fulle thik there slayne thay lay
So sore that thayre grete powere was than fayled.
Thay were so sore forfoughten and bataylde   *defeated; overcome*
Thay prayd the kynge thay myght have his lycense   *permission*
1485   To Germany to make there revertence   *return*

And leve bothe wyfe and childe, and godes fayre,
And alle thare londes, castels, toures and places,   *homes*
And never to come agayne thare to repayre.   *return*
And so thay dyd by license and his grace
1490   Thus fro Britayne he dyd thaym alle out chase
That were so hole of payenis mescreance   *pagans' misbelief*
And by advyse amendyd alle noysance   *trouble*

Restored agayn the cytese and the townes
To barons als and Bretons alle there londes
1495   With fraunchyse als and rightes by dales and downes   *liberties; valleys; hills*
And wele mayntened the fayth with lawes and bondes   *restraints*
That with the Chyrche and Cristen fayth wele stondes   *suits*
Praynge mekely Lupus and Seynt Germayne
The Cristen faythe to techen and sustayne.

1500   The Kyrke he dyd honoure at alle his myght
And it restored to alle was fro it refte   *seized*
In every place he helde justyce and right
So vertuose he was he made be lefte
Alle vices foule and vertu take up efte.   *to be adopted afterwards*
1505   Fulle wele he dyd his barons governe alle
That peple alle hym loved grete and smalle.

Bot to his high vertu and grete godenesse
Envyed so the fende who was impreste   *the devil; inscribed*
In Rowens herte so fulle of wykydnesse
1510   That by his man, whom she had so adreste   *treated*
With gyftes grete whiche she had hym promeste,
Kynge Vortymere she made bene pousond so   *to be poisoned*
For whom his men than had fulle mekylle wo.   *much*

Yit at his deth he dyd his men rewarde
1515   And bade thaym than thare londe thay shuld defende
And lay hym at the porte whare hyderwarde   *here*
Saxons dyd londe whan Engyste for thaym sende.
On high he myght ben sene and fully kende   *known*
Trustynge thay durste non nerre so come for fere   *dared; nearer*
1520   Of his body as longe as it were there.

fol. 59r   Bot than he dyed as fate of dethe it wolde
And byried was so than at Trynovaunte
By alle assent right of his Bretons bolde
Agayne his owne presumptiouse avaunte.   *vainglory*
1525   This Rowen fals, with poysouns that she haunte,   *knew about*
Thys gode kynge slewe, whare thurgh Kynge Vortigerne
The reame dyd seyse into his honde fulle yerne.   *seize; eagerly*

How the makere moveth his conceyte touchant his hardyment and presumptuous avawnte (*vainglory*)

O hardynesse of man so hiegh presumed
Agayne the wylle of hym that sitte above
1530 Whiche erthely men hath sette to be consumed
Right by his reule as clerkes wele can prove
How durstow so, lesse he thy witte reprove,   *dare you; lest*
To presume thynge men shulde thy bones drede
Whan alle thy myght is gone and waste indede?

Kynge Vortigere

1535 This Vortygerne was crouned than agayne
And regned so right in his fyrste estate
Rowen his wyfe began hym trete and prayne   *pray*
To sende than for hir fadyr arly and late   *early (i.e., continuously)*
To dwelle with hym and helpe hym fro the hate   *against*
1540 That Bretons had to hym for Vortymere
With whom thay helde as fully dyd appere.

How Engiste cam into Bretayne with grete powere by the kynges wylle

For whom sent forth the kynge Syr Vortygere
His letters so and prayd hym come anone
Hym sertifiant how dede was Vortymere   *certified*
1545 And in his come he seyde was perile none.   *coming*
For whiche he thought ben venged on his sone
Rejoysed highly with alle the haste he may
And thowsondes feel of men he brought ful gay.   *many*

For whiche Bretons with hym were greved sore
1550 And thought have fought with hym whan he shuld londe.
Whiche whan Rowen it knew she sent therefore
To warne hym so right by hyre pryvey sonde   *secret message*
For whiche he thought he might more surely stonde
Undyr hope of pese, a trety forto make
1555 With Bretons so than batayle with hem take.

And to the kynge he sente, as bokes telles,   *(i.e., Hengist)*
His message than enformed on this wyse   *shaped*
That his powere he brought for nothynge elles
Bot hym to kepe, lesse Vortymere wold ryse   *preserve, lest*
1560 At his londynge and fowly hym dispyse.
And if it to the lordes ought displese
He wold sende home thaym alle than for thaire ese.

fol. 59v	Bot more he thought hit were to thaire profyte	
	To lete thaym londe, seth they ere now so nere	*since*
1565	To chese of thaym the knyghtes moste perfyte	*perfect*
	Of werres wysest, as may by sight appere,	
	To strengh the londe agayn outwarde powere	*strengthen; against foreign*
	"For I am he," quod he, "and say thaym so	
	My doughter is quene how shulde I be thaire fo?"	*foe*

1570	The messengers unto the kynge sone come	
	And told hym alle as is afore devysed	
	Byfore the barons, who it wele undyr nomme	*received*
	And thought his witte thereof was wele advysed,	
	By hole counsaylle he came, as is comprised,	
1575	In with his flete to reste thaym and disporte	*entertain*
	After thare laboure to glad thaym and comforte.	

How Engiste treted accorde bituixe hym and the Bretons on the plane of Salesbury whare by tresoun he and his Saxons and Englisshe slew all the barons and lordes of Bretons, and putte the kynge in prisoun.

	Bot undyr this thay sette a day to mete	*meet*
	Upon the playne after of Salisbyry	
	Whiche that tyme so Caercaredot dyd hete	*was called*
1580	Bysyde the nunry ys now of Awmesbyry	
	Whare Ambrius abbot founde his cenoby	*monastic community*
	Who dwelte thereyn unto his endynge day	
	In holynesse and contemplacioun ay.	

	The day thay sette, thay mette to trete a trewe	*discuss; truce*
1585	At that same place, the friste day so of May,	*first*
	Foure hundred of the Bretons beste thay drewe	
	To that trety als fele of paynyms lay.	*many; pagans' belief*
	Bot fals Engiste unto his men gan say	
	"Loke every man of us now have his knyfe	
1590	Within his hose to refe his felaw lyfe	*stockings; take*

	"For oon of us by on of thaym shalle stonde	
	So shalle I reule whan we togedyr mete.	
	And whan I say "Nyme oure saxes," lay honde	*Take our knives*
	His fo to styke and caste hym undyrfete.	*stab*
1595	Thus shalle we sla thaym alle with moste quiete	
	And wyn this londe alle hole in governance	
	And on oure fose we shalle so take vengeance."	*foes*

	At day assygned so were thay come and mette	
	On eyther parte afore as was devysed.	
1600	A Bretoun ever afore a payen sette	

Right as Engiste afore it had avysed.
So whan he saw thay were so enteremysed   *mixed*
He sayde "Nyme oure saxes" and than anone   *Take our knives*
Eche payen slewe his make there by hym oone.   *pagan; partner*

fol. 60r   Foure hundre als and sexty of barons
1606   And erles with other whiche had the governaunce
            Of Bretayne thanne were slayne by tho larouns   *thugs*
            Whose corses alle, after that foule vengeance,   *bodies*
            Seynt Eldane so byried by Cristen ordynaunce
1610   In a kyrkeyerde bysyde the cenoby   *church yard; monastery*
            And mansioun of Abbot Ambrii.

            No wondere thof thay that no treson knewe   *though*
            Nor wapyns had thaymselff forto defende   *weapons*
            The parte adverse of wapens purvayed newe[1]
1615   Were lyghtly slayne and brought unto ane ende.
            Yit Erle Eldolle of Gloucestere so kende   *knew*
            The tresoun foule, and fro thaym went away
            And with a pale seventy he slew that day.   *stake*

**How Kynge Vortygere inprisoned gafe to the Saxons and Englisshe grete parte
of Bretayne for his delyverance fro prisoun and went into Wales**

            With that more folke of payens come fulle faste   *pagans*
1620   And toke the kynge and led to Trynovaunte.
            For fere of whiche so was he than agaste   *afraid*
            He graunte thaym alle that thay wold have and haunte   *possess*
            Castels, cytese, and forseletts evenaunte,   *advantageous little forts*
            To lette hym passe alle quyke withoute trublaunce   *difficulty*
1625   Whiche Engiste graunte bycause of thaire liance.   *alliance*

**Nota that Engiste than did call this londe Engistlonde for his name, whiche
aftir sone for shortnesse of langage men called Englonde, bot it dured noght
longe for Aurilius, Uther and Arthure put doun the name of Englond and called
it Bretayne ayeyn (*again*), to (*until*) the commynge of Gurmund, Kynge of Afrike.**

            Thay toke Ebrauke that Yorke ys called nowe
            Lyncolne that than Caerludcourte had to name
            Caergwent also unto thaym gan to bowe
            That Wynchestere is now of fulle grete fame.
1630   Engeste had alle the reme as for his hame   *realm; home*
            And dalte it forthe amonge his knyghtes wyse   *divided*
            By parcelmele as ferre as myght suffise.   *piece by piece*

---

[1] *The enemy, being newly supplied with weapons*

Wharfore so whan the kynge saw that myschefe
That payens hole distroyd the londe aboute *pagans*
1635 To Cambre went so, for socoure and relefe *support*
Whare he bygan to bygge a castelle stoute *build*
To kepe hym fro the cruelle payens route *force*
Whiche as was made the day afore certayne
Upon the nyght forthe right felle doune agayne.

1640 Wharefore his clerkes he asked why was so
Who answerd hym that he the blode shuld seke
Of a yonge chylde that never had fadyr tho *then*
With the mortere to tempre and to eke. *mortar; mix; strengthen*
The whiche thay sayde wold make the mortere steke *stick*
1645 And with the stone to byde for evermore *remain*
Alle suche cyment thay sayde was beste therefore. *cement*

fol. 60v Withoute dilay he sente to seke suche oone
Whare that he myght bene founde in any wyse.
At Caermardyn his men saw children gone
1650 Merlyne was one, who was of grete quantyse, *skill*
Dynabucyus the tother, of hiegh gentrise, *birth*
Chidynge togedur seyd Dynabucyus *Disputing*
"Who was thy fadyr wiste never man yit of us." *knew*

The kynges men whiche yede forto enquere *went*
1655 For suche a childe that fadyrlesse shuld bene
Layd honde on hym and led hym forth in fere *together*
And aske of men if thay his fadyr had sene.
Whiche answerde thus of his fadyr "We can noght mene *determine*
We have herde telle that fadyr had he none
1660 Bot iff it were men say the fende allone." *Unless; the devil*

His moder was kynges doughter of Demecy
In Cambre so is now called South Wales.
A nunne profeste was she in the nunry
Of Seynte Petirs, as we have herde by tales.
1665 Goten and borne she was in South Gales *begotten; Wales*
Wham than sent forthe the mayre of Caermardyne *mayor; Carmarthen*
Unto the kynge and als hire sonne Merlyne.

Whan Merlyne and his modyr so were come
To Vortygerne, he axed hyre anone *asked; immediately*
1670 How that hyre sonne was gote and als by whome. *begotten; also*
She answerde hym that fadyr had he none
That she couth know that ever synde with hire alone *sinned*
Sauf only thus "That in lykenesse of man
A spyrite fayre, as white as any swan,

1675	"Whan I satte with my systers and oure dores close	
	Wolde halse and kysse me in grete dulcitude	*embrace; sweetness*
	No wyght seynge oure doores ought dysclose	*person; open*
	Ne hym myght se for alle his consuetude	*custom*
	So pryvey was his nyghtes solicytude.	
1680	Amonge my systers ofte tymes he lay me by	
	And gatte this chylde that none hym couthe aspy.	*see*

	"Ne how he came, ner yede, I couthe never se	*went*
	So sodenly he vanyshit fro me away.	
	Wharefore I knew it most a spyrit be	
1685	By alle resoun that I can thynke or say."	
	Maugancyus, a philosofre that day,	
	Affermed wele how he had redde and sene	
	How spyrites had with women sogates bene.	*in this manner*

fol. 61r	And to the kynge he seyde right thus that stounde	*time*
1690	"In bokes of oure philosofres olde	
	And in storise many I have welle founde	
	Suche chyldre gote and borne monyfolde.	*begotten*
	For Ampuleyus in his bokes tolde	
	How that bytwix the mone and erthe er falle	*between; moon; are*
1695	Spirits, incubyse that clerkes so do calle.	*Demons; incubi*

	"Whiche parte of man and parte of angel als	
	In nature so ere fully constytute	*made*
	That whan thay wylle thay take a fygure fals	*desire*
	Of mannysshe fourme and women done pollute.	
1700	Suche myght thay have that tyme to execute	
	Thare nature so with woman subtyly	
	That chyldre than thay gete alle verraly.	

	"And happely of hyre so myght befalle	
	That on of thaym hath lyggen so her by	*lain*
1705	Hyre holynesse to dystayne and appalle	*defoul; destroy*
	The rather for she was in sacrary	*holy place*
	More highly sette thanne other to glorify	
	The God above who alle thynge can unfetter	*release*
	That suffred hyre to falle so for the better."	

How Merlyn, prophete of Cambre, came to Kynge Vortygere.

1710	Merlyn than sayde with wordes sad and wyse	*sober*
	"My lorde, why sende ye for my modyr and me?"	
	The kynge answerde "My clerkes say by thare advyse	
	My castelle moste be made with blode of thee	
	The cyment nedes with it moste tempred be.	

1715	So say thay alle his blode that no fadyr hadde	
	Made in mortere my werke wold make right sadde."	*steady*
	Merlyne than sayde "My lorde, it is not so.	
	Thay yow dyssayve with subtyle fals intente.	*deceive*
	Do thaym come forthe and prove it ere I go.	*Make; before*
1720	I shalle afore yow now beynge present	
	Thay bene lyers of that incontynent."	*liars; immediately*
	With that he dyd thaym sone right thare appere	
	Afore Merlyne, as now ye shalle wele here.	
	To whiche Merlyne than sayde on his manere	
1725	"My blode ye sayde moste nede attempred be	*blended*
	With cyment of thys castelle shuld be here.	
	Thynke ye no shame so openly to lee?	*lie*
	Es there ought elles bot only blode of me	
	That lette thys werke to stonde and upwarde ryse?"	*prevents*
1730	Thay answarde hym "Thy blode may it suffyse."	

fol. 61v	"Now lorde," he sayde "lete now youre mynours grave.	*miners; dig*
	Undyr this werke ye shalle so fynde a water	*pool*
	For whiche youre werke may nought stonde sure, ne save.	*safe*
	Than shalle ye se how thay yow fage and flater	*deceive*
1735	Thay ben so wyse that sum what muste thay clater	*talk nonsense*
	And els thay trowe men counte not by thare wytte.	*otherwise; believe; don't respect*
	Bot now ye shalle wele se how fals is ytte."	

	Thay grofe there doune and founde the water clere	*dug; pool*
	In manere of a staunke fulle wyde and large	*pond*
1740	Whiche made the warke to falle as dyd appere	
	And myght not ryse on high, ne yit enlarge.	*be extended*
	The grounde was fals, unstable withouten targe.	*protection*
	The kynge saw wele his wordes were alle trewe	
	And prayd hym so to telle hym that he knewe.	*what*

1745	Merlyn thaym askte what thynge was undyr more	
	That hurte som parte the werke and made it fayle.	
	Thay stode confuse for alle thaire clerkly lore	*learning*
	None answere had that myght his worde prevayle.	*overcome*
	Than sayde he thus "Wele owe ye to bewayle	*ought; regret*
1750	The fals counsaylle and imagynacioun	*conception*
	Ye gaffe the kynge thurgh youre dyssymylacioun."	*deceit*

	Than sayde he to the kynge "Have oute alle clene	
	This water fayre by stremes as may renne	
	And ye shalle fynde two caves large, I wene	*believe*
1755	With dragons two that fight and can nought blynne	*cease*

Whiche strubled have youre werke whare ye begynne."   *disturbed*
The water had oute thay founde right as he sayde
Two dragons grete of whiche thay were afrayde.

1760   The kynge gretly amervelde of his wytte   *marveled*
Hym prayd so to say how he shulde ende.
Who answerde thus "Fle fro the fyre and flytte   *keep away*
Of Constantynes sonnes and defende.   *From; protect yourself against*
For now thay come with sayles alle on ende
Whiche shalle thee brenne within thy castelle closed.   *burn*
1765   Thurgh me thou shalt nought faged ben, ne glosed."   *flattered; deceived*

Thayre fadyr right falsly thou betrayed
The Saxons als to Bretayne for thy spede.   *profit*
Thou sente so for that have thee now afrayde.   *frightened*
Thay waste thy reme thurghoute in lenghe and brede   *length and breadth*
1770   Whose sonnes two shalle pay thee now thy mede   *reward*
Whiche thare fadyrs dethe on thee shalle revenge
At Totteneys shalle thay londe thaym to avenge."

fol. 62r   Whare on the morne thay londed with grete myghte
And conquerde alle whareso thay rode or yede   *wherever; went*
1775   Tylle thay came to the kynge whare he was right
And brente hym in his castelle as I rede.   *burned*
Whiche castelle hight Genareu so indede.   *is called*
Whiche castelle stode upon the Mounte Cloarke
In Hergyge londe on Gway that renneth starke.   *Ercing; Wye; powerfully*

1780   The duke Eldolle of Gloucestere so bolde
With Bretons alle and alle the baronage
A parlement sette and in the felde dyd holde
Aurelyus to croune in that viage   *military expedition*
And to restore hym to his heritage
1785   Was thayre entent and alle thare hole desyre
The Saxons after to waste with swerd and fyre.   *destroy*

.xiiii. capitulum of Aurilius Ambrosius, Kynge of Bretayne.

Thay crouned thare Aurelyus Ambrosii
With legeance hole and fulle submysioun   *allegiance*
By hole consente of comons and clergy.
1790   So forth he yede after that deposessioun   *went; dispossession*
Of Vortygerne, so brente for his prodyssioun   *burned; treachery*
And for falshode he dyd to Kynge Constance
Who putte in hym alle hole hys governance.   *wholly*

	Than went he forthe the Saxons forto seke	
1795	Whiche fled over Humbre with alle thare myght and payne	
	Trustynge to have refute and socoure eke	*refuge*
	Of Scottes and Peghtes and Danes also to seyne.	
	The kynge pursewed with alle his hoste certayne	
	So hastly thay myght nought wele eschewe	*escape*
1800	So mette thay on a felde and togedyr drewe.	

How Engiste was take and slayne, and Saxons and Englisshe discomfyte by Kynge Aurilius Ambros.

	Thay faught fulle sore with strokes grete and grym	
	Bot at the laste the Bretons had the bettyr.	
	The Saxons fled byfore that were fulle brym	*fierce*
	Duke Eldol toke Engyste and gan to fettyr	*chain*
1805	Anone, and to the kynge he sente his letter	
	How he had take Engyste his cruelle fo	
	And shuld hym brynge to hym for wele or wo.	

	And so he dyd, he brought hym to Conan	
	That Connesburgh now hatte so in thise dayse	*was called*
1810	Whare that the kynge after his bataylle than	
	So rested hym his woundyd men to ayse	*ease*
	And with medycyne thare hurtes to appayse.	*cure*
	Duke Eldolle asket the kynge what shuld betide	*happen*
	Of fals Engiste who stode so by his syde.	

fol. 62v **How Bisshop Eldade counsaylde the kynge touchant (*touching*) Engiste**

1815	Bysshop Eldade that was Duke Eldol brother	
	Sayde "Ye shalle do with hym as Samuelle	
	Gaffe dome of oon Agag and none other	*judgment*
	Who taken was, the Bybelle doth it telle,	
	That in his werkes was fressh and cruelle felle	*fierce; villainous*
1820	And chyldre had made many so fadyrlesse	
	Withoute pyté and women hosbondelesse.	

	Whiche Agage so Samuelle the prophete	
	Demed to beheded and decollate	*Judged; decapitated*
	For the grete wronges and mekylle unquyete	*considerable*
1825	Whiche he had made in places seperate.	
	His flesshe also cutte in morcels alterate	*pieces different*
	And sende aboute to townes whare he dyd wronge	
	To make the folke remembre his dedes longe."	*for a long time*

	Wyth that the duke Eldol in his mynde thought	
1830	"Sethe the Byble thus sayth, I may the bettere	

This payen curste that mekylle wronge hath wrought *pagan; much*
Now sla," and led hym forth and dyd unfettere *slay; unshackle*
And with his sworde, by strengh of Byble lettere,
And hedyd hym by that autorité
1835 Whose corse byried was after use of his countré. *body; custom*

How the same bisshop counsailde the kynge touchant Octa and his Saxons and English

In this mene tyme Syr Octa, Engestes sonne,
His cosyn als Ebissa with in fere *together*
With many grete lordes that were wonne *accustomed*
To be wyth hym to Yorke they fled alle fere. *together*
1840 The kynge with hoste layde sege to it fulle nere
For fere of whiche Octa and his company
Came to the kynge bysekynge his mercy *beseeching*

Wyth ropes aboute thare nekkes in pytouse wyse *piteous manner*
To have his grace or turmente at his wille.
1845 The kynge so fulle of pyté asked advyse.
Bysshop Eldade was friste that spake hym tille *first; to*
"The Gabanytes whan Israelles wold thaym kylle
Mercy asked and had, and we may bene
No worse than Jewes seth we be Cristen clene." *since*

1850 The kynge thaym gafe his mercy and his grace
With pyteuse herte and humble yolden chere. *offered expresion*
A grete deserte unto thare dwellynge place *wasteland; for*
Nere Scotlonde so he gaffe thaym in powere
To his lordship ever to be famulere. *subject*
1855 So plentiouse he was alway of grace
Eche wight it had to aske it that had space. *person*

fol. 63r ### Nota how rightfully thys Kynge Aurilyus governed

So after his were, with holy herte and clene *war*
To God alle sette and wronges to refourme
The lawes profyte made jugges to sustene *uphold*
1860 The kyrkes als whiche payenis dyd disforme *churches; pagans; damage*
And cytese waste whare men wold hym enforme
He dyd amende aywhare and reparayle *everywhere; repair*
Thurgh alle his reme and alle his governayle. *dominion*

Alle heyres right and wydews to dewry *heirs; widows; dowry*
1865 Cyteyns burges to have thare olde fraunchise. *Urban freemen; liberties*
Prelates also unto thare prelacy
Agayn restored in alle that myght suffyse. *befit*

And alle that were exilde by thare enmyse
Or wrongfully fro thayre lifelode exiled   *source of livelihood*
1870   He dyd thaym calle agayn and recounsiled.   *restored*

How Merlyn broght to Bretayn the carolle (*ring of stones*) that ere called now the Stonehengles

Than sente he for the prophete hight Merlyne   *called*
To have his wytte fully and his counsayle
A towmbe to make for Bretons whare thay lyne   *lie*
Whiche Engiste slewe thurgh treson and assayle.   *attack*
1875   For whiche Bretons alway may sore bywayle   *bemoan*
So was thare blode rialle there slayne that day
In truste of pese and wasted alle away.

This Merlyne founde and brought unto the kynge
And how that tombe myght beste so be provyde   *planned*
1880   For remembrance and perpetualle durynge.   *enduring*
He sayde right thus "In Irelonde artifyde   *constructed*
Es suche a werke of stones fortyfyde   *Is*
Whiche ever wille laste and dure eternaly
Youre tombe to make and evermore magnify.

1885   "Sende forthe Utere youre brother with an hoste
And lete me with hym thedur sone forth fonde   *go*
And we shalle brynge thaym home withouten boste
And set thaym up whare ye wille that thay stonde.
With wytte I darre and sleght it take on honde."   *dare; cunning; manage*
1890   The kynge anone sente forth fiftene thousonde   *immediately*
With his brother and Merlyne to Irelonde.

Whan thay were londe the kynge Syr Guyllamare   *landed*
Of Irelond so dyd than assemble his hoste
And faught anone with Utere fersly thare.   *fiercely*
1895   Bot Bretons than withouten eny boste
The better had and victory with moste
And so thay wente to Mount Kylormare
Whare the Carolle of Geants stondynge ware.   *Ring*

fol. 63v   The whiche with strenghe that hoste couth nothynge stere.   *move*
1900   Yit Merlyn so with crafte sotyle dyd shippe   *take on board*
The whiche with wynde fulle prosperouse and clere
Into Britayne esely gan thay shyppe
Over these the wawes thay dyd over hype.   *cross*
Whiche Merlyn than with crafte so forth dyd brynge
1905   To Mounte Ambry whare that thay founde the kynge.

Whare in presence of alle rialle estate
And clergy hole assembled in that place
Unto the kynges feste solempnyyate   *feast; solemn*
This Merlyn than right in suche forme and space
1910   As at Kyllormare thay stode whan he thaym race   *extracted*
Thaym sette, the whiche geants fro Aufrike brought
Into Irelonde for vertu that thay wrought.   *power; produced*

Thus were thay sette aboute the sepulture
Of blode rialle that were bytraysed there   *betrayed*
1915   Whiche now so hight the Stonehengles fulle sure   *are called*
Bycause thay henge and somwhat bowand ere.   *hang; are bowing*
In wondre wyse men mervelle how thay bere.   *keep from falling*
The kynge than made archebysshops two that day
Whiche vacant were in Bretayne than I say.

1920   Sampson he made at Yorke religiouse
Of lyfe was ever there with a famouse clerke
Dubricyus at Caerlyoun famouse.
Whiche holy men were ever in thare werke
And seyntes ere by ought that men can merke.   *are; whatever; descry*
1925   In whiche tyme so Pascence, Vortigerne sonne,
In Bretayne londe and grete werre had begonne.

Agaynes whom the kynge his powere brought
Upon hym northe and with hym faught fulle sore
And made hym fle that he to Irelonde sought   *went*
1930   To Guyllomare that prynce and kynge was thore.   *there*
Who hym resette with right gode chere therfore   *protected*
And than thay bothe with hostes styffe and stronge   *powerful*
To Menevue came, Seynt Davyd hath ben longe,

**Nota how Eopa in munkes habite feyned hym a leche and poysond the kynge
wharof he dyed anone**

Dystroyed the toune and countrey alle aboute.   *[They]*
1935   For whiche the kynge sente Uter forth with hoste
For he myght nought for sekenes travayle oute   *illness travel*
He loked whan that he shuld yelde the goste.   *die*
In this mene while Eopa, traytoure moste
That Saxon was, so spake than with Paschence
1940   That he the kynge shuld sla with poysonment.   *slay*

fol. 64r   **Nota, make nevere unknowen man ne your executour or your haire, to bene your phisisien (*physician*), for it is presumed that thise thre wolde purvey for youre deth.**

So to the kynge he come in monkes araye   *clothing*
As he a leche had bene with alle medecyne.   *as if; doctor*
Of whom he was fulle glad and gan hym pray
Hym for to hele by his crafte and doctryne.   *learning*
1945   A drynke ful of venym gan imagyne   *poison; concoct*
The whiche fro he had drunke and lay to slepe   *as soon as*
Afore he woke away the traytoure crepe.

This traytoure so away whare no man wyste   *knew*
Was gone his gate and whan the kynge awoke   *way*
1950   He felte hymselff but dede in poynte to bryste.   *burst*
His counsaylle than anone til hym he toke   *to*
Chargynge thaym alle, for sorow of whom they quoke,   *trembled*
To byry hym in the Geants Carolle
Whan deth his soule hath fro his body stolle.

1955   Thus was he dede and byried so anone   *immediately*
At Stonehengles that alle men calle so now.
With that a sterre so bemouse by hym oone   *star; bright*
Appered grete and clere, that wondere howe   *[it was a]*
And why that it forpassynge other dyd bowe   *surpassing; send forth*
1960   His bemes bright, as was not sene afore,
For whiche men dred and mervelde wondre sore.

How Stella comata (*comet*) appered agayn the deth of Kynge Aurilyus and how Merlyn tolde Uther what it signifyed in alle thynges, and that he shuld bene Kynge of Grete Bretayne.

With that Utere Merlyne tille hym toke   *to*
And shewde hym thare the bemy sterre so bright
And askte hym what it mente, for whiche he quoke,   *trembled*
1965   Wepynge fulle sore astonyd of that sight,   *bewildered*
And sayde "The kynge is gone to God fulle right.
Loke up Utere and haste thee to thy foo   *foe*
The tryumphe now is thyne whare so thow go.   *wherever*

"Kynge of Bretayne now certanly thou arte
1970   Go to thy foose and make no more dylay.   *foes*
Yone sterre berynge the beme so southwarte
Over Fraunce thy sonne it signyfith, I say.
Who shalle over regne to Rome withouten nay   *doubt*
Alle londes for hym shalle loute, tremble and quake   *bow*
1975   Who in his tyme levynge shalle have no make.   *lifetime; peer*

Bot issue shalle he certanly have none
Of his body that worthy conqueroure.
Bot yone fyry dragoun that stonte allone   *stands*
Undyr the sterre fro whose mouth doth poure
1980   A beme bemy that dothe to Irelonde loure   *resplendent beam; scowl*
So signyfyeth thy doughters thou shalle have
Whose sonnes thy reme shalle after crepe and crave."   *come to*

fol. 64v   With that unto Menevue he wente als faste
With Guyllomare to fight and with Pascence
1985   And thay hym mette and nothynge were agaste
Bot sore thay faught and made fulle grete defence.
Bot neverthelesse by knyghtly diligence
This ilke Pascence and als this kynge Guyllamare   *same; also*
In that batayle were slayne and dede right thare.   *dead*

1990   What shulde a man of this matere say more?
The Saxons parte were slayne on every syde
Safe tho that fled to shyppe whiche hasted sore.   *Except*
This Utere than tho Saxons justifyde.   *rendered justice*
Fro thens he rode to Wynchestere that tyde   *time*
1995   In whiche way so the messengers hym sayde
The kynge was dede and in the Carolle layde.   *Ring (i.e., Stonehenge)*

.xv. capitulum offe Kynge Uter Pendragoun, brother of Auril Ambros.

Syr Utere came to Wynchester anone
And crounde was and kynge fully admytte   *recognized*
In se rialle sette up as kynge allone   *throne*
2000   Remembrynge hym with croune as he sytte
Of Merlynes speche his prophecy and wytte
Of the dragons wondere exposicioun
Two dragons made of golde by artificioun.   *artifice*

And one of hem right in the mynstere thore   *monastery; there*
2005   Of Seynte Petyr with grete solempnyté
He offerd than to byde for evermore   *endure*
In remembrance to his posterité.
The tother dragoun for his hiegh rialté
In bataylle ay aforne hym borne shuld be.

2010   For whiche thensforthe the pepyl dyd hym calle
To surname so Pendragon comonly
In Breton tonge thurghout the reme overalle.   *realm*
In Englissh tonge it is to signify
"The dragon hede" as made is memory

| 2015 | Bycause Merlyne had hym so signyfyde | *compared* |
| | To a dragon and for kynge prophecyde. | *as* |

How Octa and Oysa made werre (*war*) on Kynge Uter and how thay were discomfite in bataill

	And than anone Syr Octa Engiste sonne	
	Oysa his sonne that was to hym ful nere	
	By ridynge men that in the South dyd wonne	*dwell*
2020	Fulle certyfyed that kynge was so Utere	
	Aurelyus dede and layde upon his bere.	*bier*
	For whiche thay rode thurghoute the north contré	
	And brente and slewe with grete iniquyté.	*burned*

fol. 65r	And as thay shulde the cyté so aseged	
2025	Of Ebrauke so, that Yorke now hath to name.	
	The kynge with hoste thaym lette, it was unseged,	*obstructed*
	And with thaym faught and fersely on thaym came.	
	Bot dyscomfytte he fled with mekylle grame	*defeated; suffering*
	To Danen Hylle with alle his hoste in route	*troop*
2030	Whare Octa than hym seged alle aboute.	

	Syr Gorloys duke that than was of Cornewayle	
	Sayd "Arme us faste for now it ys at nyght	
	We shalle thaym sla slepynge and thaym assayle.	*slay*
	Thay faught fulle sore thys day and with suche myght	
2035	Thay wylle take reste and truste tomorow right	
	To wynne us sone for hungre and penury	*defeat; lack of resources*
	Sette on thaym now and have the victory."	*attack*

	By nyght thay cam upon the Saxons thare	
	Alle sodenly and slew thaym doune that bode	*remained*
2040	And Octa toke his cosyn fulle of care	
	Oysa also, and alle thare payenhode	*fellow pagans*
	Was slayn and fled for alle thare foule falshode.	
	Wherefore the kynge to Scotlonde dyd than ryde	
	Unto Alclude whare that his pese he cryde	*proclaimed*

2045	Thurghout Scotlonde his lawes welle provyde	*ordained*
	In pese and reste and voydyd tyrany.	*expelled*
	Who rob or stale or made ought homycyde	*any*
	Withoute mercy thrughoute his monarchy	
	Shuld dye therefore withouten remedy.	
2050	The North in pese, to Londoun came fulle light.	*readily*
	Octa and Oysa there he than prisonde right.	

How Kynge Uter made his feest rial at whiche he was take with lovynge of Duke Gorloys wife, on wham he gatte Arthure.

	He comaunde than thurghout alle hole Bretayne	
	That every lorde shulde bene with hym at Passhe	*Easter*
	That solempne feste to worship and obayne	*respect*
2055	Lyke Cristene folke with joy and alle solace	
	In Londoun than, that was his hiegh palace,	
	And every lorde to brynge with hym his wyfe.	
	This was his charge and wille infynytife.	*absolute*

	Amonges other Gorleys, duke of Cornewayle,	
2060	His wyfe dyd brynge, Dame Igerne fressh and pure.	
	Whose beuté thare alle others made to fayle	
	So fulle and hole avysed was Nature.	
	Hyre shappe and forme excede alle creature	
	In so ferre forthe thof Nature wold have wrought	*even if; wished; to create*
2065	The bewté more, hyre kunnynge stretched nought.	*skill*

fol. 65v	Of whose bewté and hyre godelyhode	
	The kynge so foule overcome was and oversette	*shamefully; smitten*
	That it dyd chaunge his myght and his manhode	
	And made hym seke for whiche withouten lette	*delay*
2070	The duke hyre had away sodenly than fette	*fetched*
	Parsevynge wele the kynges chyldelynesse	*Perceiving; foolishness*
	Was sette for love of hyre and wantonesse.	

	And put hyre in a castelle stronge and wight	*powerful*
	Tyntagelle hight upon the sees coste.	*named; coast*
2075	For whiche the kynge was irefulle day and nyght	*angry*
	And hight to fette hyre thens away with hoste.	*vowed; fetch; army*
	Wharfore he came with powere and with boste	
	To Dymyoke whare that the duke than lay	
	And seged it with stregh bothe nyght and day.	*military force*

2080	So segynge thare he dyd hymself dyskure	*besieging; discover*
	To oon Ulfyn and Merlyne pryvaly	*secretly*
	How bot he had the love of Igerne pure	*unless*
	He myght not leve withoute hyre company.	*live*
	Wharfore Merlyne by crafte and juglary	*conjuring*
2085	The kynge and hym and also Syr Ulfyne	
	Dyssymylde than in other lykenesse to enclyne.	*Disguised; shift*

	He made the kynge unto Duke Gorloys lyke	
	And hymselffe lyke in alle symylité	*likeness*
	To Bretelle was the dukes pryvey myke	*[who]; personal friend*
2090	And Ulfyne lyke withouten diversité	

Unto Jordan that knew the dukes pryvyté.   *private affairs*
Thus were thay thurgh his dissymylacioun
Lyke to the duke and his in symylacioun.   *his [intimates]*

This done thay sette a reule the sege to holde   *arranged*
2095   And pryvaly thise thre togedyr wente
To Tyntagelle the lady to byholde
Whom at the yate the portere in dyd hente.   *take (i.e., he allowed them in)*
The kepers alle and als the lady gente
Ful fayne were of his come and hys presence
2100   To plese hym thare with alle thare diligence.

So than to bed he and that lady fayre
Were brought to reste, bot he with besy cure   *obsessiveness*
No lenger wold of hyre be in dispayre
Bot toke anone his cely aventure   *immediately; fortunate chance*
2105   In armes with that womannysshe creature
Whiche of nature tendre was of corage   *heart*
Trustynge it was so done in clene spousage.   *marriage*

fol. 66r   That nyght he gatte on hyre the kynge Arthure
Who after his decese thurgh worthynesse
2110   Redouted was above alle creature   *Honored*
That tyme levynge in honoure and noblyesse.   *living*
Bot than the kynge after this besynesse   *enterprise*
Gan take his leve and right so came message   *leave*
That Gorloys dede was and his vassalage.   *followers*

2115   The lady couth nought so truste that message   *could*
For wele she sawe hym thare so corporaly.
His two servants brought up of tendre age
Thare were with hym and came in company
By alle lykenesse and alle gode polycy.   *counsel*
2120   Thare couthe no man fully have trusted other
So lyke thay were echone of thaym the tother.

The kynge herynge thus leugh and made gode chere   *laughed*
And in his armes hyre kyste enbrasynge faste   *kissed*
Thus sayand than "Gode wyfe I am yit here   *saying*
2125   Thof I be dede, be ye nothynge agaste.   *Even if; afraid*
For alle the harme overgone is and overpaste
That ye of me fro thys day forth shalle have
And fare welle nowe, I pray to God yow save.

"My castelle loste and als my men so slayne
2130   I drede me sore the kynge wille hyder prese.   *advance*
I wylle hym mete and trete to turne agayne   *parley*

	And by som way to trete and gete his pese.	
	And if I may hys ire and wrath not cese	
	I shalle submytte me lowly to his grace	
2135	And so I truste I shalle his love purchase."	

	With that unto his hoste he came fulle fayne	*eagerly*
	Ulfyn and als thys wyse Merlyne prophete	
	Befygurde newe in thare likenesse agayne	*Refigured*
	As thay were firste, and spake with wordes swete	
2140	Unto his men in that skarmyse and hete	*encounter; heat of battle*
	And wan that place as made is remembrance	
	And slew the duke to have his wyfe perchaunce.	

	With alle hys hoste so cam he to that place	
	Of Tyntagelle whare Igerne dyd abyde	
2145	And bade hyre thare with joy and grete solace	*beseeched*
	Hyre womannyshe sorows to layne and hyde	*disguise*
	Whiche by processe was so wele modifyde	*in time*
	That nought in haste it dried up at ones	
	Bot lyte and lyte as it were for the nones.	*little by little*

fol. 66v   **How the kynge bigan the Rounde Table in figure of the ordour of the Saint Grale that Josep made at Avalon in Bretayne**

	A feste rialle he made at his spousage	*marriage*
	And by advyse of Merlyne ordynance	
	The Rounde Table amonge his baronage	
	Bygan to make for fygure and remembrance	
	Right of the table, with alle the cyrcumstance	*in every respect*
2155	Of the Saynte Grale whiche longe tyme so afore	*Holy Grail*
	Joseph made, in Aramathy was bore.	*[who]; born*

	For right as Criste in Symonde leprous house	*Simon the Leper's*
	His soupere made amonge apostels twelve	*supper*
	At his table that was so plentyouse	
2160	At whiche he had the maystere sege hymselve	*principal seat*
	In fygure so of it Josep gan delve	
	Thurghoute his wytte of his fraternyté	*brotherhood*
	To rayse a borde of the Saynte Grale shuld be.	*construct; table; Holy Grail*

	The dysshe in whiche that Criste dyd putte his honde	
2165	The Saynte Grale he cald of his language	
	In whiche he kepte of Cristes blode he fonde	*Of which*
	A parte alway and to his hermytage	
	In Bretayne Grete it brought in his viage.	
	The whiche was thare to tyme of Kynge Arthure	
2170	That Galaad escheved his aventure.	*achieved*

For fygure so and hole remenbrance
Of that table of hole fraternyté   *brotherhood*
The Table Rounde the kynge dyd so enhaunse
Of nobleste knyghtes rialle his regalté   *royalty*
2175   In knyghthode beste and alle fortuyté   *good chance*
Approved ofte in werre and turnament
In batayls als that had grete regyment.   *domination*

Syr Octa than and Oysa bothe in fere   *together*
Thare kepers als, dyd breke oute of the toure   *guardians*
2180   Of London so and home thay yede fulle clere   *went directly*
In Germany to gete thaym there socoure
And toke on thaym agayne a new laboure
With powere grete this londe to have and wynne
And Albany distroyed ere that thay blynne.   *before; ceased*

2185   The kynge was seke and nothynge myght he ryde   *not at all*
For whiche he made Syr Loth of Louthianne   *Lothian*
With hoste to fyghte with thaym and felle there pryde   *bring low*
Who wedded had his doughter hight Dame Anne   *called*
That duke was of alle Louthianne called than
2190   A myghty prynce, hardy and corageouse,
Rightwyse and fayre, and thereto bountyuouse.   *in addition generous*

fol. 67r   Who with thaym faught by dyverse tymes sere   *many*
Some tyme the bettere and some tyme had the worse.
For whiche the kynge dyd ordeyne hym a bere   *litter*
2195   On whiche he was caried so as a corse   *corpse*
With alle his hoste aboute hym with grete forse
And founde thaym than lyggynge in Verolame   *situated*
A walled toune was that tyme of grete fame.

Now heght it so Seynte Albans verryly   *it is called; truly*
2200   Whare that the kynge thaym seged with his hoste
And dange right doun the walles myghtyly.   *knocked*
For whiche anone thay toke the felde with boste
And faught hym by halfe a day almoste.
Bot at the laste Octa and Oysa right
2205   Were slayne bothe two, thare party put to flight.

How the Kynge Uter was poysond of the water of a well that he used to drynk
medled with wyne and other licours

Bot sertayne men there were in this mene while
Saw whare the kynge had water to hym brought
Right of a welle bysyde his halle som while
To drynke with other licours for hym wrought   *drinks; made*

2210	For hys sekenesse to helpe and brynge to nought	
	It envenymde with poysoun and corupte	
	Thurgh whiche his lyfe was waste and interrupte.	*stopped*

	And dyed so in grete and sore distresse	
	And byried was in the Karolle besyde	*Ring (i.e., Stonehenge)*
2215	His brother than with honoure and noblesse	
	As conquerroure so fully glorifyde	
	In rialle wyse wele wrought and artyfyde	*constructed*
	That wondyr was the werke aboute to se	
	So was it wrought with alle nobilité.	

2220	Afore his dethe a castelle yit he made	
	Upon the marche of Scotlond stronge and fayre	*border*
	Pendragoun hight in whiche he dwelte and bade	*called; stayed*
	In that contré whan that he wolde repayre.	*go*
	Of whiche place now the Clifford is his hayre	*heir*
2225	And lorde in fe of alle the shyre aboute	*possession*
	And shiriff als of Westmerlonde thurghoute.	*sheriff*

How the makere of this comendeth this Kynge Uter Pendragoun of worthynesse for to bene myrour and remembrance to other kynges and prynces

	Allas for reuthe so gode a prynce shulde de	*sorrow; die*
	That in sekenesse nought letted for distresse	*ceased*
	Upon his fose on bere to caried be	*litter*
2230	Thaym to distroy he fonde non idelnesse.	
	Whiche to acounte was suche a worthynesse	
	As in my dome he aught of right be shryned	*judgment; enshrined*
	That fro his fose in werres never declyned.	

fol. 67v	He myght be shryned als for worthynesse	
2235	Amonges alle these noble conquerours	
	For his laboure loved none idelnesse	
	To helpe his londe and men with alle socours	*support*
	In tyme of nede agaynestonde turmentours	*withstand*
	The comyn profyte that wasted and destroyed	
2240	Or his comons vexed or yit anoyed.	

	O soverayne lorde, to whom God hath so dygned	*invested*
	The govornaylle with alle the regalté	
	Of Englonde hole to you and youres assigned	*your heirs*
	Thynke on this poynte in alle youre dygnyté	
2245	And lette no sleuthe disteyne youre soveraynté	*sloth besmirch*
	Bot ever be fresshe and grene forto defende	
	The peple hole whiche God hath to you sende.	

xvi chapitle of Arthure Kynge of Bretayne

Arthurs armes

	Arthure his son upgrowynge than pierlesse	*peerless*
	Thurghoute the worlde approved of his age	*regarded*
2250	In wytte and strength, bewté and als largesse,	*generosity*
	Of person hiegh and fayre of his visage	*tall*
	And able in alle to holde his heritage	
	At Cyrcestre than called Caercyry	
	And Caersegent som called it wytterly	*certainly*

	Who was that tyme bot fyftene yere of age	
2255	Whanne Dubrike so, Archebysshop of Caerlyoun,	
	With alle estates of alle his hole homage	
	Assembled thare duke, erle, lorde and baroun	
	By hole advise of alle the regioun	*consent*
2260	Upon his hede dyd sette the dyademe	
	In rialle wyse as dyd hym wele byseme.	*befit*

	Fortune was so frendly at his byrthe	
	That of alle folke he was ever wele beloved.	
	And rychesse als so comforte ever his myrth	
2265	That with poverte he was never sore amoved	*distressed*
	And through corage his herte was ay commoved	*stirred*
	To sette the londe in dewe obedience	
	By alle his wytte and hole intelligence.	

	And sodenly the youth of alle knyghthode	
2270	For his largesse and his liberalité	*generosity*
	Approched so, and came to his manhode	
	To bene subgyttes unto his soveraynté,	*subjects*
	So hole Fortune hyre werdes in propreté	*fate; specificity*
	Unto his helpe and honoure execute	
2275	That alle his wille was sped and insecute.	*performed; executed*

fol. 68r **How Kynge Arthure avowed to werray (*harry*) the Saxons oute of Bretayne and
on the water of Dougles discomfyte thaym**

	He made a vowe atte his coronacioun	
	That Saxons never his londe shulde enhabyte	
	Whiche slew hys eme by poysoun and toxicacioun	*uncle*
	His fadyr als, that knyghtes were perfyte.	
2280	Whose dethes so he thought revenge and quyte.	*repay*
	To Scotlonde than with alle his hole powere	
	He sped hym faste, as seyth the cronyclere.	

	Whan Colgrym knew, that was the capitayne	
	Of alle Saxons, he gatte hym Scottes and Peghtes	
2285	With his Saxons and mette the kynge to sayne	*say the truth*
	Upon the water of Douglas with grete feghtes.	
	Whare the Saxons were slayne anone dounreghtes	*down directly*
	And Colgrym fled away in pryvyté	
	Tylle that he cam to Yorke the stronge cyté.	

	Whither the kynge cam than and seged itte.	
2290	Bot Baldulf thanne his brother nereby was londe	*landed*
	With sex thousonde of men of armes fytte.	*adapted*
	Upon the kynge to falle he toke on honde	
	Of whiche the kynge was done to undurstonde.	*made to understand*
2295	Wharfore he sente Cadore, duke of Cornewayle,	
	To feght with hym who vencoust his batayle.	*vanquished*

	Wharfore Baldulf his berde and hede dyd shave	
	Feynynge hym than to bene a bordioure	*Pretending himself; jester*
	Arayed fulle lyke a fole or els a knave	*dressed; fool*
2300	With harpe in honde fulle lyke a losengeoure	*mimic*
	Amonges the hoste he yede as fals faytoure	*went; deceiver*
	And with his japes so nere the walles went	*tricks*
	That thay within hym knew and up hym hent.	*hauled*

How Cheldryke with multitude of Saxons londed in Albany whare Arthure discomfyte them, and afterwarde sone discomfyte thaym agayne.

	So cam worde to the kynge by his espy	
2305	How Duke Cheldrike with payens multitude	*pagans*
	Was comen oute than new fro Germany	
	With sexe hundre shyppes ful of juventude	*youth*
	Of armed men and archers multitude	
	And londed was that tyme in Albany	
2310	And brente the londe there thurgh his tyrany.	*burned*

	For whiche the kynge by alle his hole counsayle	
	To Londoun wente and to Kynge Howel sente	
	His syster sonne that was withouten fayle	
	Kynge of Lytylle Bretayne so fayre and gente.	*noble*
2315	And prayd hym of helpe and socourement	*requested; reinforcement*
	For whiche he came with fiftene thousond knyghtes	
	To helpe his eme with alle his force and myghtes.	*uncle*

fol. 68v	At Hamtoun londe he than with his meyné	*troop*
	Ressaved fayre as dyd hym wele beseme	*befit*
2320	Like his degré in alkyn rialté	
	That men couthe wytte or els by reson deme.	*judge*

With that anone assembled thare hostes breme.   *fierce*
In days few thay cam to Caerludcourte
That Lyncolne now ys called in every courte.

2325   And Lindcolyne dyd some men than it calle
        In cronycles as made is mencioun
        Whare Coligrym and Baldulf his brother withalle
        Seged the toun with alle intencyoun
        Brennynge the londe with strengh and subvencioun   *destructive force*
2330   Unto the tyme the kynges two ryght thore
        Dyd with thaym feght in batayle stronge and sore

        And venquyste thaym with grete humanyté.   *courage*
        Levynge the sege thay fled at alle thare myght
        Untyl a wode nereby that same cyté
2335   Hight Calidoun with grete defence to fight.   *Called*
        Whare than the kynges two thay came fulle right
        And seged thaym by alle the wode aboute
        That on no syde thay myght nowrewhare breke oute.   *nowhere*

        Whare thay so ware hungred and sore famysht
2340   Tylle thay dyd graunte oute of thare londe trewage   *payment of tribute*
        Unto the kynge so were thay almost ramyssht   *made wild with hunger*
        And prayed hym so that he wolde take hostage
        And lete thaym passe so home to thare lynage
        And never more agayn hym ought offende
2345   To whiche Arthure consent and made an ende.

**How Cheldryke, Baldulfe and Colgrym bicam Kynge Arthurs men and aftir
werred on hym agayn at Bathe whare he discomfyte thaym in bataille.**

        So than Cheldrike, Baldulf and Colgrym
        Who capteyns were to alle the Saxons hoste
        By thayre letters and seles assured hym
        Hys men to bene evermore withouten boste
2350   And Germany also thrugh alle thare coste   *country*
        To bene his men and yelde hym hole trewage   *tribute*
        And there upon delyverd hym hostage.

        And whan thay were upon the se with sayle
        As fals men shulde at Toteneys londe agayne
2355   And to Severne the countrey dyd assayle
        And so to Bathe and seged it certayne.
        Whan it was tolde the kynge he was not fayne.   *pleased*
        Thare hostage than with hym he led anone
        To the cyté of Bathe fulle faste gan gone.

fol. 69r   He hanged thare the hostage for dispyte   *contempt*
2361   Right in thaire sight and than to batayle wente
            And many slew that day withoute respyte
            Tylle Saxons alle were sore forhurte and shente.   *destroyed*
            Wherefore an hylle that toke for strengh and hente   *seized*
2365   The whiche the kynge with myght upon thaym wan
            And slew thaym doune by many thousand than.

            Wherefore thay fled away in multitude
            Unto thare shyppes, Colgryme and Baldulf slayne
            By Arthurs myght and by his fortitude.
2370   So with his swerde he dalte his strokes gayne   *skillful*
            That foure hundred he felled on the playne
            That never seth on grounde myght stonde ne ryse   *afterwards*
            His own persone so gretely dyd suffyse.

            Than sente he forth Cadore, that duke worthy,
2375   To folow on the chace who with thaym mette
            And slew Cheldrike and alle his Saxony
            Who brente and waste and strongly had oversette
            Deveshyre, Dorset and also Somersette.
            For whiche he quytte thaym than so fulle thayre mede
2380   That fro thens forthe to ryde thay had no nede.

**How whare Scottes and Peghtes biseged Howelle kynge of Lasse Bretayne in
Alclude. Kynge Arthure hym reskowed with hoste and drove thaym in to the
Oute Iles.**

            In this mene tyme Arthure herde how Howelle
            His nevew was beseged in Alclude
            By Scottes and Peghtes that ever were fals and felle   *fierce*
            But whils thay were holde lowe in servytude.   *Except*
2385   Wherefore he wente with myght of multitude
            To Alclude so his cosyn to reskowe
            Delyverde hym as he had made a vowe.

            He drofe thaym oute into a loughe so grete   *loch*
            That fourty iles within it dyd contene.
2390   From ile to ile thay fled and had no mete   *food*
            And sexty flodes partyng tho yles betwene   *isles*
            And every ile a roche so had fulle clene   *rock formation*
            Of whiche watyrs went none than to the se
            Bot oon alone in boke that I can se.

How the kynge of Irelonde with Saxons cam into Scotland wham Arthure discomfyte

2395 In whiche tyme than Syr Guyllomore the kynge
Of Irelonde so with grete powere dyd londe
In Scotlonde hole the Saxons into brynge.
Whom Arthure than so fully gan withstonde
With batayle grete that thay were fayne to fonde   *happy; go*
2400 To Irelonde than agayne and forto fle
For alle thaire pryde and contumacyté.   *rebelliousness*

fol. 69v Than came the lordes and alle the hiegh estates
Bysshops, prelates and alle the comonté
With relykes and with cros fulle desolates
2405 Besekynge hym of his humylité
On thaym so sore oppreste to have pyté.
Whom whan he sawe for mercy crie and knele
Pyté hym made to graunte thaym every dele.

How the Archebisshop of Yorke shulde bene primate and metropolitane of Scotland

To Yorke he wente and helde his Cristenmesse
2410 Sorowynge for the Chyrches desolacioun
Whiche Saxons had distroyd thurgh cursydnesse
Whan Seynt Sampson by malignacioun
The archebysshop was put fro mynystracioun
Out of the se was metropolitane   *diocese*
2415 From Humbre northe alle Albany in tane.   *included*

In whiche he sette Pyrame his chapelayne
To reule the Chyrche in alkyn holynesse
With alle the rightes of metropolitane
And kyrkes waste agayne he gan redresse   *churches*
2420 Religeouse place amendyd was I gesse
Alle folke exilde and fro thare right expelled
Agayne restored, whiche payenis had doun felled.   *pagans*

Nota how Arthure toke of the kynges of Albany homage

Thre persones were that tyme of blode rialle
In Albany: Syr Loth of Louthione
2425 That kynge was than of Louthian over alle
That is be south the Scottisshe Se allone;
Syr Aguselle of Albanactes echone;
And Urian of Murrefe was that day
Which of Arthure thare londes had holden ay.   *always*

Arthure wed Gaynore and raysed the Rounde Table of knyghtes worthy

2430 This kynge Arthure than wedded to his wyfe
   Dame Gwaynore came of worthy blode Romayne
   With Duke Cadore brought up fro byrth natyfe
   Whose bewté so alle others dyd dystayne   *exceed*
   So excelent the sothe of hyre to sayne   *truth*
2435 And forpassynge she was alle creature
   Hyre to amende than stretched noght nature.   *excel*

   The Table Rounde of knyghtes honorable
   That tyme was voyde by grete defycience.
   So few thay were thurgh werres fortunable
2440 Thay kepte no reule, ne yit obedience.
   Wherfore the kynge than by his sapience
   The worthieste of every reme aboute
   In it that tyme he put withouten doute.

fol. 70r **Names of the knyghtes of the Rounde Table and the reule of the same ordour**

   That tyme was Syr Morvyde Erle of Gloucestre
2445 And Mauron, Erle of Worcestre so stoute,
   Syr Barent, Erle was than of Circestre,
   Syr Harand, Erle of Shrewsbyry that men doute, *fear*
   Syr Jugence, Erle of Leycestre in route, *in the gathering*
   Syr Argalle, Erle of Warrewyke of grete prise,
2450 And Erle Curson of Chestere, that was so wyse,

   Kynmare, that tyme Erle of Caunterbyry,
   Urgen the Erle was than so of Bathe
   Galluc the Erle was than of Salesbyry
   Erle Jonatalle of Dorchestere so rathe *quick*
2455 Gurgoyne the Erle of Herford dyd no skathe *damage*
   And Syr Bewes, Erle of Oxenforde so wyse,
   Amorawde, Erle of Excestre of pryse, *great value*

   Kynge Aguselle, that was of Albany,
   Kynge Urian of Murref, with Ewayne
2460 His sonne who was than corageouse and manly,
   Kynge Loth that was than kynge of Louthiayne,
   Of Demecy the kynge Syr Uriayne
   That South Wales men now calle and endoce *write*
   The kynge also of North Wales called Venodoce

2465 Cadore, the duke of Cornewayle so plentyuous,
   Donand, Mapcoyl, Peredoure, and Clenyus,
   Maheridoure, Mapclaude, Griffud harageus, *stern*

Gorbonyan, Esidoure, and Heroyus,
Edlein, Masgoyd, Kymbelyne, and Cathleus,
2470   Mapcathel, Mapbangan, and Kynkare,
Colflaut, Makeclauke, Gorbodyan, Kynmare.

These were the knyghtes fully than acounted
That friste he made of the Table Rounde
Two and fourty persounes that amounted.   *came to*
2475   That tyme no mo was to that ordre bounde
Bot as oon dyed the kynge another founde.
Nota   Thare reule was than alle wronges to represse
With thare bodyse whare law myght not redresse.

Nota   Than was no knyght acounte of hiegh emprise
2480   Bot he were thrise in armes wele approved   *Unless*
Or in bataylle had grete excercyse
With ladyse els he was nothynge beloved
With whiche for thay wold not ben unbyloved
So caused thaym to haunten chyvalry   *practice*
2485   To wynne honoure and thanke of thayre lady.

fol. 70v   **How Kynge Arthure conquerde Irelonde, Iselonde, Gotlonde, Orcades,
Danmark, Freslond, with many other londes and isles.**

The somer nexte he wente into Irelonde
And with batayle and tryumphe it conquerde
And made the kynge of hym to holde that londe
That wan it so wit Caliburne his swerde   *with*
2490   With whiche he made alle londes than so ferde   *afraid*
That thay were yolde to his subjeccioun
In his servyce to byde with affeccioun.

Iselonde, Scotlonde and also Orcadese   *Iceland; Orkney Isles*
With alle the iles aboute in cyrcuyté   *ambit*
2495   Danmarke, Freselonde and Norway is no lese   *Friesland*
Alle wanne he so than with his sworde perfyte
Whare alle his knyghtes and pryncis had delyte
To prove thaymselff in batayles fulle sore smyten
As memory of thaym is made and writen.

2500   So rose of hym above alle pryncis fame
Of conqueste grete and alle nobilité
There was no prynce that had so gode a name
For whiche alle folke obeyed his sovereynté
Above alle other pryncis in Cristynté
2505   And specialy alle knyghtes of juventude   *youth*
Drew to his courte and his excelsitude.   *excellence*

Syr Loth he made the Kynge of alle Norway
Hys syster Anne had wed in trew spousage
And crouned hym with dyademe ful gay   *magnificent*
2510 To holde of hym as for his heritage
As cosyn nexte of Kynge Sychelme lynage
That of Norway dyed kynge and to hym gafe
His reme alle hole perpetualy to hafe.

How knyghtes of the Table Rounde fought and acheved aventures

Kynge Arthure than helde the gretteste hous of name
2515 Of Cristen kynges was none so plentyuouse
That thurgh the world of it than rose the fame.
Whiche tyme his knyghtes that were fulle corageouse
Of the Table Rounde thayre reule so vertuouse
To execute thay sought thayre aventure
2520 Thurgh londes fele to prove what were thaire ure.   *many; good custom*

Whiche knyghtes so had many aventure
Whiche in this boke I may not now compile
Whiche by thaymselff in many grete scripture
Bene tytled wele and bettere than I thys while   *chronicled*
2525 Can thaym pronounse, or write thaym with my style.   *pen*
Whose makynge so by me that was not fayred   *embellished*
Thurgh my symplesse I wold noght were enpayred.   *impaired*

fol. 71r For alle thare actes I have not herde ne sene
Bot wele I wote thay wolde alle comprehende
2530 More than the Byble thrise wryten dothe contene
Bot who that wylle laboure on itte expende
In the grete boke of alle the aventures
Of the Seynte Grale, he may fynde fele scriptures   *many writings*

Whiche specify fulle mony aventure
2535 Fulle mervelouse to yonge mennes wytte
Of whiche myne age ow now to have no cure.   *ought; concern*
Bot rather thaym to leven and omytte
To my masters that can thaym intermytte   *present*
Of suche thynges thurgh thaire hiegh sapience
2540 More godelily than I can make pretence.

How Arthure made al his knyghtes of the Rounde Table to telle hym al thaire aventures whiche he putte in writyng for remembrance and for noon avaunt (*boast*) be accounted

Bot whan the kynge longe tyme had so sojorned
In welthes grete and hiegh prosperité

	And alle his knyghtes were home agayn retorned	
	To his howshold fulle of alle felicité	
2545	He made echone to write his fortuyté	*adventure*
	How hym byfelle in armes in his absence	
	To tyme he came agayne to his presence.	

	And every day afore the kynge at mete	
	Amonge his prynces in open audience	
2550	An aventure of armes and a fete	*exploit*
	Reported was so for his reverence	
	That dyd that dede by suche experyence	
	And forto move his yonge knyghtes corages	
	Suche aventurs escheven in thaire viage.	*achieve; errantry*

How he made new knyghtes of the Rounde Table for cause many were spent in the werre

2555	Bycause that in his werres longe contened	
	The Table Rounde bygan aparte to fayle	
	For som were slayne in bataylle mekel mened	*sorely mourned*
	And som by age whan deth dyd thaym assayle	
	Were dede away, for whiche by hole counsayle	
2560	The kynge dyd make knyghtes new for comforte	
	Of it to kepe the honoure and comporte.	*befit*

	Syr Gawen, sonne to Lothe of Louthian,	
	Who Kynge was than of Louthian throughoute	
	And Syr Launcelot de Lake that noble man	
2565	And Kynge Pelles of North Wales than was stoute	
	Syr Persyvalle, whom mony men dyd doute,	*fear*
	Lybews Dysconus, and Syr Colygrenauntt,	
	Syr Leonelle, Degré, and Degrevaunt,	

fol. 71v	Bors and Estore, Syr Kay and Bedwere,	
2570	Guytarde, and Bewes of Corbenny, so wyse,	
	Syr Irelglas, and Mordrede als in fere,	*together*
	Who Gawayns brother was of ful grete emprise.	*action*
	Bot som bokes sayne Arthure was so unwyse	
	That he hym gatte on his syster Dame Anne	
2575	Of Louthiane that was the quene so thanne.	

Whar Kynge Arthure helde moste usualy his housholde in Bretayne

	In whiche tyme so of reste and grete sojorne	
	The knyghtes alle of the Table Rounde	
	Grete aventurs cheved and dyd perfourne	*achieved*
	And brought tyl ende thurghout alle Bretayne grounde	

2580 By enchauntements that made were firste and founde.
     Whiche tyme so than the kynge Arthure rialle
     Hys housholde helde thurghoute Grete Bretayn alle

     At Edynburgh, Stryvelyn, and Dunbretayne,
     At Cumbyrnalde, Dundonalde, and at Perte,
2585 At Bamburgh als, at Yorke the sothe to sayne,
     And at Carlele with knyghtes manly and perte.   *bold*
     And open house he kepte ay in aperte   *view*
     The Table Rounde abowte he dyd remewe   *transport*
     In every place whare that he remewed newe.   *relocated*

2590 At Londoun, als Carnarvan, and Cardyfe,
     At Herforde, als Wynchestere, and Carlyoun,
     In Cornewayle ofte, and Dovere als ful ryfe,   *often*
     And ofte within the Ile of Avaloun
     That Glasenbyry now is of religioun
2595 Thise were his places and his habitacions
     In whiche he had his hertes consolacions.

The reule of the knyghtes of the Rounde Table

     The reule so of that ordoure excellent
     In londes alle forpassynge moste desyred
     Was to distroye sorsery and enchauntement   *sorcery*
2600 And rebellyoun agayne the fayth conspyred.
     The Kyrke, wedows and maydens that required   *Church; widows*
     That wronged were with batayle to redresse
     Agayn al men that dyd thaym ought oppresse.

     Devourours als of the comoun profyte
2605 Rebelles agayne the kynges dygnyté
     Extorsioners that pore men disheryte
     Of londes or gude by myght or subtylité
     Whare suche so were within any contré
     If law myght noght thay shuld make resistence
2610 With bataylle and chyvalrouse defence.

fol. 72r And every yere upon Whisson even   *Whit Sunday (Pentecost)*
     Thay shulde come alle unto the kynges presence
     And alle that feste in his courte byleven   *remain*
     Bot if grete cause that tyme made his absence.
2615 And who cam noght his felows with grete fervence   *ardor*
     That yere shulde seke and helpe hym at thare myght
     Alle severaly echone by hymselff right.   *independently*

And at that feste the reule and ordynance
Was so that thay shulde telle thayre aventure
2620 What so thaym felle that yere and what kyns chaunce
That myght be sette in romance or scripture.
And none avaunt acounted bot nurture   *boast; good upbringing*
To cause his felaws to do so eke the same   *also*
Thaire aventure to seke and gete a name.

**How Arthure conquerde Fraunce with alle londes longynge to it, and slew Kyng
Frolle and Kynge of Fraunce corounde.**

2625 But ever as next the valey is the hille
After longe reste so comyth sharpe laboure
Kynge Arthure so fermely had sette his wille
To conquerre Fraunce as his progenitoure
Maximyan had done with grete honoure.
2630 Wharfore he sente thurghoute his homagers   *vassals*
Prynces and lordes tille come with thayre powers.   *to*

And so anone to Fraunce fulle faste he spedde
Whiche was that tyme a ful noble provynce
By senatours of Rome that powere hedde
2635 To Frolle commytte that was a manly prynce
Whom Arthure sought oute of this londe from hynce
To fyght with hym or els to have alle Fraunce
For evermore in his high governaunce.

Frolle fro hym fled and myght not with hym dele   *have dealings*
2640 And helde hym in the cyté of Parise
Whom Arthure than dyd sege with folke ful fele   *many*
And thought he shuld hym hungre and enfamyse.   *famish*
For fere of whiche Kynge Frolle by hole advyse
To Arthure sente that he wolde with hym fight
2645 With honde for honde to jugen alle the right.

Of whiche profre Kynge Arthure was ful light   *happy*
At day assyned right in an ile thay mette
Withoute the toune bothe armed wele and bright
And strokes sore ayther on other sette.
2650 Bot in affecte Kynge Frolle so sore was bette   *beaten*
That dede he was, the tale forto abbregge   *abbreviate*
Arthure hym slew with Caliburnes egge.   *edge*

fol. 72v   So was the toune of Parise to hym yolde   *surrendered*
And entred yn with alle his hole powere
2655 And kynge was thare and had it as he wolde
And gafe Howelle that was his neven dere   *nephew*

A grete parte of his hoste with hym in fere   *together*
To werre upon the duke of Aquytayne
Whiche Guyen is and Paytow eke certayne.

2660   Kynge Howelle so sore faught with Duke Guytarde
        Of Guyen so and made it alle obay
        To Kynge Arthure and stonde at his awarde   *grant*
        Servyce to do to his highnesse alway.
        And Arthure with his powere every day
2665   Hostayed the londe and with knyghthode conquerde   *Plundered*
        Alle Fraunce thurghout with Caliburne his swerde.

What prynces obeyed to Kynge Arthure and did hym homage and service

        To whom Howelle, kynge of Lesse Bretayne,
        And Geryn, erle of Chartres and Orlience,   *Orléans*
        And Duke Guytarde also of Aquytayne
2670   And alle the lordes of Fraunce to his presence
        Came and obeyed his hiegh magnyficence.
        The kynges als of Naverne and Arrogoyne,   *Navarre; Aragon*
        Of Portyngale, Castele, and Cateloyne,   *Portugal, Castile; Catalonia*

        The duke of Savoy and the duke of Burgoyne
2675   With alle the prynces in cyrcuyte aboute
        Of Ostryche eke the duke withoute essoyne   *Austria; excuse*
        Who to hym cam his lordshyp forto loute   *bow before*
        The duke also of Loreyne withouten doute   *Lorraine*
        The dukes alle and prynces of Almayne,   *Germany*
2680   Of Saxony, and als of alle Germayne,   *Saxony (Germany)*

        The dukes als of Braban and Gellerlonde   *Brabant; Gelderland*
        The duke of Bayre with rialle company   *?Bar, France*
        The erles also of Flaunders and Holande
        With mekylle folke and grete chyvalry.
2685   Of whiche he made knyghtes so than in hy   *haste*
        The worthyeste of worship and knyghthode
        In the Table Rounde than of worthihode.

        And festayde thaym by fourty days right   *feasted*
        In Paryse than with alle grete rialté   *Paris*
2690   And coronde was in alle the peples sight.
        And Quene Gaynore with hiegh nobilité
        Corounde also was in that same cyté
        At that same tyme with alle servyce rialle
        That couthe be done tille estate imperialle.

fol. 73r	With justes eche day for love of ladyse specialle	*jousts*
2696	Whiche with the quene were dwellynge in servyse	
	Whose bewté was high in universalle.	
	Some wedowes were fulle womanly and wyse	
	Some wyfes were of bewté bare emprise	
2700	And some virgyns als, fresshe as rose in May,	
	Some deflorate whiche semed maydyns gay.	*not virgins*

Bot for to speke of Gaynores grete bewté
Whiche forpassynge alle others dyd excelle
And fourmed was in alle femynyté
2705 Als ferre as couthe Nature wyrke and expelle
Of womanhode she was the floure and welle   *flower; source*
So aungellyke and so celestialle
That no bewté myght hirs in ought appalle.   *overshadow*

How Kynge Arthure dwelled nyne yeres in Fraunce, in whiche tyme the knyghtes of the Rounde Table sought and acheved many aventures.

Nyne yere he helde his rialle se in Fraunce   *seat*
2710 And open howse gretly magnyfyde
Thurghoute the worlde of welth and suffisshaunce
Was never prynce so hieghly glorifyde.
In whiche tyme so the Rounde Table multiplyde
And aventurs dyd seke cotydialy   *daily*
2715 With grete honoure as made is memory.

And whan he had so bene in Fraunce nyne yere
He toke purpose to passe home to Bretayne
At Caerlyoun his cyté fayre and clere
At Pentecoste to holde and to contayne
2720 His feste rialle thare to be crounde agayne.
For whiche he made somouns to every prynce
And lordes alle of every hole provynce

At it to bene and every worthy knyght
He sente his lettre thedyre forto come
2725 To his cyté that Carlyoun so hight.   *called*
To whiche alle men that dwelle of north halfe Rome
In Severne myght arrife both alle and some   *one and all*
So navigalle that ryvere is of streme   *navigable*
That shyppes thare myght londe of every reme.   *realm*

2730 And in that tyme Arthur helde his counsayle
At Parisse than pese and lawes to conferme   *peace*
And ordynaunce there made and governayle   *governance*
And alle customes of olde he dyd afferme.

	His londes sette for tribute and for ferme	*control*
2735	By his balifs and shirrifs alle aboute	
	Thurgh his regence that tyl hym than dyd loute.	*obey*

fol. 73v	He gaffe Bedwere that was his botyler	*butler*
	The Duchy so alle hole of Normandy.	
	And Kay he gaff that than was his pantere	*in charge of his pantry*
2740	Of alle Aungoy the noble riche duchy.	*Anjou*
	And other provynce to men that were manly	
	He gaff fulle faste in alle that myght suffise	
	For whiche his name thurghoute the world gan ryse.	

How Kynge Arthure came to Bretayn coronde at Carlioun aftir he departe oute of the reme of Fraunce

	This noble kynge to Bretayne gan retorne	
2745	And at his terme assigned so afore	
	At Carlyoun he cam there to sojorne	
	His feste to holde to prynces lesse and more	
	To lordes also prelates and clerkes of lore	
	Knyghtes and squyers with alle the comonté	*citizenry*
2750	As ordeyned was by his hiegh magesté.	

	On Whissonday that hight so Pentecoste	*Whitsunday; was called*
	Kynges and prynces thurgh his domynacioun	
	Compered there of every reme and coste	*Appeared; area*
	To se that feste and that solempnysacioun	*ceremonial celebration*
2755	And servyce als at his coronacioun.	
	And of the quene as for hyre corounement	
	That same day sette togedyr by oon assent.	

	Archebysshops thre at that feste dyd apere	
	Two hundreth als of philosophres wyse	
2760	In astronomy approved clerkes were	
	Thurgh whiche of thynge to come thay couth provyse	*foresee*
	And telle that shulde byfalle and on what wyse.	
	Suche was thayre witte and als thaire grete doctryne	
	Of thynge to come the certeyne to diffyne.	

2765	Whiche kynges and prynces everychone	
	And erles als with other noble knyghtes	
	Of the Table Rounde were knyghtes made anone	
	Whiche presed were in batayle and in fyghtes	*commended*
	Forpassynge other that moste had sene by sightes	
2770	Of honoure and travayle of knyhtlyhode	
	Of nurture als worshyp and worthyhode.	

Whiche prynces so it nede no more reherse
For alle that I have named so above
Bysyde prynces that were his offycerse
2775   That bounden were by homage and by love
To serve hym thare orwhare that he remove.   *anywhere*
Whiche were two kynges of Wales that were manly
And kynges thre also of Albany

fol. 74r Kynge Guyllomare, that kynge was of Irelonde,
2780   And Gunvase als, the kynge of Orcadese,
Kynge Malvase als that than was of Iselonde
And Doldayn kynge of Gothlonde was no lese
And Aschille, kynge of Denmarke, proude in prese,   *battle*
And Loth also that kynge was of Norway
2785   And Duke Cadore of Cornewayle redy ay

The kynge of Man, the Dusze Piers alle of Fraunce,   *Twelve Peers*
And of Bretayne alle hole the baronage
With provostes alle, that cytese governaunce   *magistrates*
In Bretayn had by auncyen pryvylage
2790   To maken joy and also sure plausage   *praise*
Of his tryumphe and coronacioun
That than shuld be with grete solempnysacioun.

Whom Seynte Dubrike the archebisshop so wyse
Of Caerlyoun that than was hyegh prymate
2795   The kynge corounde in alkyns rialle wyse
As longed to his hyegh and dygne estate   *worthy*
And as of olde it was preordynate   *ordained*
With coroun riche of golde and dyademe
That never prynce it dyd so wele beseme.   *suit*

2800   The archebysshop of Londoun helde so than
The kynges right arme, that was so his servyce.
The archebysshop of Yorke the lefte up wan   *sustained*
That tyme so was his dette and excercyse.   *duty; customary practice*
The servyce alle and als the obsequyse   *dutiful service*
2805   Seynt Dubrike dyd so in that mynstere fayre
Of Seynte Aron whare than was alle repayre.

Whiche was the se than metropolitane
Foundyd fully of gode religioun
Where byried was Seynt Dubrike not to layne   *conceal*
2810   To whom the folke in thare opynyoun
For alle desese had grete devosioun   *illnesses*
To seke hym ofte and make thaire offerynge
So gloryus was he in alle wyrkynge.

How the kynges of Albany, of Wales, and the Duke of Cornwaille, bare foure swerdes at his coronacioun afore hym.

	Kynge Aguselle of Albanyse provynce	
2815	The kynge of Demecy that South Wales hight	*was called*
	The kynge of Venodoce that worthy prynce	
	That now North Wales man calle it so fulle right	
	The duke Cadoure of Cornewayle prynce of myght	
	Foure swordes of golde afore Kynge Arthure bare	
2820	As fore thare londes so holdyn of hym ware.	

fol. 74v	It was servyce of thayre londes of right	
	Whiche thayre elders of longe antiquyté	
	Afore had done tille his auncesters of myght	*to*
	At alle suche festes of grete solempnyté	
2825	Thus fro the chyrche, that was the prymates se,	
	Thay worshyp hym so in that humble wyse	
	Of olde duté hym doynge that servyce.	

	Many thousand knyghtes homward so wente	
	Afore hym than to his palays rialle	
2830	Fresshely arayed in clothes of ryche extente	
	With thousondes fele of mynstrals pryncipalle	
	The noyse of whiche was so celestialle	
	Thare couthe no wight it fro joy of heven	
	Dyscerne in ought so were thay lyke and even.	*Distinguish; similar*

2835	And fro the chyrche of Seynt July that tyde	*time*
	The quene Gaynore the godeliest on lyve	
	With kynges led in rialle clothes and syde	*ample*
	Corounde with golde richely as his wyfe	
	With maydens fele to nombire infynytise	
2840	That no wyght couthe thaym telle, ne yit discryve,	*describe*
	Ne yit in boke no clerke that couth subscryve.	*write*

How the quenes of south Wales, north Wales, and the Duchesse of Cornwaylle, bare foure whyte culvers (*doves*) afore the quene Gaynore.

	The quenes of Northe Wales and of Albany	
	Of South Wales als than dyd hyre that servyce	
	The duchesse with of Cornewayle certanly	
2845	The fourth she was whiche dyd that obsequyse	*service*
	Thay bare afore hyre than as was the gyse	*custom*
	Foure doufes white with knyghtes multitude	*doves*
	And mynstralsy so fulle of dulcytude.	*sweetness*

	The kynge was sette in se imperialle	*throne*
2850	So was the quene with prynces of dygnyté	
	And served wele at that high feste rialle.	
	Duke Kay stewarde was than by hole decré	
	For his wysdome and his habilité	*skill*
	Afore the servyce came with a yerde in honde	*baton*
2855	Of sylvere fyne afore the kynge dyd stonde.	

A thousond knyghtes with hym to serve the halle
Both he and thay clothed alle in ermyne
From the dressoure the mete to bere over alle *counter*
With squyers, marshals and usshers gode and fyne. *porters*
2860 And ay afore a lady femynyne
A worthy knyght was sette for grete comforte
Hyre forto chere with daliance and disporte. *polite conversation; flirtation*

fol. 75r And Duke Bedwere was chefe butelere *butler*
A thousond knyghtes had clothed in a sute *matching garments*
2865 In clothe of golde as fyne as myght affere *befit*
Whiche served so the drynkes of refute *excellence*
Of dyverse wynes there spente and distribute *poured out*
So plentyuouse that wondere was to se
The grete foysoun of wynes and dyversité. *plenty*

2870 Thetys that was of waters chefe goddesse *Thetis*
Thare had of thaym that tyme no regyment *sovereignty*
For Bachus so thare regned with alle fulnesse *Bacchus*
Of myghty wynes to every mannys intente
Shad oute plenté so at that corounemente *Poured*
2875 To alle estates that there were moste and leste
For honoure so and worshyp of the feste.

The tyme so of that feste imperialle
Everiche a day justes and tournament *jousts*
Thikfolde thay made for ladyse in specialle *Aplenty*
2880 With alle maystrise provynge in thaire entente *feats*
That longed so to knyghthode and appente *pertained*
And musycanes songe notes musicalle
And poetes shewed thaire muse poeticalle. *exhibited*

The myrth and joy, the richesse and aray,
2885 The fare, the feste, the worshyp and servyse,
The nurture and the bewté of ladyse gay
There couth no wyght with alle his wytte suffise
To telle it alle by ought he couth devyse
So rialle was it alle in generalle
2890 And forpassynge estate imperialle.

And every day the quene yede sertanly   *went*
To that mynstere with many worthy man
Of Seynte July who Aarons felaw bodyly
Was whan Maxence had sent Maximyan
2895   Into this londe whare he dystroyed than
The Cristen fayth and slewe than Seynte July
And Seynte Aron thurgh his fals tyrany.

Whiche mynstere than a nuniry was devoute
Of vyrgyns clene without any vyce
2900   That served God fulle wele bothe in and oute
In prayers and in alle devyne servyce
Whiche she uphelde alway of hiegh emprice   *renown*
And thought therein to have hyr sepulture   *burial*
Whan that hyre lyfe no lengare myght endure.

fol. 75v   **Whan Saynt Dubrike dyed Saint David was made Archebisshop of Caerlyoun**

2905   But Seynte Dubrike that than archebysshop stode
Cesed mekely and hole forsoke his cure   *office*
Purposynge than in holy lyfe and gode
In ermytage whils that he myght endure   *hermitage*
Alle solitary for any aventure
2910   To plesen God in prayere wache and excuby   *nightly prayer; vigil*
Fastynge, penaunce and leve his prymacy.

In whose stede so Davyd the kynges eme   *uncle*
Was sette whose lyfe ensample of alle godenesse
Was after than, as sonne doth sprede his beme
2915   After mystes foule and grete derkenesse
Who afterwardes Seynt Davyd was doutlesse
An holy saynt and canonysed
By alle the Chyrche and autorised.

Elyden was than made Bisshop of Alclude, the whiche som say it is a litil fro Carlele at ende of the Peghte Walle, and som say it is Carlele and other some say it is Dunbretayne, bot aftir (*according to*) Policronicon it is at ende of the Peght Walle, and aftir Bede also.

The ile that was of Alclude than I gesse
2920   Whiche Dunbretayne hatte now and is named   *is called*
That tyme was voyde and also bysshoplesse.
Whiche se for sothe fulle gretely than was famed   *diocese*
Whiche at Glaskowe translate ys and hamed   *Glasgow; has its home*
The kynge gafe than estate pontificalle
2925   To Elidenne of that se cathedralle.

	And whan that feste rialle was dissolved	
	That every prynce homwarde wolde retorne	
	Within his mynde he thought and faste revolved	
	With plesance howe he myght shorte his sojorne	
2930	And to his londe agayne forto attorney.	*return*
	For whiche thay sought to his magnyficence	
	Alle holyly with alle thaire diligence	

	The kynge than dyd the grete estates rewarde	
	As dyd acorde to thaire nobilité.	
2935	So dyd he other by gode and hole awarde	
	Londes thaym gafe of grete sufficienté	
	Acordynge to thaire oportunyté	*As was appropriate to them*
	So largely that thurgh the world his name	
	Of liberalté than rose and spronge the fame.	

2940	He thonked thaym of thaire comynge so ferre	
	Prayand thaym alle eche prynce in his estate	
	To se his welfare was nothynge to hym derre.	*more precious*
	Than thaire persons with hym resociate	*associated*
	And hevy was of chere and desolate	
2945	Whan thay departe so fro his hiegh presence	
	Whiche dyd excede alle prynces regymence.	*government*

fol. 76r **How whan his knyghtes of the Rounde Table were present that Galaad sette and acheved the Sege Perlouse in the Rounde Table as the grete story of the Saynt Graal proportes in the story of the grete aventures of Arthure and his knyghtes contened, aftir Waltier of Oxenford that put in wrytynges in *Policraticon* that he made of Cornewail and Wales.**

	And at that feste than next of Whissonday	*Whitsunday*
	His knyghtes alle than of the Table Rounde	
	Within Bretayne that were reseant ay	*residing*
2950	Appered hool afore the kynge that stounde	*time*
	As by the reule of it thay were sore bounde	
	At his cyté of Carlyoun so fayre	
	Whare than his courte rialle dyd repayre.	*assemble*

	Whare Galaad of fiftene yere of age	
2955	The godelyest wyght afore that men had sene	*person*
	Whom Launselot gat by hole and fulle knowlage	
	Of Pelles doughter, that longe the kynge had bene	
	Of Venodoce, after whome she shuld be quene,	
	Came sodenly at mete into the halle	
2960	Armed fulle clene, obeyed the kynge in alle,	

And afterwarde the quene with hyegh honoure
The lordes alle, and knyghtes of worthynesse,
And ladyse fayre and fressh of thare coloure.   *complexion*
And than he yede unto the sege doutelesse   *(i.e., Galahad) went; seat*
2965   Of the Rounde Table with fulle grete hardynesse
And sette hym doune whiche was the Sege Perilouse   *Siege Perilous*
Whare never none satte bot Arthure redoutouse.   *formidable*

For alle other that it had presumed
Alle utterly were shamed and mescheved   *undone*
2970   Or brente therein or otherwyse consumed   *burned*
Saufe he allone that had it wele escheved.   *achieved*
For whiche the knyghtes echone hole beleved
He was the same persone of whom Merlyne
Sayde shulde descende of Nacyan by lyne   *Nacian*

2975   The tente persone fro hym lynyaly
Who shulde acheve and fully brynge to ende
The aventurs, as made is memory,   *chronicle*
Of the Seynte Graal whiche no man there than kende.   *Holy Grail*
For whiche thay alle anone to hym attende
2980   In alle worshyp to do hym high plesaunce
As he in whom thay truste grete governaunce.   *moral discipline*

At soupere als on Whissonday at even   *supper*
Unto his sege he wente with grete constance   *seat*
And sette hym doun his fortune forto preven   *make trial of*
2985   Whiche wele he cheved with cherefulle countenance   *achieved*
To alle the knyghtes fulle hyegh and grete plesance
Trustynge fully he shulde do grete honoure
To alle knyghthode that was in that ordoure.

fol. 76v   **How the Saynt Grale appered in Kynge Arthur hows (*house*) at soupere, and
how Galaad made a vowe to seke it to he myght knowe it clerly, to whom his
felaws gafe thaire servyce a yere, as is contened in the storie of the Seint Grale
writen by Giralde Cambrense in his *Topographie of Wales and Cornwail.***

At whiche soupere the wyndows alle dyd spere   *close*
2990   And dores als with noyse fulle merveillouse
Right by thaymselff of whiche alle men had fere
Trustynge there came som case aventurouse.   *happening*
And with that so the Saynte Graalle preciouse   *Holy Grail*
Flawe alle aboute within the halle fulle ofte   *Flew*
2995   Flyghtrande fulle faste above thaym alle on lofte.   *Flying*

And sodenly the wyndows gan to opyn
The dores also, as sayth the cronyclere,

	And forth it wente and eche man gat his wopen	*weapon*
	Bot more of it thay couth not se ne here.	
3000	Bot on the morowe Galaad dyd appere	
	Afore the kynge at mete and made a vowe	
	To seke it ever tille that he fynde it mowe.	*may (might)*

	Wyth that the knyghtes that were aventerouse	
	Of the Rounde Table thare graunted hym that yere	
3005	Thaire servyce hole his vow so corageouse	
	For to acheve and also to conquere.	
	To whiche thay made avowes syngulere	*individual*
	Praynge the kynge Galaad to make knyght	
	The whiche he dyd and gaffe hym armes right.	

3010	To whom he sayde "I shalle no shelde me take	*shield*
	Afore I have it gete by aventure	
	Ne two nyght ligge in o place for youre sake	*one*
	Whils I may ryde and with travaylle endure	
	Tylle I have founde this thynge in alle fygure	
3015	And fully know fro whyne it came and howe	*whence*
	And what it is, here make myne avowe."	

How Kynge Arthure made his compleynt at thaire departynge

	With that he toke his leve and forth he rode	
	And alle the knyghtes of the Table Rounde	
	Toke leve echone no lengare there abode.	*remained*
3020	But forth with hym thay rode as thay were bounde	
	By thare avowes whiche thay had made that stounde	*time*
	For whiche the kynge morned with dolefulle herte	
	At thare partynge with wepynge teres and smerte	*bitter*

	Saynge "Allas what shalle I do or say	
3025	My knyghtes alle that were my joy and hele	*health*
	The membres eke to kepe my body ay	*organs*
	My soules ese and alle my hertes wele	*welfare*
	My londes helpe in nede fulle trew and lele	*loyal*
	Thus sodenly from me to passe thys stounde	*time*
3030	Unto myne herte it is the dethes wounde.	

fol. 77r	"O God, seth deth wolde briste myne herte in tweyne	*since; two*
	Who shalle meyntene my coroun and my rightes?	
	I trow no more to se thaym efte agayne	*trust*
	Thus hole togedyr and so godely knyghtes.	
3035	Wold God I myght make myne avowe and hyghtes	*promises*
	To folow thaym in what londe so thay go	
	And take my parte with thaym in wele and wo."	*joy and sorrow*

How Sir Galaad had hys sheelde, swerde and his speere at Avalon, and how he achevved the Saynte Grale and made was Kynge of Sarras and made knyghtes of the ordour of Saynt Grale in significacioun of the fraternité that Joseph of Arymathy (*Arimathea*) had made afore, as Girald aforsaide specifieth in his saide *Topographie of Wales and Cornwail*.

	With that Galaad rode forthe so with his route	*troop*
	At every way he made a knyght departe	
3040	To tyme thay alle severally so were gone oute	*Until; separately*
	And none lefte than, so had echone thaire parte.	
	And iff on mette another in any arte	*one; place*
	His reule was so he shuld his felawe telle	
	His aventurs what so that hym befelle.	
3045	And als sone as thaire way lay sondry wyse	
	Thay shulde departe, and mete no more agayne	
	Bot aventure it made thurgh excercyse	*Unless*
	Of grete laboure that thaym did so constrayne	
	By dyverse stretes whiche togedir layne.	*roads*
3050	And whan he had his felawes alle convayed	*accompanied*
	He chese his way fulle like a knyght arayed.	
	Bot so Galaad than came to Avalone	
	Whare holy men he founde of grete perfeccioun	
	Whiche were fulle glad of hym than everychone	
3055	And made hym chere with alle affeccioun.	
	Thay shewed hym thare thynges in thayre subjeccioun	
	A shelde, a spere, a sworde, as thare was breved,	*noted*
	Whiche never man bare bot he were sone mescheved.	*in trouble*
	Bot than thay sayde in bokes thay founde it wreton	
3060	Kynge Evalache the shelde of olde there lefte	
	Whiche is alle white, as ye shalle se and wyten,	*know*
	With crosse of blode fro Josep nose byrefte	
	Who sayde there shulde no wyght than bere it efte	*afterwards*
	Withouten deth, mayme, or adversité,	
3065	Bot oon that shulde leve in vyrgynyté.	*Except one who*
	The spere, the swerde was by Duke Seraphe	
	There lefte that tyme who after hight Nacyen	
	Of whiche thay founde writen of antiquyté	
	The same periles who bare thaym after then	
3070	Sauf he allone that were amonge alle men	*Except*
	A vyrgyn knowe and in vyrgynyté	
	Shulde de at laste and of his blode laste be.	*die*

fol. 77v	And shulde acheve the Seynte Graalle worthyly
	And kynge so be of Sarras withouten doute
3075	Of Orboryke also duke verryly
	By heritage of auncetry thrughoute.
	And cheve he shulde amonges alle the route	*achieve; company*
	The Sege Perilouse in the Table Rounde
	That never myght knyght withouten dethes wounde.

3080   What shuld I more say of thys worthy knyght
That afterward acheved this prophecy?
For as it spake so was he after right
And verifyed fulle hole and openly
As writton had Josep off Aramathy
3085   That holy knyght with God fulle welle beloved
As by his werkes it is welle sene and proved.

The shelde he hange upon his shuldere than
And gyrde hym with that swerde of grete emprise.   *renown*
The spere in honde he toke fulle lyke a man
3090   And toke his horse right on a knyghtly wyse.
The holy men he prayed withoute fayntyse   *delay*
To pray for hym with besy herte and pure   *solicitous*
And forthe he rode to seke his aventure.

That every yere the knyghtes at Whissonday
3095   To Arthure came so by his ordynance
And tolde hym alle thaire aventures ay
Whiche he dyd putte in boke for remenbrance.
So dured thay and kepte that governance   *endured*
By yeres fele and ay agayn returned   *many*
3100   At that same feste whare that the kynge sojorned.

Bot so it felle Galaad was than kynge
Of Sarras and of Orberike alle hale   *healthy*
Upon his queste bysyly pursuyynge
Whare he sette up the Table of Seynte Grale   *Holy Grail*
3105   In whiche he made an ordre vyrgynale
Of knyghtes noble in whiche he satte as chefe
And made suche brether of it as were hym lefe.   *dear*

Syr Bors was oon, another Syr Percyvalle,
Syr Claudyus a noble knyght of Fraunce
3110   And other two nere of his blode with alle
Thre knyghtes als withouten variaunce
Of Danmarke so of noble governaunce
And thre knyghtes als of Irelonde excelente
Whiche twelve were alle of noble regymente.

fol. 78r   **What the reule of ordour of Saynt Graal was, here is expressed and notifyed, as is contened in the book of Josep of Arymathie and as it is specified in a dialoge that Gildas made, *De Gestis Arthuri*.**

3115   Whose reule was this by Galaad constytute
       To leve evermore in clennesse virginalle   *purity*
       Comon profyte alway to execute
       Alle wronges redresse with bataylle corporalle
       Whare law myght nought have course judicialle
3120   Alle fals lyvers his londe that had infecte
       Forto distroy or of thaire vice correcte

       The pese to kepe the laws als sustene
       The fayth of Criste, the Kyrke also protecte
       Wydews, maydyns aywhare forto mayntene   *everywhere*
3125   And chyldre yonge unto thare age perfecte
       That thay couthe kepe thaymselfe in alle affecte.   *manner*
       Thus sette it was in hole perfeccioun
       By gode advise and fulle cyrcumspeccioun   *deliberation*

       So endurynge fulle longe and many yere
3130   To fate of dethe and perturbacioun
       And toke his soule unto the blisse ful clere
       Therein evermore to have his habitacioun
       Eternaly withouten lamentacioun.
       Whiche tyme than so he made Syr Borse there kynge
3135   That ordre forthe to kepen over alle thynge.

       How Percyvalle broughte Kynge Galaad hert closed in gold to biry at Avalon, and alle the aventures of the Saint Gralle wryten to the Kynge Arthure, whiche he made bene remembred in Bretayn in grete writynges and notable as Giraldus Cambrensis wryteth in hys *Topographie of Cornwail and Wales*.

       So after his deth agayne the Whissonday
       Syre Percyvalle came into Grete Bretayne
       And dyverse knyghtes that were with Galaad ay
       Of that ordoure so cam with hym agayne
3140   At whiche tyme so the kynge of thaym was fayne   *joyful*
       And asked how Kynge Galaad hys compere   *companion*
       Dyd fare of hele fulle faste he dyd enquere.   *health*

       Who tolde hym alle the wondere aventures
       That never man myght acheve bot he alone
3145   Whiche Kynge Arthure thanne putte in hole scriptures
       Remembred ever to be whan he were gone
       Whiche mervelouse so were and many one

Fro tyme he wente so fro his hiegh presence
Unto his deth in knyghtly diligence.

3150   And to the kynge his herte in golde preserved
As Galaad had comaunde he than presente
Besekynge hym for that he had hym served
It to entere at Avalon anente   *near to*
The sepulture and verry monument
3155   Whare Josep lyeth of Aramathy so gode
Bysyde Nacien that nere was of his blode.

fol. 78v   And there to sette his shelde that Josep made
Whiche was the armes that we Seynt Georges calle
That aftir thare fulle many yere abade
3160   And worshypt were thurghout this reme over alle
In so ferre forthe that kynges in especialle
Thaym bare alway in batayle whare thay wente
Afore thaym ever forspede in thare entente.   *succeeded*

Whose hole requeste the kynge anone dyd spede
3165   With alle his knyghtes in honorable wyse
His herte enterde at Avaloun I rede   *interred*
Whare men sayde than that Nacyen so lyse   *lies*
With dirige and devoute exequyse   *funeral rites*
In alle suche wyse as longed to a kynge
3170   And als his shelde above hym there he hynge.

**How Templers and Hospitilers were founded in figure and significacoun of
the fraternyté and ordoure of the Saynt Grale, and the Table Rounde was made
in significacioun of the Saynte Grale.**

Of whiche ordre of Seynte Graalle so clene   *Holy Grail*
Were after longe founded than the Templers
In figure of it writen, as I have sene,
Oute of the whiche bene now Hospitulers
3175   Growen up fulle hiegh at Rodes withouten peres.   *Rhodes; equals*
Thus eche ordre were founded upon other
Alle as on and echone others brother.   *one*

So was also the Table Rounde araysed
In remembrance alle of the worthy Table
3180   Of the Seynte Grale whiche Josep afore had raysed
In hole fygure of Cristes soupere comendable.
Thus eche ordoure was grounded resonable
In grete vertu and condygne worthynesse   *proper*
To Goddes plesyre and soules heelfulnesse.   *health*

How Arthure helde hys feest at Carlioun whare the ambassiatours of Rome toke hym lettres fro Lucyus Emperoure

3185   At Pentecoste than nexte there after folowynge
        The kynge wyllynge, with hertes sore desyre
        To sene his knyghtes, olde also and yynge
        Dukes and erles thurghoute his hole empyre
        And barons alle and knyghtes he dyd requyre
3190   To ben with hym than at his feste rialle
        At Carlyoun that Camalot some dyd calle

        The kynges and prynces and prelates sprittualle
        Of Wales, Irelonde, and Iles of Orchadese,
        Of Denmarke als, and Norway than withalle,
3195   Of Albany, and of Gothlonde no lese,   *Gotland*
        Of Iselonde als, he loved so wele grete prese,
        The Dusze Piers alle thurghoute the reme of Fraunce   *Twelve Peers*
        Of Lesse Bretayne the kynge with alle plesaunce.

fol. 79r   Whiche came alle hole at his high comaundemente
3200   In grete aray for worshyp of his feste
        At whiche feste than was redde by his comaundente
        Eche day at mete, whanne served were moste and leste,
        Feel aventures of knyghtes whiche had preste   *many; fought*
        In batayls sore and had grete worthynesse
3205   In thaire laboure and knyghtly besynesse.

        This feste so dyd by fourty days endure
        With myrthe and joy with songe and mynstralsy
        Justes every day for ladyse fresshe and pure
        At tournaments his knyghtes to magnyfy
3210   And entyrludes played fulle coriously
        Revelle, daunsynge, and lovynge paramours,
        Romauns and gestes redynge of grete honours.   *Stories; narratives*

        The metes and drynkes were there so plentyuouse
        That alle men were amervelde of the feste   *astonished*
3215   The kynge also of gyftes bountyuouse
        The quene also to able men moste and leste
        Grete gyftes gafe and many men encreste   *made more prosperous*
        So godely was hyre chere and daliance
        To every wight it was a suffisshance.

3220   So at that feste whils that he helde the dese   *dais*
        Twelve knyghtes came of Romayns gode and wyse   *from Rome*
        With olyfe braunche in honde withouten prese *olive; unaccompanied*
        An esy pase as legates dyd suffise.   *Slowly*

	Upon thayre knes, with dew and hole advise	*prudence*
3225	Delyverd hym the letters to hym sente	
	By Lucyus emperoure whiche thus mente:	*read*

The Emperours lettre for truage and tribute

	"Lucyus of Rome the emperoure	
	And procuratoure for alle the hole Senate	
	Of the publyke profyte chieff governoure	
3230	By hole Senate made and denomynate	
	To Arthure kynge of Bretayne inordinate	*rebellious*
	Sendyth gretynge as thou haste deserved	
	Now late in Fraunce whiche was to us preserved	*retained*

	"Mervelynge myche of wronges whiche thou haste done	
3235	Within oure londe of Fraunce by grete rigoure	
	Withouten right that bettere had ben undone	
	Bot if thy wytte amende that foule erroure	*unless*
	Of whiche seth tyme that thou was govenoure	
	No tribute payed bot as thyne own conqueste	
3240	Haste holden it ever undre thyne arreste.	*custody*

fol. 79v	"And for thou haste no wylle it to amende	
	Or was so proude to do that cruelle dede	
	Kynge Frolle to sla tille us that dyd apende[1]	
	And mekylle more for that thou takes none hede	
3245	Of the estate imperialle we lede	
	To whiche alle londes tribute pay and trewage	
	Sauf thou allone gaynstondest of thyne outrage	*refuse to cooperate; excessive pride*

	"Wharfore straytely we byd thee and comaunde	*directly*
	That from Auguste now next within a yere	
3250	Thou come to us and pay alle oure demaunde	
	And trewage whiche thou haste of thy powere	
	Of Bretayne longe withholden so in fere	
	And thy defautes amende thou dyd in Fraunce	
	By sentence of thy lordes and ordynaunce.	

	"And els we shalle approche to thy countré	
3255	And what so that thy wodenesse hath us refte	*madness; robbed*
	With swerdes we shalle it make restored be	
	To oure Senate as friste we were enfefte	*enfiefed*
	The lyfelode that thy fadyr so thee lefte	*heritage*

---

[1] *King Frolle to slay those [who are] subject [to Arthur]*

3260	Thou arte fulle lyke for thyne intrusioun	
	To lese and brynge into confusioun.	*ruin*

"Written at Rome in the Consistory *Council Chamber*
By hole advyse of alle the wyse Senate
At Paske laste paste to byde in memory *Easter*
3265 Remembred there and fully approbate
Lesse thou foryette oure lettre and the date *forget*
And lay it so in alle foryetilnesse
Trustynge in us the same defaute I gesse."

With that the kynge wente to the Geants Toure
3270 With barons that were there of his counsaylle
To have advyse how to the emperoure
He shulde than wryte agayne for his avaylle. *advantage*
Of whiche so wyse wold not foryet, ne faylle,
So were thay made to Lucyus and endyte
3275 Whiche spake right thus for answere infenyte: *final*

The lettre and answere of Kynge Arthure to the same Emperoure and how he titled hym of right to be Emperour

"Arthure the kynge of alle the Grete Bretayne
And emperoure of Rome by alkyns right
With wronge deforced by Lucyus Romayne *deprived*
Pretendynge hym for emperoure of myght
3280 To the same Syr Lucyus of his unright
Usurpoure of the se imperialle
Sendyth gretynge as enmy moste mortalle.

fol. 80r "To the Senate of Rome it is wele knowe
How that Cesare Julyus with maystry
3285 Had trewage here Bretayne than was so lowe
By treson of Androges and trechery
That brought hym in by his grete policy
Withouten right or tytle of descente
Alle fulle agayne the barons hole consente.

Quicquid iniuste ab aliquot rapitur, numquam ab alio iuste possidetur ut in lege civili et imperatoria patet.[1]

3290 "Agayne alle right he had it by maystry *force*
And what so he with wronge so dyd possede

---

[1] *Whatever is unjustly snatched from someone, will never be justly possessed by someone else, as (it is stated) in civil and imperial law*

Lefulle to us is to withstonde forthy.   *Legal; therefore*
That lawe wylle so to it who takyth hede
What thynge by man with wronge is had indede
3295   Fro hym that aught it hole and skyllfully
By none other had may be lawfully.

"By whiche pretence thy wronge we shalle defende
And holde oure reme so in oure friste estate
Of servage fre as it to Brute appende
3300   Who had it fre afore that Rome bare date
Whose right to us is now determynate
And by suche right as thou doste now pretende
We may clayme Rome and to the Empyre ascende.   *Emperorship*

The first title by Belyne and Brenny

"For Kynge Belyne that was oure auncestre
3305   And Brenny als the kynge of Albany
Thay fully wan and hole dyd sequestre   *appropriate*
The londes hool so unto Romany
Whiche after thay had by victory
And satte right in the se imperialle
3310   Whare no prynce was that tyme to thaym egalle.   *equal*

The seconde title by Constantyne and Maximian

Cui descendebat inperium tam per mortem patris quam per eleccionem Senatoriam quam per eleccionem totius comitatus Romani.[1]

"Whose hole estate is now tille us descende   *to*
Bot yit we have a bettere tytle of right
Tylle the Empyre whiche that we wylle pretende   *To; claim*
To sette so by alle wronge conqueste and myght.
3315   Constantyne, Seynt Elyne sone so wyght,   *strong*
By right of blode of Constance doun descent
Emperoure was by Romaynes hole consent.

"Maximyan was hole the emperoure
Also by ful decré of the Senate
3320   Who next heyre was to Constantynes honoure
Whose bothe estates by law preordynate
We have wherfor of Rome we clayme estate

---

[1] *To whom rule descended as much by the death of his father as by senatorial election (and) as by election of the whole Roman people*

Of the Empyre the se imperialle
By juste tytle of law judicialle.

"Wharfore we wylle to Rome come and aproche
3326   By that same day whiche that thou haste prefyxte
         The tribute whiche thou wolde to thee acroche   *retain*
         Nought forto pay, as thou haste sette and fyxte.
         Bot of thee thare with Senate intermyxte   *together*
3330   To take tribute and holde the sovereyn se
         In alle that longe to the emperialté.   *rule of an emperor*

         "And iff thou like me sonner forto seke
         Brynge Romany with thee what day thou wille
         With me I shalle so than brynge Bretayne eke
3335   And whiche so of us two may other kylle
         Bere Rome away and Bretayne bothe ful stille.
         Writon at oure cyté of Carlyoun
         By hole advyse of alle oure regioun."

         He gafe unto that hiegh ambasshiate
3340   Fulle riche gyftes and golde ynouth to spende
         And bade thaym bere thare lordes in hool Senate
         His letters so whiche he than to thaym sende.
         And bade thaym say that sonner than thay wende
         He shulde thaym se and bade thaym nought thynke longe
3345   For in shorte tyme he shulde bene thaym amonge.

How Arthure toke his viage to feght with the Emperoure Lucius Hiberus assocyed allied with Emperoure Leo

         This noble Kynge Arthure than forth prevyde   *arranged*
         For his vyage agayne the emperoure.   *towards*
         His lettres oute he made and sygnyfyde
         To alle the londes of whiche he was protectoure
3350   Chargynge thaym alle to come for hys honoure
         On thaire beste wyse hym to acompany
         Of Rome forto conquere the monarchy.

         Whiche by processe of tyme as thay myght come
         Thay mette Arthure aywhare in place aboute
3355   To tyme thay were of myght to go to Rome
         So grete hys hoste was sembled and so stoute.   *assembled; formidable*
         And at Barbflete in Normandy no doute
         Thay londed alle with wyndes prosperouse
         Whare more powere thaym mette fulle bataylouse.

3360	Thare came the kynges of Spayne and Portyngale	
	Of Naverne als, the Kynge of Aragoyne,	
	The Dusze Piers alle of Fraunce thurghoute fulle hale	*Twelve Peers; entirely*
	The dukes also of Guyen and Burgoyne	
	Of Braban, Gelre, Savoy, and Loroyne,	
3365	The Erles also of Flaunders and Selonde	
	And dukes alle of Almayne and Holonde.	

fol. 81r **How Arthure faughte with a geant at Seynte Mighelle Mounte in Bretayne and slew hym in hys viage to Rome**

	Than was it tolde to Kynge Arthure fulle right	
	A geant grete forwaxen and horrible	*excessively large*
	Thanne ravyssht had Elyne his nece so bright	*niece*
3370	Whiche for bewté than was fulle possyble	
	For any prynce have wed and admyttible.	*acceptable*
	Kynge Howelle syster she was to Arthure nere	
	In Lesse Bretayne that tyme she had no pere.	*equal*

	Whiche geant so there durste no man assayle	*attack*
3375	Bot he thaym slewe or otherwyse dyd devoure.	
	Halfe quyke he ete thaym so it was mervayle	*alive*
	For whiche the folke aboute made grete murmoure	*complaint*
	Who on the heght of Myghel Mount dyd loure	*top; lurk*
	Whare he that mayde with in his armes had slayne	
3380	His luste to do so dyd he hyre constrayne.	

	Right so there came Bedwere by Arthure sente	
	Unto the hylle whare he a woman fonde	
	Compleynynge sore that seyde hym hyre entente	
	How Eleyne was brought so over the sonde	*shore*
3385	And she also right by a geants honde	
	And how he had so by hyre lady layne	
	That she was dede and by that tyrant slayne.	

	And so she sayde "He wille do now with me	
	At his comynge als faste, he is so grym	
3390	Therefore ye byde no lengere here bot fle	
	He is so ferse cruelle als and brym.	*fierce*
	He wylle yow ete and rife fro lymme to lym	*tear*
	So huge he is there may no wyght withstonde	
	His cruelté so hath he stroyed this londe."	

3395	Syr Bedwere than tille Arthure wente agayne	*to*
	And tolde hym alle the case how was befalle	
	For whiche Arthure wolde thedyr soth to sayne	
	To feght with hym with hande for hande at alle.	

	Syr Bedwere than and Kay dyd with hym calle	
3400	And to the mounte thay rode with right gode spede	
	When that the se was ebbe as it was nede	*ebbing*

	Thre men with thaym thare horse to kepe and holde	
	Avoydynge thaym and wente up to the hylle.	*Dismounting*
	Whare Bedwere than and Kay that were so bolde	
3405	He lafte and bad thaym byde hym there fulle stille	
	Tylle with that fende he had done alle his wille.	*fiend*
	And to hym wente with alle the ire he myghte	*vigor*
	With Caliburne his sworde hym stroke fulle righte.	

fol. 81v	Suche strokes thay gafe that woundere were to here	
3410	Syr Bedwere and Syr Kay myght here and se	
	And were fulle ferde the geants grete powere	*afraid that*
	Overcome shulde than thayre lorde thurgh grete pousté	*force*
	So huge he was and horrible on to se	
	That Arthure was bot lyke a childe to hym	
3415	So large he was and there to stoute and grym.	

	So longe thay faught and sore with strokes hatouse	*hateful*
	That Arthure had his wille and victory	
	And slew hym thare that was so vigorouse	
	That wente he to Bedwere and Kay on hy	*haste*
3420	And bade thaym there for sygne and memory	*testimony*
	Of his tryumphe and batayle conquerouse	
	Strike of the hede of that foule fende hydouse.	

	And rode so forthe unto his hoste agayne	
	Bryngand the hede with thaym for grete mervayle	*Bringing*
3425	Of whiche the hoste were alle fulle glad and fayne	
	And thankynge God gretely for that batayle.	
	Bot Elenes deth fulle sore thay dyd bywayle	*lament*
	For whom Howelle over hyre tombe dyd make	
	A chapelle fayre, whiche stonte yit for hire sake.	*stands*

3430	Whiche yit so hight Elene Tombe so named	*is called*
	On Myghel Mount within Lytille Bretayne	
	Whiche is now thare a strengh fulle gretly famed	*fortress*
	Envyrounde with the se aboute certayne	*surrounded*
	Marchynge right nere to Normandy unbayne	*Adjoining; disobedient*
3435	And enmy ever as it may be of myght	
	To take oure shyppes in pese withouten right.	

How Arthurs ambassetours with Romayns in Itaylle did feghte in bataylle

       Arthure his hoste assembled and forth wente
       Tylle that he came tille Awbe a ryvere fayre
       In Italy whiche fro the Occidente
3440   Renneth estewarde whare that he wolde repayre.
       His tentes gan sette whare was fulle holsom ayre   *wholesome air*
       With woddes by and medowes fresshe and grene
       With flowres fayre of dyvers colours sene.

       Whare he had worde the emperoure was nere
3445   To whom he sent Erle Bews of Oxenforde,
       Garyn of Chartres, the erle that was hym dere,
       And Syr Gawayne, his nevew, on whose worde
       He truste highly whom he at bed and borde
       Up brought had ay, who kynge of Louthien
3450   For sothe was than, as sayth the historien.

fol. 82r   Whiche messengers and wyse ambasiate   *deputation*
       Wente so at over that ryvere fresshe and pure
       Whare themperoure with alle the hole Senate
       Than logged was nought ferre fro Kynge Arthure.   *encamped*
3455   Bade hym remewe to Rome as he myght dure   *[They]*
       And come none nere unto the reme of Fraunce
       Elles on the morowe to fight for fulle fynaunce.   *settlement*

       Syr Lucyus than sayde "That were grete shame.
       To turne agayne I wylle noght in no wyse.
3460   It were reprefe and shamynge of my name.   *dishonour*
       To Fraunce I wille now as I may suffyse   *be able*
       And have it alle right at myne own devyse."
       With that his own neveu Quyntylian   *nephew*
       To Gawayne sayde this scornefulle wordes than: *these*

3465   "Ye Bretons alle in bragge and boste ben more
       Than youre knyghthode ever was or hardymente."
       Whom Gawayne there right with his swerde therfore
       Than slew anone, and so homwarde faste he wente
       With his felaws togedyr by hole consente
3470   Arthure to warne of bataylle and no reste.
       The emperoure had made thaym so to treste.   *trust*

       For whiche Romayns folowed upon thaym sore
       Thaym to have slayne for vengeance of that dede.
       Bot fleynge so who myghte than come afore
3475   Was slayne right doun thurgh wytte and grete manhede.
       At laste thaym sewed so fele of Romanhede   *followed; many*

      Thay wyste not how escapen in no wyse   *knew*
      Bot faught agayne fulle sore on thare enmyse.

      Out of a wode faste by sex thousond men
3480 Of Bretons bolde upon the Romayns felle
      And slew thaym doun chasynge upon thaym then
      Whiche Gawen and his men recomforte welle.   *exhort*
      Bot Petro than the senatoure fulle felle   *fierce*
      With ten thousond Romayns of grete valoure
3485 On Gawen felle fulle proudely in that stoure.   *encounter*

      And on a playne he gafe hym grete batayle
      That he and his unto a wode gan fle   *(i.e., Gawain)*
      Defendynge thaym and whan thay saw a vayle   *an advantage*
      Came oute aywhare and slew grete quantyté   *everywhere*
3490 Of Romayns ay thrugh manly juparté.   *battle*
      And at the laste thay isshed oute fulle light
      And toke Petro and slew his men doun right.

fol. 82v Whan in thare way, whare as thay shulde passe hame
      Two senatours with captayns mo in fere   *more; together*
3495 Kynges that were, lay busshed as thay came   *in ambush*
      With fyftene thousonde men of armes clere
      Trustynge thaym have rescowed with grete powere. *i.e., the Roman prisoners*
      Bot in suche pride withouten reule on brede   *in formation*
      Thay came and of the batayle toke non hede

3500 Tylle that Bretons thaym slew and toke aywhare *captured*
      And discomfyte were putte unto the flight   *defeated*
      And kynges thre with captaynes wyse and ware *knowledgeable*
      And nombre grete of Romayns party right
      The Bretons slewe and helde the felde that nyght.
3505 And on the morow came homward glad and fayne *joyful*
      Thay had so sped and of thayre syde few slayne. *prospered*

      So with thare pray and alle thare prisoners   *spoils*
      Thay came unto Kynge Arthure home agayne
      Of whiche that had so faught with smale powere
3510 Agayne so fele he was fulle glad and fayne   *many*
      "Welcome my knyghtes for me ye had grete payne."
      Bot than he sente Petro the senatoure
      Unto Parise there to be holde in toure

      Wyth other kynges and many grete capteyne
3515 That taken were in these grete batayls sere.   *various*
      Of whiche Gawen, Bewes also, and Gereyne,
      Syr Percyvalle, Ewayn, Estore, there were,

	Cadore, Guytarde, Irelgas, and Bedwere,	
	That knyghtes were of the Table Rounde	
3520	And prynces gode that sore were hurte and wounde.	*wounded*
	Lucyus so acerteyned of these dedes	*informed*
	Estoyned was if in Augustudoun	*Wondering*
	He shulde abyde for powere that hym nedes	
	Of his felawe that called was Leoun	
3525	Or to Langres he shulde his hestes boun	*plans; prepare*
	Whiche by espies was laten Arthure wete	*delayed; knew*
	Wharfore he thought how he shuld with hym mete.	
	Within that nyght he busshed in his way	*(i.e., Arthur) ambushed*
	Whare he shulde come right in a valey fayre	
3530	That Seysy hight in eght batayls fulle gay.[1]	
	To feght with hym he made there his repayre	
	The emperoure he putte oute of dyspayre	
	That passe away he shulde than in no wyse	
	Withouten batayle or els a foule supprise.	*injury*

fol. 83r	Kynge Aguselle that was of Albany	
3536	And Cadore duke that was of Cornewayle	
	The friste batayle togedyr in company	*first battalion*
	Had than al hole of men that myght avayle	*succeed*
	That couth right wele defende and eke assayle.	*also; attack*
3540	To Bewes also and Geryn of grete myght	
	Another batayle he toke, bothe stronge and wight.	*granted; vigorous*

	Aschille the kynge of Denmarke stronge and wyse	
	And to Kynge Lothe of Norway vygorouse	
	The thrid batayle he gafe of grete emprise.	
3545	Kynge Howel so and Gawayn fortunouse	
	The fourth bataylle had than fulle corregeouse.	
	Bedwere and Kay the fyfte batayle dyd holde	
	Of myghty men that hardy were and bolde.	

	Syr Holdyne and Guytarde the sexte batayle.	*[He gave]*
3550	Syr Jugens and Jonathas so famouse	
	The sevent batayle than had withouten fayle.	
	Cursale of Chestere and Urgen corageuse	
	The eght batayle had so fulle harageouse.	*violent*
	In eche batayle a legioun of knyghtes	
3555	Arrayed were alle redy for the fyghtes.	

---

[1] *That Saussy (or Val-Suzon) was called and in eight battles quite glorious*

Arthure bare a banere of sable, a dragoun of golde, and a baner of oure lady and the thrid baner of Seynt George, that were Galaad armes for remembrance of Galaad, and the fourt baner of goules (*red*) thre corouns of golde.

The nynte batale the kynge Arthure dyd lede
In whiche the erle of Gloucestere so wyse   *(i.e., Morvyde)*
A legioun thay had and dyd possede
Of knyghtes gode that were of high emprise.
3560   In whiche batayle he bare as myght suffise
In a banere a dragoun alle of golde
The castelle so to ben for yonge and olde.   *fortified camp*

The emperoure with legions fully twelve
Come thrugh that bale right as than was his way   *strife*
3565   Of Romayns fele ful stoute right with hymselve   *many*
In batayls twelve redy to fight that day.
With that eyther parte by skurours herde welle say   *scouts*
That bothe partes so nere that tyme were mette
That fyght thay muste or els to deth be bette.   *beaten*

3570   Kynge Arthure bade his knyghtes to make gode chere
Saynge right thus: "My knyghtes ye wete welle alle   *know*
Youre manhode grete and conqueste syngulere
And youre knyghthode that never yit dyd appalle   *tarnish*
So myghty was in every place over alle
3575   Have wonne and gote me thretty remes by myght
Whiche with youre honde ye have conquerde ful right.

fol. 83v   **How comforte his knyghtes to the bataylle**

"Stonde now on fete and alle youre right defende
That ye have wonne so lette it never doun falle.
Lete not this day thise Romayns us transcende.
3580   Iff thay overcome us now it wylle befalle
That we muste ever in servytute ben thralle
And tribute pay to thare domynacioun
Rather de we, than thaym do mynystracioun."   *die; service*

How the Scottes kynges and other knyghtes recomforte (*encourage*) Kynge Arthure thare

With that the kynge Agusel so vigoriouse
3585   "My lorde" he sayde "seth tyme ye thought to fight
With Romayns friste my wylle so covetouse   *first; eager*
Hath bene that woundes whiche in youre servyce right
That I shalle take for love of you I hight   *promise*

3590	Than hony so to me shalbe swetter	*honey*
	And over alle mete and drynke shalle lyke me better.	*please*

	So thruste my soule thare blode byholde and se	*thirsts*
	And Germayns als that hath us done offence	
	That ofte hath putte us from felicité	
	Thurgh thaire cruelle and cursed violence	
3595	For whiche I shalle this day thaym recompense	
	With alle myne hertes laboure and besynesse	
	Us to revenge of alle thare wykydnesse."	

	"Me thynke fulle longe" than seyde Kynge Urian	
	Of Murrefe that was fully lorde and syre	
3600	"Unto that houre whiche day myght sende so than	
	My soule dothe brenne right as it were in fyre.	*burn*
	I had lever now than have the hole Empyre	*rather*
	With thaym be mette in felde where I myght fight	
	Thayre pride to felle that bene so stronge and wyght."	*vigorous*

Howelle Kynge of Litille Bretayne

How Kynge Howelle of Lasse Bretayne comforte (*urged*) the kynge to batayle

3605	Kynge Howelle sayde to Kynge Arthure anone	
	"This taried tyme me thynke ys fully tynte	*delayed; wasted*
	Of yow thay aske no right bot wronge allone.	
	Why stonde ye thus? Go to thaym ere ye stynte	*cease*
	And for thayre wronge desyre with strokes dynte	*blow*
3610	Dyscomfyt shalle thay be and insuperate	*defeated*
	Bothe Lucyus and als his hole Senate."	

	Thus every knyght right of the Table Rounde	
	Thaire counsayle gafe to strike sone the batayle	
	And severaly made there avowes that stounde.	*individually; time*
3615	Thay shuld never spare thare ennemyse to assayle	
	For hurte, nor deth, and thought fulle grete mervayle	
	Why that thay were holden so longe in sounder	*apart*
	So longe thay thought to se who shulde ben undre.	

fol. 84r	**How Kynge Arthure and the Emperour Lucyus faughte in grete bataille in Itaylle whare Lucius was slayne and Arthure had the victory**	

	Thanne to that vale whare Kynge Arthure so lay	*valley*
3620	The emperoure came holy with his hoste.	
	And thare thay faught whils thousandes dede that day	*died*
	On ayther parte were, bot of Romayns moste.	
	Many thousonde Romayne thare yelde the goste.	*spirit*

3625   Bot Duke Bedwere and als Duke Kay were slayne
       In that batayle and suffred dethes payne.

       Whose corses so brought were to the dragoun   *bodies; i.e., fortified camp*
       By Aguselle and Duke Cadore with myght.
       And of Romayns two kynges that bare the croun
       And prynces foure that senatours were wight   *strong*
3630   Were slayne that houre that manly were in fight.
       With thaire fresshe hostes layde on alle new fulle faste
       Was no wyght there of deth that was agaste.   *person*

       Now here, now thare, on every syde aboute
       Thay stroke men doun to deth ay as thay mette
3635   Some tyme Romayns the worse had there thurghoute
       Some tyme Bretons with Romayns were oversette.
       On ayther parte so were thay alle wele bette.
       Than Kynge Howelle and Gawen corageouse
       With thaire batayle came Bretons to rescouse.   *rescue*

3640   A sore batayle was than on every syde
       Whare Holdyne erle of Flaunders than was slayne.
       The erle also of Boloyne in that tyde   *time*
       Syr Cursale, erle of Chestere, sothe to sayne,
       Of Salisbyry, erle Gwaluk, nought to layne,
3645   Urgen of Bathe, that was fulle bataylouse,
       Alle slayne were than in that stoure dolorouse.   *sorrowful encounter*

       And of Romayns were dede foure prynces grete
       With thousondes fele of other low estate.   *many*
       So Gawen and Howelle thaym gan rehete   *attack*
3650   And thre knyghtes than thay slewe of the Senate
       Whiche for manhode myght have ben socyate   *raised*
       Tylle kynges degré for noble regyment   *With*
       And ben lyfte up to estate excellent.

       Than came Arthure right with his grete dragoun
3655   The emperoure als with his egle of golde   *eagle*
       Thare myght men se fele knyghtes stryken doun   *many*
       On bothe sydes that were fulle stoute and bolde.
       Ayther on other that day than fought thykfolde   *in large numbers*
       And faught fulle sore whanne they togeder mette
3660   And many knyghtes thay bothe to dethe doun bette.

fol. 84v   Bot at the laste to passe unto an ende
       The Bretons so upon the Romayns hewe   *attacked*
       With comynge of Morvyde to thaym fulle hende   *noble*
       Behynde Romayns and at thare bakkes theym slew

3665   As Kynge Arthure hym bade and layde on newe
        Tylle Romayns faste began to waxen thynne
        And Lucyus slayne, and many of his kynne.

        Bot who hym slew there wyste no wyght so than   *knew*
        Bot Syr Gawayne of it dyd bere the name
3670   For ayther of thaym hurte other ay whan and whan   *alternately*
        By dyvers tymes as thay togedyr came
        Whanne thay departe ayther gafe other fame
        For worthyest that ever he dyd with mete   *meet*
        Suche ennemyse love eyther other dyd behete.   *grant*

3675   Of whose dethe so the Romayns were dismayed
        And fled fulle faste on every syde aboute.
        Some unto tounes and some to wodes strayed
        And some to toures and castels in grete route   *bands*
        Grete multitude there slayne withouten doute.
3680   There was never prynce that dyd so manly fight
        As Kynge Arthure thare dyd in alle mennes sight.

        So dyd his kynges and prynces for his right
        His Bretons alle thurghout alle hole his hoste
        His knyghtes hole also that were fulle wight   *strong*
3685   Right of the Rounde Table withouten boste
        Ful doughtly thaym bare with myghtes moste
        His ennemyse so to felle and wyn the felde
        With alle honoure and vyctory to weelde.   *possess*

        Than sente he forthe the corse of Lucyus   *body*
3690   To Rome that was emperoure than doutelesse
        Who called was Lucyus Hiberus
        Associate with Leo as I gesse
        To holde hym in imperialle worthynesse
        Of whiche in youthe and tendre innocence
3695   He was putte oute by myghty violence.

        He bade thaym take that corse for thare truage   *(i.e., the Senate); body; tribute*
        And holde thaym payed and be nought daungerouse   *satisfied; haughty*
        And iff thay wylle have alle the supplusage   *extra payment*
        He shulde thaym pay of corses preciouse   *bodies*
3700   Of senatours and princes gloriouse
        In that same wyse, and prayed thaym it alowe   *recognize*
        For with suche gode he shulde thaym welle endowe.   *gifts*

fol. 85r For fere offe whiche thay dyd hym than relese
        The trewage alle and servyce every dele   *tribute; part*
3705   Renounsynge it of suche payment to cese.

Thay prayed hym so gode lordeship thay myght fele   *enjoy*
And iff he wolde the publike unyversele
With alle thare hertes the hole imperialté
Thay wolde hym graunte with alle the dygnyté.

3710   Kynge Arthure than unto thayre graunte consente
And Bedwere sente to bery at Bayoun   *bury; Bayeux*
And Kay unto Chynoun his castelle gente   *Chinon; noble*
Whare beried was his corse with devocioun   *body*
In an abbay thereby of religioun
3715   And every lorde unto thayre sepulture   *tombs*
He sente so home whare was thare kynde nature.

Bot he abode in Italy so thane   *remained*
That wynter helde his men in dyverse place
Tylle somer came at whiche tyme he beganne
3720   To passe to Rome on Leo forto chace
The Empire hole unto hymselfe enbrace
And Leon putte in reule of his regence
As myght acorde so with his innocence.

How Kynge Arthure had worde of Modrede that purposed (*intended*) to bene Kynge of Bretayne, wharfore he cam home and slew Modrede and had his dethes wounde.

Bot tythandes cam than oute of Grete Bretayne   *news*
3725   To Kynge Arthure how Modrede had aspyred
To have the croune of Bretayne for certayne
And wedden wold the quene, and had conspyred
With Duke Cheldrike fulle bysyly requyred
To helpe hym so with alle his payenhede   *pagan troops*
3730   And Albany he gafe hym to his mede.   *reward*

For whiche to Kynge Howelle his neveu dere   *nephew*
His hoste he toke on that syde on the se
And bade hym ride the Romayns to conquere
And he wolde with his insulans pousté   *insular force*
3735   To Bretayne wende to chastyse that contré
The fals Modrede whom he had made regent
As traytoure honge and draw by jugyment.

Whare Arthure faughte first with Modrede atte Whytsonde

In this mene while the traytoure Modrede
And Cheldrike als who came with grete powere
3740   Assembled were with Cristen and payenhede
Foure score thousonde of men of armes clere   *armed men*

Whare Kynge Arthure and his hoste londed were
At Porte Rupyne whare Whitesonde is fulle ryght   *Richborough; Wissant, France*
Thay faught with hym in batayle stronge and wight.   *vigorous*

fol. 85v   Bot Aguselle the kynge of Albany
3746   And Syr Gawayn the kynges neven dere   *nephew*
                Of Louthian kynge than by auncetry
                With many other were slayne that day in fere.   *together*
                Bot Arthure had the felde with his powere
3750   And putte thaym to the flight and made grete chace
                In whiche he slewe grete peple withouten grace.

How Arthure faughte with Modrede at Wynchestre and putte Modrede to the flyghte

                Bot Modrede than to Wynchester so fledde
                With grete peple to whom Arthure came right
                With alle his hoste whom Modred bataylle bedde   *offered*
3755   And redy was anone with hym to fight.
                Bot there Modrede was putte unto the flight
                And fled fulle faste to Cornewayle with powere
                Whom in that chace Kynge Arthure sought so nere

How Arthure faught with Modred the thryd tyme bysyde Camblayne in Cornewaylle

                That he sawe whare he lay with his powere
3760   Upon a water that called is Camblayne
                With sexty thousonde Cristen and payenis clere   *pagans*
                That with hym were redy to fight agayne
                With whom Arthure with alle his hoste fulle fayne
                Thare faught and slewe fulle mekylle multitude
3765   Thurgh powere of his hoste and fortitude.

                Bot Arthure was in herte so sore anoyed
                For Gawayns deth and of Kynge Aguselle
                Which were afore by Modrede slayne and stroyed
                And myght not mete with swerdes for to dele
3770   His foule tresoun and falsede to cansele
                And his persone to hangen and to drawe
                As hyegh traytoure by jugyment of his lawe.

                For ire of whiche he faughte so in that stoure   *encounter*
                That thousondes fele he slew there and his knyghtes   *many*
3775   Thare was never kynge, nor prynce, no conqueroure,
                That dyd so wele as thay in any fightes
                Bot Arthure thare at laste with alle his myghtes

Slew Modrede than with Caliburne his swerde
And Duke Cheldrike so Fortune made his werde.   *fate*

3780   Than fled thay faste thaire captayns were alle slayne.
The Saxons hole and alle the payenhede   *pagan troops*
And Arthure helde the felde and was fulle fayne
With vyctory of alle his fose I rede   *foes*
So hole Fortune was his frende at nede
3785   That Mars the god of armes and of batayle
No better myght have done withouten fayle.

fol. 86r   Bot dethes wounde, as cronycle doth expresse,
Modrede hym gafe that was his syster sunne
And as some sayne his owne sonne als doutlesse.
3790   Bot certaynté thereof no bokes kunne   *can*
Declare it wele that I have sene or funne.   *found*
Bot lyke it ys by alle estymacioun
That he cam never of his generacioun.

The quene Gaynore whanne she persayved wele
3795   That Modrede so discomfyt was and slayne
Fro Yorke dyd fle by nyght than every dele
Tylle that she came to Carlyoun with payne
Whare she hyre made a nonne the soth to sayne
In pryvyté thare hyd for fere of deth   *secret*
3800   For shame and sorow almoste she yalde the brethe.   *died*

In the temple of Seynte July Martyre
Whare she corounde was with solempnyté
Amonges nunnes fro whom none shulde departe hire
She toke hyre lyfe with alle stabilité   *accepted; steadfastness*
3805   Thare to abyde and leve in chastyté
Hyre synne to clenge to God and yelde hyre goste   *cleanse; spirit*
Whiche eternaly ay is of myghtes moste.

In whiche batayle the floure of alle knyghhede   *flower; knighthood*
Dede was and slayne on Arthurs syde so dygne   *worthy*
3810   The knyghtes alle that were of worthihede
To kynges egalle and compers were condygne   *equal; companions; distinguished*
Whiche for Arthure thare lyfe did there resygne   *give up*
That knyghtes were right of the Table Rounde
That were alle slayne echone with dethes wounde.

3815   For whiche Arthure formerred in his thought   *distraught*
Never after had comforte, ne yit gladnesse,
To thynke on thaym so dere his love had bought.
Fulle fayne he wolde so than have be lyfelesse   *joyful*

	Whyche he byried with grete and high noblesse	
3820	With herte fulle sore his sorows to complayne	
	His dethes woundes fulle sore bygan dystrayne.	*oppress*

	He gafe his reme and alle his domynacioun	
	To Constantyne the sonne of Duke Cadore	
	Whiche Cadore slayne was in that adversacioun	*battle*
3825	With Arthure so at Camblayne than afore	
	Whose brother he was alle of a moder bore	*born*
	Bot Gorloys sonne, that duke was of Cornewayle,	
	He was sertayne and heyre withouten fayle.	

fol. 86v	Kynge Arthure than so wounded mortaly	
3830	Was led forth thanne to Avalon fulle sore	
	To lechen thare his woundes pryvely	*tend to; secretly*
	Whare than he dyed and byried was right thore	*there*
	As yit this day ys sene and shalle evermore	
	Within the chirche and mynstere of Glastynbyry	
3835	In tombe rialle made sufficiantly.	

	Who dyed so in the yere of Cristes date	
	Fyve hundred was acounted than in fere	*together*
	And fourty more and two associate	
	As cronyclers expressed have fulle clere	
3840	Fro whiche tyme forth he dyd no more apere	
	Nought wythstondynge Merlyne seyde of hym thus	
	His deth shuld be unknow and ay doutous.	*uncertain*

De quo Merlinus dicit inter prophecias suas exitus eius erit dubius et quidam propheta Britonum fecit pro epitaphio super tumbam suam versum istum: Hic iacet Arthurus rex quondam rexque futurus.[1]

	Bot of his dethe the story of Seynt Grale	*Holy Grail*
	Sayth that he dyed in Avalon fulle fayre	
3845	And byried there his body was alle hale	*healthy*
	Within the Blake Chapelle whare was his layre	*burial place*
	Whiche Geryn made whare than was grete repayre	*spiritual retreat*
	For Seynt Davyd, Arthurs uncle dere,	
	It halowed had in name of Mary clere.	*pure*

---

[1] *Concerning which Merlin says, among his prophecies, that his death will be uncertain and a certain prophet of the Britons made as an epitaph on his tomb this verse: "Here lies Arthur, the once and future king"*

Nota how Geryn went with Arthure into Avalon, to whom Sir Launcelot de Lake cam of aventure folowyng on the chace and thay toke ordere of preest and wox (*became*) recluses ther to pray for Arthure time of thaire lyves.

3850	Whare Geryn so abode than alle his lyfe	
	Aboute his tombe with devoute exequyse	*rites*
	So was he than ay forth contemplatife	
	He lyfte no more the worlde to excercyse	
	Bot only there to serve at his advyse	
3855	Allemyghty God whils he on lyfe myght dure	
	Of his erledome he had none other cure.	*concern*

	And as that same story aftyr doth contene	
	That Syr Launcelot de Lake the worthy knyght	
	Of the Rounde Table fulle longe a knyght had bene	
3860	Folowynge on the Saxons in that flight	
	Thare foonde the tombe of Kynge Arthure so wyght	*vigorous*
	And fro the tyme that Geryn had hym tolde	
	Of Arthurs tombe his herte began to colde.	

	Of Seynt Davyd archebisshop of Carlyoun	
3865	Ordres of preste with gode devocyoun	
	He toke, and als sone as he myght be boun	*ready*
	His servyce hole gostely withoute remocioun	*delay*
	He made his lorde of his owne commocioun	*motivation*
	In that chapelle with Geryn his compere	*companion*
3870	In penaunce grete recluses were foure yere.	

fol. 87r   **The compleynt of the makere for the dethe of Kynge Arthure and of hys noble prynces and knyghtes of the Rounde Table**

	O gode lorde God, suche tresoun and unrightes	
	Whi suffred so devyne omnipotence	
	Whiche had of it precyence and forsightes	*prescience*
	And myght have lette that cursed violence	*prevented*
3875	Of Modredes pryde and alle his exsolence	*insolence*
	That noble kynge forpassynge conqueroure	
	So to dystroy and waste thurgh his erroure?	

	O thou Fortune, executrice of werdes,	*arbiter of fate*
	That evermore so with thy subtylité	
3880	To alle debates so strongly thou enherdes	*participate in*
	That men that wolde ay leve in charité	*live*
	Thou dooste perturbe with mutabilité	
	Why stretched so thy whele upon Modrede	*wheel*
	Agayne his eme to do so cruelle dede?	*uncle*

3885	Whare thurgh that hiegh and noble conqueroure	
	Withouten cause shulde sogates perisshit be	*in this manner*
	With so fele kynges and prynces of honoure	*many*
	That alle the worlde myght never thare better se.	
	O fals fallace of Modredes propreté	*deceit; nature*
3890	How myght thou so in Gaynore have suche myghtes	*power of attractiveness*
	That she the dethe caused of so fele knyghtes?	*many*

	Bot O Modrede that was so gode a knyght	
	In grete manhode and proudely ay approved	
	In whom thyne eme the nobleste prynce of myght	*uncle*
3895	Putte alle his truste so gretely he thee loved	
	What unhappe so thy manly goste hath moved	*ill-chance; spirit*
	Unto so foule and cruelle hardynesse	
	So fele be slayne thurgh thyne unhappynesse?	*evil*

	The highnesse of thyne honoure had a falle	
3900	Whanne thou beganne to do that injury.	
	That grete falshode thy prowesse dyd apalle	
	Alsone as in thee entred perjury	*As soon*
	By consequent tresoun and traytory	
	Thy lorde and eme also thy kynge soverayne	*uncle*
3905	So to bytrayse thy felaws als sertayne.	

.xvii. capitulum of the Kynge Constantyne, the son of Cador of Cornewaylle.

	Kynge Constantyne his brother son was crounde	
	Duke Cadore sonne a knyght fulle aventurouse	
	And chosen was oon of the Table Rounde	
	In Arthure tyme for knyght ful corageouse	
3910	In trone rialle was sette fulle preciouse	*throne*
	With dyademe on his hed signyfyde	
	At Trynovaunt whare no wight it replyde.	*person; objected to*

fol. 87v	Whiche Constantyne with Saxons sore dyd fight	
	Assembled than with Modredes sonnes two	
3915	By dyverse tymes and putte thaym to the flight	
	Of whiche oon fled to Wynchestere right so	
	Whare Constantyne hym slewe as for his fo	
	Right in the kyrke than of Saynte Amphibale	*church*
	At the awtere withoute lengere tale.	*altar*

Nota de data mortis sancti David Archiepiscopi de Caerlioun[1]

3920   The tother hyd than in a chyrch fulle fayre
At Trynovant behynde the high autere.
He slew anone withoute any dispayre
And Saxons putte in subjeccioun clere.
In whose tyme so, as sayth the cronyclere,
3925   Seynt Davyd dyed archebisshop of Carlyoun
In his mynstyre at Meneu of religioun

Whare he ys byried now in fayre sepulture
Of whiche the name so for his byrialle
Es called now with every creature
3930   Seynt Davys so by name especialle
Whare now is sette the se pontyficalle
In name of hym for his solempnysacioun
Of his gode lyfe to make comendacioun.

At Bangore als bysshop Seynt Danyele   *Bangor*
3935   That holy was and ful religeouse
Decesed than of lyfe had leved wele   *lived*
And honourd thare his body preciouse
Amonge the folke for his werkes vertuouse
Eternaly muste bene in memory
3940   Remembred hole within that cenoby.   *monastery*

Bot Constantyne his reme dyd wele governe
In reste and pese so after in grete noblesse
By foure yere hole after he couth descerne
Whanne thurgh sentence of devyne myghtynesse
3945   He dyed so and byried was doutelesse
In the Carolle by Utere Pendragoun
As cronyclers have made in mencioun.

.xviii. capitulum of Aurelius Conan, Rex Britannie[2]

Aurelyus Conan his cosyn fayre
The se rialle than helde and dyd succede   *royal see (i.e., jurisdiction)*
3950   To hym as next than of his blode and hayre.   *heir*
His eme and eke his sonnes two indede   *uncle*
In prisoun slew which after Constantyne I rede
Shulde have bene kynges of alle the Grete Bretayne
The dyademe and coroune to obtayne.

---

[1] *Note the date of the death of David Archbishop of Caerleon*

[2] *Chapter of Aurelius Conan, King of Britain*

fol. 88r	Forpassynge fayre he was in alle beuté	
3956	Bot strife betwyx cytese and alle cuntrese	*cities*
	He cherisshit ay thurghoute, of his pousté.	*promoted; power*
	Cyvyle batayls amonges alle his cytese	
	He maynteynd sore thurgh his hye dygnytese	
3960	And bot thre yere his regne dyd so endure	
	Whanne deth hym toke and layde in sepulture.	

The makers wordes to lordes for mayntenance of quereles and debates

	Bewarre ye lordes that ben in hygh estates	
	And thynke upon this worldes transmutacioun	
	And cherisshe not contencions, no debates,	
3965	In youre countrese, lesse it be youre confusioun.	*lest; ruin*
	For fals Fortune with hyre permutacioun	
	Fulle lyghtely wille caste doun that ys above	
	Whose nature is to chaungen and remove.	*be inconstant*

.xix. capitulum of Kynge Vortypore and Malgo kynges, and Kynge Careys.

	Than Vortypore succeded aftyr hym	
3970	And helde the se of alle the rialté	*seat of judgement*
	Agayns whom the Saxons stronge and grym	
	Made fulle grete werre and grete malignyté	
	Whiche by batayle and grete humanyté	
	He overcame wele and kepte the londe in pese	
3975	Unto the tyme that deth made hym decese.	

	Malgo next hym to the croune atteyned	
	Fayrest of other that ever were in his day	
	Alle tyrany fully he restreyned	
	And conquerde hole sex iles, the sothe to say,	
3980	With force of werre Denmarke and eke Norway.	*also*
	Irelonde, Iselonde, Gothlonde, and Orkadese,	
	With bataylle stronge obeyed his rialtese.	*royal authority*

	Stronge he was and myghty of powere	
	Excedynge other of hiegh and large stature	
3985	In alle worshyp and fredome syngulere	
	And wele beloved with every creature	
	Bot only so by grete mysaventure	
	And thurgh his foule acursed appetyte	
	He haunted ay the synne of sodomyte.	*practiced; sodomy*

3990	In whiche synne so at Wynchestere he dyed	
	Within a bathe by Goddes own vengeaunce	
	And how his soule was in his deth applyed	

None wote bot God oonly of his pusaunce.   *knows; power*
The thrid yere of his regne and governaunce
3995   The cruelle deth hym stale away anone
Fro his coroune and fro his rialle trone.   *throne*

fol. 88v   **Kynge Careyse**

Careys was than corouned kynge anone
That loved wele in alle cytese debate
And als bytwyxe the cytese everychone
4000   He suffred werre and ofte it made for hate
Engendred of his ire imoderate   *extreme wrath*
So ferre that werre in every grete cyté
Fulle comoun was thurgh his maliciousté.

For whiche Bretons than made hym mekylle were
4005   That whanne Gurmonde of Aufrike payen stronge   *pagan*
Irelonde had wonne thay sente to hym for fere
Of Kynge Careys and prayde hym byde not longe
Bot that in haste he wolde come thaym amonge.
So dyd Saxons, thay hight hym alle the londe   *promised*
4010   Of Bretayne hole if he wolde with theym stonde.

EXPLANATORY NOTES

ABBREVIATIONS: *Alliterative Morte*: *Alliterative Morte Arthure*, ed. Benson; **Arthur**: *Arthur: A Short Sketch of His Life and History in English Verse*; **Bede**: Bede, *Ecclesiastical History of the English People*; **Brut**: *The Brut or The Chronicles of England*, ed. Brie; **CT**: *Canterbury Tales*; **CPL**: Peter Langtoft, *The Chronicle of Pierre de Langtoft*; **EH**: *Eulogium Historiarum sive Temporis*, ed. Haydon; **FH**: *Flores Historiarum*, ed. Luard; **FP**: John Lydgate, *Fall of Princes*; **HA**: Henry of Huntingdon, *Historia Anglorum*; **HB**: Nennius, *Historia Brittonum*; **HRB**: Geoffrey of Monmouth, *Historia Regum Brittanniae*; **HRBVV**: Geoffrey of Monmouth, *Historia Regum Brittanniae, Variant Version*; **JG**: John of Glastonbury, *The Chronicle of Glastonbury Abbey*; **LB**: Layamon's *Brut*, trans. Allen; **m**: marginalia; **Mort Artu**: *La Morte Artu*, ed. Lacy; **MED**: *Middle English Dictionary*; **MO**: Martin of Troppau, *Martini Oppaviensis Chronicon Pontificum et Imperatorum*; **NC**: *Þe New Croniclis Compendiusli Ydrawe of Þe Gestis of Kyngis of Ingelond*; **OED**: *Oxford English Dictionary*; **OV**: *The Oldest Anglo-Norman Prose Brut Chronicle*, ed. Marvin; **P**: Ranulf Higden, *Polychronicon*; **PRO**: Public Record Office; **Queste**: *La Queste del Saint Graal*, trans. Burns; **RB**: Wace, *Roman de Brut*; **RMB**: Robert Mannyng of Brunne, *The Chronicle*; **TB**: John Lydgate, *Troy Book*; **TC**: Geoffrey Chaucer, *Troilus and Criseyde*; **TNA**: The National Archives of the UK; **Whiting**: Whiting, *Proverbs, Sentences, and Proverbial Phrases*.

PROLOGUE

1–14   *O soverayne . . . withouten variance.* The *Chronicle* is dedicated to King Henry VI (1421–71), his wife, Margaret of Anjou (1429–82), and their son, Edward of Lancaster (1453–71), prince of Wales. Hardyng appears to have based the opening line of his prologue on line 531 of John Lydgate's "King Henry VI's Triumphant Entry into London" ("O noble Meir! be yt vnto youre pleasaunce"); this is the first of several borrowings from the poem. For further discussion of Hardyng's use of Middle English poetry in the *Chronicle*, see Introduction and Peverley, "Chronicling the Fortunes of Kings."

2   *of my symplicité.* The term "symplicité" can mean "meekness," "plainness of style," or "lack of sophistication" (*MED simplicite* (n.)). Hardyng's affected modesty is a rhetorical topos common to medieval prologues.

4   *Whiche no man hath in worlde bot oonly ye.* This reference to the uniqueness of the *Chronicle* may be a rhetorical feature, but it also supports the assumption that Lansdowne 204 was the presentation copy made for Henry VI (see Manuscript Description).

11   *With baronage and lordes.* This is the first of many references to the nobility
            helping the king to govern effectively.

20–21   *Of Scotland . . . prowdly straye.* The topic of English hegemony over Scotland
            is raised frequently throughout the *Chronicle* (see Introduction and Peverley,
            "Anglo-Scottish Relations"). A number of English kings attempted to bring
            the smaller kingdom under English rule, the most important being Edward
            I, whom Hardyng mentions in the following stanza. For an overview of Anglo-
            Scottish relations in the Middle Ages see Stones, *Anglo-Scottish Relations*,
            Nicholson, *Scotland*, and Brown, *Wars of Scotland*.

22–28   *Wythin thre . . . hool proteccioun.* Hardyng's optimistic estimation that the king
            could conquer Scotland within three years anticipates his account of how "the
            kynge may moste esely conquere Scotlonde" at the end of Book 7 (lines
            1170–1330). Revised estimates are given at 7.1327 and 7.1711. For the
            Scottish campaigns waged by Edward I, see Prestwich, *Edward I*.

29–35   *Who hath . . . an idyote.* The medical metaphor employed here has its origins
            in Boethius' *The Consolation of Philosophy*, where Lady Philosophy advises the
            narrator to divulge his sorrows to her. It is common in medieval literature
            (see Whiting L173), but Hardyng probably encountered it in Book 1, Prosa
            4 of John Walton's Middle English translation of Boethius's work (p. 29), or
            Chaucer's *TC* 1.857–58, two texts that he utilizes elsewhere in the *Chronicle*.
            In this instance he uses it to heighten his appeal to Henry VI for the reward
            promised by the king's father, Henry V. The sovereign is depicted as the only
            man capable of remunerating Hardyng and curing the metaphorical sickness
            brought about by his lack of reward. See Peverley, "Chronicling the Fortunes
            of Kings."

33   *erande.* "Erande" refers to the reconnaissance Hardyng allegedly undertook
            for Henry V in Scotland between 1418 and 1421. (For further information see
            Introduction).

45   *maymed.* Hardyng is referring to an injury that he received during his Scottish
            mission.

49   *Esthamstede.* The patent rolls confirm that Hardyng presented documents to
            Henry VI at Easthampstead manor, and that he received an annuity of £10
            from the king (*Calendar of Patent Rolls: Henry VI 1436–1441*, p. 431, m. 15).

50–56   *a lettre . . . sovereynté expressynge.* The document referred to is the submission
            of the competitors for the Scottish crown at Norham in 1291, acknowledging
            their deference to Edward I. For this and other documents supposedly
            recovered in Scotland by Hardyng, see Stones and Simpson (*Edward I and the
            Throne*, II:385–87) and Hiatt (*Medieval Forgeries*, pp. 104, 112–13).

54   *Long Shankes.* Longshankes (literally "long legs") was the soubriquet given to
            Edward I on account of his height.

57–63   *two patents rial . . . made memory.* Hardyng refers to two letters patent from
            David II of Scotland and Robert II of Scotland acknowledging English

suzerainty. Several forged documents relating to David and Robert are associated with Hardyng: they survive in TNA: PRO E 39/2/5, E 39/96/4, E 39/96/5, E 39/97/4, and E 39/4/3a. For further information see Stones and Simpson (*Edward I and the Throne*, II:385–87) and Hiatt (*Medieval Forgeries*, pp. 103–11).

64–70   *the relees . . . hieghness wroght*. This is a reference to the Treaty of Northampton (1328), an Anglo-Scottish peace treaty that recognized Scotland as an independent nation; see Stones, *Anglo-Scottish Relations*, document 41a (pp. 323–27), and Hiatt (*Medieval Forgeries*, p. 105). In the second version of the *Chronicle* Hardyng also claims to have submitted a copy to Edward IV, most probably in 1463 (see Oxford, Bodleian Library MS Arch. Selden B. 10, fol. 139v, and *The Chronicle of Iohn Hardyng*, ed. Ellis, p. 317).

67   *Umfrevile*. Hardyng claims that the treaty was immersed in oil while in the custody of a member of the Umfraville family.

71–77   *tho lettres . . . withoute difficulté*. Hardyng refers to the forged letters of David Bruce that he retrieved exemplifying a charter of Alexander of Scotland in which English overlordship is acknowledged and the ecclesiastical rights of York and Durham are reserved. The document in question is preserved in TNA: PRO E 39/2/7 and in Oxford, Bodleian Library MS Ashmole 789, fols. 161r–161v (See Hiatt, "Forgeries of John Hardyng," p. 9). Another reference to the rights of York occurs in the reign of King Arthur (3.2409m–2415).

76   *Cuthbertes ryght*. St. Cuthbert (circa 635–87) was bishop of Lindisfarne in the kingdom of Northumbria. Since Northumbria extended up to the Firth of Forth in Cuthbert's time, his "ryght" refers to the powers that the episcopal see gave the saint over south-east Scotland. For Cuthbert's life see Rollason and Dobson, "Cuthbert [St Cuthbert] (*c.*635–687)."

93   *figure*. The word *figure* refers to Hardyng's map of Scotland occurring on fols. 226v–227r.

99–105   *Now seth . . . verry demonstracioun*. By emphasizing Henry VI's descent from the celebrated Henry V, Hardyng implies that he inherits a responsibility to continue his father's work, not only in the form of fulfilling his promise to reward Hardyng, but by continuing the successful campaigns of his father and following his example of good leadership (compare also Prol.134–47).

113   *Sex yere now go*. The Dedication and Prologue appear to have been composed after the main body of the *Chronicle*, but before the text was presented to Henry VI in 1457; "Sex yere now go" probably refers to 1451. Hardyng's description of John Kemp seems to corroborate this date (see the Introduction and notes to Prol.120 and Prol.148–49).

114–15   *lettres secretary . . . pryvy seel*. Hardyng refers to the royal seals, particularly the king's personal seal, indicating that his grant was authorized in the correct manner and should not have been canceled. The Privy Seal was originally the king's personal seal, but over time it was adopted for other government functions, and new "secret" seals, most notably the Signet Seal, took its place to enable the king to exercise his authority and authenticate correspondence. The Signet Seal was kept by the king's secretary, hence "lettres secretary"; for further information, see Otway-Ruthven, *King's Secretary and the Signet*.

117   *Gedyngtoun*. Geddington Manor, Northamptonshire, is no longer extant. In the late medieval period it was a royal hunting lodge and was often granted to the queen of England as dowager land. See the second version of the *Chronicle*, where Hardyng attributes his loss of Geddington to Henry Beaufort and states that he was promised "recompense" (Oxford, Bodleian Library MS Arch. Selden B. 10, fol. 129v; *Chronicle of Iohn Hardyng*, ed. Ellis, p. 292). The estimated annual revenue of Geddington at this time was approximately £32 (see *Chronicle of Iohn Hardyng*, ed. Ellis, p. vi, and the Sheriffs' accounts for 1436–41 in TNA: PRO E 199/32/19); it would therefore have been a substantial reward for Hardyng's services.

120   *noble chaunccellere*. John Kemp (c.1375–1454), cardinal (1439), archbishop of York (1425), archbishop of Canterbury (1452), and chancellor of England (1426–32 and 1450). Hardyng's description of Kemp as "cardinall" of York (Prol.122) is a conflation of two of his titles. Given that he makes no reference to Kemp's position as archbishop of Canterbury, it is likely that Hardyng is describing events that took place in 1451; at this time Kemp held the office of chancellor, cardinal, and archbishop of York, but was not yet archbishop of Canterbury (Kingsford, "First Version," p. 465). However, see the Textual Notes for evidence that the scribe erased a previous line occupying the space of Prol.122 before adding the line that identified Kemp as Chancellor.

134–47 *Bot undirnethe . . . thys cace*. Once again Hardyng compares the rule of Henry VI with that of his father in order to demonstrate that Henry VI has the power to continue his father's good rule.

148–49 *Whiche evydence . . . yow take*. Hardyng's reference to the main body of the *Chronicle* being "afore comprised" suggests that the prologue was added after the history had been compiled and before it was presented to the king (other evidence supporting this assumption is discussed in the Manuscript Description).

        These lines also suggest that the *Chronicle* and the documents that Hardyng delivered to the Treasury in November 1457 (the "other mo" mentioned at Prol.149) were meant to form a package attesting to Henry VI's dominion, and that the *Chronicle* was submitted to the king at, or around, the same time as the forgeries. The Patent Roll entry recording Hardyng's 1457 annuity further supports this: dated three days after Hardyng submitted the documents, it alludes to the content of the prologue, particularly James I's bribery and Hardyng's losses (see Introduction; *Calendar of Patent Rolls: Henry VI, 1452–61*, p. 393. m. 8 [18 November 1457]; *Calendar of Close Rolls: Henry VI, 1454–61*, p. 235, m. 28; Kingsford, "First Version," p. 465; and Riddy, "Wars of the Roses," p. 96). For Hardyng's repeated foregrounding of "the Scottish issue" and the relationship between the *Chronicle* and documents, see the Introduction, Hiatt, *Medieval Forgeries*, and Peverley, "Anglo-Scottish Relations."

150   *Foure hundre mark and fyfty*. It is highly improbable that Hardyng had this much capital. Rather, he has inflated the cost to demonstrate the documents' financial and figurative value to the English crown. His expenses contrast effectively with the alleged bribe offered to him by James I, which is more than double the amount paid by Hardyng. The distinction between the expenses and bribe similarly underscores Hardyng's loyalty, despite a lack of financial recompense from his "natyfe" king, Henry VI (Prol.144).

BOOK 1

1m   *How thay . . . eldest sustire*. The pre-Trojan foundation myth of Albyne and her sisters has a long and complicated textual history, which appears to be linked with the classical tale of the Danaïds and the biblical account of the giants before the deluge in Genesis 6:1–6 (see Cohen, *Of Giants*, pp. 52–54 for the latter). Its first notable appearance in England is in the fourteenth-century Anglo-Norman poem *Des Grantz Geantz*, which survives in a long and short version, a unique prose redaction in Oxford Corpus Christi College MS 78, and a Latin prose adaptation, *De Origine Gigantum*. The story was attached to the Long and Short versions of the Anglo-Norman Prose *Brut*, *FH*, *The Short English Metrical Chronicle*, the *Anonimalle Chronicle*, Castleford's *Chronicle*, *Scalacronica*, *Mohun Chronicle*, Thomas Sprott's *Chronicle*, *EH*, the Latin *Brut*, the Middle English Prose *Brut*, *NC*, the *Liber Monasterii de Hyda*, John Rous's *Historia Regum Anglie*, the *Ynglis Chronicle*, and Jean Waurin's *Chroniques*. The story also occurs in the romance *Guiron le Courtois* and the unique text about Brutus and Albyne in London, College of Arms L6. For further information on the myth and its different forms see *Des Grantz Geantz*, ed. Brereton; Reynolds, "Medieval *Origines Gentium*"; Carley and Crick, "Constructing Albion's Past"; Evans, "Gigantic Origins"; Matheson, *Prose Brut*; and Marvin, "Albine and Isabelle."

           Hardyng's adaptation, which is similar to *Des Grantz Geansz*, contains some interesting and unique embellishments (see 1.20–61, 1.172–82, 1.232m, and 1.257–80). Though the accompanying marginalia demonstrate awareness of other versions of the story (see note 1.176m), Hardyng only pursues the issue of conflicting sources in his second *Chronicle*.

           Seynt Colman. Hardyng appears to be referring to Saint Colman (d. 676), bishop of Lindisfarne; however, the "Dialoge" that he refers to as a source for the foundation myth of Albion does not correspond with any known texts written by the bishop. Since Hardyng later cites Colman as a source for events that occurred after his death in 676, he may be deliberately misrepresenting him to lend authenticity to his history. On the other hand, he may have encountered a text that erroneously attributed certain information to Colman, or confused him with Saint Columba, who is linked with a number of writings, but not a "Dialoge" including Albyne.

Trogus Pompeyus. Pompeius Trogus, an historian and naturalist from Gallia Narbonensis, composed the *Philippic History* during the reign of the emperor Augustus. The history, comprising forty-four books, is now known only from references to it by other writers and an abbreviated version, or *Epitome*, compiled by Marcus Junianus Justinus, or Justin, c. 200 AD. (For further information see Howatson, *Classical Literature,* pp. 308 and 582, and *Justin, Epitome,* ed. Yardley and Heckel). If Hardyng really had been instructed in Justin's *Epitome*, his recollection of it is very poor; it is not a source for the legend of Albyne and her sisters, or indeed for any of the other passages that Hardyng attributes to Trogus and Justin (see 1.176m, and 2.554m). Hardyng may have made an erroneous connection between the proud Grecian princesses and the origin myth of the Amazon women recounted in Book Two of the *Epitome*, but it is more likely that he altered the work to lend authority to the early part of the *Chronicle*. Equally, he may have cited Trogus, like Colman, after seeing him mentioned as a source for ancient history in other chronicles, such as *FH* or *P*.

Julyus Cesaryne . . . and discripcion. Cesarini (1398–1444), an eminent scholar and humanist, had a prominent career in the service of the Papal Curia and was created cardinal in 1426. Pope Martin V (c. 1368–1431), whom Cesarini served, was elected on 11 November 1417. For further details on Cesarini and Martin, see Cross and Livingstone (*Christian Church,* pp. 314 and 1045).

the cardynal of Wynchester. The "cardynal of Wynchester" is Henry Beaufort (c. 1376–1447), bishop of Lincoln (1398–1404), bishop of Winchester (1404–47), and cardinal (from 1426/27). Hardyng also mentions Beaufort in the second version of his *Chronicle*; see note Prol.117 above. For Beaufort's life and career see Harriss, *Cardinal Beaufort*.

1   *The while that Troy was regnyng in his myghte.* This line appears to be a reworking of the opening of John Walton's verse translation of Boethius's *De Consolatione Philosophiae*, which begins "The while þat Rome was reignyng in hir floures" (p. 4). For Hardyng's probable knowledge and use of Walton's text see note 2.14–56 and Peverley, "Chronicling the Fortunes."

3   *thretty.* The number of daughters is usually thirty or thirty-three. The later reference to fifty daughters at 1.176m shows Hardyng's awareness of the story's association with the myth of the Danaïds.

20–61   *Save only . . . alle fortorne.* Whilst the presentation of the youngest daughter corresponds with that in *Des Grantz Geanz, De Origine Gigantum,* and *NC* (compare her declaration that she agreed to Albyne's plan with her mouth but not her heart), Hardyng draws upon the romance tradition to develop her character further. She discloses her sisters' plan out of "pyté" for the husbands (1.29), a desideratum in romance heroines, and she trembles, faints, cries "allase" (1.57), and scratches her face in the same manner as distressed romance heroines; see, for example, Queen Heroudis in *Sir Orfeo*, lines 78–82, and Chrétien de Troyes' *Erec and Enide*, lines 4285 ff. and line 4560 ff.

62–99   *And fro . . . me tolde.* The dialogue between the king and his daughter is omitted from the second version of Hardyng's *Chronicle.*

148–68   *Thus in . . . right fayne.* By comparing the sisters' former and present states during the long sea voyage Hardyng highlights the sisters' shift in status and prepares us for a change in landscape, as we move from the civilization of their father's kingdom to the wilderness of Albion. The detailed description of the sea voyage does not occur in the second version.

172–82   *Bot Albyne . . . gode policy.* The succession laws of ancient Greece that Hardyng describes are really those that governed the inheritance of lay property and titles in medieval England. When the male line failed, as it so often did in the late Middle Ages, an "heir general," or daughter, could inherit or pass on a claim over a younger male member of the family. In Hardyng's time there were no explicit laws regulating the descent of the monarchy so, technically, either an "heir male" or an "heir general" could inherit it. However, in practice, the inheritance of the crown followed the rules of primogeniture governing the "heir male" principle, ensuring that the inheritance of titles and lands passed to the oldest male.

176m   *Nota that . . . xliiii bookes.* The different names assigned to the king show Hardyng's awareness of alternative versions of the Albyne myth. While he does not pursue the issue in this version, he discusses the conflicting stories in the second version of the *Chronicle.* Diocletian appears most commonly in the Middle English Prose *Brut,* where he is king of Syria, not Greece, and Albyne's mother is Labana, not Albyne. He also appears in some manuscripts of the Anglo-Norman Prose Brut, the Latin Brut, and in several conflated versions of the Greek and Syrian story prefacing the Middle English Prose Brut.

The association of King Danaus with the Grecian king, who is usually unnamed, connects the sisters with the classical myth of the Danaïds; the same myth is alluded to in *FH* I:15. For further information about the different versions see the items listed at 1.1m above.

The chronicle Hardyng cites by Martin is *MO,* but this does not include the myth of the Danaïds; neither does Justin's *Epitome* of Pompeius Trogus (see note 1.1m). Although some of the *Chronicle*'s material does correspond with that in *MO* (see, for example, 1.202–03, 2.163–205, 2.229–31), Hardyng probably encountered it via another source that acknowledged its debt to *MO* (and Trogus), and misappropriated its attributions to enhance the authority of his text. For the influence of *MO* in the Middle Ages see Ikas, "Martinus Polonus' Chronicle."

197m   *Nota whan . . . sayde Dialoge.* For the "law of Greece" see note 1.172–82; for Colman see note 1.1m.

202–03   *As Omer . . . his entent.* We have been unable to find a satisfactory explanation for this remark. It may be an erroneous response to *HRB* §25, which states that "Omerus clarus rethor et poeta habebatur" ("Homer was considered to be a famous rhetorician and poet") at the end of the reign of Guendolyne, but, this would not explain Hardyng's correct use of the passage at 2.940–53. Conversely, it could be a serious misreading of the passage in *MO* (p. 399), *FH* (I:42–43), and *EH* (I:304), which states that Homer flourished in Greece during the forty-year reign of Agrippa Silvius.

211–17   *Thus Fortune . . . withoute disobeyshance.* This is the first of many references to the "mutabilité" of Fortune. For further discussion of Hardyng's attitude to Fortune and its importance see Peverley, "Chronicling the Fortunes." Compare also the reference to Fortune in *Des Grantz Geantz* (pp. 328–40).

232m   *How the . . . destroyed hem.* Hardyng's reference to God taking vengeance on those who embrace evil and fail to keep the "pese amonge thaymselfe" lays the foundation for later warnings about the perils that face the English if contemporary injustices and civil unrest are not resolved. This is further supported by the reference at 1.267–80 to contemporary men retreating to the "kaves" where the giants used to dwell in times of civil unrest (see note 1.257–80). By alluding to Brute's overthrowing of the giants before we reach that part of the narrative, Hardyng initiates a pattern common in chronicles whereby Providence is consistently shown to punish the wicked. See also note 2.575–659 below.

251–52   *Thus gat . . . and wight.* This part of the Albyne legend alludes to Genesis 6:4, where the sons of God beget giants on the daughters of man. For giants in medieval literature, see Cohen, *Of Giants.*

257–80   *Of peple . . . by waste.* Hardyng appears to be suggesting that humans lived alongside the giants and were oppressed by them. This is an interesting adjustment to the usual story, because the description that ensues of the wild places where the giants make their "grete edificaciouns" (1.268) invites the audience to see a correlation between the civil unrest in Albion and that in late fifteenth-century England. Whilst other chronicles contain allusions to the giants' dwelling in caves and on hills, Hardyng's narrative makes a distinct connection between the "kaves" (1.272, 1.275) that giants once lived in and those where his contemporaries retreat with their goods in times of war. This shifts the theme of oppression and societal strife from the giants' era to the present, where another type of "giant" — the self-serving lord — oppresses the people and maintains disorder (compare also note 2.560–61).

283–308   *From Dame . . . very computacioun.* Compare with *CPL* (I:20), and RMB (1.1745–48). See also note 2.570–74 below.

310   *Til tyme come efte that Brutus have thaym slayne.* These lines anticipate events in Book 2, where Hardyng describes the arrival of Brute in Albion, and he and Coryneus slay the last remaining giants (see note 2.575–659).

BOOK 2

1m   *the genology as is comprised in the grete Brute.* The "genology" referred to here is the genealogy of the Trojans contained in several manuscripts of *HRB*, in RMB, and in a number of the *Prose Bruts* in Latin and English (see note 2.57–96). In all likelihood the "grete Brute" is one of these texts.

     the cronicles of Itaylle. Possibly a reference to *MO* or a text dealing with the Trojan war (see note 2.97–144 below).

     De Gestis Enee Regis Latinorum. Hardyng may be referring to a romance dealing with the events surrounding the Trojan war (see note 2.97–144 below). Identification of the illegible "Pli[?]" might shed further light on this matter.

     Cronica Bruti . . . primi Anglie. This alludes to *HRB* §§1–4.

14–56   *I shalle . . . my fone.* Hardyng employs two rhetorical features common to fifteenth-century literature to lend authority to himself, as an author, and his text. His claim to be "symple" and devoid of skill (2.15, 2.48) should not be taken at face value; it is part of a humility topos found in many late medieval prologues (on this topic see Lawton, "Dullness," p. 762). Equally, his call to God for help with completing the *Chronicle* blends affected modesty with the topos of invoking classical deities. Like Osbern Bokenham in his *Legendys of Hooly Wummen* and John Walton, whose translation of Boethius's *De Consolatione Philosophiae* appears to have influencd 2.24–39, Hardyng sets himself apart from previous authors, like Chaucer and Lydgate, whom he imitates elsewhere, but attains a moral victory over them by emphasizing his own piety over their partiality for pagan assistance. At the same time, Hardyng adds unquestionable authority to his text by indicating that it is inspired by God and therefore aligned with truth. Hardyng's use of poetry by Chaucer, Lydgate and Walton is explored in Peverley, "Chronicling the Fortunes." For other examples of the topos see Chaucer's *TC* 1.6–14, 4.22–28; *TB*, Prol.36–62; and Bokenham's *Life of Mary Magdalene* in the *Legendys of Hooly Wummen*, lines 5214–24. For contemporary criticism by preachers on the use of classical authorities see Owst, *Literature and Pulpit*, pp. 178–80.

24   *welles of Caliope.* Calliope is the muse of epic poetry. In stating that he has not tasted, or drank, from her wells, Hardyng means that he lacks poetic eloquence. Compare Chaucer's Franklin, *CT* V(F)716–22, and *TC* III.45. He appears to have based the phrase on Walton's *Boethius*, p. 3 ("And certayn I haue tasted wonder lyte / As of the welles of calliope"), but other poets similarly called upon Calliope for inspiration; compare, for example, Lydgate, *FP*, 3.8–9.

25–32   *Saturnus. . . Protheus.* The gods and goddesses that Hardyng refuses to invoke are as follows: Saturn, Titan god of time and father of Jupiter; Jupiter, king of the gods and sky in Roman mythology; Mars, Roman god of war; Mercury, messenger of the gods in Roman mythology; Venus, Roman goddess of love; Ceres, Roman goddess of the earth; Phoebus, the sun god, also known as

Apollo; Seneus, a god we have been unable to identify positively, though it may, unusually, be Cenaeus, a surname of Zeus derived from Cape Cenaeum in Euboea (see Smith, *Dictionary of Greek and Roman Biography*, I:663–64); Pallas Athena, the Greek goddess of war and wisdom (her Roman counterpart, Minerva, also occurs in this list); Alecto, one of the three Furies or Erinyes in Greek mythology; Megaera, one of the three Furies or Erinyes in Greek mythology; Genius, the daimon, or spiritual essence, of an individual; Tisiphone, one of the three Furies or Erinyes in Greek mythology; Cupid, Roman god of love and son of Venus; Hymen or Hymenaeus, Greek god of marriage; Minerva, Roman goddess of wisdom (her Greek counterpart Pallas Athena is also listed); Diana, Roman goddess of the moon; Bacchus, Roman god of wine and festivities; Cerberus, three-headed dog of the underworld in Greek and Roman mythology; Manes, spirits of the dead; Glaucus, a Greek sea god; Vulcane, Roman god of fire; and Protheus, Greek prophetic sea god and herdsman of Poseidon's seals.

46   *Guyen.* Guyenne was a province in southwest France.

49–52   Here Hardyng's modesty topos again echoes Chaucer, *CT* X(I)55–60, among others.

57–96   *Bot of . . . so gloryus.* In tracing the lineage of Brute's ancestors back to Adam, Hardyng appears to follow the same genealogy as RMB 1.209–428. However, similar genealogies of the Trojans occur in several manuscripts of *HRB* (see Crick, "*Historia*," pp. 43–44), and in some manuscripts of the Latin and English *Prose Brut*, making it difficult to ascertain which specific source(s) Hardyng utilized. Selective parts of the lineage also appear in other chronicles, such as *HB, MO, P, EH,* and *NC*.

97–144   *Whom Ercules . . . rial toure.* Reference to the first destruction of Troy is also made in RMB 1.339–40, 1.439–50, and *P* II:406–07, which Hardyng may have used; however, given that he goes on to include details not found in these chronicles, such as the width of new Troy and the height of its walls (1.137–44), this part of the text could have been influenced by a non-chronicle source, such as Lydgate's *TB* (2.82–96, 2.571–88), another account of the fall of Troy similar to the *Laud Troy Book* (1825–26), or the alliterative "*Gest hystoriale*" *of the Destruction of Troy* (1007 ff., 1538, 1546–48), all of which are based on Guido delle Colonne's *Historia destructionis Troiae*, pp. 46–47. Crick notes that some manuscripts of the *HRB* contain Guido's Troy story or the *Historia de excidio Troie* attributed to Dares Phrygius (*Historia*, pp. 37–39 and 47–48), so it is possible that a similar manuscript supplied Hardyng with the information for this section. Nevertheless, there is sufficient correspondence between Lydgate's work and the *Chronicle* to recommend *TB* as a potential source for Hardyng's description of Priam's Troy, as well as his "Conceyte" on the fall of Troy (2.105m) and his address to Laomedon ("Leamedon"). Further investigation of the sources used by RMB might help to ascertain whether Hardyng utilized a single text, which combined all of the aforementioned elements, or blended two separate works; for a discussion of RMB's possible sources see RMB, ed. Sullens (pp. 695–96). The temporary switch to eight-line stanzas at the start of Book 2 may indicate that Hardyng was using a source written in eight-line stanzas for this section of the work, although it is possible that this change was influenced by Walton's translation of Boethius's *De Consolatione Philosophiae*, which Hardyng knew and used at the start of Book 2 (see note 2.14–56).

99   *Destroyed Troy*. The pun is irresistible in implying that Troy, through fate and bad decisions, undoes itself. See 104m, "Troy for litil myght hafe," and line 118, "distroynge Troys cyté." Compare Chaucer's *TC* (1.68), "Troie sholde destroied be."

129   *Exiona*. Possibly an error for Polyxena, Priam's daughter, or a misreading of Hesione ("Esionam"), daughter of Laomedon, who is taken by the Greeks after the first destruction of Troy. See, for example, *P* II:406; RMB 1.346; *TB,* 1.4343; *Laud Troy Book*, line 1709; and *"Gest hystoriale" of the Destruction of Troy*, line1387.

163–205   *With alle . . . more discordance*. Aeneas's encounter with Dido does not occur in *HRB*, *HRBVV*, *RB*, RMB, *Brut*, or *NC*, but Hardyng could have known the story from a number of sources, including *MO* (pp. 398–99) and *P* (II:432–33), which mention Dido's great love for Aeneas, and from those works dealing with the fall of Troy mentioned above (see notes 2.97–144 and 2.129), or from Chaucer's *House of Fame*, part 1, which divagates extensively and amusingly on their relationship. Lydgate's *FP* briefly touches upon Dido's encounter with Aeneas, but makes no reference, as Hardyng does, to Dido's desire to make Aeneas her "husbonde" or the fact that he "stale fro hire" (2.168–69). Aeneas's vision and his helping King Evander are absent in *HRB*, *HRBVV*, *RB*, RMB, *Brut*, and *NC*, where only King Latinus and Turnus are mentioned, but Evander is present in *MO*, p. 399, *P* II:434–35, and *EH* I:43. Interestingly, *P* II:434–35 also contains a reference to Pompeius Trogus, whom Hardyng mentions as a source at 1.1m, 1.176m, and 2.554m.

217–20   *This Eneas . . . was hayre*. The castle named after Lavinia, "Lavynyon" (2.219), is mentioned in *HRBVV* §6, *RB* lines 70–72, *LB* lines 96–97, RMB 1.790–92, and *P* II:434–35, but not *HRB*, *Brut*, and *NC*.

221–24   *Of whom . . . londes echone*. The child referred to is Silvius Posthumus, so called because he was born after Aeneas's death. In *HRB* §6, lines *OV* 17–22, *Brut* p. 5, *NC* fol. 3v, only one Silvius, son of Ascanius, is mentioned, but Hardyng, like *HRBVV* §6, *HA* p. 24–27, *RB* lines 74–117, *LB* lines 99–133, and RMB 1.797–834 includes two: one, Silvius Posthumous, the son of Aeneas by Lavinia; the other, Silvius Julius, son of Ascanius and father of Brute. Interestingly, *P* (II:442–43) goes on to discuss the conflicting information about the two Silvii in its sources, and *MO* (p. 399) provides a list of the many Silvii who reigned in Italy. Wright believes that the introduction of two Silvii derives from a lost text of *HRBVV* (see *HRBVV*, pp. xcix–ci).

229–32   *Whan Abdon . . . of sentement*. Abdon is also mentioned in *FH* I:19, *MO* p. 398, *P* II:418–19, and *EH* I:43. *FH* and *P* record Abdon as judge in Israel during and after destruction of Troy, but they do not mention Homer in the same section; *MO* and *EH* on the other hand do. *MO* is of particular interest here because its dating of Abdon's reign against other events matches Hardyng's reckoning of 330 years before the foundation of Rome (2.228).

236   *House of Fame*. The concept of a house of fame was made most famous by Chaucer's work of the same name, which retells the story of Aeneas in part 1. Lydgate also mentions it in his *TB* (3.4254, Envoy 14), and *FP* (3.2352, 4.122, 5.420, 6.109, 6.514, 6.3093, 8.26).

246   *corporaly*. Hardyng's use of corporally as an adverb is earlier than the first instance recorded in the *OED* by Caxton in 1483 (s.v. *corporally*). He appears to be using it to designate the passing of time in this world, much like one would use the adverb "temporally."

250   *Creusa, Lavynes nese*. There is some confusion here, either on Hardyng's part or in a hitherto unidentified source used by him. In classical mythology Lavinia's niece is usually unnamed, and Creusa is the name of Aeneas's first wife, mother of Ascanius and daughter of Priam; she is left behind as Aeneas flees from Troy. See *HRBVV* §6, *RB* lines 84–88, *FH* I:19, *P* II:436–37, RMB 1.733–36, and *EH* I:304. Hardyng may also have encountered her in the romances dealing with Troy mentioned in note 2.97–144 above or in Chaucer's *Legend of Good Women*, although there is no evidence within the *Chronicle* to suggest that he knew the latter.

253   *hire pitese*. Hardyng associates female virtue with the quality of pity once again (see note 1.20–61 above), but this stanza is critical of women's abuse of that quality. Creusa is deflowered because of Silvius's "subtilitese" (2.252) not because she willingly gave herself to him out of pity, as Hardyng implies some women are prone to doing when they encounter a man in adversity; compare, Chaucer's Merchant's Tale, where May decides to take Damian as her lover because she is "fulfilled of pitee" (*CT* IV[E]1995). Hardyng's portrayal of Silvius may have been influenced by a text such as *CPL* I:4, where the words "enchaunta" and "larcenus" are used to describe his seduction of Lavinia's niece.

257–64 *Askanyus whan . . . his humanyté*. The prophecies made here about Brute are later linked with destiny, Fortune, and divine providence. See 2.280, 2.321–36 and 2.512.

269–72 *In whiche . . . no mo*. Although the syntax is unclear, Hardyng appears to ascribe the foundation of Alba ("Aube") to Silvius Posthumous, not Ascanius, who builds the city in *HRB* §6, *RB* lines 91–92, *LB* line 111, *MO* p. 399, and RMB 1.807–08. In these chronicles Alba is mentioned before the prophecies concerning Brute, but Hardyng, or the source he is using, switches the order. Alba is not mentioned in *OV*, *Brut*, or *NC*.

280   *predestinate*. The reference to destiny recalls Hardyng's earlier explanation of the prophecies governing Brute's life and Fortune's role in shaping his future. See 2.257–64, 2.321–36, 2.512.

281–312   *His fadir . . . to dispende*. The wide range of social, literary, and military skills
           encompassed in Brute's education corresponds with the sort of curriculum
           followed by a noble youth in the later Middle Ages. This passage is unique to
           Hardyng and may reflect the kind of education that he received whilst in the
           service of the Percy family, since servants of gentle and high rank in noble
           households often received tuition similar to their young masters. In reality
           the biennial sequence prescribed by Hardyng would not have been so rigid,
           but the approximate ages provided for the start of each new activity do
           correspond with extant examples of medieval instruction and with the
           recommended ages for similar activities in late medieval educational
           treatises. Hardyng's suggestion that hunting and military training should
           commence at fourteen and sixteen respectively echoes the suggestions made
           in Christine de Pisan's *Book of the Fayttes of Armes* (p. 29) and the earliest
           English prose translation of Vegetius's *De Re Militari* (p. 52) both of which
           draw upon Giles of Rome's *De Regimine Principum*, which, in turn, was known
           in both its Latin form and in a Middle English translation by John Trevisa
           (see *Governance of Kings and Princes*, pp. 242–43, 399). For the accuracy of
           ages given by Hardyng, see Orme, *From Childhood to Chivalry* (pp. 51–60,
           144–56, 182), and Green, *Poets and Princepleasers, passim*.

287   *fiftene yere age*. Hardyng's source for Brute's age is RMB, which in turn follows
           RB and *HRB*. Several other kings and knights are singled out in the *Chronicle*
           for achieving remarkable feats in their youth: see, for example, Constantine,
           the first Christian king of Britain, who is said to show "Grete manhode" in his
           "chyldissh yeres" (3.505–11); King Arthur, who is fifteen when he inherits the
           throne and expels the Saxons from his land (3.2248–49); Galahad, who is
           also fifteen when he joins Arthur's court, achieves the Siege Perilous, and
           embarks on his Grail quest (3.2954–55); Thomas Umfraville, who is sixteen
           when he defeats the Scots (6.2391–2400); and Gilbert Umfraville, who
           completes his rite of passage on the Scottish borders and gains a fearsome
           reputation amongst his enemies (6.3436–49). Hardyng's decision to
           emphasize the age of such figures may indicate that he wished to make them
           comparable with the chivalric heroes of medieval romance, who frequently
           surpass their peers and achieve great things in adolescence. Equally, he may
           have planned to associate the potential for greatness in young men with
           Henry VI, who ascended the throne as a child and whose minority ended, not
           inconsequentially, where Hardyng chose to end this version of the *Chronicle*.

313–44   *So was . . . with joy*. Hardyng's presentation of Brute as a constant, virtuous
           young man "withoute mutabilité" (2.320) contrasts with the capriciousness of
           Fortune and introduces one of the principal themes of the *Chronicle*: the
           notion that no man can eschew the mutability of Fortune, but steadfastness
           and virtue provide the best defense against her. At 2.326–28 Hardyng puns
           on the word "herte," as Brute brings "unquyet" to his own heart by shooting
           at a hart and accidentally killing his father. Of greater interest, however, are
           2.322 and 2.344, where Hardyng appropriates phrases from Chaucer's *TC*
           1.1, 1.54, and 3.617. His depiction of Brute as physician to the Trojans'
           "double sorowe" (2.344) recalls the Boethian sickness imagery used in the

prologue to describe Hardyng's twofold distress at being unrewarded and injured from his royal service (see note Prol.29–35 above). This may imply that Hardyng intended to align Henry VI's potential to "leche" his subjects' sorrows (2.344) with Brute's ability to help and emancipate the Trojans. For further discussion of Hardyng's use of *TC* see Peverley, "Chronicling the Fortunes."

321–36   *Hir fadir ... alle retribute.* For other references to Brute's destiny see 2.257–64, 2.280, and 2.512.

339   *fortuyté.* The earliest recorded use of the noun fortuity in the *OED* dates from circa 1747 (s.v. *fortuity* (n.), meaning "accident, chance, an accidental occurrence"), but Hardyng uses it much earlier here to refer to Brute's accidental killing of his father. Compare also *MED* s.v. *fortunite* (n.), where Hardyng is the only source cited.

345–52   *Syr Helenus ... and morow.* The details here correspond most closely with *CPL* I:6, and RMB 1.865–66, although Anchises is not mentioned in RMB.

353–553   *For pyté ... be repigned.* Hardyng's version of the story offered by *HRB*, *RB*, *CPL*, and RMB is greatly condensed. He omits all reference to Assaracus, the Greek lord who sympathizes with the Trojans and allows Brute to use his castles, and Membritius, the wise Trojan who suggests freeing Pandrasus and leaving Greece to seek a new land; in so doing the narrative loses some of the coherence that the other chronicles have. The fight between Coryneus and Himbert is similarly absent. On balance, a number of features suggest that Hardyng was using a version of *CPL*, RMB, or an intermediate source linked to them, rather than the other texts (see notes 2.381–84, 2.441, 2.444–45, and 2.545 below), but his narrative is also distinct from other texts in terms of the additional emphasis that he places on Brute's noble characteristics by presenting him as the sole saviour of the Trojans and the wisest and strongest of leaders (see also note 2.431–32).

381–84   *For whiche ... o way.* Both Hardyng and RMB 1.1021 place Brute in his castle as it is besieged by Pandrasus, whereas *HRB* and *RB* do not. *CPL* omits the siege entirely.

431–32   *To whiche ... grete defence.* Hardyng's Pandrasus grants Brute's requests "with gode wille," rather than out of fear as in other sources.

441   *So saylynge forthe by two days and two nyghtes.* Hardyng, *LB* line 559, and RMB 1.1311 give the length of Brute's first sea voyage as two days and two nights, whereas *HRB* §16, *HRBVV* §16, *RB* line 617 and *EH* II:209 specify two days and one night. In lines *OV* 79–80 and *Brut* p. 8, Brute arrives in Leogetia on the third day.

444–45   *His wyfe ... and swete.* These lines echo *HRB* §15, *CPL* I:10, and *EH* II:209, where Brute comforts his distressed wife during the sea voyage.

455–56   *Bothe herte . . . sene overalle.* Diana is the goddess of the moon, hunting, and chastity in Roman mythology; the presence of many deer in the island underlines her association with hunting.

461   *exspectaunce.* The *MED* does not record the form "exspectaunce." Hardyng appears to have used the adjective "expectaunt" as a noun (*MED* s.v. *expectaunt* and *OED* s.v. *expectant*) to rhyme with "observaunce," which would mean that Brute offers his prayers to Diana with "expectation" or "hope" that she will respond. If this is the case, his form of "expectance" is earlier than those examples given in the *OED*. Another possibility is that Hardyng's "exspectaunce" is a form of the noun "aspectaunce" (see *MED* s.v. *aspectaunce*) meaning "expression (of the face)." This would mean that Brute offers his prayers with expression. The former seems most likely given that Brute goes to Diana to ask for guidance.

489   *Columpnes of Ercules.* The Columns, or Pillars, of Hercules is the ancient name for the Straights of Gibraltar.

512   *werdes of desteny.* Hardyng refers once again to the role of Fortune and destiny in Brute's life. Compare 2.257–64, 2.280 and 2.321–36.

524   *Dusze Piers.* The "Twelve Peers" is a collective title usually given to the twelve paladins of Charlemagne; it is also used, more generally, as here, to refer to the twelve great peers of France (temporal, and ecclesiastic). See *MED* s.v. *dousse-per* (n.).

545   *Ovyde.* Hardyng's allusion to Ovid may be derived from *CPL* I:10 and RMB 1.1363–64, where he is mentioned just before Brute prays to Diana.

554m   *Nota how . . . armes of Eneas.* The description of Brute's arms given here does not occur in Justin's *Epitome* of Pompeius Trogus or Gerald of Wales's *Topography of Ireland*, as Hardyng maintains. An identification of the enigmatic *cronycles of Romanye* may shed further light on this matter, but given his penchant for heraldry, Hardyng may have invented the arms himself. It is not unusual for medieval romances and genealogies to provide descriptions of the arms belonging to classical heroes; see, for example, the *Laud Troy Book* 4538–39, 4775–78; *The "Gest Hystoriale" of the Destruction of Troy* 5926–28, 6144–46; and the genealogical roll made for Edward IV extant in Philadelphia Free Library, MS Lewis E201, which includes the banners of Brute and Pandrasus.

560–61   *Whiche by . . . and oppreste.* This is Hardyng's second reference to the giants oppressing the inhabitants of Albion (see note 1.257–80 above).

570–74   *Into this . . . ought enquere.* Compare with *CPL* I:20, and RMB 1.1745–48.

575–659   *Thus Brutus . . . lyfe inordynate.* Hardyng's account of Coryneus's victory over Gogmagog and Brute's establishment of Britain is comparable with, although much shorter than, *HRB* §21, *CPL* I:20–22, RMB 1.1757–1919 and *EH* II:218–19. Of greater interest, perhaps, is the way in which Hardyng reflects on the episode to establish what makes a kingdom flourish or fail. A good strong leader, like Brute, who provides for his people, offers a solid foundation for a successful civilization; Albine's society on the other hand is founded on sin (namely pride, a failed murder plot, and lust) and is therefore destined to fall. Hardyng makes a point of explaining that the destruction of the giants and the foundation of a new civilization was made possible because of God's will. Lines 639–52 are a reworking of Chaucer's *TC* 5.1828–41, but instead of warning his audience to turn their thoughts away from earthly love and look to heaven, Hardyng adapts Chaucer's verse to suit the moral of his narrative by admonishing pride and evil living. His observation that God will take "vengeance" (2.654) on those who sin and embrace misrule — further emphasized by 2.639m and the plethora of proverbial wisdom at 2.653–59 — echoes the earlier notice of the giants' malevolence at 1.301, and prefigures his later allusions to God destroying the wicked (see, for example, 2.1004, 2.1388, 2.1937, 3.335; for more on this topic see Peverley, "Chronicling the Fortunes"). Hardyng may have been struck by the biblical connotations of the name Gogmagog, for in Ezekiel 38–39 God threatens to inflict "Gog, the land of Magog" upon the Israelites as punishment for their sins (see also Ezekiel 38:2; Apocalypse 20:7–9). If so, he would undoubtedly have interpreted the Trojans' journey as a classical parallel of the biblical Exodus and quest for the Promised Land.

Significantly, the interjection at 2.639 is the only one that is not directly addressed to lords and princes; in essence the phrase "fresshe and lusty creatures" is general enough to apply to all levels of the social spectrum, but since it is appropriated from Chaucer's romance, Hardyng may have intended it to apply more specifically to members of the middle to high social strata.

625–31   *Rewardynge ever . . . withouten fayle.* Hardyng may have intended to invite a parallel between Brute's gifting of land to his loyal men and his own plea to be rewarded with Geddington Manor for his loyalty.

633   *kalendes of a chaunge.* This phrase appears to be taken from Chaucer's *TC* 5.1634 (see note 2.575–659 above).

639–45   *O ye . . . abd gay.* Compare *TC* 5.1835–41.

646–52   *Suche fyne . . . fals array.* Compare *TC* 5.1828–32.

667–743   *Thus Kynge . . . onto se.* This section has more in common with the details given in RMB 1.1845–1940, than *HRB* §22 and *RB* lines 1169–1246, but Hardyng omits RMB's references to Gurmund and Lud, and moves the notice of Coryneus's naming of Cornwall to the end of his fight with Gogmagog. Whilst *RB* and RMB include references to Brute's tending the land, the civilizing effect that Hardyng's Brute has on the realm is more emphatic and offers a striking contrast to fifteenth-century England under Henry VI. Hardyng accentuates the establishment of Trojan law in Britain to a greater degree than other chroniclers, highlighting the peace and stability that this brings to the realm after the iniquities and unrest suffered under the giants of Albion. In so doing, he is able to underscore a greater contrast between the Trojans' cultivation of the land and the wilderness that was there "before" (2.684). The depiction of the Trojans participating in chivalric activities, such as jousting, feasting, and hunting, may derive from *TC* (see, for example, 3.1718 and 3.1779–80) or Lydgate's *TB* (2.784–804). Hardyng's justification for disliking the French form "Novel Troy" (2.719) is unique.

676–80   *In whiche. . . townes edifyde.* In contrast with Albyne's kingdom, Brute's realm is governed by "rytes and lawes" (2.676). This is the first of many references within the *Chronicle* where the establishment and maintenance of just laws is shown to be conducive to peace, a point strongly emphasized in *HRB* as the mark of kingship.

703   *On his language.* That is, his Celtic dialect. Hardyng seems to recognize that *Thamyse* is not a Latin word (it is a Celtic term for river). He knows little of Celtic languages, of course, but explains the peculiarity "Of his language" (2.708) in terms of its descent from "Of Troys language as Turkes yit use and haunte" (2.718).

720–22   *That Frenshe. . . and unkynde.* The lack of "tendyrnesse" (2.721) shown to Brute and his men in France would undoubtedly have resonated with Hardyng's audience; following severe territorial losses across the Channel, anti-French sentiment in England was rife in the 1450s.

730–36   *That tyme . . . in Italy.* This information ultimately comes from *HB* §11, but Hardyng presumably knew it through another source such as *HRB* §22. The material is also contained in *RB* lines 1247–50, *FH* I:25, and *EH* II:219, but it does not occur in *OV*, *CPL*, RMB, *Brut*, or *NC*. The erroneous attribution of information in *HB* to Gildas is common in medieval chronicles.

744–71   *And at . . . of nature.* In describing Brute's division of the kingdom between his sons, Hardyng follows the tradition represented by *OV*, *CPL*, *EH*, and *Brut*, not *HRB*, *HRBVV*, *RB*, RMB, and *NC*, which have the sons divide the kingdom after their father's death. In giving the length of Brute's reign as twenty-four years, the *Chronicle* provides the same information as *HRB* §23; *HRBVV* §23; *RB* line 1257; *P* II:444–45; *CPL* I:22; RMB 1.1933–34; *EH* II:220; and *NC* fol. 6v, but not *OV* and Brut.

          Hardyng makes more of Brute's burial than the aforementioned texts by assigning him a tomb in the temple of Apollo, which he equates with St. Paul's Cathedral, London, and placing Brute's death in the year 1176 BC, a calculation which may help to identify a more specific source for these passages in the future.

751m   *But Giraldus . . . this balade.* Gerald of Wales says nothing of the sort, but Hardyng offers a reasonable justification for believing that Brute had a longer reign, even if his own *Chronicle* contradicts this marginalia by giving his reign as twenty-four years.

772–85   *O gude. . . dyd love.* Hardyng's interjection emphasizes the fact that Brute's good governance makes him worthy of God's eternal salvation, even though he was a pagan born before Christ.

786–834   *Of Brutus . . . his successory*. The order in which Hardyng presents Brute's sons
            is the same as that in *HRB* §23, *RB* lines 1259–60, Gerald of Wales's
            Description of Wales p. 232, *LB* lines 1054–66, *FH* I:27, *P* II:444–45, *CPL* I:22,
            RMB 1.1942–43, and *NC* fols. 6v–7r, where Locryne is the eldest, then
            Camber, then Albanacte. This is important because it allows Hardyng to
            accentuate the additional authority that Locryne has over his younger
            brothers, particularly Albanacte, the first king of Scotland, who is older than
            Camber in *HRBVV* §23; *OV* lines 187–88; *EH* II:220; and *Brut* p. 12.
            Hardyng stresses the sovereignty of Loegria (England) over Albany (Scotland)
            more than any of the aforementioned chroniclers, because it allows him to
            stress the theme of English suzerainty that was first introduced in the
            Prologue and that permeates the entire *Chronicle*.
                Though Brute's establishment of Trojan law in Britain first occurs in *HRB*,
            Hardyng uses it to parallel his earlier reference to Greek inheritance laws
            legitimizing Albyne's claim to Albion and reinforce Locryne's supremacy over
            his brothers. In describing how the poet "Mewyne" later set down "the lawes
            of Troy" in a work called "Infynytes" (2.822–31), Hardyng establishes the
            importance of law to society, paves the way for later accounts of rulers who
            have established new laws and had them written down, such as Dunwallo
            (2.1521m), Marcyan, and Alfred (2.1855–58), and provides precedents to
            allude to in later appeals to Henry VI to uphold the law and rectify
            contemporary injustices.
                We have been unable to identify "Infynytes" (2.831). It could have been
            invented by Hardyng, especially since the title emphasizes the eternal nature
            of the law, and thereby England's enduring right to rule Scotland according
            to Trojan law. However, the title may derive from a lost source, because, as
            Richard Moll has noted, the enigmatic Mewyn credited with copying his
            books at Glastonbury ("Mewytryne") probably results from Hardyng's
            misreading "of a Welsh placename, Inis-witrin, and the associated prophet,
            Melkin," who appears in *JG* ("Another Reference," p. 298). For further
            discussion of Melkin, the texts attributed to him by other authors, and the
            possible influence of *JG*, or a related "florilegium of Glastonbury lore," on
            Hardyng, see Carley, "Melkin the Bard"; *JG*, pp. lii–lx; and Riddy,
            "Glastonbury." See also note 2.2611–47 below.

835–953   *Bot as . . . and curiouse*. Hardyng's account of the death of Albanacte, his
            brothers' battle against Humber, and Locryne's affair with Estrilde follows
            HRB §§24–25, but omits a number of the details in Geoffrey of Monmouth's
            story, such as Coryneus brandishing his axe at Locryne and the length of
            Locryne's affair with Estrilde, which is also omitted in *CPL* I:26. Instead,
            Hardyng emphasises Locryne's position as overlord of Scotland (2.870–76),
            names the god that Locryne pretends to worship as Jupiter, and notes that
            Guendolyne sent Maddan to Cornwall *after* the death of Coryneus.

844   *thare sores to complayne*. This phrase echoes both the prologue, where Hardyng
            reveals that the king is the only man who can heal his sorrow (Prol.29–30),
            and 2.343–44, where the Trojans have their "double sorowe" healed by Brute.

849m   *eschete.* This term refers to the "reversion of land to the king or lord of a fee;" see *MED* s.v. *eschete* (n.).

954–1016   *This Maddan . . . in Lacedemonya.* Hardyng's version of the reigns of Maddan and Membrice is very similar to RMB 1.2115–2142. Both give the length of the kings' reigns as forty and twenty years respectively, present Manlyn as the elder brother, mention Membrice's bestiality, and conclude with reference to "Eristens" (Eurysthenes) reigning in "Lacedemonya" (Sparta). Hardyng's account is nevertheless exceptional for the striking contrast it creates between Maddan's peaceful reign and the strife witnessed under Membrice. The observation that under Maddan no man would dare to "displese" (2.969) his neighbor is comparable with the *Chronicle*'s praise of Henry V and Sir Robert Umfraville (7.586–88, 7.592, 7.906–07), and with later criticism of contemporary strife in England, where "In every shire, with jakkes and salades clene / Missereule doth ryse and maketh neyghbours were" (7.1009–10; see also 7.643–44). The suggestion that Maddan's two sons were born to defend the realm from war and strife likewise parallels Hardyng's later criticisms of Henry VI and his magnates failing to use their privileged position to serve the common weal and bring an end to civil unrest. Finally, while Hardyng's reference to God taking vengeance on Membrice for his perversion is consistent with the interpretation of his savage end in *OV* (lines 263–67) and in *Brut* (p. 14), he builds upon the notion of divine retribution by depicting the pagan goddess Minerva ("Mynerve") as God's scourge, and describing the hellish torments she inflicts upon Membrice's soul.

1017–1114 *Ebrauke his . . . cyté pryncipalle.* For the most part, the narrative concerning Ebrauke is analogous to *HRB* §27 and RMB 1.2143–2202, although neither source contains all of the details that Hardyng includes here. Like *RB* line 1539; *CPL* I:30; *P* III:14–15; RMB 1.2165; *OV* line 271; and *Brut* p. 15, Hardyng gives the length of the king's reign as sixty years, but he follows *HRB*, *P*, and *EH* II:226, by explaining the rationale behind Ebrauke's sending his daughters to Italy and by putting events into a universal context. The account in RMB agrees with the first etymological explanation Hardyng gives concerning Maiden Castle, but the connections he makes between Ebrauke's foundations and the castles of Arthurian romance are unique, as is his reference to the folklore associated with Saint Patrick at Dumbarton (see notes 2.1033–44, 2.1052–65 and 2.1066–72 below). However, see also *Le Petit Bruit* (p. 6), which makes reference to Ebrauke's two castles and attributes the information to the testimony of the Saint Grail ("a la testemoinaunce Seint Graal"), presumably an allusion to the Vulgate Cycle, or a similar Arthurian text.

1033–44   *A castelle . . . tho wones.* These lines allude to the death of the Lady of Escalot, who falls in love with Sir Lancelot and dies when he rejects her. In the Vulgate *La Mort le Roi Artu* (p. 113), which Hardyng shows familiarity with elsewhere, the boat on which the lady's dead body is placed sails to Camelot, not Lancelot's castle, Dolorouse Garde (or Joyous Garde as he later renames it; see *Lancelot*, II:103). For further discussion of Hardyng's association of Dolorouse Garde with Bamburgh, and related sources, see Moll, "Ebrauke."

1052–65   *High on . . . that awarde*. Hardyng appears to be conflating two episodes from Arthurian romance involving Ywain, a knight of the Round Table, who defeats a giant named Harpin of the Mountain, travels to the town of Dire Adventure ("Pesme Aventure"), and rescues a host of ladies kept in servitude by the king of the Isle of Maidens ("li rois de l'Isle as Puceles"); see Chrétien de Troyes' *Chevalier au Lion*, 5111 ff. and the Middle English *Ywain and Gawain*, 2931 ff. (it is unlikely that he knew the Welsh analogue *Owain*). Hardyng aligns the Isle of Maidens in the romance with the "Mayden Castelle" (2.1064) he knows as Edinburgh and casts the two demons that Ywain must defeat to free the women as a giant, possibly confusing this episode with Ywain's earlier encounter with Harpin.

           The Vulgate Grail quest, during which Yvain helps Gawain to liberate the Castle of Maidens from seven wicked knights, could, alternatively, have inspired Hardyng's anecdote, but, on balance, the presence of a giant makes Chrétien de Troyes' *Le Chevalier au Lion* a more likely source. Lines 3.3012–16 and 3.3191 may also have been influenced by Chrétien's works.

1066m   *Nota quod . . . vocatur Dunbretayne*. The marginalia alludes to *P* II:64–69. The reference to Sulwath may indicate that Hardyng was using Trevisa's translation of *P* rather than Higden's text (see also note 2.1017–1114 above, where other correspondences between Hardyng's text and *P* in this section are noted).

1066–72   *The cyté . . . donge therein*. Saint Patrick was purportedly born in Dumbarton (see MacPhail, *Dumbarton Castle*, p. 4). The miracles that Hardyng attributes to the saint are no doubt derived from folk tradition (compare also 7.1296–97), but we have only been able to locate one other reference to Saint Patrick's proscription that no horse should dung in Dumbarton Castle in what appears to be a sixteenth-century paraphrase of Hardyng's itinerary of Scotland. The document, which survives in three copies, provides "An abstracte for Englyschemen to knowe the realme of Scotlande thorowe oute," giving the distances between the towns through which an invading army should pass and some notes about local features. One of the features mentioned is that Dumbarton is the strongest castle in Scotland and that at Saint Patrick's request "there should never horse dung in it." The document appears to be associated with a memorandum of 1542 made in preparation for Henry VIII's invasion of Scotland (see Gairdner and Brodie, *Letters and Papers*, 17, pp. 584–85).

1115–98   *Hys sonne . . . his hire*. For the reigns of Brute Grenesheelde, Leyle, Rudhudibrace, and Bladud, Hardyng's text is comparable with *HRB* §§28–30, RMB 1.2203–2260, and *EH* II:226–27 (which also equates the Temple of Apollo with St. Paul's). The references to Gildas and Walter of Oxford at 2.1128 and 2.1189–90 appear to be Hardyng's own; by referring to Walter, archdeacon of Oxford, as a source, Hardyng actually means Geoffrey of Monmouth, who claims to have drawn upon a work given to him by Walter (see 2.1m above). Other chronicles to make this mistake include the *Scalacronica* and Geffrei Gaimar's *L'Estoire des Engleis*, see Moll, *Before Malory*, (p. 43).

1199–1303   *Aftyr hym . . . had deserved.* Hardyng's account of King Leyre omits a number of details found in most other chronicles, particularly *HRB* §31 and RMB 1.2261–2549. It does not remark on Leyre's partiality for Cordele; Leyre's retinue is only downsized once before Ragawe asks him to disband it completely; Leyre does not return to Goneril after Ragawe upsets him; and the king's lengthy lament on Fortune is excluded. There are nevertheless some interesting additions: Hardyng describes the way in which the "r" in the pronunciation of "Leyrecestre" was set aside "to make the language swettre" (2.1203–05); Leyre is advised to seek Cordele's help by his friends; Cordele is touchingly buried next to her father as her soul ascends to Janus and Minerva; and, perhaps most idiosyncratic of all, marginalia is added to show how the story of Leyre underscores England's suzerainty over Scotland.

1304–52   *Syr Margan . . . and mortalyté.* Hardyng appropriates his information from *HRB* §§32–33, RMB 1.2550–2608, or a similar source. The observation that Britain was established 599 years before the foundation of Rome is comparable with RMB 1.2595–2600, which makes a similar statement but provides a date of 397 years, perhaps indicating that Hardyng's source was a lost version of RMB containing a different reading, or an analogous text drawn upon by both RMB and Hardyng.

1353–1408   *Gurgustius his . . . grete myght.* The characteristics Hardyng ascribes to Gurgustius, Sisilius, Iago, and Kymar are unique. Through assigning good or bad qualities to each monarch, he is able to contrast good and bad kingship and stress the role of divine providence in determining a monarch's fate. His warning that those sovereigns who fail to uphold the law and protect the peace are "In moste perile . . . forto be slayne / Or els put doun right by his undirloute" (2.1404–05) encapsulates one of the *Chronicle*'s most important themes and anticipates later cautions that Henry VI's monarchy is in danger if he fails to restore justice and peace to the realm. Also of interest is the fact that Hardyng, like *CPL* I:40, makes Kymar the son of Iago.

1409–92   *Gorbodyan that . . . youre sovereynté.* Unlike their counterparts in other sources, Hardyng's Ferrex is sent to France in his father's lifetime for causing discord and Queen Judon kills Porrex without the help of her handmaidens. The *Chronicle* is similar to *RB* lines 2195–98, *OV* line 441–43, *EH* II:234, and *Brut* pp. 22–23, in stating that the kingdom was divided between four kings, but only Hardyng and RMB 1.2658 give the length of the conflict as forty years. The most notable feature of this section is Hardyng's amplification of the break-down of social order and his use of the exemplarity of the ancient civil war to warn contemporary "prynces and lordes of hye estate" (2.1486) about the importance of exercising their power to uphold law and peace.

1491   *Iff pese and lawe be layde and unyté.* In this line, "unyté" — with "pese" and "lawe" — is a subject of "be layde."

1493–1555   *And whils . . . hym come.* The text follows the basic outline of Dunwallo's military campaign and his subsequent reign as presented in RMB 1.2673–2768, which, like *P* III:246–47, and *EH* II:236, locates Dunwallo's burial *inside* his temple of peace rather than adjacent to it (as in *HRB*, *RB*, and *FH*). *EH* is unlikely to have been a source for this section because it gives the length of Dunwallo's reign as forty-three years and comments on the cities he founded (as do *OV*, *Brut*, *NC*), but *P* may have been used alongside a version of RMB or a related text. Gildas, mentioned at 2.1546, is similarly cited as a source in *HRB* §34, *P* III:246–47, and later in *EH*. Hardyng's unique address to the "prynce" (2.1549), either Henry VI or his son Edward, serves to highlight the *Chronicle*'s repeated appeal for good governance and justice from the contemporary sovereign.

1556–1800   *Than felle . . . and laste.* The history of Belyn and Brenny appears to draw upon *HRB* §§35–44, *RB* lines 2313–3240, RMB 1.2769–3598, or a similar source, rather than the shorter, alternative accounts found in *OV* and *Brut*. Hardyng omits the detailed descriptions of the brothers' military campaigns found in *HRB*, *RB*, and RMB, and abbreviates the rest of the narrative. His text is remarkably close to *RB* and RMB in its reference to the extreme sadness of the people upon Belyn's death, and like *CPL*, it omits all reference to the brothers' having to fight on two fronts — against Germany and Italy — when the Romans repudiate their treaty. The references to Geoffrey of Monmouth (2.1689m), Alfred of Beverley (2.1689m), the River Allia ("Awbe," 2.1722), King Assuere (2.1748), Socrates (2.1749), and Orosius (2.1738m) are probably taken from *P* III:260–61, 264–75, and 294–95, although Martin of Troppau (2.1746), whom Hardyng lists as a source, is not mentioned at this point in the printed edition of *P*. Since *MO* was a source for *P*, Hardyng may have been working from a manuscript of *P* that acknowledged its debt to *MO* for this information, or he may have included "Martyne" after finding references to the Allia, King Assuere, Socrates, Orosius, and the dating from the foundation of Rome in *MO* (p. 403). Given the reference to *P* at 2.1801m and the possible correspondence between the *Chronicle* and *P* at 2.1801–1940, it is more likely that *P* is being used here. Hardyng's personal touches include the marginalia drawing attention to Brenny's deference to Belyn as overlord of Albany (Scotland) and the rebuke addressed to Fortune on account of her mutability.

1689m   *secundum Alfridum . . . Monemutensem.* See note 2.1556–1800 above.

1738m   *Secundum computacionem Orosii ad Augustinum.* "According to the computation of Orosius to Augustine." See note 2.1556–1800 above. This marginalia occurs alongside line 1742.

1801m   *Nota that . . . Radulphi Cestrensis.* Although Hardyng appears to have known and used *P* I:344–45 and III:328–29, for some of the details given in the section this marginalia accompanies, it is not his only source. See also notes 2.1556–1800 and 2.1801–1940.

1801–1940   *Gurguyn his . . . I gesse.* None of the individual sources considered here contains all of the details given by Hardyng. In all likelihood *HRB* §§45–48 provided the information for the reigns of Gurguyn, Guytelyn, and Morvyde, but it is silent about the nature of Danyus's reign. RMB 1.3599–3775, or a text related to it and *CPL* I:50–55, seems to have supplied the length of each king's reign, but it lacks the anachronistic reference to Alfred at 2.1857 and does not name Morvide's mother. *P* is the only source to match Hardyng in placing Sysilius's accession *after* his mother's death (see II:92–93 and III: 381–83), but this, like other details, could equally have filtered into a hitherto unidentified source employed by Hardyng. The marginalia on pity, the notices of Scotland's homage to England, and the interjection on God's vengeance are Hardyng's own.

1809   *unto his friste degré*. The suggestion here seems to be that there is a direct line of fealty. In rebelling against the king the rebels break their oath of fealty to him. See also line 2.1826.

1941–2045   *Gorbonyan his . . . and specyfyed*. Although this section ultimately derives from *HRB* §§49–51, Hardyng's account is closer to RMB 1.3776–3911 in that it places the burials of Argalle and Elydoure at Carlisle and Aldburgh respectively. *CPL* I:54–56 also mentions these burial places, but it lacks many of the other details included in RMB, which Hardyng repeats. The reference to few people knowing where Alclude is echoes the information at 2.1066m.

2046–2231   *Gorbonyan whiche . . . fulle bounteuus*. Hardyng appears to be following *HRB* §§52–53 and RMB 1.3912–4113. He almost certainly obtained the notice of Cheryn's drunkenness (also in *RB*), and Ely's burial at Castor (also in *CPL* I:58) from RMB, but he develops both details in a unique manner. The conceit on drunkenness serves as a warning to princes about the dangers of intoxication, whilst simultaneously providing an explanation for the weakness of Cheryn's sons. By the same token, the discussion about the location of Ely's burial allows Hardyng to show his discerning nature at work by defending his rationale for dismissing those sources that place Ely at Castor, Lincolnshire (i.e., *CPL* and RMB). In incorporating additional, albeit brief, information about how good or bad a number of the kings were, Hardyng is able to adjust the monotonous list of names provided by his sources into useful examples of good and bad kingship.

2232–2451   *So felle . . . his excelence*. Hardyng abbreviates the story of Cassibalan's reign and Caesar's invasions found in *HRB* §§54–63 and RMB 1.4127–5245, apparently combining details from each, or using an intermediate source that drew upon both. See, for example, the reference to Caesar fighting Pompey, which occurs in *HRB* (possibly the "Boke of Brute" referred to at 2.2431) and in one of the manuscripts of RMB (London, Lambeth Palace MS 131; see RMB, pp. 216–17). The dating attributed to Bede's "Gestes of Englonde" (2.2418) is also found in RMB (compare Bede p. 47). Although Hardyng is not alone in presenting Cassibalan's celebratory feast at 2.2326–64 in chivalric terms (see *RB* and RMB), he accentuates the courtly nature of the festivities more than other texts by describing how beautiful women were seated in front of the king's men to "chere" them (compare with the later description of King Arthur's celebrations at 3.2856–62). At lines 2.2347–53, in the second of several borrowings from John Lydgate's "King Henry VI's Triumphant Entry into London" (1432), Hardyng similarly emphasizes the importance of commemorating military conquests and royal power through public spectacles by comparing Cassibalan's celebrations with Caesar's triumphant entry into Rome and Scipio Africanus's entry into Carthage (Lydgate, "Henry VI," 517–20). For further discussion of Hardyng's use of Lydgate's poem see Peverley, "Chronicling the Fortunes." Hardyng is correct in stating that Martin of Troppau does not mention Caesar's being in Britain (2.2422–23).

2354–55   *Bot ever . . . ay adversité*. For this proverb, which Hardyng may have taken from Chaucer's *TC* 1.950, see Whiting V2.

2452–2710   *Tenvancius that . . . withouten lese.* This section is remarkably similar to RMB 1.5246–5631, albeit in an abridged form. It appears to be indebted to it for details such as Caesar's knighting Kymbelyn (also in *RB*); the dating of Christ's birth and Kymbelyn's death to 1200 years after Brute's arrival in Albion; the prophet Thelofyne (Teselyn in RMB and Teleusin *RB*); Claudius's sending for his daughter forty-six years after Christ's birth; Marius's forty-nine year reign and burial at Salisbury (also in *CPL* I:66); and Coile's ten year reign and burial at Norwich (likewise in *CPL* I:68). Aspects taken from another source, or unique to Hardyng, include his reference to translating a chronicle "Oute of Latyne" into "balade" (see note 2.2545–49 below); the attribution of Vespasian's coming to Britain to Gildas at 2.2573–74 (see note below); the marginalia before 2.2599 (see Textual Note 2599m) noting women's desire for sovereignty over their husbands (compare with the sovereignty desired by Albyne and her sisters at 1.14 and 1.212); the material concerning Joseph of Arimathea (see note 2.2611–47 below); the deliberation on the Virgin's assumption at 2.2655–61; and the information about Rey Cross (see note 2.2676–82 below).

2466–72   *Whiche Cesare . . . dyd de.* This information may have come from *MO* (pp. 443–44).

2545–49   *As cronycle . . . me submytte.* There is no reason to doubt Hardyng's claim to be using a Latin source; however, unless he is using a hitherto unidentified Latin text closely linked to RMB, he is probably using *HRB* alongside a copy of Mannyng's English chronicle. *HRB* §§68 makes reference to Claudius's sending for Genvyse but does not give the date found in RMB.

2573–74   *as sayth . . . and remembrance.* Neither Gildas nor *HB* — the work commonly attributed to Gildas in medieval chronicles — mentions Vespasian's coming to Britain.

2611–47   *In whose . . . thurgh meschaunce.* It is unclear where Hardyng obtained his information about Joseph of Arimathea, but, as Kennedy has suggested, he seems to have included this and other material relating to the Grail in response to "Scotland's claims to preeminence as a Christian nation" ("John Hardyng and the Holy Grail," p. 199). Hardyng may have known *JG* (pp. 2–3, 30–31, 54–55), as some critics have argued, or had access to a related text — a chronicle or a romance — that incorporated similar details about Joseph's association with Glastonbury. Since *EH* I:157, *NC* fols. 21r–21v, several Latin *Bruts* (including the source of *NC*), and *English Chronicle* (see Marx "Aberystwyth" pp. 4–5), all describe Joseph's burial with two phials of the bloody sweat of Christ, Hardyng could have drawn on a chronicle for the details or amalgamated information from more than one source. Similar material concerning Joseph has been interpolated into William of Malmesbury's *Antiquitate Glastonie Ecclesie*, a manuscript of *FH* I:127, the version of Robert of Gloucester's *Chronicle* in London College of Arms MS Arundel 58, and later works attesting to an ongoing interest in Joseph include the unusual Prose *Brut* extant in Lambeth Palace Library MS 84, William Worcester's *Itineraries* (p. 298), and the life of Joseph printed in the *Nova Legenda Anglie* by Wynkyn de Worde in 1516, though Hardyng did not know these.

Importantly, none of the aforementioned chronicles makes reference to the "rode of the north dore" (2.2613m), a cross that Joseph made which was later cast into the sea by Agrestes, only to appear again in the reign of Lucius at St. Paul's, London (see 3.96–119 and 3.99m). Hardyng's marginal reference to the story being contained in the "book of Joseph of Arymathi lyfe" (2.2613m) implies that he knew a separate version of Joseph's story, similar to, but doubtless fuller than, *Lyfe of St Joseph of Armathia* printed by Pynson in 1520, which also refers to the "rode" (see 217–24). Such a text was presumably based on *Lestoire del Saint Graal*, which makes reference to Agrestes (pp. 136–37), and *Queste*, which incorporates the story of the shield Galahad inherits on his Grail quest, something that Hardyng recounts later in the *Chronicle* (see 3.3052ff). If Hardyng did use a source of this kind, it may also have inspired his reference to the Virgin's assumption, as *Lyfe of St Joseph of Armathia* (line 117) mentions this event, though the unedited part of an *English Chronicle* in National Library of Wales, MS 21608, ff. 25v–26r also includes it so, again, it could have come from a chronicle (see Marx, "Aberystwyth," pp. 4–5). The tantalizing, but brief, reference to "þe Auenturus of Brutayne" (line 232) in the extant fragment of *Joseph of Arimathie*, a fourteenth-century English alliterative romance extant in the famous Vernon manuscript, seems to indicate that Joseph's coming to Britain was covered in the missing text, so Hardyng may well have drawn on a similar lost vernacular romance containing the story of the cross. Henry Lovelich's *History of the Holy Grail* offers another example of a romance which associates Joseph with Glastonbury (IV:324) and includes an account of Agrestes and a 'red cross' (III:211–13), but in this version Agrestes does not throw the cross into the sea and it is not lost or associated with Lucius.

In the fifteenth century, the cross of the "north dore" was very popular with pilgrims, a fact that Reginald Pecock notes in his *The Repressor of Over Much Blaming of the Clergy* (I:194); this may have influenced Hardyng's decision to include it in the *Chronicle*. For another reference to Joseph's burial at Glastonbury, see 6.2317–23.

2676–82   *In signe . . . over alle*. Although some chronicles give Stainmore as the location of the stone Marius erects to commend his victory over Redryke the Pict (see *OV* lines 757–59, and *EH* II:261), the information provided by Hardyng, who describes the stone as the ancient boundary marker known as Rey Cross ("Rerecrosse"), appears to come from his own knowledge of the border regions.

BOOK 3

1–196   *Aftyr Kynge . . . his exeqyse.* For the most part Hardyng follows *HRB* §§72–74, but the date of Lucius's coronation appears to come from *MO* (p. 412), which gives the year 184 as the start of Pope Eleutherius' rule and mentions Lucius's appeal to him. Hardyng incorrectly claims that *MO* records Severus's death in the year 235, perhaps indicating that he misread a later entry, had a corrupt text, or took the reference from another source citing Martin (*MO*, pp. 447–48, gives the year as 212). However, another emperor with the name Severus — Alexander Severus — died in 235, so Hardyng may have used an unidentified source that confused the two emperors. In *MO*, Alexander Severus dies in 236, but he is not named "Severus" (p. 448).

        Other writers attributing a seventeen-year reign to Severus include Bede (p. 50), who also mentions his burial at York, and RMB 1.5776–5779.

29m   *Nota of . . . of goules.* Hardyng links Lucius's shield with the shield made by Joseph of Arimathea. It is later owned by St. George, Constantine, and Galahad. See 3.505m, 3.575m, 3.694m, 3.3059, 3.3157.

83–88   *Whose names . . . for memory.* According to Gildas, Christianity first came to Britain in the reign of the Emperor Tiberius, not Lucius, who first appears in Bede (p. 49). Hardyng has taken the reference to Gildas from *HRB* §72 (it also occurs in *FH* I:147), where it may be a mistake for the pseudo-Nennius *HB* §22. *HB* mentions Lucius's baptism, but not Fagan and Duvian.

89–91   *And Mewytryne . . . his dyspence.* Reference to Lucius's giving Glastonbury to Fagan and Duvian is also made in *JG* (pp. 38–39). The inclusion of the episode here provides further evidence that Hardyng knew a similar source detailing Glastonbury's legendary past. See also notes 3.29m, 3.96–119, and 3.99m.

96–119   *Bot now . . . dyd apere.* See notes to 2.2611–47 and 3.99m.

99m   *How the . . . sayd rode.* Having already mentioned the story of the crucifix made by Joseph of Arimathea at 2.2611–47, Hardyng develops his account by describing its miraculous arrival at St. Paul's. His reference to the "table" and stained glass window depicting the story of the crucifix at St. Paul's demonstrates the importance of the cross to the medieval cathedral. The information probably derives from Hardyng's own knowledge of the rood, from a work on Joseph's life, or, given its close proximity to lines 3.89–91, from an unidentified source containing the early history of Glastonbury (see notes 2.2611–47 and 3.89–91).

197–329   *Getan his . . . foule meschaunce.* This section contains one of the most topical interjections in the *Chronicle* (3.246–80). The essence of the story of Bassian and Carauce is most likely taken from *HRB* §§75–76 and RMB 1.5780–5921, but Hardyng removes all reference to Carauce's courage and his dealings with the Roman Senate. Instead he uses the example of Carauce's ambition and treachery to warn Henry VI and contemporary lords about the problems they face if the lawlessness plaguing late fifteenth-century England is allowed to continue. Hardyng's caution about lower-born men rebelling above their station and rebelling against their social betters when oppressed is particularly significant given that he was writing this version of his *Chronicle* at the time of, or shortly after, the Kentish rebellion led by Jack Cade. Moreover, his criticism of "mayntenaunce" (3.263), a corrupt process by which a lord would trade on his influence to abet wrong-doers under his protection, complements complaints and advice found in other fifteenth-century works. Lydgate's *FP*, for example, frequently warns lords and princes to protect the poor, maintain the law, and be aware of the dangers of allowing low-born men to take positions of power (see 2.1423–29, 3.3108–14, 3.3129–35, 3.3262–82, 5.2362–75, 7.270–77, 9.3022–56). Since Hardyng knew Lydgate's work, such comments may have inspired his own interjections. For further discussion of Caraunce's reign and other sections relating to civil unrest see Peverley, "Dynasty and Division" and "Political Consciousness."

263   *mayntenaunce*. See note 3.197–329 above.

264–66   *The pore . . . sore ban*. Hardyng appears to be referring to the citizens of the Tuscan city states who had considerable rights of access and redress at law, even if they were poor. We are grateful to Alan Crosby for this suggestion.

288–308   *A prynce . . . it alterate*. Hardyng develops the brief comment about the Picts intermarrying with Britons in *HRB* §75 to emphasize the bellicose nature of the Scots and present a more general, xenophobic point about the danger of having "aliens" within a kingdom. Such sentiments would have been particularly topical in light of the riots that took place against alien merchants in London in the late 1450s (see Griffiths, *Henry VI*, pp. 790–95).

292   *kyng Maryus*. The reference to King Marius alludes to 2.2662–89.

330–36   *Suche fyne . . . thayre hame*. An echo of 2.645–51, where Hardyng attributes the downfall of Albion's giants to Providence.

335   *And after olde synne so commyth ay new shame*. Proverbial. See Whiting S338 and Tilley S471.

336   *And wronge lawes make lordes forsake thayre hame*. Proverbial. See Whiting L111.

337–504   *The Bretons . . . the felde*. This section is similar to *HRB* §§76–78 and RMB 1.5922–6095, although neither source remarks on St. Amphilbalus's martyrdom ("Amphybale"), mentions Galerius ruling the Empire with Constance, or gives the year of Constance's death as 306 AD, as Hardyng and *FH* I:173–75 do. A linguistic echo of Hardyng's "engynes and magnels" (3.359) occurs in RMB 1.5966–67.

499   *Galeryus*. Galerius is also mentioned in *HA* (pp. 536–37) and *MO* (p. 450).

505m   *Constantynes armes . . . the aire*. This marginalia is accompanied by an illustration of Constantine's coat of arms, but the colors of the shield have been accidentally reversed (i.e., the cross is colored argent [silver] when it should be gules [red], and the background is gules when it should be argent). For other decoration in the manuscript see the Manuscript Description. Other references to the arms, which are associated with St. George, occur at 3.575m, 3.694m, 3.3059, and 3.3157–70.

505–25   *Constantyne that . . . nought transcende.* The beginning of Hardyng's account of Constantine's reign (3.505–74) relies on HRB §78–79, or a text derived from it, such as *RB* lines 5688–5730, which mentions Constantine's coronation by the British barons and his noble, "lion-like" countenance. The emperor's laudable ability to live from his own resources (3.521) and the suggestion that financial prudence is a desideratum in a sovereign (3.524–25) appear to be Hardyng's own embellishments. Though his additions are typical of the opinions expressed in advice literature, or "mirrors for princes," Hardyng may have included them in light of his own experience of the financial difficulties faced by the Lancastrian government in the late 1440s and early 1450s. At this time, a series of Resumption Acts were passed to counteract Henry VI's crippling household expenditure and inept distribution of privileges: Hardyng's royal grant was among those resumed.

526–74   *And so . . . wele biloved.* Hardyng, like *CPL* I:78, has the Roman Senate appeal to Constantine for help instead of following the structure of HRB, in which a number of Romans flee to Britain because of Maxcence's tyranny and persuade Constantine to wage war on him. Among the chronicles considered for this edition, only Hardyng makes reference to the Romans' promise to cease their request for Britain's tribute, paving the way for King Arthur's decision to defy Lucius's request for tribute later in the *Chronicle*.

575–677   *The yere ... were felle.* The Chronicle either draws directly upon *MO* (pp. 450–52) and the *Legenda Aurea* ("The Life of Saint Silvester" and "The Invention of the Cross"), or uses an intermediate source, such as *P* (V: 114–151), which borrows from these texts and contains many of the details found here (see notes 3.645m and 715m below). Whatever the case, Hardyng builds upon Constantine's refusal to slaughter innocent children in order to cure his leprosy by turning his reported comment about imperial dignity being born out of pity in "The Life of Saint Silvester" and *P* (V:124) ("Dignitas Romani imperii de fonte nascitur pietatis") into an appeal to contemporary lords to show pity to those in distress. He goes on to explain that Constantine deferred baptism because of his desire to be baptized in the River Jordan; this story does not occur in *MO* or the *Legenda Aurea*, but it is mentioned in *P* V:128–29, where it is attributed to Ambrose and Jerome, although it actually originates from Eusebius's *Vita Constantini* (Book 4, Chapter 62). Of all of these texts, only Hardyng's explicitly aligns the emperor's desire for baptism in the Jordan with his aspiration of conquering the "Jewry hool" (3.608).

575m   *How Kynge . . . or borne.* See note 3.505m.

582m   *As in . . . hoc vinces.* The legend of St. Helen referred to here appears to be "The Invention of the Cross" in the *Legenda Aurea*; see note 3.575–677 above.

645m   *How Seynt . . . cronicas Martini.* The source for Silvester's healing of Constantine could have been the *Legenda Aurea*'s "Life of Saint Silvester," *MO* (pp. 450–51) or *P* (V:122–29), which also acknowledges its debt to the "Life of

Saint Silvester" (see note 3.575–677 above). Hardyng's claim to have seen the holy water used at Constantine's baptism may indicate that he had been to Rome in 1424, as suggested by 1.1m, because, in the second version of the *Chronicle*, he states that the water can be seen there. However, the holy water was clearly a well-known relic, and in *FP*, which Hardyng knew, Lydgate also mentions the font at St. Peter's, Rome, containing the water used on Constantine (*FP* 8.2140–67). The story of Constantine's leprosy and miraculous baptism is also told by Gower in *Confessio Amantis* 2.3187–3464.

659m   *secundum cronicas Martini*. The number of bishops given in this marginalia, 300, does not correspond with the number given in the following stanza, 318 (3.660).

678–79   *She dyed ... and sely*. Hardyng may have used an unidentified source for his account of St. Helen's burial at Santa Maria in Ara Coeli, the city church in Rome dedicated to the Virgin Mary. However, Helen's relics were allegedly moved to the church in 1140, so if Hardyng did travel to Rome in 1424, as suggested by 1.1m and 3.645m, it is also possible that he saw the relics firsthand and added this information from his own knowledge. For St. Helen and Ara Coeli, see Drijvers, *Helena Augusta*, p. 75 and Harbus, *Helena of Britain*, p. 46.

680–86   *But now ... were unkynde*. Gildas does not mention Constantine. Hardyng may have meant *HB*, which was commonly attributed to Gildas by medieval chroniclers, in which case he is correct in stating that it does not describe Constantine's life (see *HB* §25, where he is mentioned very briefly). Henry of Huntingdon does include some of Constantine's deeds, but his account is succinct in comparison with Hardyng's (see *HA* pp. 60–63, 574–75).

694m   *And than ... Georges armes*. Hardyng links Constantine's arms with the arms of St. George and, therefore, with the arms of Lucius (who is said to bear arms "in fourme of Seynt Georges armes"; see 3.29m). Later, he will associate the same heraldic device with Galahad. See 3.3056 ff. and notes 3.505m and 3.3157–70.

715m   *How this ... Martyne Romayn*. Hardyng has taken this information, including the reference to Isidore, from *MO* (pp. 450–51) or *P* (V:148–51). *MO* is the more likely source; if Hardyng had used *P* he would have had to have a manuscript that attributed the information to *MO* and gave the correct date of 21 May rather than the incorrect date of 11 May given in the manuscript used by Babington and Lumby for their edition of *P*. A survey of extant manuscripts of *P* would shed further light on this matter.

717–28   *A saynt ... Chyrche promocioun*. See note 715m above.

729–812   *But in ... withouten fayle*. This section has much in common with *HRB* §§80–81, although it differs in a number of smaller details. Like *OV* (lines 883–87) and *EH* (II:269), Hardyng locates Traherne's battle with Octave at Stainmore, rather than the less specific Westmorland of *HRB*; he also attributes the plan to persuade one of Octave's friends to kill Traherne to

Gunbert, an alteration that does not occur in any of the chronicles considered in this edition, and he clarifies that Kaerperis is Porchester (compare *FH* I:178). Such changes may indicate that Hardyng was using a source based on *HRB* rather than *HRB* itself.

771m   *Unde Seneca . . . periculo est.* Hoccleve's *Regiment of Princes*, 1114 ff., which Hardyng may have known, includes a similar statement attributed to Seneca, but as Blyth, Hoccleve's editor, notes, it does not occur in Seneca: "the idea, though not the language, is in Boethius" (see note to 1114 ff.). If Hardyng's marginalia was not inspired by Hoccleve, his quotation may be an allusion to Seneca's *De Clementia* (Book I, chapter viii, §§ 1–5 or Book I, chapter xix, §§ 2–8), in which the dangers facing a prince are discussed. It is also possible that the sententia was obtained from a florilegium, which failed to identify the source correctly.

813–925   *The kynge . . . fully assocyate.* Hardyng's account of Maximian's reign is closest to *HRB* §§83–88 and RMB 1.6290–6543, although neither text is an entirely satisfactory match. The *Chronicle* offers a noticeably shorter version of the longer accounts of Maximian's campaign given in *HRB*, RMB, and other texts associated with them, omitting all reference to Maximian's encounter with the king of the Franks and the subsequent attacks made on Conan before the British women are sent to Brittany. The 10,000 men that Maximian requests to populate Brittany does not match any of the figures given in *HRB*, *RB*, RMB, *OV*, *EH*, or *FH*, but the description of Gwaynes and Melga as Saracens (3.896) corresponds with RMB 1.6484–94, as does the reference to the eleven noble women accompanying Ursula in the marginalia before line 3.855 (compare RMB 1.6456 and 1.6482, although, arguably, this could also be a shared mistake for eleven thousand). Hardyng's reference to Gwaynes and Melga's hatred of Britain is not part of their motive for executing the virgins in other sources, nor have we been able to find a textual parallel for Hardyng's reference to St. Ursula's burial in the choir at a church in Cologne, but it may have been widely known that her relics were at the church dedicated to her in Cologne. Only Hardyng refers to Maximian's killing of Valentinian instead of Gracian.

926–60   *Gracyan, whan . . . cronycle historialle.* Of the chronicles considered here, Hardyng alone provides specific details of Gracian's tyranny and states that Melga and Gwaynes invaded Britain because they believed Maximian was still king. His reference to Melga and Gwaynes ravaging Britain to avenge Maximian's slighting of Gracian may stem from the observation that Melga and Gwaynes ravaged the coasts for Gracian in *HRB* §88 and *P* (V:202–03).

961–1107   *Gwayns and . . . is memory.* Hardyng's source(s) here is unclear; for the most part his account corresponds with *HRB* §§89–93, but some elements are closer to *P* (V:224–27, 250–53) and RMB (1.6564–6885), suggesting that he combined two or more sources or was following a text that had already done this. He omits the speech made by Bishop Guthelyne in *HRB* just before the Romans leave Britain for the last time, thus removing the criticism levied at the British for being weak and not defending their realm properly, and similarly fails to include the alternative speech made by the wise Roman in texts such as *RB* and RMB. This allows him to present the plight of the British in a sympathetic light, which is further enhanced by his accentuation of the treachery of Melga and Gwaynes and the indifference of the Romans. Guthelyne's request for help from Aldroene is shorter than that in most other sources and has much in common with the petition in RMB, whilst Aldroene's reply is closer to that in *HRB*.

975m   *How Bretons . . . Gestis Anglorum.* Reference to the wall built by Severus is also made in Bede (p. 59), *P* (V:226–27), and *NC* (fol. 28v). It is difficult to tell whether Hardyng obtained the information directly from Bede or from another text that attributed it to him.

1024m   *How Bretons . . . Gestis Anglorum.* Compare Bede (pp. 60–61), although there the Britons' sending for help from Egicyo (Aetius) is ascribed to the year 446 (see note 3.1045–48).

1045–48   *The tyme . . . and compilacioun.* This date is given in Bede (p. 325) and RMB (1.6758–61), though neither of the extant copies of RMB attribute the date to Bede. Hardyng, or his source, appears to confuse the year that Roman rule in Britain comes to an end in Bede with the year of the Britons' request for help from Egicyo.

1108–42   *This Constantyne . . . had conspyred.* Hardyng, *FH* (I:209), *P* (V:252–53), *CPL* (I:94), RMB (1.6886), and *NC* (fol. 29v) place Constantine's coronation at Cirencester ("Cyrcester") rather than Silchester (as in *HRB* §93 and *RB* line 6437), but only Hardyng supplements this information with the ancient name for Cirencester, Caerceri ("Caersyry"). Hardyng and RMB 1.6890–91, 1.6904–27 are the only texts in the aforementioned group to give Constantine's wife Roman and British ancestry and attribute Constantine's death to Vortigern's treachery.

1143–1219   *Constans than . . . bene sene.* Hardyng is probably following *HRB* §§94–96 and RMB 1.6928–7168, but his account of Constance's election and coronation is more succinct than their detailed version of events. He omits all of the material dealing with the barons' concerns about Constance and Vortigern's discussion with him at Winchester (like *P* [V:254–55]). The *Chronicle* resembles *HRB* in its reference to the kingdom being devoid of older leaders and the future leaders (Aurelius and Uther) being too young to rule; however, it appears to emulate RMB in making Vortigern a duke of Wales and accentuating his ability to flatter.

1145   *the mynstere of Seynte Amphibale.* Other texts that make reference to Constance's being in a church dedicated to St. Amphibalus include *HRB* §93, *FH* (I:209), *P* (V:252–53), *EH* (II:274), and *NC* (fol. 29v).

1220–1443   *This Vortygere . . . quenes supportacioun.* This section has most in common with *HRB* §§97–100, although the reference to Engist's landing at Sandwich suggests knowledge of *RB* lines 6704–05 and/or RMB 1.7183–85, and Vortimer's sending for saints Germanus and Lupus occurs in RMB 1.7641–42.

Hardyng omits some of the information found in *HRB*, including the reference to Satan entering Vortigern when he sees Rowen, and adds a number of unique details, such as the description of Engist being as meek as a lamb (3.1243), the notification at 3.1402m that "Thwongcastre" is Caistor in Lincolnshire, and Engist's prayer of thanks to Mercury and Venus for bringing the eighteen Saxon ships safely to Britain (3.1371–73). Two other points are worth noting: having elected not to include the Latin and Welsh names for "Thwongcastre" found in *HRB*, *RB*, and RMB, Hardyng provides an etymological description of the name, claiming that Engist named it "Thwongcastre" (3.1403) to ensure that he never forgot the wisdom, or clever trick, that helped him to obtain the land (i.e., cutting a continuous strip of leather, or "thong," from a bull skin to measure out the greatest possible territory). This helps to underscore Engist's intelligence and his ability to manipulate Vortigern, paving the way for his subsequent treachery. Likewise, whilst other texts stress that Engist asked for Kent as Rowen's dowry, Hardyng does not; he merely states that Vortigern gave her the land as "dowere" (3.1401). This may be an attempt to reduce the narrative on Hardyng's part, but it also has the effect of showing how blinded Vortigern is by his desire for Rowen; only a few stanzas before, he would not grant Engist land because he was a foreign pagan and he did not want to upset the British barons, but here he gives a whole county to his pagan wife.

1290m   *Nota also . . . of golde.* This marginalia offers another example of Hardyng's interest in heraldry as he includes a coat of arms for Engist and Horsa. Compare, for example, the arms he ascribes to Aeneas and Brute at 2.554m and the genuine coat of arms belonging to Sir Robert Umfraville at 7.889.

1444–1534   *This Engiste . . . waste indede.* The majority of this section corresponds to *HRB* §§101–02; however, there is sufficient correlation with RMB to suppose that Hardyng was combining elements of *HRB* and RMB, or using another text that had already done so. Compare, for example, Engist's suggestion of sending for Octa, his cousin Ebissa (a brother in *HRB*) and Cherdyke with RMB 1.7541–46, and Vortimer's request for Germanus to preach again with RMB 1.7641–42. Hardyng's conceit on Vortimer's presumption is unique.

1535–1632   *This Vortygerne . . . myght suffise.* Although Hardyng's account of Engist's return is close to *HRB* §§103–05 in many respects, such as its inclusion of Eldane's burial of the dead at Salisbury plain and Earl Eldolle's defeat of seventy Saxons, it nevertheless contains several aspects yet to be found elsewhere. Unlike other sources, Hardyng comments on Engist's joy upon hearing of Vortimer's death and emphasizes the Saxon's rhetorical skills by reporting his insincere statement about not wanting to hurt the British because of his consanguinity with their queen (3.1568–69). Correspondingly, Hardyng places greater emphasis on the role of the British barons — they are present when Engist's messenger arrives and they approve of his alleged plan to "strengh the londe agayn" (3.1567) — and he supplements Engist's plot to kill the British by adding a new stratagem whereby each "Bretoun" is "afore a payen sette" to make them easier to kill (3.1600).

1626m   *Nota that . . . of Afrike.* Like *OV* (lines 1238–40) and *EH* (I:280), the *Chronicle* mentions the etymology of England at this point in the narrative. Hardyng adds that the name was set aside shortly afterwards and not used again until Gurmond was king. The subsequent reference to the land being divided up "parcelmele" (3.1632) may indicate that Hardyng had some version of the Prose *Brut* to hand, or another text that drew upon it, since *OV* also mentions the apportionment of the realm.

1633–1786   *Wharfore so . . . swerd and fyre.* Compare with *HRB* §§105–08 and RMB 1.7689–8202. Hardyng supplements his account of Merlin's birth with several details: he alone uses the simile "as white as any swan" to describe the spirit that visited Merlin's mother (3.1674) and makes reference to the popular opinion that his father could have been a "fende" (3.1660). Likewise, he has Maugancyus suggest that the spirit may have chosen to "dystayne and appalle" his mother's "holynesse" because God selected her to fall "for the better" (3.1703–09). Hardyng may have included the latter because he had seen references to demons wanting to shame women in RMB 1.7973 and 1.7976, or he may have emphasized the spirit's fiendish nature because he knew the Vulgate *Lestoire de Merlin*, which focuses on Merlin's demonic father and his attempt to dishonor a secular virgin. Other aspects that Hardyng may have appropriated from RMB include the restyling of *HRB*'s governor of Caermardyn ("prefectum") as "mayre" (see RMB 1.7917) and the naming of the castle Aurelius burns (see *RB* lines 7601–06 and RMB 1.8187–92). Elements not found in any of the sources considered here include Vortigern's clerks defiantly answering Merlin (3.1730) and Duke Eldolle's responsibility for the assembly that crowns Aurelius king (3.1780–86).

1757–72   *The water . . . to avenge.* Hardyng reduces the significance of the two dragons, which subsequently fight in *HRB* §§111–12 and signify the forthcoming battle between the Britons and the Saxons. He similarly omits all of the other prophecies found in *HRB* §§112–17 and condenses the divination concerning Vortigern's end in §118 by passing over the fates of Aurelius and Uther, and excluding notice of the coming of Arthur. In the second version of the *Chronicle*, Hardyng states that he cannot write affirmatively about Merlin's birth or his prophecies, so he omits them entirely.

1787–1835   *Thay crouned . . . his countré.* Generally speaking, Hardyng follows *HRB* §§120–25, but he radically reduces the account of Aurelius's battle with Engist, omits Aurelius's promise to restore the churches if victorious and removes Eldolle's prayer to meet Engist on the field. Hardyng similarly alters *HRB*'s statement about the north of England being open to attack from Scots, Picts, Danes, and Norwegians, and recasts it as a justification for the Saxons' northerly retreat; they choose this area because they can seek refuge in Scotland and obtain help from Britain's foreign enemies if necessary (compare RMB 1.8255–56). Only Hardyng's Eldolle sends a letter to Aurelius noting Engist's capture and only here does he ask what his punishment will be.

1816–28   *Sayde "Ye . . . dedes longe."* This alludes to Samuel 1 15:33. Hardyng adapts his source to imitate the contemporary practice of quartering high-profile criminals and sending their body parts to various cities for display to deter prospective felons.

1836–70   *In this . . . and recounsiled.* Compare *HRB* §§126–27 and RMB 1.8517–8611. Hardyng's Octa submits himself to Aurelius's mercy with a rope around his neck instead of a chain, as in RMB 1.8534–35, but the *Chronicle* follows RMB in having Bishop Eldade offer the king advice first (Eldade is presumably a variation of the earlier character "Eldane," as he is in other sources). The gift of land to the Saxons is similarly attributed to Aurelius's own free will, rather than in response to the bishop's request as in *HRB* §126 and *RB* lines 7957–59. For the biblical story of the Gibeonites, see Joshua 9:26.

1871–1924   *Than sente . . . can merke.* Compare *HRB* §§128–30 and RMB 1.8612–8817, although the *Chronicle* may be drawing upon a related, but more succinct, text linked to *RB* and *EH*. Hardyng appears to condense and simplify the episode explaining how Stonehenge was brought across from Ireland; however, further investigation into unpublished chronicles, particularly the Latin *Bruts*, may reveal that the following alterations do not originate with him at all. Hardyng has Aurelius send for Merlin without the advice of his bishop, and he removes any material that makes the king appear foolish, such as his desire to know the future and his laughter at Merlin's suggestion of bringing the immovable stones to Britain. In so doing, Hardyng creates a stronger, more decisive Aurelius, whose qualities are more in keeping with those already seen. Hardyng alone has Merlin offer to travel with Uther, and by excluding the scene whereby the Britons amuse the prophet with their hopeless attempt to move the stones, he introduces a more obliging Merlin than *HRB* and RMB. Whilst *RB* (lines 8175–78), *OV* (lines 1425–26), *EH* (II: 302), and *NC* (fol. 38v) explain that the stones are known as Stonehenge, only *RB* and *EH* come close to matching Hardyng's etymological explanation for the name. Finally, reference to the saintliness of bishops Sampson and Dubricius is also made in *RB* (lines 8169–70) and RMB (1.8805–07).

1925–54   *In whiche . . . body stolle.* Hardyng appears to emulate RMB 1.8818–8913. He omits all reference to Paschance's being in Germany, describes "Menevue" (3.1933) as St. David's (RMB 1.8841–43; see also *RB* lines 8213–14) and has Aurelius request burial at Stonehenge instead of dying in his sleep, as he does in *HRB* §132. The advice concerning unsuitable physicians in the marginalia before 3.1941 is Hardyng's own.

1955–2149   *Thus was . . . the nones.* Hardyng's rendering of Uther's reign combines elements of *HRB* §§133–42 and RMB 1.8914–9599. He probably adapted Merlin's prophecy to accommodate his later account of Arthur's victory over Lucius (3.3619 ff.), for in *HRB* the beam that extends from the comet across the territories destined to be conquered by Uther's son stretches only to Gaul. On the other hand, Hardyng may have known that the place the beam extends to in *RB* (line 8298) and RMB (1.8929) — the Great St. Bernard's Pass or "Muntgieu" — leads to Italy and changed his text accordingly to include the more familiar Rome. Other alterations to the prophecy that appear to originate with Hardyng include the prediction that Arthur will have no issue (3.1976) — an interesting addition, which looks forward to the succession of Constantine, the son of Duke Cador (3.3822–28) — and the reference to Uther having more than one daughter at 3.1981. If authorial, the latter is presumably an attempt to reconcile the incongruity in *HRB* §144, whereby the mother of King Hoel of Brittany, Arthur's nephew, does not appear to be Anna, daughter of Uther and wife of Loth. Regrettably, Hardyng's reference to Arthur and Hoel's consanguinity at 3.2312–13 adds nothing to support this assumption, but the second version of the *Chronicle* also refers to Uther's having more than one daughter, suggesting that the change was intentional or the result of Hardyng following a source with such a reading.

The *Chronicle* follows RMB 1.9029 in naming the church at Winchester St. Peter's (compare also *CPL* [I:132]), and the speech given by Hardyng's Gorlois is similar to, but noticeably shorter than, that in RMB 1.9110–19. Reference to Uther declaring peace at Alclud and punishing criminals severely is made in *HRB* §137, as is the name of Gorlois's stronghold "Dymyoke" (but compare *RB* line 8636, where it also occurs in three manuscripts of that text). Unfortunately, Hardyng's narrative is confused about the manner of Gorlois's death. He is slain twice: first by Uther's men (3.2113–14), and again by Uther (3.2142). This error probably arose because Hardyng decided to omit the episode in his sources whereby the king's men breach Gorlois's camp, kill the duke, and win the siege whilst Uther is with Igerne. In passing over this and attributing the victory to Uther, Hardyng may have hoped to enhance the king's military prowess, which is somewhat overshadowed by his lust in other texts. However, if this was his intention, his failure to omit the messenger's speech reporting the duke's demise at 3.2113–14 has spoilt the effect.

Finally, Hardyng omits those parts of his sources that cast the British barons in an unfavorable light; see, for example, *HRB* §139 and RMB 1.9450–59, where they refuse to follow Loth's orders.

2061–65   *Whose beuté . . . stretched nought*. Hardyng's observation that Nature surpassed itself when it fashioned Igerne is comparable with the descriptions of feminine beauty in romance (see, for example, Chrétien de Troyes' *Chevalier au Lion* 1495–98, where we are told that Laudine is of "such immeasurable beauty, for in her Nature has surpassed all limit"; *TB* 5.1910–15; and Brewer, "Feminine Beauty," pp. 258, 268).

2063   *Hyre shappe and forme excede alle creature*. Compare *TC* 5.807–08.

2106   *Whiche of nature tendre was of corage*. Compare *TC* 5.825.

2150–77   *A feste . . . grete regyment*. Unlike other chroniclers, Hardyng follows the Vulgate *Lestoire de Merlin* (pp. 196–97) in placing the foundation of the Round Table in Uther's reign. However, whereas *Lestoire de Merlin* locates the first appearance of the Table at Uther's Whitsunday feast, Hardyng's Uther establishes it during his wedding feast. The description of the Grail as "The dysshe in whiche that Criste dyd putte his honde" and the vessel that Joseph of Arimathea used to collect Christ's blood is taken from *Lestoire de Merlin*, (pp. 196–97, 352), but it is at odds with Hardyng's earlier account of Joseph's coming to Britain with two vials of the bloody sweat of Christ (2.2611–19).

Whilst it is not inconceivable that Hardyng viewed the vials and the Grail as separate relics, it is more likely that the inconsistency arose from his use of disparate sources. For the Grail as blood relic see Barber, *Holy Grail*, pp. 127–34, and Vincent, *Holy Blood*. For Joseph's arrival in Britain see note 2.2611–47 above. For the Round Table in literature and legend see Fleming, "Round Table" and the works cited therein. The reference to Christ at the house of Simon the leper alludes to Mark 14:3.

2220–26   *Afore his . . . Westmerlonde thurghoute.* The Middle English Prose Bruts found in Dublin, Trinity College MS 489 and Cleveland Public Library MS John G. White Collection W Q091.92–C468 (classified by Lister Matheson as *PV–1419: A* and *PV–1451/1460*) also connect Uther's stronghold with Pendragon Castle. The castle, which probably dates from the twelfth century, belonged to the Clifford family, who held the shrievalty of Westmorland by hereditary right and had close familial ties with the Percies, whom Hardyng once served. If this portion of the *Chronicle* was composed before the first Battle of St. Albans (22 May 1455), which seems most likely, "the Clifford" (3.2224) mentioned here is Thomas Clifford, eighth Baron Clifford (1414–55), son of John Clifford (1388/89–1422) and Elizabeth Percy (d. 1436). Thomas played an important role in fifteenth-century politics and was one of the men who supported Henry VI against Richard, duke of York at the Battle of St. Albans, where he was killed. Conversely, if Hardyng was at work on this section after Thomas's death, "the Clifford" is Thomas's son John Clifford, ninth Baron Clifford (1435–61), who came of age and inherited his father's legacy in July 1456.

2227–47   *Allas for . . . you sende.* Like the stanza before it, this unique commendation of Uther's achievements enhances the significance of his reign and underlines the continuity between past and present. Uther, like other sovereigns throughout the *Chronicle*, is to be a "myrour and remembrance to other kynges and prynces" because he protected his realm and opposed those who "vexed" his people, even when sick (3.2227m and 3.2240). The correlation between the difficulties in Uther's reign and those lamented elsewhere in the *Chronicle* relating to Hardyng's own time are implicit, but Henry VI is asked to "Thynke on this poynte" and ensure that he remains active in defending the realm and people that God entrusted to his care (compare 7.1051–78). Uther's sickness and subsequent battle at St. Albans may have reminded Hardyng of the mental illness suffered by Henry VI in 1453–54, which preceded the battle of St. Albans in 1455, where one of the Cliffords mentioned above died (see note 3.2220–26).

2247m   *Arthurs armes.* The illustrated arms of King Arthur — gules (red), three crowns or (gold) — occur alongside this marginalia.

2248–80   *Arthure his . . . and quyte.* Hardyng's portrait of Arthur's excellent features and his pledge to free the land of Saxons echoes *RB* lines 9013–38 and RMB 1.9614–37, although the inclusion of Fortune favoring the king is Hardyng's own expansion, perhaps inspired by references to Fortune in Lydgate's *FP*, and it anticipates his later diatribe on her fickleness (for more on this topic see Peverley, "Chronicling the Fortunes"). The location of Arthur's coronation at

Cirencester ("Cyrcestre," 3.2253), presumably a misreading of "Silcestrie" in *HRB* §143, similarly demonstrates the *Chronicle*'s debt to *RB* and/or RMB, for the same reading occurs in four extant manuscripts of *RB* (line 9012) and the surviving copies of RMB (1.9605, 1.9610). Whilst the presence of "Caercyry" (3.2253) merely repeats the information at 3.1110, the observation that "som" call Cirencester "Caersegent" (3.2254) indicates some confusion, either on Hardyng's part or in one of his sources. *HB* §66a lists Cair Segeint as one of the twenty-eight British cities and *HA* (pp. 14–15) equates it with Silchester, but neither text mentions it in relation to Arthur. Hardyng may have conflated his "Cyrcestre" with *HRB*'s Silchester and decided to supplement his text with the information in *HA*, or, perhaps more likely, he obtained "Caersegent" from a text that drew upon the identification in *HA* to supplement its own reference to Arthur's coronation at Silchester.

2255   *fyftene yere*. Arthur is fifteen at his accession in *HRB* and RMB.

2281–2380   *To Scotlonde . . . no nede*. Arthur's campaign against the Saxons follows *HRB* §§143–48 and RMB 1.9638–10020, but Hardyng reduces the narrative considerably, omitting Hoel's illness, the speeches made by Arthur and Dubricius, Arthur's arming scene, and the detailed descriptions of combat. On one occasion his concision loses the coherence of his sources, for in omitting the scene in which Baldulf flees from battle and decides to try to reach his brother while disguised as a jester to plot their next move (3.2297–2303), it is not immediately apparent why Baldulf adopts his disguise.

2348   *By thayre letters and seles*. Only Hardyng refers to Cheldryke, Baldulf, and Colgrym ratifying their treaty with Arthur by "letters and seles."

2360–61   *He hanged . . . batayle wente*. Hardyng diverges from his sources, where the Saxon hostages are hanged before Arthur journeys to Bath, and has them executed in full sight of their kinsmen to press home the Saxons' perfidy.

2378   *Deveshyre, Dorset and also Somersette*. RMB 1.9845–48 appears to have inspired the *Chronicle*'s reference to the Saxons ravaging Devonshire, Somerset, and Dorset, although the information ultimately derives from *RB* lines 9245–48. Hardyng has removed it from its original context, where the pillaging precedes the siege of Bath.

2381–2401   *In this . . . and contumacyté*. Compare *HRB* §§149–52 and RMB 1.10021–10244. Details apparently taken from *HRB* include Hardyng's reckoning of forty islands in the loch, as opposed to sixty in *RB* line 9427 and RMB 1.10039, and the remark about Bishop Sampson. RMB 1.10077–10130 presumably supplied the reference to all levels of society petitioning the king, not just the bishops as in *HRB* (see also *RB* lines 9465–9526). It may also have prompted Hardyng's observation that Guyllomore came to assist the Saxons, for one of the manuscripts of RMB has him coming to help the Saxons instead of the Scots (1.10067). Hardyng omits his sources' report of the eagles at the loch and their reference to Arthur restoring the three Scottish kings' inheritance, electing to emphasize their homage to Arthur as king of Britain instead. In so doing, he makes the Scots the first men to show deference to Arthur, a detail that suits the *Chronicle*'s repetitive assertion that English kings have always had suzerainty over Scotland.

2430–76   *This kynge . . . another founde.* Although the details of Arthur's marriage to Guinevere are ultimately derived from *HRB* §152, Hardyng adapts his narrative to parallel Uther's earlier marriage to Igerne. Hardyng describes Guinevere's beauty in the same terms as Igerne's (see note 3.2061–65) and mentions Arthur's reestablishment of the Round Table, justifying his creation of new knights with the statement that the Order of the Round Table had become depleted through war. This is a shrewd way of reconciling the disparate accounts that Hardyng encountered in his chronicle and romance sources concerning how the Round Table was formed and by whom. It also allows Hardyng to present Arthur as a king who restores order and brings stability to his realm by regulating the conduct of his knights and uniting them under a common cause.

Whilst the number of Arthur's new knights — forty-two — may have come from the additional companions that join the order of the Round Table in *Lestoire de Merlin* (see pp. 245–49 and the accompanying notes), the majority of their names are taken from *HRB* §156 and RMB 1.10879–10908, where a list of those attending the plenary court at Caerleon later in Arthur's reign is given. *RB* lines 10249–82, one of RMB's sources, and *Arthur* also contain the names, but Hardyng's "Syr Barent" earl of "Circestre" (3.2446), "Syr Jugence" (3.2448), and "Syr Bewes" (3.2456) are closer to the forms given in RMB. The knights at lines 2466–71 have been appropriated from the Welsh names in *HRB*, but Hardyng has misunderstood the Welsh prefix "map," meaning "son of," and produced a number of erroneous names; for clarification of individual names, see the notes that follow. Several knights have no clear source.

Finally, Hardyng may have had the processes governing the election of new Garter Knights in mind at line 2476, for there is nothing immediately apparent in his sources matching his statement about the selection of new knights (see Keen, *Chivalry*, pp. 196–97, for the election process). New members were only admitted into the Order of the Garter upon the death of one of the knights, a fact that Hardyng would have been aware of because his former patron, Sir Robert Umfraville, was a member of the Order.

2447   *Syr Harand, Erle of Shrewsbyry.* We have been unable to locate a precise match for this name, but *RB*, RMB, and *Arthur* have an "Anaraud," "Amorand" (or "Emoraund"), and "Euerad Erl of Salesbury" respectively (see note 3.2457 below).

2453   *Galluc . . . of Salesbyry. HRB* §156 has "Galluc Guintoniensis," but interestingly *EH* (II:326) is closer to Hardyng's knight with "Galluc Saresburiensis."

2455   *Gurgoyne the Erle of Herford.* See *RB* line 10259, RMB 1.10889, and *Arthur* line 155.

2457   *Amorawde, Erle of Excestre.* A variation of RMB's "Amorand" of Salisbury (1.10895), although it is not clear whether Hardyng changed the knight's place of origin because he already had a knight from Salisbury, or whether he took this information from another source (see also *HRB* §156, *RB* line 10263, and *Arthur* line 159).

2459   *Ewayne*. See *RB* line 10252 and RMB 1.10882. *Arthur* lines 141–42 has "Vrweyn þe kynge / Of scottes."

2462   *Of Demecy the kynge Syr Uriayne*. Of the sources considered here, only Hardyng presents Uriayne as the king of South Wales. *RB* line 10253, RMB 1.10883, and *Arthur* line 143 call the king of South Wales Stater.

2466   *Donand, Mapcoyl, Peredoure, and Clenyus*. Compare *HRB* §156 "Donaut Mappapo," "Cheneus Mapcoil," and "Peredur Maheridur" respectively. "Clenyus" may be a variation of the first part of "Cheneus Mapcoil," used here as a separate name.

2467   *Maheridoure, Mapclaude, Griffud*. For "Maheridoure" see note 3.2466 above. The other names ("Regin Mapclaud" and "Grifud Mapnogoid") derive from *HRB* §156.

2468   *Gorbonyan, Esidoure and Heroyus*. "Gorbonyan" is taken from *HRB* §156 "Gorbonian Masgoit"; the second part of this name is used at 3.2469 and a variation of Gorbonyan occurs again at 3.2471. We have been unable to locate a source for "Esidoure," but "Heroyus" may be Hervi of Rivel, who appears in several Arthurian romances, including the Vulgate *Lestoire de Merlin*, pp. 289–90 (see Bruce, *Arthurian Name Dictionary*, p. 265, which gives Herui(s) as a form of Hervi).

2469   *Edlein, Masgoyd, Kymbelyne*. Compare *HRB* §156 "Eddelein Mapcledauc," "Gorbonian Masgoit," and "Kinbelin"; see also 3.2468 and 3.2471, where the first part of "Gorbonian Masgoit" has been used for two other knights.

2469–70   *Cathleus / Mapcathel, Mapbangan, and Kynkare*. Compare *HRB* §156 "Cathleus Mapcatel" and "Kingar Mapbangan."

2471   *Colflaut, Makeclauke, Gorbodyan*. Compare *HRB* §156 for "Clofaut." "Makeclauke" may be a corruption of "Regin Mapclaud" or "Eddelein Mapcledauc." For "Gorbodyan" see notes 3.2468 and 3.2469 above.

2477–85   *Thare reule . . . thayre lady*. Compare *HRB* §157, *RB* lines 10511–20, and RMB 1.11095–11114.

2486–2513 *The somer . . . to hafe*. These details are drawn from either *HRB* §§153–55 or RMB 1.10259–10519, although Arthur's sword "Caliburne" (3.2489) is named much earlier in both texts (*HRB* §147 and RMB 1.9883). Hardyng radically condenses his source's account of Arthur's conquest of Ireland and Norway, omitting the Norwegians' attempt to defy Arthur's installation of Loth as their king. He also adds Scotland and Friesland ("Freseland") to the list of conquered realms.

2511   *Kynge Sychelme*. King Sichelm, Lot's Norwegian grandfather (or uncle?), cited in *HRB* 9.11.

2514–40   *Kynge Arthure . . . make pretence.* Hardyng's idiosyncratic description of the vast corpus of Arthurian literature available in his own time may have been inspired by RMB 1.10391–10420, which in turn develops a passage in *RB* lines 9785–98. By directing his readers to "the grete boke of alle the aventures / Of the Seynte Grale" (3.2532–33), a source also mentioned in Lydgate's *FP* (8.2788), Hardyng simultaneously shows his own knowledge of, and fondness for, Arthurian literature, whilst introducing the notion that such stories are for "yonge mennes wytte" (3.2535) and not for seasoned old men like himself. The "grete boke" referred to is presumably a manuscript containing several Vulgate romances similar to that mentioned in the will of Sir Richard Roos (d. 1481/82), which contained the *Estoire del Saint Graal*, *Mort Artu*, and *Queste* (now British Library MS Royal 14 E. iii); (see Meale, "Manuscripts," p. 103, and "Patrons," p. 207; and Moll, *Before Malory*, pp. 170, 304). Moll has suggested that the individual tales alluded to at 3.2523 refer "to romances of individual achievement" (p. 170), a point that appears to be supported by the fact that Hardyng probably knew several of the knights listed at 3.2555–75 from their own romances.

2541–54   *Bot whan . . . thaire viage.* The suggestion that the knights' exploits were recorded in Arthur's time probably comes from *Queste* (p. 87), which refers to clerks writing down the adventures of the Grail quest (see also *Lestoire de Merlin*, p. 345), or Lydgate's *FP*, which mentions a clerk chronicling the deeds reported to him by pursuivants so that the stories could be read and sung at court to give folk "gret confort" (8.2780–86 and 8.2829–35). Even so, only Hardyng's knights write down their own adventures (3.2545), possibly, as Harker suggests, to reflect "a changed social context in which knightly literacy had become less uncommon" ("John Hardyng's Arthur," p. 252). Hardyng is similarly unique in stating that the adventures were recorded and read to stir young knights to perform chivalric deeds, a detail that sustains the contrast between youth and old age introduced at 3.2534–36. Lydgate mentions a "scoole of marcial doctrine / For yonge knihtes to lernen al the guise" (*FP*, 8.2815–21), but he fails to connect the education of new knights with the exemplary activities of tested knights.

2555–75   *Bycause that . . . so thanne.* Whereas Hardyng's first register of the Round Table knights was compiled from those names occurring in his chronicle sources (see note 3.2430–76 above), this roll call consists mainly of figures from Arthurian romance, thus complementing Hardyng's previous allusion to romances concerning the adventures of individual knights (see note 3.2514–40). Gawain, Lancelot, Pelles, Percival, Calogrenant ("Colygrenauntt," 3.2567), Lionel, Bors, Kay, and Mordred all appear in the Vulgate Cycle, as well as other romances, although there is also a chronicle precedent for Percival in *Le Petit Bruit* (p. 12). Libeaus Desconus ("Lybews Dysconus," 3.2567), Degare ("Degré," 3.2568), and Degrevaunt feature in their own English romances. Bedivere also occurs in English romance, but like his nephew Hirelglas ("Irelglas," 3.2571), and Guytarde, Hardyng would have known him from *HRB*. "Estore" (3.2569) is Ector, another romance figure, but it is unclear whether he is meant to be the father of Sir Kay and foster father of Arthur, or another Ector, such as the half-brother of Sir Lancelot. We have been unable to locate Hardyng's source for "Bewes of Corbenny" (3.2570); one Escant, or Escans, duke of Cambenic is mentioned in *Lestoire de Merlin* (see, for example, pp. 227, 230–32, 270), where Cambenic is one of the northern duchies against Arthur, but Corbenny is more likely to be a variant of Corbenic, the Grail Castle in the Vulgate Cycle. The allusion to Arthur's incestuous relationship with his sister at 3.2573–75 provides another example of Hardyng's knowledge of the Vulgate Cycle, for, with the exception of the *Stanzaic Morte Arthur* which is derived from *Mort Artu*, early English sources tend to depict Mordred as Arthur's nephew (see 3.3787–93).

2576–96   *In whiche . . . hertes consolacions*. Arthur's movable household mimics that of a medieval king, but the number of places he holds court is excessive, as the various locations serve to emphasize Arthur's supremacy "thurghout alle Bretayne grounde" (3.2579). Hardyng's inclusion of Glastonbury is particularly striking, because his interest in it usually centers on its association with Joseph of Arimathea and the Grail: that is, as a place of religious, as opposed to secular, authority. It is also the location of Arthur's court in *Libeaus Desconus*, a romance that Hardyng might have known given his reference to the hero at 3.2567.

2597–2624   *The reule . . . a name*. Having briefly touched upon the "reule" of the Round Table at 3.2477–78, Hardyng establishes the principles governing the order in greater detail. Three elements of the oath (helping maidens, seeking out absent knights, and describing their adventures) ultimately derive from the vows made by the knights in *Lestoire de Merlin* (p. 345), whilst other aspects of the pledge show the knights addressing common fifteenth-century problems by offering their services against those who commit heresy, oppress the common weal, rebel against the king's "dygnyté" (3.2605), and commit extortion, particularly against the poor. Hardyng may have been inspired by Lydgate's account of the Round Table statutes in *FP* 8.2728–2849, which list amongst other things the knights' duty to resist tyranny, protect widows and maidens, restore children to their "trewe heritage," defend "comoun proffit" and the "liberté" of the church, and help companions in need. The reference to the knights' deeds being recorded in "romance or scripture" (3.2621) to inspire others likewise bears some resemblance to Lydgate's text and echoes Hardyng's earlier observation at 3.2541–54 (see note 3.2541–54 above).

     In Arthurian literature Pentecost is a common time for the knights to gather at court and Hardyng appears to make use of this convention later on to invite comparisons between Arthur's court and that of Edward I, who is also said to hold a great feast at Pentecost, second only to Arthur's (6.798–867).

2625–26   *But ever . . . sharpe laboure*. See note 2.2354–55.

2625–2715   *But ever . . . is memory*. Having already changed the order of events in RMB 1.10391–10470 (which follows *HRB* §155 and *RB* lines 9731–9886) by recounting Arthur's conquest of Norway before the first period of peace and knightly adventures, Hardyng moves straight to the king's conquest of France and provides an abbreviated account of Arthur's victory over Frolle, which appears to be drawn from RMB 1.10520–10792. The ensuing list of the European kings and princes that pay homage to Arthur is Hardyng's own addition, as is Arthur's coronation in Paris, an event which may have been added to prefigure Henry VI's coronation in Paris as dual monarch of England and France and create a connection between the two kings (see note 3.2716–2946 below, though compare Lydgate's *FP* 8.2892–98, which mentions Arthur's feast in Paris).

Other unique aspects of Hardyng's narrative include the description of Guinevere's beauty, which resembles that of Chaucer's Criseyde in *TC* 1.99–105, and the declaration that the tournaments took place for "love of ladyse" (3.2695). The description of Arthur's sojourn in France follows *RB* and RMB, rather than *HRB*, in that it enhances Arthur's prestige by depicting his nine-year stay as a time of peace and adventure; on this topic see Putter, "Finding Time for Romance."

2716–2946	*And whan . . . prynces regymence.* Compare *HRB* §§155–57, *RB* lines 10147–10620, and RMB 1.10775–11192, though each of these places the events at 3.2730–43 *before* Arthur makes a decision to return to Britain. Although the basic details of the celebrations at Caerleon ultimately derive from *HRB*'s account of Arthur's plenary court, where the king wears his crown in state, Hardyng recasts the episode as a *second* British coronation. This alteration might indicate that he was following *RB* line 10204 or RMB 1.10828, since both texts phrase Arthur's wish to be crowned in such a way that it could be interpreted as a desire to have another coronation, rather than simply to wear the crown at court. RMB 1.10873–74 may have added to this confusion with its later reference to a "legate fro Rome" being sent to crown Arthur. In addition to this, Hardyng embellishes his account of the abundance of wine at Arthur's feast by reworking lines 314–320 and 333–34 of Lydgate's "Henry VI's Triumphant Entry into London" (see 3.2869–76). Having recycled parts of the same poem earlier in the *Chronicle*, Hardyng presumably utilizes it here to underscore subtle links between King Arthur's celebrations and those witnessed related to Henry VI's dual coronation in England and France. See Peverley, "Chronicling the Fortunes" for further discussion of Hardyng's use of Lydgate's poem. For other uses of the poem see Prol.1–14, 2.2232–2451, 6.812–67, 7.708–14.
2726	*north halfe Rome.* This detail is unique to Hardyng. It may have been inspired by the comparison of Caerleon and Rome in *HRB* §156 and other texts, or perhaps from RMB's reference to a papal legate being sent for (1.10873–74).
2727	*Severne.* In *HRB* §156 and elsewhere Arthur's guests sail down the River Usk, which is said to be close to the Severn. Hardyng just mentions the Severn.
2786	*The kynge of Man.* Compare *RB* line 10321 and RMB 1.10934, both of which mention the king of "Mans."
2800–03	*The archebysshop . . . and excercyse.* Hardyng, like *LB* lines 12206–07, places the archbishop of London on Arthur's right and the archbishop of York on

Arthur's left; neither *HRB*, *RB* nor RMB mention which side the archbishops walked on or which of Arthur's arms they held.

2809–13   *Where byried . . . alle wyrkynge.* Reference to Dubrike's burial is not made in the equivalent passages in *HRB* §157, *HRBVV* §157, *CPL* I:176, *EH* II:329, and RMB 1.11543–48, where the archbishop resigns from his office to become a hermit. See note 3.2905–18 below.

2814–27   *Kynge Aguselle . . . that servyce.* Hardyng places additional emphasis on the symbolic nature of the swords carried by the four kings, making it clear to his audience that the swords represent the lands that the kings "holdyn" for Arthur (3.2820).

2837   *With kynges led.* Presumably a misreading of *HRB* §157, which describes Guinevere being led by the consorts of the four kings accompanying Arthur.

2852–55   *Duke Kay . . . dyd stonde.* Hardyng's reference to Kay's carrying a silver baton, or "yerde" (3.2854), before the king appears to be unique. It may be an allusion to the ceremonial white staff carried by the king's steward in the Middle Ages.

2860–62   *And ay . . . and disporte.* Arthur's court is said to follow Trojan custom in *HRB* §157, *RB* lines 10445–58, and RMB 1.11049–60, where the men and women attend separate feasts; however, Hardyng emphasizes the fact that both sexes sit together so that the knights can "comforte" and "chere" the ladies "with daliance." Compare with the seating arrangements at Cassibalan's feast at 2.2340–46.

2865   *In clothe of golde.* In *HRB* §157, *RB* lines 10471–78, and RMB 1.11073–76, Bedivere and his men are clad in ermine like Sir Kay; Hardyng's reference to their golden attire appears to be unique.

2870–76   *Thetys that . . . the feste.* See note 3.2716–2946 above.

2891–2904   *And every . . . myght endure.* Only Hardyng appears to mention Guinevere's special relationship with the church dedicated to St. Julian. For Guinevere's flight to St. Julian's at the end of Arthur's reign see 3.3801–07; for the martyrdom of saints Julian and Aaron see 3.386–92, where, contrary to what Hardyng says here, the saints' martyrdom is said to have taken place under the Emperor Diocletian, not Maxence.

2905–18   *But Seynte . . . and autorised.* Compare note 3.2809–13 above. Dubrike's retirement and David's consecration are also mentioned briefly in *HRB* §157, *CPL* I:176, *EH* II:329, and RMB 1.11543–48. Although Sullens has noted that RMB's reference to Dubrike is "conspicuously out of order" with the rest of the narrative (see p. 704n11543–48) Hardyng's record of the archbishop's fate points towards the likelihood that he was using a version of *HRB*, RMB, or an unknown text related to them, rather than *RB*, which does not refer to Dubrike's resignation or burial. The allusion to David's canonization and the use of the simile at 3.2914–15 to describe the saint's exemplary life appear to be unique to Hardyng.

2919m   *Elyden was . . . Bede also.* For Elyden as bishop of Alclud see *HRB* §157. The
             debate about Alclud's location echoes similar comments at 2.1066m and
             2.1941–2045, and draws upon *P* (II:64–69) and Bede (pp. 58–59) (although
             Bede is cited as a source in *P*, so Hardyng may not have used Bede directly
             here).

2926–46   *And whan . . . prynces regymence.* Compare with *RB* lines 10589–10620 and
             RMB 1.11159–92, where Arthur's generosity is described. Hardyng's account
             of the king's "liberalté" (3.2939) is notably different in its emphasis on the
             respect that other princes have for Arthur and the growth of his reputation.

2947m   *How whan . . . and Wales.* Hardyng's account of Galahad's Grail Quest is
             unparalleled in the chronicle tradition and has attracted a great deal of
             attention from scholars. Whereas other chronicles, such as *HRB* and RMB,
             describe the arrival of the Emperor Lucius's envoy immediately after Arthur's
             plenary court, Hardyng's text takes a detour into the world of romance,
             delaying the onset of Arthur's war with Lucius until Galahad has achieved the
             Grail. Kennedy argues, quite convincingly, that Hardyng imbues the quest
             with political significance by transforming his source, the Vulgate *Queste*, into
             "something creditable to Arthur and his court," which enhances "the spiritual
             authority of Arthur's reign" and repudiates "Scottish writers who boasted of
             Scotland's preeminence as a Christian nation and who stressed the illegitimacy
             of Arthur's rule" ("John Hardyng and the Holy Grail," pp. 203, 205, 206).
             Riddy, on the other hand, makes an equally compelling case for Hardyng's
             demystification of the Grail, claiming that it "is not a religious symbol at all
             but [. . .] a heraldic emblem that harks back through history to Joseph of
             Arimathea, binding together the British past rather than transcending history
             in the Eucharist" ("John Hardyng in Search of the Grail," p. 426; see also her
             "Glastonbury" and "Chivalric Nationalism").
                 In this particular marginalia Hardyng attempts to lend historical authenticity
             to the romance material by linking "the grete story of the Saynt Graal" (i.e.,
             Queste) with the "Policraticon" of "Waltier of Oxenford." Elsewhere in the
             Chronicle Hardyng's allusions to Walter of Oxford imply that he was thinking
             of *HRB*, a text that he probably had in mind here given his observation that
             Walter's text deals with "Cornewail and Wales" (see 2.1m, 2.1115–98, 4.2754),
             but which certainly did not furnish him with the story of the Grail. In
             connecting the "grete story" of the Grail with an author named Walter,
             Hardyng may be referring to Walter Map, alleged author of the Vulgate *Queste*
             and *Mort Artu* (see *Queste*, p. 87 and *Mort Artu*, pp. 91, 160). This hypothesis,
             however, does not explain the reference to Cornwall and Wales or Walter's
             association with Oxford, unless Hardyng was confusing Map with the Walter
             mentioned in *HRB* (see Moll, *Before Malory*, pp. 186–87). The enigmatic
             "Policraticon" is similarly opaque, and Moll may be correct in suggesting that
             Hardyng intended *Polychronicon* (p. 187). Nevertheless, if Hardyng had
             Higden's work of that name in mind he must have been attempting to lend
             spurious authority to the romance material because the information about
             Galahad and the Grail did not come from that text (compare notes 3.2989m,
             3.2989–3016, 3.3038m, and 3.3136m, for other erroneous sources).

Since Hardyng is not the only author to cite the story of the Grail as a source (compare *JG*, p. 48, *Le Petit Bruit*, p. 6, and Lovelich, V:306), it is likely that he is drawing upon a genuine Grail text — probably a romance from the French Vulgate cycle — or repeating the information after seeing it cited elsewhere. Equally, John Lydgate's reference to a "Sang Real" in his account of Sege Perilous in *FP* 8.2788, may have influenced Hardyng. Futher information about this marginalia is available in the Textual Notes.

2947–88 *And at . . . that ordoure*. Hardyng's main source for this section is the Vulgate Cycle. In the Vulgate *Lancelot*, Galahad stays at an abbey until he is fifteen, then he leaves to become a knight (III:338), and in *Queste* (pp. 3–5), he arrives at Arthur's court on Whitsunday (Pentecost). The story of "Sege Perilouse" (3.2966) and the prophecy about Galahad are found in *Lestoire de Merlin* (pp. 196–97, 352, 359) and *Queste* (pp. 5, 26–27), but only Hardyng uses the story of the seat's destructive power to enhance Arthur's reputation by claiming that, until Galahad arrived, nobody except the king had sat in it without being "shamed and mescheved" (3.2969). Hardyng's description of Lancelot's begetting Galahad "by hole and fulle knowlage / Of Pelles doughter" (3.2956–57) likewise deviates from the traditional account of his conception by implying that Lancelot loved "Pelles doughter" willingly, rather than being duped into sleeping with her as he is in other romances (see, for example, *Lancelot*, III:164–65). In the second version of the *Chronicle*, Hardyng makes the purity of Galahad's conception clearer still by stating that Galahad was conceived "in verray clene spousage / On Pelles doghter" (see Arch. Selden B. 10, fol. 56r; *Chronicle of Iohn Hardyng*, ed. Ellis, p. 131).

2954 *fiftene yere of age*. Compare with the Vulgate *Lancelot*, vol. 3, VI:338.

2989m *How the . . . and Cornwail*. Hardyng's spurious reference to Gerald of Wales ("Giralde Cambrense") writing about the Grail in his "Topographie of Wales and Cornwail" is another attempt to give historical authenticity to the romance material in this section of the *Chronicle*. Similar references to Gerald occur at 3.3038m and 3.3136m. See also note 3.2947m above and Moll, who suggests that Hardyng could have been "aware that Giraldus's work contained information relating to Glastonbury and that the rubrics are based on this" (*Before Malory*, p. 187).

2989–3016 *At whiche . . . myne avowe*. The account of the Grail's appearance is based on *Queste* (p. 5), where the doors and windows shut by themselves as Galahad is brought to Arthur's court, but Hardyng invents an erroneous source for it in the chronicle tradition at 3.2997 ("as sayth the cronyclere"; compare also notes 3.2947m and 3.2989m above). Besides adapting this episode to herald the Grail's entrance rather than Galahad's, Hardyng disregards the solemn procession of the Grail described in *Queste* (p. 7), and instead depicts it flying in, around, and out of the hall. Other alterations include Galahad's pledge to take up the quest before any other knight (in *Queste* Gawain is the first, pp. 7–8), and Arthur's knighting of Galahad (Lancelot confers this honor in *Queste*, p. 3). The king's gift of "armes" (3.3009) and Galahad's refusal of a shield echo *Queste* (p. 7), where Galahad dons a hauberk and helmet at the king and queen's request, but refuses to carry a shield until he has won his own.

3012–16   *Ne two . . . myne avowe.* As Harker notes, Galahad's pledge not to stay "two nyght" in one place until he has learnt about the Grail is the same as the vow made by Percival in Chrétien de Troyes' *Li Contes del Graal*, 4693 ff. ("John Hardyng's Arthur," p. 275). Compare also Arthur's vow not to spend two nights at the same place until he has found Percival (4099 ff.).

3022–37   *For whiche . . . and wo.* Arthur's lament at the knights' leaving echoes *Queste* (p. 8), but Hardyng supplies the king's aspiration to "folow thaym" (3.3036) and expands on the importance of the knights by employing the well-known image of the body politic, whereby the knights are the "membres" (3.3026), limbs or organs, that sustain Arthur's body (i.e., the realm) and maintain his "coroun" and sovereign "rightes" (3.3032).

3038m   *How Sir . . . and Cornwail.* See note 3.2989m above and Textual Notes.

3038–49   *With that . . . togedir layne.* The concept of knights exchanging stories about their adventures may have been inspired by *Queste* (pp. 10, 87), *Lestoire de Merlin* (p. 345), or, more generally, by the plot of *Queste*, whereby the knights often encounter each other again after separating on their quest.

3052–82   *Bot so . . . after right.* Hardyng follows *Queste* (pp. 11–13), although he changes several details (see the notes below).

3052   *Avalone.* Instead of finding the shield that once belonged to Evalache, king of Sarras, at a Cistercian abbey, as in *Queste*, Galahad acquires it at the Benedictine house at Glastonbury, which Hardyng equates with Avalon. For Glastonbury's association with Avalon and the Grail see Lagorio, "Evolving Legend"; Robinson, *Two Glastonbury Legends*; Abrams and Carley, *Archaeology and History*; and Barber, *Holy Grail*.

3057   *A shelde, a spere, a sworde.* Hardyng's source, *Queste*, makes no reference to Galahad obtaining a sword and spear at the abbey; Galahad obtains his sword before setting out on his quest (p. 6), and encounters a bleeding lance much later in the narrative when he uses it to cure the maimed king (p. 85). The *Queste* does describe a tomb at the abbey containing the cadaver of a knight in full armor, with a sword and other "chivalric accoutrements" (p. 14), but Galahad does not take the items and the dead knight is later revealed to be a symbol of sinful mankind. This episode may have inspired Hardyng to include the other weapons here, especially since Nascien (Seraphe) is said to be buried with the shield (p. 13), but he may simply have incorporated them because of their prominence in Grail lore at large.

3059   *thay sayde . . . it wreton.* In *Queste* a White Knight explains the shield's history to Galahad, but in Hardyng's text the holy men find the information written "in bokes."

3060   *Kynge Evalache.* Evalache is a pagan king of Sarras, who converts to Christianity after receiving a shield from Josephus, son of Joseph of Arimathea, which enables him to defeat his enemy. After converting he changes his name to Mordrain. See *Estoire del Saint Graal* (pp. 14–49) and *Queste* (pp. 12–13).

3062–64   *With crosse . . . or adversité.* Either deliberately or in confusion, Hardyng changes the character responsible for drawing the "crosse of blode" (3.3062) on the shield from Josephus — the son of Joseph of Arimathea in the Vulgate Cycle — to Joseph of Arimathea. The observation that no man except Galahad could bare the shield without suffering "deth, mayme or adversité" (3.3064) alludes to *Queste* (pp. 11–13).

3065   *Bot oon . . . in vyrgynyté.* The themes of virginity and spiritual purity are ubiquitous throughout the Vulgate Cycle; see, for example, *Lestoire de Merlin*, (p. 359), where King Pelles predicts that three knights are needed to fulfil the Grail quest, two of which must be virgins and the third chaste.

3066   *Duke Seraphe.* Seraphe, duke of Orberica, brother-in-law of King Evalache, and ancestor of Galahad. Upon converting to the Christian faith, Seraphe changes his name to Nascien. See *Estoire del Saint Graal* (p. 47) and *Queste* (pp. 12–13).

3075   *Orboryke.* Orberica, the land ruled by Nascien and converted by Joseph of Arimathea in the Vulgate Cycle (see, for example, *Estoire del Saint Graal*, pp. 42, 44, 50, 69, 73). It is also mentioned at 3.3102.

3080–81   *What shuld . . . this prophecy.* In this version of the *Chronicle*, Hardyng does not elaborate on how, or where, Galahad finds the Grail, only that he fulfils his destiny; in the second version, Galahad finds the Grail in Wales.

3094–3100   *That every . . . kynge sojorned.* Hardyng probably appropriates the idea that the knights' adventures were recorded by the court from *Queste* (p. 87) or *Lestoire de Merlin* (p. 345), but see notes 3.2541–54 and 3.2597–2624.

3101–28   *Bot so . . . fulle cyrcumspeccioun.* The nine companions that join Galahad, Percival, and Bors at the "Table of Seynte Grale" originate from *Queste* (pp. 84–85), but Hardyng ignores the brief role that they play in his source, whereby they re-enact the Last Supper with Galahad, Percival, and Bors and receive the Eucharist from Josephus. Instead, Hardyng credits Galahad with establishing a new chivalric order to equal that of the Round Table. The "reule" of Galahad's Grail Order (3.3114m, 3.3115) differs from that of the Round Table in only a few details: Galahad's knights swear "To leve evermore in clennesse virginalle" (3.3116), and young children are added to the list of people that they should protect. Several aspects of the Round Table oath — the vow to protect against sorcery, defend the king's dignity, meet annually to recount adventures, and seek absent knights — are similarly omitted, but, for the most part, the codes upheld by both orders are the same. Compare 3.2477–78 and 3.2597–2624.

3102   *Orberike.* See note 3.3075 above.

3115m   *What the . . . Gestis Arthuri.* The enigmatic sources alluded to in this marginalia have prompted some debate amongst scholars. Riddy suggests that "the dialogue 'de gestis Arthur' is conceivably 'de gestis Britonum', an alternative title for the *Historia Brittonum*," which was "frequently attributed to Gildas in medieval manuscripts" ("Glastonbury," p. 322n17). In contrast, Moll posits that the reference to "De Gestis Arthuri" is a "poor reading" of the *Description of Wales*, where Gerald of Wales "explains why Gildas did not mention Arthur in his *De Excidio Britonum*" (*Before Malory*, pp. 188). However, he concedes that the accompanying marginalia, which could have been written in two stages, may represent Hardyng's "own attempts, late in the production of the manuscript, to provide authority for his suspect history" (p. 189).

Carley, on the other hand, notes that Hardyng's alleged sources "correspond very closely" to the *Tractatus de Sancto Ioseph ab Arimathia* (The Treatise of St. Joseph of Arimathea) and *Liber de gestis incliti regis Arthuri* (The book of the deeds of the glorious King Arthur) cited in *JG*. He surmises that Hardyng's references are drawn from "some sort of compendium concocted at Glastonbury separate from John's chronicle [*JG*] (but into which it was partially incorporated)." See Barron, ed., *Arthur of the English* (p. 54) and *JG* (pp. 46, 52, and 278n69); see also the interpolation in William of Malmesbury's *De Antiquitate Glastonie Ecclesie* (p. 47), from which *JG*'s reference to the *Liber de gestis incliti regis Arthuri* is taken. Although *JG* does not attribute the *Gestis* to Gildas directly, it does celebrate Glastonbury's connections with the saint and draws upon Caradoc of Llancarvan's *Life of Gildas*, so if Hardyng did use "some sort of compendium" related to Glastonbury, there is a small possibility that such a work may have attributed a *Gestis* to Gildas; see, for example, Geffrei Gaimar's *L'Estoire des Engleis* (lines 39–42).

Given that other similarities occur elsewhere between Hardyng's work and that of *JG* (or a related text), Carley's proposal best explains how Hardyng might have encountered a reference to the works cited here, but, for all this, it is highly unlikely that he obtained any information about the "reule" of Galahad's Grail order from such a text; he appears to have invented the "reule" himself based on Arthur's Round Table oath and material in *Queste* (see notes 3.2597–2624 and 3.3101–28). For the possibility of Hardyng using, or having knowledge of, a romance dealing with Joseph of Arimathea see note 2.2611–47 above. In sum, all that can be said with any degree of certainty is that the "book of Josep of Arymathie" and "De Gestis Arthur" are cited to add authority to the narrative, whether they are real or spurious sources (compare notes 3.2989m, 3.2989–3016, 3.3038m, and 3.3136m). Additional information about this marginalia can be found in the Textual Notes.

3129   *So endurynge fulle longe and many yere*. In Hardyng's source, *Queste* (p. 87), Galahad has no desire for worldly sovereignty and reigns for a single year before receiving the Eucharist from Josephus and dying of joy. Since Hardyng's presentation of Galahad is much more secular in its orientation, he may have refrained from mentioning Galahad's reluctance to be king and extended the length of his reign to present a more positive portrait of kingship and English rule over a foreign land (see Riddy, "Chivalric Nationalism," pp. 407–08).

3134–49   *Whiche tyme . . . knyghtly diligence*. In *Queste*, Galahad does not make Bors king of Sarras. After witnessing Galahad's death Bors remains with Percival until he dies; he then returns to Arthur's court, where he recounts Galahad's adventures and they are recorded for posterity (p. 87).

3136m   *How Percyvall . . . and Wales.* See note 3.2989m and Textual Notes. As Kennedy notes, the spurious sources cited in this marginalia have been falsified to lend authority to Hardyng's own account of the burial of Galahad's heart ("John Hardyng and the Holy Grail," p. 204).

3150–56   *And to . . . his blode.* Kennedy argues that Hardyng's inimitable reference to Galahad's heart being encased in gold could have been inspired by "the well known story of the death of Robert Bruce, whose heart was encased in silver, taken on a pilgrimage against the Saracens, and brought back to Scotland and buried with great ceremony at Melrose Abbey" ("John Hardyng and the Holy Grail," pp. 204–05). In contrast, Riddy proposes another analogue, suggesting that Hardyng "must have known" about Emperor Sigismund's presentation of St. George's heart to Henry V in 1416 "through his 'good lord,' the Garter knight Sir Robert Umfraville" ("Chivalric Nationalism," p. 409). Given the reference to St. George's arms in the following stanza (see note 3.3157–70 below), Riddy may be correct, or Hardyng could be conflating both episodes. Wherever his inspiration came from, his account of Galahad's interment at Avalon (Glastonbury) serves to bolster the connections he makes elsewhere between Glastonbury, Joseph of Arimathea, Galahad and the Grail. In *Queste*, Galahad is buried in Sarras.

3157–70   *And there . . . he hynge.* English interest in St. George arose in the fourteenth and fifteenth centuries, first under Edward III, who created the Order of the Garter in his honor and may have helped to establish St. George as the patron saint of England, and later under Henry V, who had a "personal devotion" to the saint and who carried his banner during his campaign against France (see Riddy, "Glastonbury," p. 330n37). Up to this point in the *Chronicle*, Hardyng has taken care to associate St. George's arms with Joseph of Arimathea, the legendary Christian kings Lucius, Constantine, Arthur, and Galahad, but here he makes an explicit link between the monarchs of the past who have borne the "armes that we Seynt Georges calle" (3.3158) and all subsequent kings who have fought under the saint's banner. It is likely that Hardyng, who fought for Henry V in France, had his former sovereign in mind when composing these lines. For earlier references to St. George's arms see 3.505m, 3.575m, 3.694m, 3.3059, and 3.3157–70. By emphasizing the connection between past and present uses of heraldry, Hardyng similarly paves the way for his subsequent description of how all chivalric orders are connected (see note 3.3171–84 below).

3171–84   *Of whiche . . . soules heelfulnesse.* Earlier in the *Chronicle*, Hardyng followed the Vulgate *Lestoire de Merlin* (pp. 196–97) and *Queste* (pp. 26–27), stating that the chivalric orders of the Round Table and the Holy Grail were made in imitation of the table at the Last Supper. In this section he builds upon the notion of a chivalric genealogy connecting past and present orders of knighthood by claiming that the twelfth-century order of the Knights Templar was formed "in figure" of Galahad's Grail Order (3.3173), and that Knights

Hospitaller are, in turn, related to the Templars, who were disbanded in 1312. Whilst the Hospitallers, who also originated in the twelfth century, did indeed model their rule on the Templars, it is likely that Hardyng's lines reflect an interest in, and awareness of, the "historical mythology" of chivalry (see Keen, *Chivalry*, pp. 50, 124), rather than any detailed knowledge of the Templars' and Hospitallers' statutes. Consequently, these stanzas underscore Hardyng's careful attempt to chronicle the ancestry of chivalry alongside the ancestry of his sovereign; moreover, they provide an insight into why Hardyng may have elected to weave romance materials into this and earlier sections of the *Chronicle*. As Keen has noted, the stories of Joseph of Arimathea, the Grail, and Arthur's court played a significant role in helping to underpin "the values of chivalry by providing them with a faultlessly antique and highly evocative pedigree" (*Chivalry*, p. 102); thus, just as Hardyng traces Henry VI's lineage from Adam, he is also able to chart the development of knighthood and chivalry from Joseph of Arimathea and the Last Supper by appropriating and adapting the Vulgate stories and explaining the history of the arms of St. George, patron saint of the Order of the Garter to which Sir Robert Umfraville, who is held up as a perfect proponent of chivalry at the end of the *Chronicle*, belonged. For similar correlations between past and present orders see Keen, *Chivalry*, (pp. 190–92), who cites some interesting examples of the Order of the Garter being made in honor of Arthur's Round Table. Compare also, Wolfram von Eschenbach's *Parzival*, which also links the Templars to the Grail by making them the guardians of the Grail Castle (Keen, *Chivalry*, p. 59).

3185–3219   *At Pentecoste . . . a suffisshance*. Compare with 3.2744–2890. Having interpolated a Grail Quest and account of Galahad's achievements, Hardyng picks up his chronicle sources where he left them. By incorporating a second Pentecostal feast at Caerleon, he is able to follow *HRB* and RMB and describe the arrival of the Roman delegates during the festivities at court (see note 3.3220–73 below).

3191   *Camalot*. Hardyng may be alluding to an oral tradition that associates Caerleon with Camelot, or he may be conflating the disparate locations of Arthur's principal court found in chronicles, such as *HRB*, and romance, such as the Vulgate *Mort Artu*. Camelot first appears in Chrétien de Troyes' *Chevalier de la Charette*, but it is a separate location to Caerleon.

3192–98   *The kynges . . . alle plesaunce*. Compare 3.2777–88, where the same kings are mentioned alongside Duke Cador and the King of Man.

3220–72   *So at . . . his avaylle*. On the whole, Hardyng's account of the arrival of Lucius's envoy and his letter appears to draw upon *HRB* §158 and RMB 1.11195–11314, although the wording of *RB* lines 10621–10730 is also of interest (see note 3.3227–32). Lucius is "procuratoure" of Rome (3.3228) in *HRB* and *EH* (II:330), and Emperor in *RB*, *Lestoire de Merlin* (p. 401), RMB, and *EH* (II:330) (in the chapter heading), but see also note 3.3346m. *CPL* refers to him as senator and emperor (I:176, 192). "Kynge Frolle" (3.3243) is mentioned in Lucius's letter in *RB* and RMB, but not *HRB*. *LB*, *OV*, and *Brut* also refer to Lucius as emperor, mention Frolle, and have Arthur reply by letter (see *LB* lines 12356–12627, *OV* lines 1808–45, *Brut* pp. 81–82), but they do not appear to be Hardyng's sources.

3220   *dese*. RB and RMB also place Arthur on the dais when the envoy arrives.

3222–23   *With olyfe . . . esy pase*. Compare RMB 1.11204–05, "with olyue branches in handes born / with softe pas."

3224   *Upon thayre knes*. This detail appears to be unique to Hardyng.

3227–32   *Lucyus of . . . haste deserved*. Compare *HRB* §158 and *EH* (II:330), "Lucius rei publice procurator Arturo regi Britannie quod meruit" (Lucius, Procurator of the Republic, wishes that Arthur, King of Britain, [may receive such treatment] as he has deserved) and *RB* (lines 10641–42) "Luces, ki Rome ad en baillie / E des Romains la seinurie / Mande ço qu'il ad deservi / Al rei Artur, sun enemi" (Luces, the ruler of Rome and lord of the Romans, sends King Arthur, his enemy, what he has deserved).

3249   *Auguste*. *HRB* §158, *RB* line 10691, and *EH* (II:330) contain August, but RMB 1.11269 refers to "next heruest."

3259   *The lyfelode . . . thee lefte*. This detail does not occur in *HRB*, *RB*, or RMB. Although the *Alliterative Morte* (line 112) touches upon Uther's tribute ("Thy fader made fewtee we find in our rolles / In the regestre of Rome"), there is nothing in this section to suggest that Hardyng knew or used the romance. See Harker, "John Hardyng's Arthur," p. 285, who seems to imply that Hardyng knew the text.

3262–68   *"Written at . . . I gesse."* This stanza is unique to Hardyng and may reflect, as Harker has suggested, "the kind of officiating tag which Hardyng in his capacity as a forger of documents could be expected to add" ("John Hardyng's Arthur," p. 286).

3269   *Geants Toure*. Compare *HRB* §158 ("giganteam turrim"), *RB* line 10730 ("Tur gigantine"), RMB 1.11314 ("Toure Geaunt"), and *EH* II:331 ("gigantaeam").

3272   *He shulde than wryte*. Despite the fact that *HRB* §§158–162 elucidates Arthur's rights and mentions that Arthur used Lucius's messengers to relay his reply, there is no explicit reference to Arthur writing a letter. *RB* lines 11045–47 briefly mentions the composition of a letter after Arthur has discussed the matter with his men, but RMB 1.11405–10, 1.11611–18, and *Arthur* lines 247–70 make more of Arthur's writing, dedicating several lines to the composition of the letter. Hardyng may have been inspired by RMB (see note 3.3273–3345 below for a linguistic echo to support this assumption) or another unidentified source related to *RB* (as *Arthur* appears to be). Equally, the decision to present Arthur's response to Lucius solely in letter form may originate from a desire to link Arthur's epistolary exchange with other instances in the *Chronicle* where kings have asserted their territorial claims through letters; see, for example, 6.1990–94, where Edward III uses letters to establish his claim to France, and Edward I's letter to Pope Boniface at 7.1401–14, which Hardyng urges Henry VI to use if he ever wishes to insist on his right to Scotland.

3273–3345   *Of whiche . . . thaym amonge.* Hardyng omits the speeches made by Arthur's men in *HRB* §§158–162, *RB* lines 10711–11058, RMB 1.11315–11628, and *EH* II:331–35. There are linguistic echoes between the letter at 3.3333–36 and Arthur's response in RMB 1.11494–96 ("bring Rome & I salle Bretayn bring, / & whilk of vs most may / bere Rome and Bretayn boþe away"). See also note 3.3272 above.

3286   *By treson of Androges.* This is an allusion to 2.2354 ff. Androges is not named in *HRB*, *RB*, *OV*, RMB, *EH*, or *Brut.*

3290m   *Quicquid iniuste . . . imperatoria patet.* Compare with *HRB* §159: "Nichil enim quod ui et uiolentia adquiritur iuste ab ullo possidetur" (Nothing that is acquired by force and violence can ever be held legally by anyone). Similar statements occur in *RB* lines 10829–34 and RMB 1.11415–18.

3299   *Brute.* Brute is not mentioned in *HRB*, *RB*, *LB*, *OV*, *CPL*, RMB, *EH*, *Brut*, *Arthur*, or *NC* at this point.

3311m   *Cui descendebat . . . comitatus Romani.* The editors thank Neil Wright for his help in elucidating this text.

3346m   *How Arthure . . . Emperoure Leo.* In *HRB* Lucius is the Procurator of Rome and Leo is the emperor. However, in §162, Arthur sends a reply to "Imperatoribus" (emperors), stating that he has no intention of paying *them* tribute, and later, in the description of the battles that ensue, the narrative contains frequent references to the emperor, the emperor's camp, and the emperor's bodyguard, which presumably refer to Leo, but could equally be mistaken for references to Lucius. This appears to have led to the confusion that arises about Lucius's status as an emperor in this and other texts (see, for example, *RB*, *CPL*, RMB, and *Arthur*).

3346–66   *This noble . . . and Holonde.* Hardyng omits the details found in *HRB* §§162–64, *RB* lines 11085–11286, RMB 1.11653–11848, and *EH* II:336 concerning Lucius's army, Arthur's dream, and Mordred's love of Guinevere (not in *HRB*), and instead emphasizes how Arthur mustered his troops and who supported him. With the exception of the references to Flanders (lacking in *HRB* and *EH*) and the Twelve Peers of France, Hardyng's account of the men supporting Arthur is different to that in *HRB*, *RB*, RMB, and *EH*. Interestingly, *HRB* and *CPL* list the king of Spain as one of Lucius's supporters, whilst *RB*, *EH*, and RMB refer to one Aliphatima of Spain in Lucius's retinue; Hardyng, like the *Brut* (p. 83), has the king of Spain supporting Arthur.

3367–3436   *Than was . . . withouten right.* Hardyng alone describes "Elyne" as Arthur's niece and Hoel's sister (3.3369–73), although the *Brut* (p. 84), *Arthur* (line 355), and *NC* (fol. 41r), refer to her as Hoel's "cosyn," which could mean kinswoman, niece, or cousin. In *HRB*, *RB*, *OV*, RMB, and *EH*, she is Hoel's niece; in *LB* she is Hoel's daughter (line 12924). Nonetheless, on the whole, Arthur's encounter with the giant at Mont St. Michel is similar to *HRB* §165 and RMB 1.11849–12170. See additional notes to this section below.

3370–73   *Whiche for . . . no pere*. Compare RMB (1.11961–62) and *Arthur* (line 356),
           which also mention Helen's fairness. Harker notes that the *Alliterative Morte*
           (lines 860–63) similarly refers to Helen's beauty, but there is no further
           correspondence to indicate that Hardyng knew this source ("John Hardyng's
           Arthur," p. 289).

3375–76   *Bot he . . . ete thaym*. Compare *HRB* §165 and *EH* II:338, which draws upon
           HRB.

3390–94   *Therefore ye . . . this londe*. Compare *HRB* §165, where the giant eats men half-
           alive and the woman tells Bedivere to flee or the giant will tear him to pieces,
           and *CPL* I:188, where Bedivere is warned that the giant will eat him.

3401–03   *When that . . . the hylle*. Compare *RB* lines 11461–68 and RMB 1.12014–20.

3408   *With Caliburne his sworde*. Compare *RB* line 11547, *CPL* I:190, RMB 1.12071,
           12104, and *EH* II:340, all of which refer to Arthur's sword by name at this
           point in the narrative.

3413–15   *So huge . . . and grym*. Reference to Arthur's stature being like that of a child
           beside the giant does not occur in *HRB*, *RB*, *OV*, *CPL*, RMB, *EH*, or *Brut*.

3419–22   *That wente . . . fende hydouse*. Only Bedivere is told to sever the giant's head in
           HRB, *RB*, *LB*, *OV*, RMB, *EH*, and *Brut*; in *CPL* Arthur removes the head.

3432–36   *Whiche is . . . withouten right*. Throughout the Hundred Years War, Mont St.
           Michel withstood repeated attacks from the English, hence Hardyng's
           reference to it as a "strengh fulle gretly famed" (3.3432). The last two lines of
           this stanza are comparable with the *Libelle of Englysche Policy*, lines 198–210 (c.
           1436–38), which similarly criticizes the people of Mont St. Michel for capturing
           English ships in peacetime, albeit during the reign of Edward III.
                Whilst Hardyng may be alluding to the importance of keeping the seas, a
           topic that engaged writers in the mid-1430s and 1440s (see the *Libelle* and
           John Capgrave's *Liber de Illustribus Henricis*, pp. 134–35), two extant petitions
           made to the Chancellor, John Kemp, between 1450 and 1452 illustrate that
           the problem of piracy near Mont St. Michel was very real at the time Hardyng
           was writing this version of the *Chronicle*. Two petitions for alms made by John
           Sterlyng of Horning reveal that his ship had been captured by Bretons and
           taken to Mont St. Michel where he was ransomed (see TNA; PRO, SC
           8/304/15182 and SC 8/305/15208). Similar cases in the Chancery Proceedings,
           nevertheless, demonstrate that the capture of vessels was common on both
           sides of the Channel during periods of truce, and that the English were just
           as guilty of seizing ships as their foreign counterparts (see, for example, TNA;
           PRO, C 1/43/53).
                Hardyng's reference to "pese" (3.3436) may indicate that this part of the
           Chronicle was composed between 1444 and 1449, when the Truce of Tours
           technically protected interests on either side of the Channel. Correspondingly,
           the notion that Normandy is "unbayne" (3.3434) might imply that Hardyng
           wrote this section before 1450, when the English lost Normandy. Then again,
           as a patriotic Englishman, Hardyng may be speaking more generally about the

nefarious character of the French and could conceivably have been writing
after the fall of Normandy in the early 1450s, when the loss of Lancastrian
France was still keenly felt but no hostile action was being taken to retrieve it.
For further information about the increase of piracy around England's shores
from the mid-1430s onwards, and the wider debate about the importance of
keeping the seas, see Griffiths, *Henry VI*, pp. 424–33.

3437m   *in Itaylle did feghte*. See note 3.3438–43 below.

3437–3520   *Arthure his . . . and wounde*. Hardyng's account of the Roman war is more
             succinct than his probable sources; compare, for example, *HRB* §§166–67, *RB*
             lines 11609–12262, and RMB 1.12171–12775. See the notes that follow for
             additional comments.

3438–43   *Awbe a . . . colours sene*. In *HRB* §166, *RB* lines 11616–24, *Lestoire de Merlin* p.
             405, and RMB 1.12178–84, Arthur makes his camp by the River Aube in
             Autun, or Augustodunum, Burgundy (compare note 3.3522 below). Hardyng
             has either confused the Aube with the River Allia, a tributary of the Tiber in
             Italy, where Belin and Brenny fight against the Romans and conquer Rome
             earlier in the *Chronicle* (see 2.1556–1800), or he has deliberately altered his
             source to make Arthur's war against the Romans echo Belin and Brenny's
             campaign. Three later references to Arthur fighting against Lucius in Italy
             seem to indicate that the change was intentional (see notes 3.3437m, 3.3619m,
             and 3.3717–19); however, if this is the case, Hardyng's attempt to relocate the
             action has been impeded by his appropriation of Augustodunum (3.3522) and
             Saussy (3.3530) from one of his sources.
                 The description of the landscape's natural beauty at lines 3441–43 appears
             to be Hardyng's own addition, but the imagery used is conventional and
             similar descriptions can be found in other medieval texts, particularly those
             evoking a spring setting, such as dream visions, lyrics, and romances.

3447–50   *Syr Gawayne . . . the historien*. Only Hardyng makes reference to Gawain being
             brought up in Arthur's household at this point in the narrative, but compare
             HRB §166 and *Lestoire de Merlin* (p. 405), which stress Gawain's consanguinity
             to Arthur. *RB*, *LB*, *CPL*, and RMB enhance Gawain's usefulness by claiming
             that he had either spent time in Rome (*RB* lines 11653–54, *LB* line 13100) or
             that he could speak "speche Romeyn" (*LB* line 13099, *CPL* I:194, RMB
             1.12214). *LB* line 13099 also credits Gawain with knowledge of Celtic.

3459–61   *To turne . . . may suffyse*. Compare RMB 1.12306–07: "To turne agayn, it salle
             not be. / ffrance is myn, þider wille I go."

3463   *Quyntylian*. In *HRB* §166 and *HRBVV* §166, Lucius's nephew is Gaius
             Quintillianus, but Hardyng refers to him by surname only, like *RB* line 11741,
             LB line 13197, *CPL* I:194, and RMB 1.12311.

3465–66   *"Ye Bretons . . . or hardymente."* Although Quintillian's speech is similar to that
             reported in *HRB* §166, and the direct discourse developed by *RB* lines
             11745–48 and RMB 1.12315–20, Hardyng alone places emphasis on the
             quality of "knyghthode" (3.3466).

3467–3520   *Whom Gawayne . . . and wounde.* Whilst this section is based on *HRB* §§166–67, Hardyng greatly reduces the narrative and omits all reference to the fact that Arthur did not authorize his men to fight, an issue that causes anxiety for the knights in Hardyng's sources, but which Hardyng manages to sidestep here by having the "felaws" attempt to travel "homwarde" to "warne" Arthur of "bataylle and no reste" (3.3468–70). Hardyng similarly alters the circumstances leading to the ambush described from 3.3493 onwards and downplays the number of Briton casualties. In *HRB* §167 the Britons are ambushed the day after the first battle, as they prepare to take the Roman captives to Paris, and Arthur loses many troops in the first stage of battle. Here the Roman ambush occurs before the Britons have reached Arthur to give him the prisoners and "few" of them are slain (3.3506). Whilst the first of these changes may result, unintentionally, from Hardyng's abridgement of the narrative, the deliberate attempt to downplay the Briton casualties suggests that Hardyng wanted to present Arthur's men as formidable warriors.

3494–97   *Two senatours . . . grete powere.* Hardyng, like *HRB* §167 and *CPL* I:200, refers to the emperor sending two senators, the kings of Syria and Libya, and fifteen thousand men to ambush the Britons, whereas *RB* line 12105, *HRBVV* §167, and RMB 1.12641 state that ten thousand men were sent. RMB similarly mistakes *RB*'s senator "Catellus Waltereius" (line 12112) for two individuals, thus listing three senators and two kings (1.12647–50). *EH* (II:345), also refers to fifteen thousand men, but makes a similar mistake to RMB and interprets *HRB*'s "Vulteius Catellus" and "Quintus Carucius," as three or four individuals.

3502   *kynges thre.* It is unclear where Hardyng obtained this figure from, as *HRB* §167, *RB* lines 12237–40, and RMB 1.12755–58 only list two high-born Roman casualties. Harker has suggested that this might be a transposition error for "ther" ("John Hardyng's Arthur," p. 294).

3511   *"Welcome my . . . grete payne."* Arthur's speech appears to be unique to the *Chronicle*.

3516–18   *Gawen, Bewes . . . and Bedwere.* Hardyng's list of wounded knights combines several of the knights mentioned in *HRB* §167 — Gawain, Beus, Bedivere, Gerin, Cador (either Duke Cador of Cornwall or Maurice Cador of Cahors), Guitard, and Irelglas — with three of Hardyng's own choosing. However, of these, only Maurice Cador of Cahors and Irelglas occur in the list of four princes killed in *HRB*, making Hardyng's list unique.

3521–62   *Lucyus so . . . and olde.* Hardyng follows *HRB* §168. In condensing his source the only significant changes he makes include the addition of marginalia describing Arthur's four banners (see note 3556m below) and the repositioning of the reference to the earl of Gloucester's battalion, which is mentioned before the other battalions in *HRB*, but last here.

3522   *Augustudoun.* Augustodunum is the Latin name for Autun given in *HRB* §168. See note 3438–43 above.

3530   *Seysy*. Probably Saussy or Val-Suzon in France; see Matthews, "Where was Siesia-Sessoyne?" and Keller, "Two Toponymical Problems" for further discussion.

3556m   *Arthure bare . . . of golde*. Of the four heraldic devices mentioned in this marginalia three are referred to elsewhere in the *Chronicle*: the dragon banner (3.2008–09), the three crowns (3.2248m), and Saint George's Cross (3.3157–63). The dragon and three crowns are common in Arthurian heraldry. The image of Mary is ultimately derived from *HB* §56, but Hardyng presumably encountered it in *HRB* §147, where it is painted on Arthur's shield. Morris believes that Hardyng's transferral of the Virgin's image from the shield to the banner indicates that "it is no longer [a] personal insignia, but a focus for allegiance, belonging to Arthur only insofar as he represents England, and proclaiming the whole nation's devotion to the Christian cause" (*Character of King Arthur*, p. 127). The inclusion of St. George's arms in remembrance of Galahad is clearly Hardyng's invention, and may have been inspired by Henry V's use of the arms during his French campaign.

3556–62   *The nynte . . . and olde*. Hardyng has amalgamated what appear to be two battalions in *HRB*, one headed by Arthur and one by Morvide. In *HRB* §168 Morvide is given his own company of men and told to wait in reserve until needed, so that Arthur's men can withdraw to him if necessary, regroup, and launch new attacks. Arthur then leads his own company, which he positions behind the other battalions and identifies with his dragon banner to designate it as a fortified camp to which the wounded can withdraw. See also note 3.3661–65 below.

3563–66   *The emperoure . . . that day*. These lines are based on the twelve Roman legions mentioned in *HRB* §170 after the speeches of Arthur and Lucius. Hardyng omits Lucius's speech and *HRB*'s description of the structure of the Roman army.

3567–69   *With that . . . be bette*. This appears to be Hardyng's own addition, but see RMB 1.12985–96.

3570–83   *Kynge Arthure . . . do mynystracioun*. Hardyng radically reduces the rousing speech attributed to Arthur in *HRB* §169, and, in keeping with RMB 1.12923–24, emphasizes the great conquests made by the Britons and the "servytute" (3.3581) that they will suffer if the Romans are victorious in battle. Lines 3577–78 are particularly interesting, as they accentuate the threat of losing territorial possessions and failing to defend the king's "right," two themes that would doubtless have had a strong resonance with Hardyng's original audience, who, by the time the *Chronicle* was completed, had witnessed the loss of Henry VI's possessions in France.

3584–97   *With that . . . thare wykydnesse*. Hardyng has taken King Auguselus's speech out of its original context in *HRB* §161 and abbreviated it; in the source Auguselus speaks to Arthur and his men in the Giants' Tower just after Lucius's emissaries arrive demanding tribute. Compare 3.3605–11 and 3.3612–18, which are also taken out of context here.

3598–3604   *"Me thynke . . . and wyght."* Urian's speech has no equivalent in *HRB* or its derivative texts. It is probably unique to Hardyng.

3605–11   *Kynge Howelle . . . hole Senate.* In *HRB* §160 Hoel, like Auguselus, speaks at the meeting Arthur holds in the Giants' Tower following Lucius's demand for tribute. While Hardyng may have taken his inspiration for this speech from this earlier section of *HRB*, the content is only loosely related. Compare 3.3584–97 and 3.3612–18, which are also taken out of context.

3612–18   *Thus every . . . ben undre.* Like 3.3584–97 and 3.3605–11, these lines appear to be based on the vows made by Arthur's knights in the Giants' Tower in *HRB* §162; but compare the end of *HRB* §169, *RB* lines 12441–50, and RMB 1.12937–44.

3619m   *in Itaylle.* See note 3.3438–43 above.

3619–88   *Thanne to . . . to weelde.* For the most part Hardyng follows, and severely condenses, *HRB* §§171–75, but see notes 3.3626 and 3.3668–69 below for the possible influence of RMB.

3626   *Whose corses so brought were to the dragoun.* In *HRB* §171 it is Kay who takes Bedivere's body back to the golden dragon that marks Arthur's fortified camp. Hardyng assigns this task to Auguselus and Cador instead, possibly because he omits that part of *HRB* where Kay attempts to avenge Bedivere and rescue his body. The phrasing of this line is also interesting because of its similarity to RMB 1.13133, "þe body to þe dragon brouht," which may have influenced Hardyng here.

3628–30   *And of . . . in fight.* *HRB* §172 states that two kings and two senators were killed at this point.

3647   *foure prynces.* See note 3.3628–30 above. Hardyng appears to be repeating information here.

3650   *And thre knyghtes than thay slewe of the Senate.* The equivalent section of *HRB* §173 does not relay any specifics about the high-born Romans lost when Hoel and Gawain attack; instead we are told that the Briton casualties include Chinmarchocus, duke of Tréguier, and three other leaders, Riddomarcus, Bloctonius, and Iaginvius. Assuming that Hardyng was not using an unidentified source, he either misread *HRB* or a chronicle related to it, such as RMB, or he deliberately altered it to reflect more favorably on the Britons.

3655   *egle of golde.* Lucius's golden eagle is mentioned much earlier in *HRB* §170, where it has the same function as Arthur's dragon: that is, to act as a rallying point, where men can withdraw to and regroup (see also *CPL* I:206). It also occurs in *RB* line 12866 and RMB 1.13294, just after Gawain begins to fight Lucius, although RMB does not call the device an eagle, but a "standard."

3661–65   *Bot at . . . on newe.* Hardyng's reduction of his source obscures some of the sense behind Morvide's actions here. In *HRB* §168 Morvide is asked to lead a reserve company of men that the Romans are not aware of; see note 3.3556–62 above.

3668–69   *Bot who . . . the name.* Hardyng may have taken this detail from *Lestoire de Merlin* (p. 410), where Gawain kills Lucius in battle; however, it is more likely that he is following RMB 1.13405 ff., which builds upon a similar assertion in *CPL* I:216, by stating "I kan not say who did him falle, / bot Sir Wawayn, said þei alle" (1.13405–06) and "Þe certeyn can þer noman ame / But sire Wawayn bar þe name" (1.13408–09, additional text supplied in the margins of Sullen's edition from London, Lambeth Palace Library, MS Lambeth 131).

3680–88   *There was . . . to weelde.* Hardyng's own addition.

3690–3723   *To Rome . . . his innocence.* Hardyng bases this section on *HRB* §176 and RMB 1.13433–13468, making several additions of his own. The lines concerning Lucius's association with Leo are his (see 3.3346m for further details), but they are in keeping with other texts that present Lucius as emperor, such as *RB*, *CPL*, and RMB. Hardyng seems to follow RMB, rather than *RB*, in expanding *HRB*'s reference to Arthur sending Lucius's body to the Senate as "truage" (3.3696), though he makes more of Arthur's grim irony by using the word "gode" (3.3702), meaning "gifts" or "wealth," to describe the additional corpses that he will send if Rome demands further payment. Finally, and perhaps most importantly, Hardyng introduces a scene in which the Senate offers Arthur the emperorship in return for "gode lordeship" (3.3706); although Arthur falls short of conquering the "Empire hole" in this version of the *Chronicle* because news of Mordred's usurpation necessitates his return to Britain, Hardyng's reference to the king wintering in Italy after accepting the Senate's offer implies that Arthur has all of Italy, except Rome, under his control. In the second version of the *Chronicle*, Hardyng's Arthur enters Rome, where he is crowned emperor and resides for the winter.

3717–19   *Bot he . . . somer came.* See notes 3.3438–43 and 3.3690–3723 above. In *HRB*, *RB*, *LB*, *OV*, *CPL*, RMB, and *Brut*, Arthur sojourns in Burgundy.

3724–3870   *Bot tythandes . . . foure yere.* Hardyng's main sources for the account of Arthur's return to Britain and ensuing death appear to be *HRB* §§176–78 and RMB 1.13469–13744 (or an unidentified text linked to them), and *Mort Artu*; see the notes that follow for specific examples and for features unique to Hardyng.

3725–27   *Modrede had . . . the quene.* In other texts Mordred has already taken the crown and, in most cases, the queen. Here the use of "aspyred / To have the croune" and "wedden wold the quene" implies that he has yet to secure both.

3730   *And Albany he gafe hym to his mede.* HRB, RB, OV, CPL, Castleford's *Chronicle*, RMB, *EH*, and *Brut* all refer to Mordred offering Cheldrike Scotland for his assistance, but only Hardyng and *CPL* I:218 call it "Albany."

3733   *And bade . . . to conquere.* In *HRB* §177 Arthur cancels his attack on Rome and sends Hoel to restore peace. Hardyng's Arthur appears to be unique in sending Hoel to conquer Rome on his behalf instead.

3737   *As traytoure . . . by jugyment.* Arthur's desire to "honge and draw" Mordred, the medieval punishment for high treason, appears to be unique, but see *LB* lines

14065–85, where Gawain wishes to hang Mordred and have the queen drawn apart by horses. See also 3.3770–72.

3740–41   *Assembled were . . . armes clere*. *HRB* §177 and *EH* II:360 mention the 80,000 pagans and Christians, but Hardyng uses the same phrasing as *CPL* I:218 ("quatre vint myl") and RMB 1.13492 ("fourscore þousand") to describe them.

3743   *Porte Rupyne whare Whitesonde is*. "Rupini Portu" (Richborough) is given in *HRB* §177 and *EH* II:360 ("Rutupi portu"), whereas Wissant is given in *RB* line 13049 ("Witsant"), *LB* line 14091 ("Wissant"; the manuscript used for Barron and Weinberg's edition contains "Whitsond"), *OV* line 1986 ("Whitsonde"), RMB 1.13518 ("Whitsand"), and *Arthur* line 559 ("Whytsond"). Hardyng tries to reconcile the two disparate places by conflating the two.

3752   *Wynchester*. Like *HRB* §177, *CPL* I:220 and *EH* II:361, Hardyng's Mordred goes straight to Winchester. In *RB*, *LB*, *OV*, RMB, *Brut*, and *Arthur* he travels to London first where he is refused entry.

3760   *Camblayne*. Hardyng's text is closest to *HRB* §178 ("fluuium Camblani"); compare *RB* line 13253 ("Juste Cambe"), RMB 1.13687 ("a water, Tambre"), and *EH* II:361 ("fluvium Cambla").

3761   *sexty thousonde*. Compare *HRB* §178, *LB* line 14240, *CPL* I:222, and *EH* II:361. *RB* line 13070 and *OV* line 1980 also number the troops at 60,000 when Mordred first musters his soldiers for Arthur's return.

3766–68   *Bot Arthure . . . and stroyed*. Compare *RB* lines 13143–48 and RMB 1.13587–94.

3770–72   *His foule . . . his lawe*. See note 3.3737 above.

3777–93   *Bot Arthure . . . his generacioun*. Hardyng, like *CPL* (I:222), Castleford's *Chronicle* (line 23924), *P* (V:332–33), RMB (1.13693–700), *Mort Artu* (p. 154), and the *Alliterative Morte* (lines 4224 ff.), states unequivocally that Mordred was slain by Arthur and that Arthur received his "dethes wounde" (3.3787) from Mordred (compare also *EH* II:363). In claiming that he can find no books attesting to Mordred's incestuous birth, Hardyng follows the chronicle tradition, in which Mordred is Arthur's nephew (see, for example, *HRB* §176 and RMB 1.13475), as opposed to the romance tradition, which presents him as Arthur's son. In so doing, Hardyng distorts the truth about his own knowledge of Arthurian literature — deliberately overlooking the fact that *Mort Artu*, a romance that he clearly knew, emphasizes Mordred's status as Arthur's son — and makes his king morally superior to his sinful counterpart in romance. Hardyng's attribution of Cheldrike's death to Arthur similarly increases the king's prestige; *HRB*, *CPL*, Castleford's *Chronicle* (line 23937), RMB, and *EH* list the Saxon amongst those that fell at the battle, but fail to elaborate on who killed him. In other sources, such as *JG* and *P*, Cheldrike does not die in this battle. Also of interest here is Hardyng's idiosyncratic comparison of Arthur and Mars, the god of war, and his allusion to Fortune's role in Arthur's victory, which prefigures the complaint addressed to Fortune at 3.3878–88.

3778   *Caliburne*. The *Alliterative Morte* (lines 4230, 4242) also mentions the king's sword by name in its description of Arthur slaying Mordred.

3787   *as cronycle doth expresse*. Compare *RB* line 13275 ("si la geste ne ment") and RMB 1.13706 ("men sais").

3794–3807   *The quene . . . myghtes moste*. In *HRB* Guinevere flees to Caerleon upon hearing of Mordred's initial defeat, that is, before the siege at Winchester. In *RB*, *OV*, RMB, *EH*, *Brut*, and *Arthur*, she leaves after learning of Mordred's flight from Winchester and before the final battle. In *CPL* she flees when she hears of Arthur's return, after Mordred has retreated to Winchester, whilst in the *Mort Artu* the news of Arthur's imminent return prompts her to abscond, but this time prior to the king's arrival in Britain. *NC* concludes Arthur's reign with a brief description of Guinevere's fate, but the moment of her flight is not given. In contrast, Hardyng's queen escapes out of fear for her own life only upon hearing of Mordred's death. This, together with the references to "shame" (3.3800) and "synne" (3.3806) — possibly inspired by the use of the same words in *RB* lines 13221–22 and RMB 1.13648–50 — suggests that Hardyng is following other chronicles in presenting Guinevere as an adulteress despite his knowledge of the *Mort Artu*, where, having locked herself in the Tower to avoid Mordred's attentions, Guinevere elects to join the nunnery because she fears that Arthur will not believe she is innocent. Whilst this version of the *Chronicle* does not condemn the queen as overtly as the second version, Hardyng's later "compleynt . . . for the dethe of Kynge Arthure" (3.3871m) emphasizes her culpability by lamenting the fact that she caused the death of "so fele knyghtes" (3.3891) because of the power she allowed Mordred to exert over her. Hardyng similarly accentuates her fall by expanding the reference to the church of St. Julius the Martyr in *HRB* §177 and *EH* II:361 and reminding his audience that this was where she was crowned.

3808–14   *In whiche . . . dethes wounde*. Compare *RB* lines 13266–74, *OV* lines 2017–19, RMB 1.13701–04, and *Brut* p. 90; Hardyng's phrasing is similar to *RB* and RMB.

3815–21   *For whiche . . . bygan dystrayne*. The account of Arthur's distress echoes the king's sadness when the knights leave him in pursuit of the Grail (see 3.3022–37). Hardyng may have drawn upon *HRB* §178, where an angry Arthur buries his dead knights before attacking Winchester, or *Mort Artu* (pp. 154–55), where Arthur laments the loss of his men at the Black Chapel.

3824   *Whiche Cadore . . . that adversacioun*. Hardyng is presumably following either *HRB* §178, *CPL* I:224, or RMB 1.13732 in saying that Cador died in battle, although in *HRB* it is not Cador of Cornwall listed amongst the dead, but "Cador Limenic."

3826–28   *Whose brother . . . withouten fayle*. Hardyng provides more detail about Cador's lineage than his regular sources; his Cador is Arthur's half-brother, the son of Arthur's mother, Igerne, and her first husband Gorlois. Cador is also Arthur's half-brother in Thomas Gray's *Scalacronica* (Moll, *Before Malory*, pp. 165–66), in the *Brut y Brenhinedd* in the *Black Book of Basingwerk* (National Library of

Wales MS 7006D, p. 182b), and, according to Fletcher, in the *Brut Tysilio* (see Fletcher, *Arthurian Material*, pp. 117–18, 283), although there is no evidence to suggest that Hardyng knew any of these texts. Cador's son, Constantine, is Arthur's nephew in the *Vita Merlini* (p. 268), *OV* (lines 2027–28), *EH* (II:363), and *Brut* (p. 90) (which also uses "cosyn"), implying that Cador is Arthur's sibling, but most chronicles simply describe Constantine as Arthur's kinsman or cousin (see, for example, *HRB* §178, *RB* line 13296, Robert of Gloucester's *Chronicle* lines 4585–86, *CPL* I:224, RMB 1.13742, *P* V:338–39, and *NC* fol. 41r).

3829–35   *Kynge Arthure . . . made sufficiantly.* Hardyng links Avalon with Glastonbury once again and places Arthur's tomb there, along with the grave of Joseph of Arimathea and Galahad (see 2.2611–47, 3.3052–82, 3.3150–56). For Arthur's association with Glastonbury and the alleged discovery of his remains in 1190–91 see Robinson, *Two Glastonbury Legends*; Lagorio, "Evolving Legend"; and Abrams and Carley, *Archaeology and History*. Other texts mentioning Arthur's burial at Glastonbury include William of Malmesbury's *De antiquitate Glastonie ecclesie*, p. 82–83; Gerald of Wales' *De principis instructione*, I:20 and *Speculum ecclesiae* II:8–10; Ralph of Coggeshall's *Chronicon Anglicanum*, p. 36; Adam of Domerham's *Historia de rebus gestis Glastoniensibus*, pp. 341–42; Robert of Gloucester's *Chronicle*, lines 4592–94; the fourteenth-century copy of William of Malmesbury's *Gesta Regum Anglorum* in Oxford Bodleian Library MS Bodley 712 (II:261–62); *An Anonymous Short English Metrical Chronicle*, lines 239–48; *Petit Bruit*, p. 13; *Castleford's Chronicle*, lines 23988–89; *JG*, pp. 80–81; John of Fordun, *Chronica gentis Scotorum*, pp. 110–11; *P* V:332–33; *EH* II:363; the *Alliterative Morte* lines 4308–09; *Arthur* lines 612–24; *NC* fol. 41r; the Middle English Prose Bruts extant in Cleveland Public Library MS John G. White Collection W Q091.92–C468 and Dublin Trinity College MS 489; and a Cornish folktale (see Barber, "*Vera Historia*," p. 77). Gray's *Scalacronica* and Capgrave's *Chronicle* can be also added to this list, as they mention the discovery of Arthur's tomb at Glastonbury.

3833   *As yit this day ys sene and shalle evermore.* This statement links the Arthurian past with Hardyng's own time. Compare with Caxton's preface to Malory's *Morte Darthur*, in which relics of the Arthurian past provide evidence of Arthur's existence in the late fifteenth-century (see *Works of Sir Thomas Malory*, ed. Vinaver, I:cxliii–cxlvii).

3836–39   *Who dyed . . . fulle clere.* This is the date given in *HRB* §178.

3840–42   *Fro whiche . . . ay doutous.* A number of chronicles mention Merlin's prediction about the uncertainty surrounding Arthur's death; see, for example, *RB* lines 13279–93, *OV* lines 2022–23, RMB 1.13714–22, and *Brut* p. 90. The reference ultimately stems from the prophecy in *HRB* §112 that Arthur, the "Boar of Cornwall," will have an uncertain end ("exitus eius dubius erit"). Hardyng presumably followed RMB, but see also note 3.3843m below.

3843m   *De quo . . . rexque futurus.* For a study of this epitaph and its history see Withrington, "Arthurian Epitaph" and Barber, "*Vera Historia.*" It occurs in several texts: the *Vera Historia de Morte Arthuri*; the *Chronicon de Monasterii de Hailes*; *Arthur* lines 619–24, which may be based on a lost version of *RB*; at the end of the unique copy of the *Alliterative Morte*; in a version of John of Fordun's *Chronica gentis Scotorum*, p. 111; in a manuscript gloss accompanying Lydgate's *FP* in British Library MS Royal 18 B. xxxi (fol. 193r); and in Malory's *Morte Darthur* (*Works of Sir Thomas Malory*, ed. Vinaver, III:1242). The epitaph appears to have gained some currency in the fifteenth century, and it probably circulated in oral form too, which Hardyng may have known. If Hardyng encountered it in written form, he may have known it from a lost text based on *RB*, linked with the source of *Arthur*, or a manuscript of the *FP* containing similar marginalia (see note 7.491–97 for a possible borrowing from the stanza in *FP* against which the epitaph occurs).

3843–70   *Bot of . . . foure yere.* Hardyng completes his account of Arthur's passing by leaving his chronicle sources and turning, once again, to romance. In this instance, the "story of Seynt Grale" (3.3843) refers to *Mort Artu*, pp. 154–59, which locates Arthur's tomb at a Black Chapel, describes how Girflet lived at the chapel as a hermit for eighteen days before dying, and relates how Lancelot and his companion Hector spent their last four years in religious contemplation with the archbishop of Canterbury and Lancelot's cousin, Bliobleris. Hardyng, who may have been recalling *Mort Artu* from memory, adapts his source, linking the Black Chapel with the chapel at Glastonbury reputedly dedicated to the Virgin Mary by St. David, and he claims that Geryn (who takes the place of the Vulgate Girflet) spent four years there as hermit with Lancelot. It is unclear whether the phrase "Whiche Geryn made" (3.3847) refers to his building Arthur's tomb or the chapel dedicated to Mary, which is normally attributed to St. David (see, for example, *JG*, pp. 2–3), but in the *Mort Artu* neither is constructed by Girflet, so unless Hardyng was using a source linked to Glastonbury that incorporated material from *Mort Artu*, the suggestion may originate with him.

3871–3905 *O gode . . . als sertayne.* Hardyng's "compleynt" (3.3871m) questions the role of divine prescience and Fortune in the demise of Arthur *and* Mordred, who is portrayed, rather surprisingly, as a "gode" knight (3.3892) who falls from a state of "grete manhode" (3.3893) and "honoure" (3.3899) to "pryde" (3.3875) and "falshode" (3.3901) through "unhappe" (3.3896). Line 3878 is clearly influenced by Chaucer's *TC* 3.617, a text that Hardyng uses elsewhere to infuse his narrative with Boethian wisdom; however, whilst the tragic implications of Fortune lamented here were undoubtedly inspired by *TC*, the account of Arthur's reign in Lydgate's *FP* may have been equally influential on Hardyng, ending as it does with an envoy warning "princis" against treason and Fortune's mutability (8.3130–3206). For Hardyng's knowledge of Boethian narratives see Peverley, "Chronicling the Fortunes."

3889–91   *O fals . . . fele knyghtes.* See note 3.3794–3807 above.

3904   *Thy lorde . . . kynge soverayne.* Hardyng emphasizes the triple nature of Mordred's treachery; when he commits treason by betraying his sovereign, Mordred also breaks the oath he made to Arthur as a feudal "lorde" and his obligations to him as a blood-relative. Cooper makes a similar observation about the wording of Gawain's appeal to Arthur in Malory's *Morte Darthur*, as he requests Arthur help as "My king, my lord, and mine uncle" (*Sir Thomas Malory*, ed. Cooper, p. 560).

3906–47   *Kynge Constantyne . . . in mencioun.* Hardyng expands the account of Constantine's reign in *HRB* §§179–80 and instead of condemning the king for killing Mordred's sons at the "high autere" (3.3921), as *HRB* and *RB* do, Hardyng presents him as a good king who governs well in "reste and pese" (3.3942). The brief description of Constantine's coronation at 3.3910–12 appears to be original to the *Chronicle*, as does the reference to Constantine being a knight of the Round Table (3.3906–08). For Constantine's consanguinity to Arthur see note 3.3826–28 above.

3924–40   *In whose . . . that cenoby.* Compare *HRB* §179, which Hardyng augments with additional information.

3948–68   *Aurelyus Conan . . . and remove.* Despite the fact that Hardyng's narrative is similar to both *HRB* §181, which gives the length of Conan's reign as three years, and RMB 1.13777, which refers to Conan as Constantine's "cosyn," neither source provides all of the details found here; this suggests that Hardyng was conflating two or more sources, supplementing the narrative himself by referring to Conan's "beuté" at line 3955 (an observation that is absent from all of the sources considered here), or using an unidentified source. The stanza warning "lordes that ben in hygh estates" (3.3962) to avoid quarrels is unique to Hardyng, but it may have been inspired by similar advice in Lydgate's *FP*.

3969–75   *Than Vortypore . . . hym decese.* Compare *HRB* §182.

3976–96   *Malgo next . . . rialle trone.* Although this section has its origins in *HRB* §183, lines 3990–96 are based on RMB 1.13823–26.

3997–4010 *Careys was . . . theym stonde.* Compare with the beginning of *HRB* §184. Hardyng's account of Careys and Gurmond continues in Book 4.

Figure 9. Folio 196r. Facial details observed at different wave lengths. Additional emphasis on upper lip observed at 420 nm on the electromagnetic spectrum (left) and curls in the hair become visible at 780 nm on the electromagnetic spectrum (right). Photos courtesy of Dr. Christina Duffy, Conservation Science Team, The British Library and The British Library.

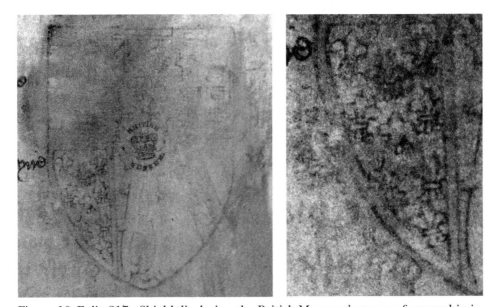

Figure 10. Folio 217v. Shield displaying the British Museum's stamp of ownership in the center (left) and the erased arms of Margaret of Anjou. Pattern of multiple fleurde-lis designs in the lower left hand quarter of Margaret Anjou's arms (right). Images captured at 420 nm on the electromagnetic spectrum. Photos courtesy of Dr. Christina Duffy, Conservation Science Team, The British Library and The British Library.

TEXTUAL NOTES

ABBREVIATIONS: m: marginalia; **MS**: London, British Library MS Lansdowne 204 (base manuscript).

Throughout the manuscript, the marginalia, book and chapter headings, and the running heads featuring the names of the reigning kings, are written in red ink; often the first letter of each stanza of the main text is also written in red ink. Because of the consistency of the scribe's use of red in these areas, we have only recorded exceptions to this rule in the notes. Other features, such as scribal corrections, illumination, annotations by hands other than the scribe(s), and editiorial emendations are recorded as they occur.

Occasionally, background smudges and traces of letters or words occur behind the current text of Lansdowne 204. Though beyond the scope of this edition, a comprehensive study of each instance of smudging is desireable, as some may have been caused by underwriting, indicating that the scribe(s) altered the work. The British Library analyzed ten examples of potential underwriting for us, using multispectral imaging equipment and Digital USB microscopy. Our selections fell into one of three categories. 1) Examples that did contain underwriting: the background shadows were caused by the scribe scraping the parchment to remove a word or phrase and writing different text over the erasure (or, as in two cases, simply erasing text that was no longer required). In such instances, traces of the original iron gall ink burn-through have survived, leaving partial letter-forms or words visible at a wavelength of 420 nanometers (hereafter nm) on the electromagnetic spectrum; sadly, it is often impossible to discern complete letters or words, and ink burn-through from text overleaf further obscures the original writing, making it largely unrecoverable. 2) Examples that do not contain underwriting: the shadows behind the text are caused by ink-burn through from text overleaf, which, to the naked eye, gives the impression of underwriting. 3) Examples that do not contain underwriting: the shadows behind the text are again due to degradation caused by the iron gall ink flaking away from the surface of the parchment and leaving the shape of the original letter below; to the naked eye, the spread of the burn-through can look like underwriting beneath the thinner flakes of surviving ink. The following textual notes make references to confirmed instances of underwriting only; we do not highlight *potential* cases because, given the degredation of the ink, we feel that this could be misleading.

PROLOGUE

1–28	MS: The scribe adds rhyme bands in the same colored ink as the verse and draws lines between each stanza.
29–154	MS: The scribe adds red rhyme bands and draws each stanza. With the exception of line 29 (which begins with an illuminated initial), the

	first letter of each stanza has been written in the same black ink as the rest of the stanza, then written over again in red ink.
29	*Who*. MS: illuminated initial.
30	*compleyne*. MS: *compley*; the corner of the folio is missing.
71–93	The corner of the folio is missing. The text has been reconstructed using Charles Kingsford's "Extracts" and the epilogue of Lansdowne 204 (7.1093–1169) as a guide.
122	MS: This line shows evidence of some alteration to the text. Before the present line was added, the parchment was scraped away removing the ink of a previous line. During the multispectral analysis carried out by the British Library, partial letters were observed in the underwriting, but the original text was unrecoverable. The nature of this particular change is important because it may indicate that Hardyng asked the scribe to add or correct the reference to John Kemp's titles ("cardinalle" and archbishop of "York") at a later stage of production.
155–61	MS: This stanza is partially legible under ultraviolet light and may have been intentionally erased by the scribe(s). Traces of the text are observed at a wavelength of 420 nm on the electromagnetic spectrum, but are not always legible. We have reconstructed illegible words speculatively. Evidence of red rhyme bands is present, and there is a small trace of red ink near the first letter of the stanza (visible in a false color image), suggesting that it was rendered in red ink like the stanzas covering Prol.29–54.

CONTENTS PAGE

The incomplete contents page is written entirely in red ink on one folio; it is divided into two columns, the second of which begins with the entry for Book 3, chapter 7. Each of the headings denoting a new book is enclosed by a red box.

The First Book.   MS: The corner of the folio is missing.
xxvi capitulum Of Arvyragus. MS: This appears on the same line as the previous entry.
viii capitulum . . . Seint Elene. MS: The text runs into the gutter, which is too tight to see the final letters of *Elene*.
xx capitulum of Elfride of Westsex sovereyn. MS: An early reader has added a small manicule pointing to this line.
xxii capitulum Of Edward, sovereyn. MS: *xxii capitulum Of Edward sover*.
xxiiii capitulum.   MS: *xxiiii*.
xxv capitulum.   MS: *xxv*.
xxvi capitulum.   MS: *xxvi*.
xxvii capitulum.   MS: *xxvii*.
xxviii capitulum.   MS: *xxviii*.
xxix capitulum.   MS: *xxix*.

BOOK 1

1m	*How thay . . . hys Dialoge.* MS: This part of the marginalia (in red ink) appears to have been written over an earlier note in iron gall ink, traces of which can still be seen, although it is not legible. In most cases the red ink traces the orignal ink underneath, though regions of the marginalia at the start and the end of the present selection do contain illegible underwriting, partially visible at a wavelenghth of 420 nm of the electromagnetic spectrum.
	Lyndisfarn. MS: *Lyndifarn.*
	Wynchester. MS: *Wynchest.*
1	*The.* MS: illuminated initial.
176m	*Nota that . . . exiled thaym.* MS: This part of the marginalia was originally copied in iron gall ink, but has been written over in red.
	as Trogus . . . xliiii bookes. MS: This part of the marginalia appears to have been added when the scribe traced over the rest of the marginalia with red ink.
197–203	An early hand has copied a version of the first two lines into the left-hand margin: 'Thys was the yere afore the incarnacyon a thousand iiii c v yere.' Other annotations by this hand occur at 3.4004, 4.42, 6.1, 6.295, 6.332, and 6.346.
212	*soveraynté.* MS: *soveraraynte.*
266	*So that.* MS: *That.*
283	*From Dame Albyne.* MS: *From.*
286	*Two hundre yere.* MS: A contemporary hand has written "ii c yere" by the side of this text in the left-hand margin.
295–2.14	The stanzas on this folio, covering 1.295–2.14, have red rhyme bands.
308	A contemporary hand has written "x ii c yere afore the encarnacyon" in the left-hand margin next to this line.

BOOK 2

1m	*Pli(?).* MS: This word is difficult to read. It appears to be an abbreviation of an author's name. It could be an erroneous abbreviation for Pompeius Trogus, who is later mentioned with regards to Aeneas.
	translata. MS: *tranlata.*
1	*As.* MS: an illuminated initial.
1–512	Hardyng writes in eight-line stanzas here and at 2.522–617.
68	*Japhet cam.* MS: *Japhet.*
89	An early hand, possibly that of John Stow, writes "Eryctonnus frost edified Troy" in the left-hand margin beside this line. See Manuscript Description for futher information from Stow.
151	*disposicioun.* MS: *disposicoun.*
258	An early hand has written "Nota how Brutus was borne" in the gutter of the right-hand margin of this folio.
330	*fallible.* MS: *fallibe.*

417	*Brutus*. MS: an illuminated initial.
513–21	A nine-line stanza.
522–617	Hardyng writes in eight-line stanzas here and at 2.1–512.
543	The name "Brute" has been erased in the right-hand margin next to this line; a contemporary hand has rewritten it underneath the original annotation.
630	*Cornewayle*. MS: A contemporary hand has copied the word "Cornewall" below this word.
639m	*conceyte of.* MS: *of* has been inserted above line.
667	*Thus*. MS: an illuminated initial.
730m	Originally copied in iron gall ink, this marginalia has been overwritten in red.
786	*Of.* MS: an illuminated initial.
822	*Mewyne*. MS: An early hand has copied this name into the right-hand margin.
902	*fylde*. This sentence requires the infinitive *fylen*. The needs of rhyme have produced a grammatical error.
919	*After*. MS: an illuminated initial.
954	*This*. MS: an illuminated initial.
975	*Manlyn*. MS: an illuminated initial.
989	*Membrice*. MS: an illuminated initial.
1017	*Ebrauke*. MS: an illuminated initial.
1062	*myschaunce*. MS: *myschaune*.
1066m	MS: This marginalia was originally copied in iron gall ink, but has been overwritten in red.
1115	*Hys*. MS: an illuminated initial.
1128	An early hand, apparently that of John Stow, writes "Gyldas" in the right-hand margin beside this line. See Manuscript Description.
1129	*So*. MS: an illuminated initial.
1153	*Hys*. MS: an illuminated initial.
1171	*Bladud*. MS: an illuminated initial.
1185	An early hand, apparently that of John Stow, writes "Gyldas" in the left-hand margin beside this line. See Manuscript Description.
1199	*Aftyr*. MS: an illuminated initial.
1234m	*Nota, for homage of Scotland*. MS: This part of the marginalia was originally copied in iron gall ink; it has been overwritten in red.
1290m	*How Margan . . . of hym*. MS: This part of the marginalia was originally copied in iron gall ink; it has been overwritten in red.
1290	*Margan*. MS: an illuminated initial.
1339	*Ryval*. MS: an illuminated initial.
1353m	*Nota of drunkenes*. MS: This marginalia occurs beside 2.1358–59.
1353	*Gurgustius*. MS: an illuminated initial.
1367	*Sisilius*. MS: an illuminated initial.
1381	*Iago*. MS: an illuminated initial.
1395	*Kymar*. MS: an illuminated initial.
1409	*Gorbodyan*. MS: an illuminated initial.
1437	*Cloten*. MS: an illuminated initial.

1493	*And*. MS: an illuminated initial.
1556	*Than*. MS: an illuminated initial.
1654m	*hoste*. MS: This word is inserted above the line.
1676	*conquerours*. MS: *conquerous*.
1689m	An early hand, apparently that of John Stow, has written "Alfryd and Galfryd" after the marginalia. See Manuscript Description.
1718	*And*. MS: *Ane*.
1738m	This marginalia occurs alongside 2.1742.
1801	*Gurguyn*. MS: an illuminated initial.
1850	*Guytelyn*. MS: an illuminated initial.
1864	*Sysilius*. MS: an illuminated initial.
1878	*Kymar*. MS: an illuminated initial.
1885	*Danyus*. MS: an illuminated initial.
1892	*Morvyde*. MS: an illuminated initial.
1941m	*first*. MS: This word is inserted above the line.
1941	*Gorbonyan*. MS: an illuminated initial.
1955	*Argalle*. MS: an illuminated initial.
1962	*Elydoure*. MS: an illuminated initial.
1997	*Argalle*. MS: an illuminated initial.
2004	*The*. MS: an illuminated initial.
2011	*But*. MS: an illuminated initial.
2025	*Peridoure*. MS: an illuminated initial.
2032	*Elydoure*. MS: an illuminated initial.
2046	*Gorbonyan*$_1$. MS: an illuminated initial.
2053	*Margan*. MS: an illuminated initial.
2060	*Enniaunus*. MS: an illuminated initial.
2067	*Ivalle*. MS: an illuminated initial.
2074	*Rymo*. MS: an illuminated initial.
2081	*Geyennes*. MS: an illuminated initial.
2088	*Katellus*. MS: an illuminated initial.
2095	*Coyle*. MS: an illuminated initial.
2102	*Porrex*. MS: an illuminated initial.
2109m	*Nota of drunkenes*. MS: This marginalia occurs beside 2.2114.
2109	*Cheryn*. MS: an illuminated initial.
2116	*His*. MS: an illuminated initial.
2137	*Urian*. MS: an illuminated initial.
2144	*Elyud*. MS: an illuminated initial; the rest of the name was originally in iron gall ink, but has been overwritten in red.
2146	*Detonus*. MS: originally written in iron gall ink, but overwritten in red.
2151	*Detonus*. MS: an illuminated initial.
2152–2259	The following words and proper names have an initial letter in red ink: *Gurgucyus* (2.2152); *Meryan* (2.2153); *Bledudo* (2.2154); *Cappe* (2.2156); *Oenus* (2.2156); *Sisilyus* (2.2157); *Bledud* (2.2158); *Than* (2.2165); *Archyvalle* (2.2165); *Eldolle* (2.2166); *Redyon* (2.2167); *Redrike* (2.2168); *Samuel* (2.2169); *Pyrre* (2.2170); *Penysselle* (2.2170); *Capoyre* (2.2171); *Elyguelle* (2.2171); *Tenvancyus* (2.2229); *Cesar Julyus* (2.2232); *O* (2.2237); *For* (2.2259).

2178	*greteste*. MS: *gretete*.
2179	*Hely*. MS: an illuminated initial.
2193	*Than*. MS: an illuminated initial.
2221	*Cassibalan*. MS: an illuminated initial.
2238	*Belyne*. MS: initial letter originally written in iron gall ink and overwritten in red.
2452	*Tenvancius*. MS: an illuminated initial.
2459m	*Kymbelyn Kynge*. MS: This part of the marginalia appears to have been added at a later stage of production.
2459	*Kymbelyne*. MS: an illuminated initial.
2487	*Guydere*. MS: an illuminated initial.
2526	*Arviragus*. MS: an illuminated initial.
2527	*Claudius*. MS: *Claudus*.
2550	*At*. MS: an illuminated initial.
2574	An early hand, apparently that of John Stow, writes "Gyldas" in the left-hand margin next to this line. See Manuscript Description.
2599m	This marginalia occurs beside 2.2604.
2599–2633	MS: The stanzas from 2.2599–2633 are quite close together, so the scribe has drawn red lines between each of them to show that they are separate.
2662	*Maryus*. MS: an illuminated initial.
2697	*Coyle*. MS: an illuminated initial.

BOOK 3

1	*Aftyr*. MS: an illuminated initial.
39	An early hand, apparently that of John Stow, writes the word "Gildas" in the left-hand margin beside this line. See Manuscript Description.
84	An early hand, apparently that of John Stow, writes the word "Gildas" in the left-hand margin beside this line. See Manuscript Description.
86	The first letter of this line has been overwritten in red ink. An early hand, apparently that of John Stow, writes the words "de victoria Aurelii Ambrosii" in the left-hand margin beside this line. See Manuscript Description.
141	*The*. MS: an illuminated initial.
197	*Getan*. MS: an illuminated initial.
204	*This*. MS: an illuminated initial.
253	*Nota*. The word "Nota" occurs in the right-hand margin beside the text.
274m	*Principio . . . cadas*. This marginalia occurs alongside 3.279.
281	*Thurgh*. MS: an illuminated initial.
281–94	The first letter of each line has been overwritten in red ink.
288m	*regno*. MS: *regn*, due to marginal cropping.
309	*But*. MS: an illuminated initial.
311	*and*. MS: *ad*.
316m	This marginalia occurs alongside 3.320.
337	*The*. MS: an illuminated initial.

342	*Asclepiadote*. MS: The first letter of this word has been overwritten in red ink.
351m	*How the*. MS: *the* has been inserted above the line.
435	*Than*. MS: an illuminated initial.
477m	*Kynge Constance*. MS: This part of the marginalia appears to have been added at a later stage of production.
477	*Constance*. MS: an illuminated initial.
Before 505m	*Constantynes armes*. MS: The armes of Constantine (gules [red], a cross argent [silver]) appear in the left-hand margin.
505	*Constantyne*. MS: an illuminated initial.
525	*Nota*. This word presumably draws attention to the fact that the king lived by his own means.
553	*That what*. MS: *That*.
680–81	An early hand, apparently that of John Stow, has written "Gyldas" and "Henry Huntyngdon" in the right-hand margin beside these lines. See Manuscript Description.
729	*But*. MS: an illuminated initial.
750	*So*. MS: an illuminated initial.
771m	*Unde . . . est*. This marginalia occurs beside 3.776–77.
785	*This*. MS: an illuminated initial.
813	*The*. MS: an illuminated initial.
848	*Conan*. MS: an illuminated initial.
875	*ese*. MS: this word appears to have been added at a later stage of production.
883–90	An eight-line stanza.
926	*Gracyan*. MS: an illuminated initial.
961	*Gwayns*. MS: an illuminated initial.
979	*senatours*. MS: *sanatours*.
1108	*This*. MS: an illuminated initial.
1143	*Constans*. MS: an illuminated initial.
1220	*This*. MS: an illuminated initial.
1278	*knyghthede*. MS: *knyghhede*.
1290m	MS: Multispectral analysis reveals traces of underwriting beneath the current text (observed at a wavelength of 420 nm), which originally continued for several lines after the current marginalia, but was erased by the scribe before being partially overwritten. The original text contained similar information to the current marginalia (referring to the arms containing Woden and Fry), but also cited Saint Colman as a source for the information.
1402m	*called*. MS: *called called*. This marginalia occurs beside 3.1403.
	Sapiencia . . . suaviter. This marginalia occurs beside 3.1408.
1458m	*of Bretayne, son of Vortygere*. MS: This part of the marginalia may have been added at a later stage of production.
1458	*Syr*. MS: an illuminated initial.
1535	*This*. MS: an illuminated initial.
1553	*surely*. MS: This word appears to have been added at a later stage of production.

1626m	This marginalia was originally copied in iron gall ink, but has been overwritten in red.
1710	*Merlyn*. MS: an illuminated initial.
1787	*Thay*. MS: an illuminated initial.
1847	*Israelles*. MS: *Isarelles*.
1997	*Syr*. MS: an illuminated initial.
2004–09	A six-line stanza.
2059	*Gorleys, duke of Cornewayle*. MS: The capital *G* and *C* have been overwritten in red ink.
2099	*of*. MS: *of of*.
2145	*And bade*. MS: *And*. We have followed Harker's conjectural restoration of *bade* (meaning *beseeched*), which restores the meter and is further supported by the presence of *bade* in the second version of the *Chronicle* (see Harker, "John Hardyng's Arthur," p. 226 and Oxford, Bodleian Library MS Arch Selden B. 10, fol. 50r).
2150m	*How the*. MS: *the* inserted above the line.
2164	An early hand, apparently that of John Stow, has written "The Saynt Grale what it is" in the left-hand margin next to this line. See Manuscript Description.
2197	An early hand, apparently that of John Stow, has written "Verolame, is name of Saint Albons" in the right-hand margin next to this line. See Manuscript Description.
2248m	*Bretayne*. MS: *Br*. This marginalia is accompanied by an illustration of King Arthur's arms (with gules [red], three crowns or [gold]).
2248	*Arthure*. MS: an illuminated initial.
2407	*whan*. MS: *than*.
2409m	*Scotland*. MS: *Scoland*.
2414	*Out*. The first letter of this line has red ink in the center.
2430	*This*. MS: an illuminated initial.
2444–57	Originally written in iron gall ink, the first letter of each line, the first letter of the proper names, and the first *e* of *erle* in each of these lines have been overwritten in red.
2514	*Kynge*. MS: an illuminated initial.
	the. MS: inserted above the line.
2528–33	A six-line stanza.
2541m	*he*. MS: inserted above the line.
2564–71	The first letter of each proper name is overwritten in red.
2567	*Colygrenauntt*. MS: *Colgrenauitt*.
2625	*But*. MS: an illuminated initial.
2668	*Chartres*. MS: *Chartes*.
2709m	*Table*. MS: inserted above the line.
2715	*is*. MS: *his*.
2744	*This*. MS: an illuminated initial.
2759	*philosophres*. MS: *phlosophres*.
2947m	MS: The multispectral analysis of this marginalia undertaken by The British Library was unable to clarify whether the smudge observed

behind *as the grete story of þe Saynt Graal proportes* was indicative of underwriting. The shadows may be from the text overleaf.

Perlouse. MS: *Pelouse*, due to cropping.

Table₂. MS: *Tabl*, due to cropping.

the₇. MS: *the of*.

contened. MS: *contene*, due to cropping.

2979–81	The first letter of each line has been overwritten in red.
3038m	*swerde*. MS: inserted above the line.
3115m	Underneath this marginalia an early hand, apparently that of John Stow, has written "Gildas de gestis arthur." See Manuscript Description.
3136m	*he*. MS: inserted above the line.
3207	*mynstralsy*. MS: *mystralsy*.
3227	*Lucyus*. MS: an illuminated initial.
3276	*Arthure*. MS: an illuminated initial.
3311m	*inperium*. MS: *in*. The rest of the text appears to be in the gutter of the manuscript, but it is difficult to see due to the tight binding.
	totius. MS: *to*. The rest of the text appears to be in the gutter of the manuscript, but it is difficult to see due to the tight binding.
	Romani. MS: *Romane*.
3319	*Senate*. MS: *Sanate*.
3419	*to*. MS: *to to*.
3463	*Quyntylian*. MS: *Quytylian*.
3535–76	Each stanza begins with an illuminated initial. Some of the proper names in the text begin with a red initial up to to *kynge Arthure* at 3.3556.
3605	*Kynge₁*. MS: an illuminated initial.
3615	*ennemyse*. MS: *enmemyse*.
3634	*doun*. MS: *doum*.
3843m	This marginalia occurs alongside 3.3842.
3906	*Kynge*. MS: an illuminated initial.
3907	*aventurouse*. MS: *aventrorise*.
3920m	This marginalia occurs alongside 3.3924.
3948	*Aurelyus*. MS: an illuminated initial.
3963	*transmutacioun*. MS: *transmuitacioun*.
3969	*Than*. MS: an illuminated initial.
3976	*Malgo*. MS: an illuminated initial.
3997	*Careys*. MS: an illuminated initial.
4004	An early hand has written "Bretons" in large letters in the left-hand margin next to this line. Other annotations by this hand include 1.197–203, 4.42, 6.1, 6.295, 6.332, and 6.346.

Figure 11. Folio 225v, stanza 6. Underwriting is observed in between the lines. Image captured at 420 nm on the electromagnetic spectrum. Photo courtesy of Dr. Christina Duffy, Conservation Science Team, The British Library and The British Library.

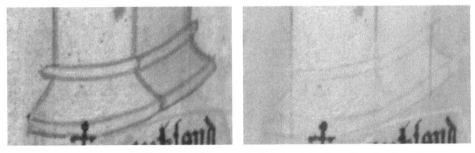

Figure 12. Folio 226v–227r, Map of Scotland. Original designs for the building structures are observed at 1000 nm on the electromagnetic spectrum. Photo courtesy of Dr. Christina Duffy, Conservation Science Team, The British Library and The British Library.

INDEX OF NAMES AND PLACES

ABBREVIATIONS: *HB*: Nennius, *Historia Brittonum*; *HRB*: Geoffrey of Monmouth, *Hisoria Regum Brittanniae*; **m**: marginalia; **RMB**: Robert Mannyng of Brunne, *The Chronicle*.

Aldroene: 3.1060, 3.1087.
Aldroenus, fourth King of
Brittany.

Alecte: 2.28. Alecto, one of the
Erinyes, or Furies, in Greek
mythology.

Alfridum Beverlaicensem: 2.1689m.
Alfred of Beverley.

Allecte: 3.309m, 3.316m, 3.317,
3.351. Allectus, King of Britain.

Almayne: 2.1689m, 2.1690, 2.1695,
3.827m, 3.913, 3.2679, 3.3366.
Germany.

Alsynges: 2.1599. Elsingius, King of
Norway, whose daughter is
coveted by Brenny.

Alverede: 2.1857. King Alfred.

Ambrius (Ambrii): 3.1581, 3.1611.
Ambrius, alleged founder of a
religious house at Mount Ambri
(equated with Amesbury).

Ambry, Mounte: 3.1905. Mount
Ambri, the location of the
religious house founded by
Ambrius.

Amorawde: 3.2457. Amoraud, Earl of
Exeter, Knight of the Round
Table. Possibly derived from
Amorand in RMB 1.10895.

Amos: 2.1141, 2.1166, 2.1181. Amos,
prophet at the time of King Leyle.

Amphybale (Amphibale): 3.393,
3.1145, 3.3918. Saint
Amphibalus.

Ampuleyus: 3. 1693. Apuleius; the
work referred to by him in the
text is *De deo Socratis*.

Anacletoun (Anacletus): 2.378,
2.387, 2.393, 2.426. Anacletus,
comrade of King Pandrase.

Anchises: 2.122, 2.148, 2.158, 2.346.
Anchises, father of Eneas.

Andragius (Andragyus): 2.2116m,
2.2117, 2.2121. Andragius, King
of Britain, youngest son of
Cheryn.

**Androgyus (Andragyus, Andragius,
Andrage, Androge)**: 2.2226,
2.2228, 2.2326m, 2.2354m,
2.2360, 2.2363, 2.2368, 2.2389m,
2.2390, 2.2399, 2.2401, 2.2409,
2.2438, 3.3286. Androgeus, Lord
of London, Duke of Kent, eldest
son of Lud.

Anglia: 2.730m. England.

Anne: 3.2188, 3.2508, 3.2574. Anne,
daughter of Utere Pendragon and
Igerne, sister of King Arthure,
wife of Loth of Louthianne.

Anthenores Posterieus: 2.734.
Antenor, a Trojan lord.

Antigonus (Antigonyse, Antigone):
2.377, 2.389, 2.426. Antigonus,
brother of King Pandrase.

Antioche (Antyoche): 2.2571m,
2.2579. Antioch.

Appolyne: 2.765, 2.1192. The god
Apollo.

Aquitayne (Aquytayne): 2.513,
3.2658. Aquitaine.

Ara Cely: 3.678. The church of Santa
Maria in Ara Coeli, Rome.

Archyvalle: 2.2165m, 2.2165.
Archmail, King of Britain.

Argalle: 2.1955m, 2.1955, 2.1962m,
2.1972, 2.1989, 2.1997m, 2.1997,
2.2053m, 2.2053, 2.2060m.
Archgallo, King of Britain, second
son of Movyde.

Argalle: 3.2449. Argall, or
Artgualchar, Earl of Warwick,
Knight of the Round Table.

Armoryke: 3.827m, 3.834. Armorica,
the ancient name for Brittany.

Arriens erresyes: 3.659m, 3.661,
3.664. The Arian heresy.

Arrogoyne (Aragoyne): 3.2672.
3.3361. Aragon.

Arthure (Arthuri, Arthur, Arthurus):
2.1061, 3.1626m, 3.2052m,
3.2108, 3.2169, 3.2248m,
3.2276m, 3.2304m, 3.2345,
3.2346m, 3.2369, 3.2381m,

Brenny's battle against the Romans. At 3.3438 Hardyng confuses the River Aube in Burgundy for the Allia.

Awmesbury: 3.1580. Amesbury, or more specifically the religious house allegedly founded there by Ambrius.

Azarius (Azarias): 2.1141, 2.1167, 2.1182. Azariah, prophet at the time of King Leyle.

Bachus: 2.31, 3.2872. Bacchus, God of wine.

Baldulf (Baldulfe): 3.2291, 3.2297, 3.2327, 3.2346m, 3.2346, 3.2368. Baldulf, brother of Colgrym, the Saxon leader.

Bamburgh: 2.1035, 3.2585. Bamburgh Castle, Northumberland; also called Mounte Dolorouse.

Bangore: 3.3934. Bangor.

Barbflete: 3.3357. Barfleur.

Barent: 3.2446. Barent, Earl of Cirencester, Knight of the Round Table (possibly derived from Baruc of Cirencester in RMB 1.10897).

Bassian (Bassyan): 3.197m, 3.201, 3.204m, 3.204, 3.206, 3.211m, 3.233, 3.240, 3.325. Bassanius, son of Severe by a British woman and brother of Getan.

Bathe: 2.1173, 3.2346m, 3.2356, 3.2359. Bath; see also **Caerbladon**.

Bayoun: 3.3711. Bayeux.

Bayre, 3.2682. ?The ancient Duchy of Bar (Bar-le-duc), France; ?Baar, Germany; or ?Bavaria, from the German Beiern.

Beaufort, Henry: 1.1m. Henry Beaufort, Bishop of Winchester and Cardinal.

Bede (Bedam): 2.2418, 3.176m, 3.178, 3.189, 3.975m, 3.1024m, 3.1047, 3.2919m. Bede.

Bedwere: 3.2569, 3.2737, 3.2863, 3.3381, 3.3395, 3.3399, 3.3404, 3.3410, 3.3419, 3.3518, 3.3547, 3.3624, 3.3711. Sir Bedivere, Knight of the Round Table, Duke of Normandy.

Belyn (Belyne): 2.1556m, 2.1560, 2.1563m, 2.1567, 2.1570, 2.1577m, 2.1602, 2.1612m, 2.1619, 2.1624, 2.1627, 2.1633, 2.1654m, 2.1658, 2.1662, 2.1683, 2.1689m, 2.1708, 2.1713, 2.1722, 2.1732, 2.1752m, 2.1752, 2.1759, 2.2238, 3.3304m, 3.3304. Belinus, King of Britain and elder son of King Dunwallo.

Besaunse: 3.669. Byzantium.

Bewes: 3.2456, 3.3445, 3.3516, 3.3540. Beus, Earl of Oxford, Knight of the Round Table (possibly derived from Beus of Oxford in RMB 1.10890).

Bewes of Corbenny: 3.2570. A knight of the Round Table.

Bilyngate (Belyngate): 2.1773m, 2.1785. Billingsgate, London.

Bladud: 2.1171m, 2.1171, 2.1185. Bladud, King of Loegria.

Blake Chapelle: 3.3846. The Black Chapel at Glastonbury.

Bledud Gabred: 2.2151m, 2.2158. Beldgabred, King of Britain.

Bledudo: 2.2151m, 2.2154. Bledudo, King of Britain.

Boloyne: 2.2234, 3.3642. Boulogne.

Bors (Borse): 3.2569, 3.3108, 3.3134. Sir Bors, Knight of the Round Table.

Braban: 3.2681, 3.3364. Brabant.

Brenny (Brenne): 2.1563m, 2.1563, 2.1577m, 2.1591m, 2.1595, 2.1612m, 2.1626, 2.1640, 2.1654m, 2.1655, 2.1680, 2.1689m, 2.1708, 2.1713, 2.1722,

Duke of Cornwall, son of Gorloys, Knight of the Round Table, and father of Constantyne III.

Caerbladon: 2.1173. Bath.

Caercaredot: 3.1579. Salisbury.

Caercolim: 3.436. Colchester.

Caerglou (Caergloy): 2.2558, 2.2560, 3.134. Gloucester.

Caergwent: 2.1158, 3.1143, 3.1628, 3.746, 3.748, Winchester.

Caerkent: 2.1157, 3.1235. Canterbury. See also **Cauntyrbyry** and **Doroberny**.

Caerlegion (Caerlegioun, Caerlegyoun): 2.2634, 3.70, 3.99. The City of Legions, equated with Caerleon, see also **Caerlioun**.

Caerleyle (Caerleyl, Carlele): 2.1066m, 2.1131, 2.1132, 2.1150, 2.2003, 3.2586, 3.2919m. Carlisle.

Caerleyre: 2.1201, 2.1279, 2.1301. Leicester.

Caerlioun (Carlyoun, Caerlyoun, Carlioun): 2.1752m, 2.1768, 2.1848, 2.1877, 2.2613m, 3.43m, 3.64m, 3.1922, 3.2256, 3.2591, 3.2718, 3.2725, 3.2744m, 3.2746, 3.2794, 3.2905m, 3.2952, 3.3185m, 3.3191, 3.3337, 3.3797, 3.3864, 3.3920m, 3.3925. Caerleon. See also **Caerlegion**.

Caerludcourte: 3.1627, 3.2323. Lincoln.

Caermardyn: 3.1649, 3.1666. Carmarthen.

Caerpaladoure: 2.1159. Shaftsbury.

Caerpenelgorte: 2.2593. Exeter.

Caerperis (Kaereperis): 2.2502, 3.744. Porchester.

Caersegent: 3.2254. A correct identification of this location is difficult because the context of Hardyng's reference to it is hindered by his use of two confused sources (see Explanatory Note 3.2448–80). He may have

believed it was the ancient name for Silchester, but the correct identification is probably Caernarfon.

Caersyry (Caercyry): 3.1110, 3.2253. Cirencester.

Caeruske: 2.1752m, 2.1769, 2.1772. The City of Legions, associated with Caerleon. See also **Caerlegion** and **Caerlioun**.

Calabre: 2.1702. Calabria, Italy.

Calathere: 2.1638, 2.1971. The forest of Calaterium in Albany, where Belyn and Brenny fight, and Elydoure meets his brother. Taken from Geoffrey of Monmouth, it may derive from Calatria, an area of the Scottish lowlands associated with the Calders in Midlothian.

Caliburne: 3.2489, 3.2652, 3.2666, 3.3408, 3.3778. Caliburn, the name of Arthure's sword.

Calidoun: 3.2335. Celidon Wood, Lincoln.

Caliope: 2.24. The goddess Calliope, muse of epic poetry.

Camalot: 3.3191. Camelot. Hardyng equates this with Caerleon; see **Caerlioun**.

Camber (Cambre): 2.793m, 2.793, 2.805, 2.807m. Camber, or Kamber, second son of Brute. See also **Gales**.

Camblayne: 3.3759m, 3.3760, 3.3825. The scene of Arthure's last battle with Mordrede, which Hardyng appears to identify with the River Camel in Cornwall.

Cambre (Camber, Cambry, Kambre): 2.786m, 2.794, 2.795, 2.849, 2.1442, 2.1561, 2.2334, 2.2635, 3.70, 3.344, 3.1158, 3.1635, 3.1662, 3.1710m. Wales; see also **Gales**.

Campany: 2.1702. Campania, Italy.

Clenyus: 3.2466. A Knight of the
Round Table. The name is
probably derived from Cheneus
Mapcoil in *HRB* §156.

Clifford: 3.2224. Either Thomas
Clifford, Eighth Baron Clifford, or
his son John, Ninth Baron Clifford
(see Explanatory Note 3.2220–26).

Cloarke, Mounte: 3.1778. The hill on
which Vortygere's castle stands;
possibly associated with Little
Doward, Herefordshire.

Cloten: 2.1437m, 2.1437, 2.1498,
2.1500. Cloten, King of Cornwall
during the civil war that follows
the death of Porrex.

Coile II (Coule, Coyle, Coylus):
2.2662m, 2.2697, 3.1, 3.3. Coilus,
King of Britain, son of **Marius**.

Colayn: 3.899. Cologne.

Colchester: 3.436. Colchester.

Colegrenauntt: 3.2567. Sir
Calogrenant or Colgrevance, a
Knight of the Round Table.

Colflaut: 3.2471. Clofaut, a Knight of
the Round Table.

Colgrym (Coligrym, Colgryme):
3.2283, 3.2288, 3.2327, 3.2346m,
3.2346, 3.2368. Colgrin, a Saxon
leader, brother to Baldulf.

Colman: 1.1m, 1.197m. Saint
Colman, bishop of Lindisfarne.
See Explanatory Note 1.1m.

Conan: 3.1808. Conisbrough.

Conan Mariadoch: 3.792, 3.816,
3.822, 3.838, 3.848, 3.855m,
3.855, 3.874, 3.1062. Conanus
Meridiadocus, King of Brittany.

Condage (Cundage): 2.1290m,
2.1291, 2.1306, 2.1310, 2.1315,
2.1318m, 2.1320. Cunedagius,
Duke of Cornwall, son of Ragawe.

Connesburgh: 3.1809. Conisbrough.

Constance (Constans): 3.1124,
3.1129, 3.1143m, 3.1143,
3.1157m, 3.1281, 3.1325, 3.1792.
Constance, eldest son of

Constantyne II, King of Britain,
and brother to Aurilyus
Ambrosius and Utere Pendragon.

Constance (Constans, Constaunce):
3.463m, 3.465, 3.473, 3.477m,
3.477, 3.499, 3.503, 3.3316.
Constantius, Roman Senator,
King of Britain, father of
Constantyne I.

Constantyne I (Constantine): 3.491,
3.505m, 3.505, 3.526m, 3.532,
3.543, 3.554, 3.575m, 3.576,
3.582m, 3.583, 3.603, 3.617m,
3.659m, 3.665, 3.670, 3.680,
3.687m, 3.705, 3.715m, 3.730,
3.732, 3.804, 3.3311m, 3.3315,
3.3320. Constantine I, Emperor
and King of Britain.

Constantyne II (Constantine):
3.1052m, 3.1094m, 3.1094,
3.1108m, 3.1108, 3.1143m, 3.1762.
Constantine II, King of Britain,
brother of Aldroene, King of
Brittany.

Constantyne III: 3.3823, 3.3906m,
3.3906, 3.3913, 3.3917, 3.3941,
3.3952. Constantine, son of
Cadore, King of Britain after
King Arthure.

Conwen: 2.1666. Queen Conwenna,
mother of Belyn and Brenny.

Cordele (Cordeyle): 2.1227, 2.1243,
2.1263. Cordelia, youngest
daughter of King Leyre.

**Cornewayle (Cornwail, Cornwaille,
Cornwaylle, Cornewail,
Cornewaylle)**: Cornwall, 2.630,
2.751m, 2.917, 2.922, 2.938,
2.1020, 2.1234m, 2.1240, 2.1291,
2.1437, 2.2227, 2.2452, 3.65,
3.341, 3.799, 3.856, 3.2031,
3.2059, 3.2295, 3.2465, 3.2592,
3.2785, 3.2814m, 3.2818,
3.2842m, 3.2844, 3.2947m,
3.2989m, 3.3038m, 3.3536,
3.3757, 3.3759m, 3.3827,
3.3906m. Cornwall.

Coryneus: 2.497m, 2.505, 2.520, 2.540, 2.543, 2.563, 2.586m, 2.595, 2.602, 2.629, 2.631, 2.884, 2.912, 2.919, 2.960. Corineus, a Trojan leader, companion to Brute, and eponymous founder of Cornwall.

Coyle I: 2.2095m, 2.2095. Coilus, King of Britain, son of Katellus.

Coyle III: 3.435m, 3.437, 3.449, 3.471, 3.475. Coel, Duke of Colchester, King of Britain, father of Seynt Elene.

Cradocke, see **Carodoch**.

Crete: 2.71, 2.73. According to the genealogy that Hardyng follows, Crete is the mythical founder of Crete.

Creusa: 2.250, 2.261, 2.273. Hardyng's Creusa is the mother of Brute, but in Greek mythology she is the daughter of Priamus.

Crocea Mors: 2.2301. "Yellow Death," the name of Julius Caesar's sword.

Cronica Bruti: 2.1m. The Chronicles of Brute, a reference to the *HRB*. See also **Brute, the grete**.

Cryste (Criste, Cryste, Jhesu): 2.572, 2.1740, 2.2459m, 2.2468, 2.2471, 2.2473m, 2.2474, 2.2479, 2.2480, 2.2483, 2.2487m, 2.2495, 2.2544, 2.2613, 2.2617, 2.2637, 2.2640, 3.18, 3.29m, 3.29, 3.37, 3.42, 3.71, 3.73, 3.80, 3.179, 3.184, 3.372m, 3.385, 3.397, 3.421, 3.498, 3.575, 3.596, 3.609, 3.651, 3.667, 3.673, 3.676, 3.694m, 3.703, 3.894, 3.931, 3.938, 3.1046, 3.2157, 3.2164, 3.2166, 3.3123, 3.3181, 3.3836. Christ.

Cumbyrnalde: 3.2584. An error for Cumbyrlande (Cumberland).

Cupido: 2.30. Cupid, the god of Love.

Curson (Cursale): 3.2450, 3.3552, 3.3643. Cursalem, Earl of Chester, Knight of the Round Table.

Cypre: 2.70. According to the genealogy that Hardyng follows, Cypre is the mythical founder of Cyprus.

Cypres: 2.70. Cyprus.

Cyrcester (Cyrcestre): 3.1110, 3.2253. Cirencester. See also **Caersyry**.

Cythym: 2.69. Kittim, son of Javan.

Danaus: 1.176m. Danaus, King of Greece, father of Albyne. In classical mythology he is the father of the Danaïds.

Danen Hylle: 3.2029. Mount Damen, the site of one of Utere's battles.

Danmarke (Denmarke, Danmark, Dannemarke): 2.1612m, 2.1612, 2.1801m, 2.1815, 2.1819, 3.2486m, 3.2495, 3.2783, 3.3112, 3.3194, 3.3542, 3.3980. Denmark.

Danos: 2.1066m. The Danes.

Danyele, Seynt: 3.3934. Saint Deiniol.

Danyus: 2.1885m, 2.1885. Danius, King of Britain, brother of Kymar II.

Dardanus: 2.85. Dardanus, father of Eryctonius.

David (Davyd): 3.2905m, 3.2912, 3.2916, 3.3920m. Saint David, Archbishop of Caerleon, and uncle to King Arthure.

Davyd: 2.1101. The biblical king, David.

Degré: 3.2568. Sir Degare, Knight of the Round Table.

Degrevaunt: 3.2568. Sir Degrevant, Knight of the Round Table.

Demecy: 3.1661, 3.2462, 3.2815. Demetia, ancient name for South Wales.

Dephebus: 2.124. Deiphobus, son of Priamus.

Derwent: 3.1465. The River Derwent.

Detonus: 2.2146, 2.2151m, 2.2151. An error for Clotenus (?), King of Britain.

Deveshyre: 3.2378. Devonshire.
Diane (Dyane): 2.31, 2.417m, 2.453, 2.460, 2.468, 2.554m, 2.767, 2.768. Diane, goddess of the hunt, the moon, and virginity.
Didone: 2.167. Dido, Queen of Carthage.
Dioclican (Dioclycian, Dioclicyen, Dioclycien): 3.379m, 3.379, 3.386, 3.577. The Emperor Diocletian.
Dioclician: 1.176m. Diocletian, King of Syria, father of Albyne.
Doldayn: 3.2782. Doldavius, King of Gotland.
Dolorous, Mounte (Mounte Dolorouse): 2.1031m, 2.1034. Bamburgh Castle.
Dolorouse Garde: 2.1036. The name of a tower at Mount Dolorous.
Donand: 3.2466. Donand, Knight of the Round Table. The name derives from Donaut Mappapo in *HRB* §156.
Doroberny: 3.1236. Canterbury. See also **Caerkent** and **Cauntyrbyry**.
Dorset: 3.2378. Dorset.
Dougles, water of (water of Douglas): 3.2276m, 3.2286. The River Douglas.
Dovere: 2.2394, 2.2585, 3.2592. Dover.
Dubricyus (Dubrike): 3.1922, 3.2256, 3.2793, 3.2805, 3.2809, 3.2905m, 3.2905. Dubricius, Archbishop of Caerleon.
Dunbretayne: 2.1066m, 2.1069, 3.2583, 3.2919m, 3.1920. Dumbarton, Scotland.
Dundonalde: 3.2584. Dundonald Castle, Ayrshire.
Dunwallo (Dunwallo Molmucyus): 2.1493m, 2.1499, 2.1505, 2.1507, 2.1513, 2.1520, 2.1521m. Dunvallo Molmutius, son of Cloten, King of Cornwall, and King of Britain.

Dusze Piers: 2.524, 2.539, 2.541, 3.2786, 3.3197, 3.3362. The Douze Peers, twelve peers of France.
Duvian (Duvyan): 3.8m, 3.25. Duvianus, a Christian sent to Britain by Pope Eleuthery.
Dymyoke: 3.2078. Dimilioc, the place where Utere besieges Gorloys.
Dynabucyus: 3.1651, 3.1652. Dinabutius, the child who plays with Merlyne at Carmarthen.
Dyonote: 3.856, 3.869. Dionotus, Duke of Cornwall, father of Saint Ursula.

Ebissa: 3.1447, 3.1837. Ebissa, cousin of Hengest.
Ebrauke (Ebrauk): 2.1031, 2.1113, 2.1991, 2.2451, 3.64m, 3.66, 3.169, 3.191, 3.494, 3.1626, 3.2025. York, founded by King Ebrauke.
Ebrauke (Ebrauk, Ebrauc): 2. 1010, 2.1017m, 2.1017, 2.1031m, 2.1039, 2.1073m, 2.1087m, 2.1108. Ebraucus, son of Membrice and King of Loegria.
Eccuba: 2.131. Hecuba, wife of King Priamus.
Ector: 2.123, 2.733. Hector, son of Priamus.
Edlem: 3.2469. A Knight of the Round Table. The name derives from Eddelein Mapcledauc in *HRB* §156.
Edynburgh: 2.1050. Edinburgh Castle.
Edynburgh: 3.2583. Edinburgh.
Egicio (Egicyo): 3.1024m, 3.1025. Agicius, a Roman to whom the Britons appeal for help.
Egistus: 1.176m. Aegyptus, King of Egypt and brother of Danaus.
Eldade, see **Eldane**.

Evalache: 3.3060. Evalach, the pagan king of Sarras, who converted to Christianity in the time of Joseph of Arimathea, and who possessed the shield inherited by Galaad.

Evandre: 2.174, 2.185, 2.193, 2.196, 2.199, 2.201. King Evander, adversary of King Latyne.

Ewayn: 2.1058. Ywain, Knight of the Round Table.

Ewayn: 2.1234m, 2.1240, 2.1246. Henwinus, duke of Cornwall, married to the second daughter of King Leyre, Ragawe.

Ewayne: 3.2459. Ywain, son of Urian of Moray, Knight of the Round Table.

Excestere: 2.2592. Exeter.

Exiona: 2.129. Possibly Hesione, daughter of Leamedon, King of Troy.

Faggan: 3.8m, 3.24. Faganus, a Christian sent to Britain by Pope Eleuthery.

Fenycia: 1.176m. Phoenicia.

Ferrex: 2.1415, 2.1416. Ferrex, son of King Gorbodian, brother of Porrex.

Flaunders: 2.2260, 3.2683, 3.3365, 3.3641. Flanders.

Fortune: 1.211m, 1.211, 1.214, 1.225, 2.127, 2.322, 2.330, 2.1577m, 2.1577, 3.2262, 3.2273, 3.3779, 3.3784, 3.3878, 3.3966. Fortuna, the goddess of fortune.

Fraunce: 2.46, 2.523, 2.1645, 2.1687, 2.1689m, 2.2320, 2.2435, 3.827m, 3.913, 3.1972, 3.2625m, 3.2627, 3.2632, 3.2637, 3.2666, 3.2670, 3.2709m, 3.2709, 3.2716, 3.2744m, 3.2786, 3.3109, 3.3197, 3.3233, 3.3235, 3.3253, 3.3362, 3.3456, 3.3461. France.

Freslond (Freselonde): 3.2486m, 3.2495. Friesland.

Frolle: 3.2625m, 3.2635, 3.2639, 3.2643, 3.2650, 3.3243. Frollo, King of France.

Frye (Fry, Frie): 3.1290m, 3.1300, 3.1373. Freyja, the Norse goddess, also associated with Venus.

Frygy (Fryge): 2.81, 2.87. Phrygia (Turkey).

Fulgen: 3.141m, 3.154, 3.169m, 3.174. Fulgen, King of Scotland at the time of Severe.

Fulgyn: 2.2116m, 2.2116, 2.2118. Fulgenius, King of Britain, eldest son of Cheryn.

Gabanytes: 3.1847. The biblical Gibeonites.

Gabas: 2.1705, 2.1720, 2.1729. Gabius, Roman Consul who fights against Belyn and Brenny.

Gad: 2.1103. Gad, prophet in Israel at the time of King Ebrauke.

Galaad: 3.2170, 3.2947m, 3.2954, 3.2989m, 3.3000, 3.3008, 3.3038m, 3.3038, 3.3052, 3.3101, 3.3115, 3.3136m, 3.2170, 3.3138, 3.3141, 3.3151, 3.3556m. Galahad, Knight of the Round Table, son of Lancelot, and achiever of the Holy Grail.

Galbroke: 3.369. Walbrook, named after the Roman, Gallus.

Galeryus: 3.499. The Emperor Galerius.

Gales: 2.796, 3.1665. Wales. See also **Cambre**.

Galfridum Monmentensem: 2.1m. Geoffrey of Monmouth, author of *HRB*.

Galilea: 1.176m. Galilee.

Galluc (Gwaluk): 3.2453, 3.3644. Galluc, Earl of Salisbury, Knight of the Round Table.

Gallus: 3.351m, 3.353, 3.362, 3.366, 3.370. Gallus, the Roman after whom Walbrook is named.

Gaule (Galle): 2.469, 2.522, 2.544, 2.1021. Gaul, the name given to an ancient region of Western Europe. It is often used here to refer to France.

Gawen (Gawayn, Gawayne): 3.2562, 3.2572, 3.3447, 3.3464, 3.3467, 3.3482, 3.3485, 3.3516, 3.3545, 3.3638, 3.3649, 3.3669, 3.3746, 3.3767. Gawain, Knight of the Round Table, son of King Loth, and King of Lothian.

Gaynore (Gwaynore): 3.2430m, 3.2431, 3.2691, 3.2702, 3.2836, 3.2842m, 3.3794, 3.3890. Guinevere, Queen of Britain, wife of King Arthure.

Geants Toure: 3.3269. The Giants' Tower.

Gedyngtoun: Prol.117, Prol.124, Prol.138. Geddington Manor, Northamptonshire.

Gellerlonde: 3.2681. Gelderland.

Gelre: 3.3364. Guelders.

Genareu: 3.1777. The name of Vortygere's castle; it may be associated with Ganarew, Herefordshire.

Gene: 2.1701. Genoa, Italy.

Genvyse: 2.2537, 2.2550m, 2.2597, 2.2663. Queen Genvissa, daughter of the Emperor Claudyus and wife of Arvyragere.

Genyus: 2.29. The god Genius.

George, Seynt: 3.29m, 3.575m, 3.694m, 3.3158, 3.3556m. Saint George.

Gerald of Wales, see **Giraldus Cambrensis**.

Germany (Germayne): 2.1073m, 2.1085, 2.1096, 3.881, 3.988, 3.1246, 3.1330, 3.1360, 3.1370, 3.1485, 3.2181, 3.2306, 3.2350, 3.2680. Germany. See also **Almayne**.

Germayn: 3.1423m, 3.1431, 3.1498. Saint Germanus, bishop of Auxerre.

Geryn (Garyn, Gereyne): 3.2668, 3.3446, 3.3516, 3.3540, 3.3847, 3.3850m, 3.3850, 3.3862, 3.3869. Gerin, Earl of Chartres and Orléans.

Getan: 3.197m, 3.197, 3.204, 3.205. Geta, son of Severe by a Roman woman.

Geyennes: 2.2081m, 2.2081. Gerennus, King of Britain, son of Elydoure.

Gildas (Gyldas): 2.735, 2.1128, 2.1185, 2.1546, 2.2574, 3.39, 3.84, 3.681, 3.3115m. Gildas, the historian. NB: medieval writers often cite Gildas when they really mean the pseudo-Nennius *HB*; Hardyng is no exception.

Giraldus Cambrensis (Giralde Cambrense, Girald): 2.554m, 2.751m, 3.2989m, 3.3038m, 3.3136m. Gerald of Wales.

Glamorgan (Glamargan): 2.1316, 2.1318, 2.1319, 2.1770. Glamorgan, Scotland.

Glaskowe, 3.2923. Glasgow.

Glassynbyry (Glasenbyry, Glastynbyry): 2.2632, 3.2594, 3.3834. Glastonbury; see also **Mewytryne**.

Glaucus: 2.32. Glaucus, a sea god.

Gloucestere (Gloucester): 2.2553, 2.2557m, 2.2652, 3.134, 3.1616, 3.1780, 3.3557. Gloucester.

Gloy: 2.2562. Gloius, son of the Emperor Claudyus.

Goffore: 2.497m, 2.518, 2.522. Goffar, King of Aquitaine.

Gogmagog: 2.579, 2.586m, 2.593, 2.602, 2.612. Gogmagog, the giant killed by Coryneus.

Goneryle (Gonerile): 2.1213, 2.1238, 2.1253. Goneril, eldest daughter of King Leyre.

Gorbodian (Gorbodyan): 2.1409m, 2.1409. Gorboduc, King of Britain, son of King Kymar.

Gorbodyan: 3.2471. A Knight of the Round Table. The name probably derives from Gorbonian Masgoit in *HRB* §156.

Gorbonyan: 3.2468. A Knight of the Round Table. The name derives from Gorbonian Masgoit in *HRB* §156.

Gorbonyan I: 2.1941m, 2.1941, 2.2046m, 2.2046. Gorbonian, King of Britain, eldest son of Morvyde.

Gorbonyan II: 2.2046m, 2.2046. Gorbonian, King of Britain, son of Gorbonyan I.

Gorloys (Gorleys): 3.2031, 3.2052m, 3.2059, 3.2087, 3.2114, 3.3827. Gorlois, Duke of Cornwall, husband of Igerne.

Gotlonde (Gothlonde): 3.2486m, 3.2782, 3.3195, 3.3981. Gotland.

Gracyan (Gracyane, Gracian): 3.813m, 3.917, 3.922, 3.926m, 3.926, 3.939, 3.947m, 3.947, 3.963. Gratian, King of Britain and Emperor.

Grece: 1.2, 1.176, 1.197m, 1.203, 2.46, 2.71, 2.130, 2.337, 2.341, 2.365. Greece.

Griffud: 3.2467. A Knight of the Round Table. The name is derived from Grifud Mapnogoid in *HRB* §156.

Guendolyne (Guendolene, Guendelyne): 2.896, 2.917, 2.919m. Queen Gwendolen, daughter of Coryneus, first wife of Locryne, mother of Maddan.

Guinevere, see **Gaynore**.

Gunberte: 3.765. Gunbert, King of Norway.

Gunthelyne (Guntelyne, Guthelyn): 3.1053, 3.1059m, 3.1066, 3.1095, 3.1115, 3.1121, 3.1132.

Guithelinus, Archbishop of London.

Gunvase: 3.2780. Gunhpar, King of the Orkneys.

Gurgoyne: 3.2455. Gurguint, Earl of Hereford, Knight of the Round Table. Possibly derived from Gurguynt in RMB 1.10889.

Gurgucius (Gurgucyus): 2.2151m, 2.2152. Gurgintius, King of Britain.

Gurgustius: 2.1353m, 2.1353. Gurgustius, King of Britain.

Gurguyn (Gurguyne Batrus): 2.1801m, 2.1801, 2.1836, 2.1843. Gurguit Barbtruc, son of Belyn and King of Britain.

Gurmund (Gurmonde): 3.1626m, 3.4005. Gormund, King of Africa.

Guthlake: 2.1612m, 2.1612, 2.1617. Ginchtalacus, King of Denmark.

Guydere (Guyder): 2.2487m, 2.2487, 2.2494, 2.2506, 2.2511, 2.2515. Guiderius, King of Britain, son of Kymbelyn.

Guyen: 2.46, 2.514, 3.2659, 3.2661, 3.3363. Guyenne, an ancient province of southwest France.

Guyllamare (Guyllomare): 3.1892, 3.1930, 3.1984, 3.1988. Gillomanius, the Irish king killed in battle against Utere.

Guyllomore (Guyllomare): 3.2395, 3.2779. Gilmaurius, the Irish king that attacks King Arthure in Scotland.

Guytarde: 3.2570, 3.2660, 3.2669, 3.3518, 3.3549. Guitard, Knight of the Round Table.

Guytelyn (Guytelyne): 2.1850m, 2.1850, 2.1859. Guithelin, King of Britain, husband of Queen Marcyan.

Gway: 3.1779. The River Wye.

Gwayns (Gwaynes, Gwayne, Gwaynus): 3.876m, 3.882, 3.928, 3.947m, 3.961m, 3.961, 3.975m,

Irelglas (Irelgas): 3.2571, 3.3518.
   Hirelglas, one of King Arthure's
   knights, nephew to Bedwere.
Irelglas (Irelglasse): 2.2358, 2.2361.
   Hirelglas, nephew of Cassibalan.
**Irelonde (Irelande, Ireland,
   Irelond)**: 2.1801m, 2.1836,
   2.2335, 2.2685, 3.1881, 3.1891,
   3.1893, 3.1912, 3.1929, 3.1980,
   3.2395m, 3.2396, 3.2400,
   3.2486m, 3.2486, 3.2779, 3.3113,
   3.3193, 3.3981, 3.4006. Ireland.
Irisshe se: 2.1920. The Irish Sea.
Isaye: 2.1325. Isaiah, the prophet.
Iselonde: 3.2486m, 3.2493, 3.3981,
   3.3196. Iceland.
Isrelle (Israell, Israelle): 2.229,
   2.942, 2.1102. Israel.
Isydorus: 3.719. Isidore of Seville.
**Itaylle (Italy, Itayly, Itale, Itayl,
   Itaille)**: 2.1m, 2.45, 2.75,
   2.153m, 2.163, 2.170, 2.178,
   2.337m, 2.736, 2.948, 2.1073m,
   2.1073, 2.1105, 2.1689m, 2.1698,
   2.1735, 2.1755, 2.1758, 3.740,
   3.914, 3.3437m, 3.3439, 3.3619m,
   3.3718. Italy.
Ivalle: 2.2067m, 2.2067. Idvallo,
   King of Britain, son of Ingen.

Janus: 2.1281, 2.1302. Janus, the
   Roman god of beginnings and
   endings.
Japhet: 2.68. Japheth, son of Noe.
Jareth: 2.63. Jared, father of Enoch.
Jason: 2.98, 2.106. Jason, the Greek
   hero and leader of the Argonauts.
Javan: 2.68. Javan, son of Japhet.
Jerusaleme: 2.1136, 3.666.
   Jerusalem.
Jhesu, see **Cryste**.
Joel (Joelle): 2.1141, 2.1166, 2.1181.
   Joel, prophet at the time of King
   Leyle.
Jonatalle (Jonathas): 3.2454, 3.3550.
   Jonathel, Earl of Dorchester,
   Knight of the Round Table.

Jordan: 3.2091. Jordan, a servant of
   Gorloys whose resemblance Ulfyn
   adopts through Merlyne's magic to
   help Utere infiltrate Tintagel
   Castle.
Jordan, Flum: 3.607. The River
   Jordan.
**Josep Aramathy (Joseph of
   Arymathy, Joseph of Arymathi)**:
   2.1612, 2.2613m, 2.2620, 3.8m,
   3.91, 3.96, 3.2150m, 3.2156,
   3.2161, 3.3038m, 3.3062, 3.3084,
   3.3115, 3.3155, 3.3157, 3.3180.
   Joseph of Arimathea.
Jubiter (Jubyter): 2.26, 2.81, 2.914.
   Jupiter, the principal Roman god,
   son of Saturnus.
Judea (Judé, Jude): 1.176m, 2.730,
   2.1015, 2.1101, 2.1134. Judea.
Judon: 2.1423. Queen Judon, wife of
   Gorbodian and mother of Ferrex
   and Porrex.
Jugence (Jugens): 3.2448, 3.3550.
   Jugein, Earl of Leicester, Knight
   of the Round Table.
Julius Cesar, see **Cesar, Julyus**.
Julyus (July): 3.387, 3.2835, 3.2893,
   3.2896, 3.3801. Saint Julius.
Julyus Cesaryne: 1.1m. Julian
   Cesarini, scholar and humanist.
Justynus (Justyne): 1.1m, 1.176m.
   Marcus Junianus Justinus, author
   of an *Epitome* of Pompieus
   Trogus's *Philippic History*.

Katellus: 2.2088m, 2.2088. Catellus,
   King of Britain, son of Geyennes.
Kay: 3.2569, 3.2739, 3.2852, 3.3399,
   3.3404, 3.3410, 3.3419, 3.3547,
   3.3624, 3.3712. Sir Kay, Knight of
   the Round Table and Duke of
   Anjou.
Kent (Kente): 2.2226, 2.2312,
   3.1234m, 3.1237, 3.1401, 3.1442.
   Kent.
Kylormare, Mount (Lyllormare):
   3.1897, 3.1910. Mount Killaraus,

the legendary location of
Stonehenge before Merlyne
transports it to Britain; possibly
associated with Kildare.

Kymar I: 2.1395m, 2.1395. Kimar,
King of Britain.

Kymar II: 2.1878m, 2.1878. Kimar,
King of Britain, son of Sisilyus II.

Kymbelyn (Kymbelyne): 2.2459m,
2.2459, 2.2473, 2.2478.
Cymbeline, son of Tenvancyus,
also known as Cunobelinus.

Kymbelyne: 3.2469. Kimbelin,
Knight of the Round Table.

Kynkare: 3.2470. Kingar, Knight of
the Round Table. The name
derives from Kingar MapBangan
in *HRB* §156.

Kynmare: 3.2451. Kynmarc, Earl of
Canterbury, Knight of the Round
Table.

Kynmare: 3.2471. Kinmar, Knight of
the Round Table.

Lacedemonya: 2.1016. Lacedaemon,
ancient name for Sparta.

Lameke: 2.65. Lamech, son of
Matussaleel and father of Noe.

Langres: 3.3525. Langres.

Latyne (Latyn): 2.153m, 2.554m,
2.949, 2.1076. Latium in the
Kingdom of Alba Longa.

Latyne (Latyns): 2.193, 2.201, 2.203,
2.209. King Latinus, father of
Lavynyane, wife of Eneas.

**Launcelot (Launcelot de Lake,
Launselot)**: 2.1042, 3.2564,
3.2956, 3.3850m, 3.3858. Sir
Lancelot, Knight of the Round
Table.

Lavynyane (Lavyne): 2.153m, 2.203,
2.208, 2.220, 2.250. Lavinia,
second wife of Eneas.

Lavynyon: 2.219. Lavinium, an
ancient city founded by Eneas.

Leamedon (Leamedoun): 2.95,
2.113, 2.121. Laomedon, King of
Troy, father of Priamus.

Leo (Leoun): 3.3346m, 3.3524,
3.3692, 3.3720, 3.3722. The
Emperor Leo.

Leogice (Leogyce): 2.417m, 2.446,
2.769. From Geoffrey of
Monmouth's Leogetia, an island
where Brute visits the temple of
Diana. Possibly the Greek Island
of Lefkada.

Leonelle: 3.2568. Sir Lionel, Knight
of the Round Table.

Leycestre (Leyrecestre, Leycester):
2.1202, 2.1203, 2.1301. Leicester.

Leyle (Leyl): 2.1129m, 2.1129,
2.1139, 2.1165. Leil, King of
Loegria.

Leyre: 2.1199m, 2.1199, 2.1206m,
2.1206, 2.1234m. Lear, King of
Britain.

Lincolneshire: 3.1402m.
Lincolnshire.

**Litel Bretayne (Lesse Bretayne,
Lytylle Bretayne, Lesse Bretayn,
Litille Bretayne, Bretayne the
Lesse, Litil Bretayne, Lasse
Bretayne, Bretayne Lesse, Litle
Bretayne, Bretayne Lasse, Lytille
Bretayne)**: 3.827m, 3.835, 3.847,
3.848, 3.855m, 3.878, 3.967,
3.1052m, 3.1057, 3.1060,
3.1094m, 3.1108m, 3.1216,
3.2314, 3.2381m, 3.2667, 3.3198,
3.3373, 3.3431. Brittany.

Locryne (Locrine): 2.786m, 2.787,
2.791, 2.804, 2.807m, 2.807, 2.
844, 2.849m, 2.849, 2.861, 2.863,
2.919m, 2.920, 2.924, 2.933.
Locrin, eldest son of Brute.

Loeline: 3.561, 3.568. Ioelinus,
brother of King Coyle and father
of Maximyan.

Logres (Loegres): 2.786m, 2.788,
2.789, 2.791, 2.954, 2.1502,
2.1561, 2.1601, 2.1609, 2.1618,

2.2334, 3.65, 3.345, 3.998,
3.1012. Loegria or Loegres, the
name given to the land ruled by
Locryne, eldest son of Brute,
approximating to the area covered
by England (minus Cornwall).
London (Londoun): 2.667m, 2.724,
2.751m, 2.1773m, 2.1786,
2.2193m, 3.43, 3.99m, 3.351,
3.1052m, 3.2050, 3.2056, 3.2180,
3.2183, 3.2312, 3.2590, 3.2800.
See also **New Troy** and **Carlud**.
Loreyne: 3.2678. Lorraine.
Loth of Louthianne: 3.2186, 3.2424,
3.2461, 3.2507, 3.2562, 3.2784,
3.3543. Loth, King of Lothian
and of Norway.
Louthianne (Louthian, Louthien):
3.2186, 3.2189, 3.2425, 3.2461,
3.2563, 3.2575, 3.3449, 3.3747.
An ancient region in Scotland
covering the current Lothian and
part of the border areas.
Lucius (Lucyus): 3.1m, 3.1, 3.8m,
3.26, 3.29m, 3.43m, 3.72, 3.94,
3.98, 3.99m, 3.103, 3.106,
3.120m, 3.120. Lucius, King of
Britain.
Lucyus (Lucius): 3.3185m, 3.3226,
3.3227, 3.3274, 3.3278, 3.3280,
3.3346m, 3.3458, 3.3521, 3.3611,
3.3619m, 3.3667, 3.3689, 3.3691.
The Emperor Lucius, whom King
Arthure defeats.
Lud: 2.2193m, 2.2193, 2.2210,
2.2385. Lud, King of Britain, son
of Ely.
Ludgate: 2.2200m, 2.2205, 2.2212.
Ludgate, London.
Lumbardy: 2.1696, 3.264.
Lombardy, Italy.
Lupe (Lupus): 3.1423m, 3.1432,
3.1498. Saint Lupus, Bishop of
Troyes.
Lybews Dysconus: 3.2567. Libeaus
Desconus, Knight of the Round
Table.

Lyncolne (Lindcolyne): 3.1627,
3.2324, 3.2325. Lincoln.
Lyndsay, 3.1234m. Lindsey,
Lincolnshire.

Maddan: 2.898, 2.917, 2.936, 2.954m,
2.954. Maddan, King of Loegria,
son of Guendolyne and Locryne.
Maglane (Maglayne): 2.1234m,
2.1237, 2.1239, 2.1246.
Maglaurus, duke of Albany,
married to King Leyre's eldest
daughter, Goneryle.
Maheridoure: 3.2467. A Knight of
the Round Table. The name
derives from Peredur Maheridur
in *HRB* §156.
Makeclauke: 3.2471. A Knight of the
Round Table. The name probably
derives from Regin Mapclaud in
HRB §156.
Malaleel: 2.62. Mahalalel, son of
Caynaan.
Malgo: 3.3969m, 3.3976. King Malgo.
Malvase, 3.2781. Malvasius, King of
Iceland.
Man: 3.2786. The Isle of Man.
Manes: 2.32. Manes, the spirits of the
dead in Roman mythology.
Manlyn: 2.963, 2.975m, 2.975.
Malin, son of King Maddan.
Mapbangan: 3.2470. A Knight of the
Round Table. The name derives
from Kingar Mapbangan in *HRB*
§156.
Mapcathel: 3.2470. A Knight of the
Round Table. The name derives
from Cathleus Mapcatel in *HRB*
§156.
Mapclaude: 3.2467. A Knight of the
Round Table. The name derives
from Regin Mapclaud in *HRB*
§156.
Mapcoyl: 3.2466. A Knight of the
Round Table. The name derives
from Cheneus Mapcoil in *HRB*
§156.

Marcyan (Marcian, Marcyane):
2.1850m, 2.1853, 2.1866.
Marcian, Queen of Britain, wife of
Guytelyn.

Margan: 2.1290m, 2.1290, 2.1304,
2.1309, 2.1317, 2.1318m.
Marganus, duke of Albany, son of
Goneryle.

Margan: 2.2053m, 2.2053.
Marganus, King of Britain, son of
Argalle.

Marius (Maryus): 2.2662m, 2.2662,
2.2690, 3.292. Marius, King of
Britain, son of Arvyragere.

Mars: 2.26, 3.3785. Mars, the god of
war.

Martyne: 1.1m. Pope Martin V.

Martyne (Martyn, Martini): 1.176m,
2.1746, 2.2422, 3.8m, 3.31,
3.183m, 3.183, 3.645m, 3.659m,
3.660, 3.673m, 3.687m, 3.701,
3.705m, 3.719. Martin of
Troppau (aka Martinus Polonus,
or Martini Oppaviensis), author
of *Chronicon Pontificum et
Imperatorum*.

Mary: 2.572, 2.2480, 2.2655m,
2.2656, 3.703, 3.3849. Mary,
mother of Christ.

Maryn: 3.562. Marius, brother of
King Coyle.

Masgoyd: 3.2469. A Knight of the
Round Table. The name derives
from Gorbonian Masgoit in *HRB*
§156.

Matussaleel: 2.64. Methuselah, son
of Enoch.

Maugancyus: 3.1686. Maugantius.

Mauron: 3.2445. Mauron, Earl of
Worcester, Knight of the Round
Table.

Maxcence (Maxence): 3.501, 3.527,
3.532, 3.578, 3.2894. Maxentius,
a Roman dictator at the time of
Constantyne I.

**Maximyan (Maximyane,
Maxymyan)**: 3.571, 3.578, 3.801,
3.808, 3.813m, 3.814, 3.827m,
3.859, 3.912, 3.926, 3.938, 3.940,
3.965, 3.1075, 3.3311m, 3.3318,
3.2629. Maximianus, a Roman
senator and Emperor, son of
Loeline (brother of King Coyle),
King of Britain.

**Maximyan (Maxymyan, Maxymyan
Herculyus)**: 3.372m, 3.379m,
3.380, 3.421m, 3.440, 3.2894.
Maximianus Herculius, a Roman
sent by Dioclican to persecute the
British Christians.

Mayden Castelle: 2.1046, 2.1064.
Maiden Castle, an alternative
name for Edinburgh Castle.

Megary: 2.28. Megaera, one of the
Erinyes, or Furies, in Greek
mythology.

Melga: 3.876m, 3.883, 3.928,
3.947m, 3.961m, 3.961, 3.975m,
3.986, 3.1005, 3.1010, 3.1106.
Melga, King of the Picts.

Membrice (Membryce): 2.963,
2.975m, 2.978, 2.982, 2.989m,
2.989, 2.1012. Mempricius, son of
Maddan and King of Loegria.

Menevue (Meneu): 3.1933, 3.1983,
3.3926. Menevia, or Saint David's,
Wales.

Mercury (Mercure): 2.26, 3.1258,
3.1283m, 3.1283, 3.1288, 3.1371.
The Roman god Mercury also
associated with the Norse god,
Woden. See **Woden**.

Merlyne (Merlyn, Merlinus): 2.824,
3.1650, 3.1667, 3.1668, 3.1710m,
3.1710, 3.1717, 3.1723, 3.1724,
3.1745, 3.1871m, 3.1871, 3.1878,
3.1891, 3.1900, 3.1904, 3.1909,
3.1962m, 3.1962, 3.2001, 3.2015,
3.2081, 3.2084, 3.2137, 3.2151,
3.2973, 3.3841, 3.3843. Merlin.

Meryan: 2.2151m, 2.2153. Merianus,
King of Britain.

Mewyne: 2.822. Possibly a corruption of the name Melkin, a prophet associated with Glastonbury.

Mewytryne: 2.821, 2.2625, 3.89. Glastonbury (a probable corruption of Inis Witrin).

Mordrede (Modrede, Modred): 3.2571, 3.3724m, 3.3725, 3.3736, 3.3738m, 3.3738, 3.3752m, 3.3752, 3.3754, 3.3756, 3.3759m, 3.3768, 3.3778, 3.3788, 3.3795, 3.3875, 3.3883, 3.3889, 3.3892, 3.3914. Mordred, nephew to King Arthure.

Morvyde: 2.1892m, 2.1892, 2.1910. Morvide, King of Britain, son of Danyus.

Morvyde: 3.2444, 3.3557, 3.3663. Morvid, Earl of Gloucester, Knight of the Round Table.

Murreve (Murrefe): 2.1906, 3.2428. Moray, Scotland.

Mynerve: 2.31, 2.1014, 2.1303. Minerva, goddess of creativity and wisdom.

Nacyan (Nacyen, Nacien): 3.2974, 3.3067, 3.3156, 3.3167. Nascien, or Seraphe, an ancestor of Galaad.

Nathan: 2.1103. Nathan, prophet in Israel at the time of King Ebrauke.

Naverne: 3.2672, 3.3361. Navarre.

Nemynus: 2.2302, 2.2307. Nennius, brother of Lud, son of Ely.

New Troy (Novel Troy, Trynovant, Troynovant, Troynovaunte, Trynovaunte, Trynovaunt): 2.475, 2.667, 2.705, 2.707, 2.709, 2.716, 2.717, 2.719, 2.724, 2.753, 2.1543, 2.1773, 2.1953, 2.2015, 2.2193m, 2.2200m, 2.2201, 2.2226, 2.2312, 3.64m, 3.64, 3.108, 3.346, 3.876, 3.1051, 3.1054, 3.1522, 3.1620, 3.3912, 3.3921. New Troy, the ancient name for London. See also **Carlud**.

Nicholas, Seynt: 3.659m, 3.663. Saint Nicholas.

Noe: 2.67. Noah, son of Lameke.

Normandy: 2.2318, 3.2738, 3.3357, 3.3434. Normandy.

Northumbreland (Northumbrelonde): 2.1565, 2.1907. Northumberland.

Norway (Northway): 2.1591m, 2.1598, 2.1605, 3.764, 3.2495, 3.2507, 3.2512, 3.3194, 3.3980. Norway.

Norwyche: 2.2704. Norwich.

Nychomede: 3.716. Nicomedia, the place of Constantyne I's death.

Octa: 3.1446, 3.1836m, 3.1836, 3.1841, 3.2017m, 3.2017, 3.2030, 3.2040, 3.2051, 3.2178, 3.2204. Octa, son of Hengest.

Octave (Octavyus): 3.729m, 3.729, 3.736, 3.751, 3.764, 3.785m, 3.785, 3.813. Octavius, seizes Britain during the reign of Constantyne I.

Octovain, see **Cesare Auguste**.

Odnea: 2.2319. The place where Julius Caesar builds his tower in Normandy.

Oenus: 2.2151m, 2.2156. Oenus, King of Britain.

Omer: 1.202, 2.231, 2.951. Homer, the poet.

Orboryke (Orberike): 3.3075, 3.3102. Orberica, the land ruled by Nacyan and converted by Joseph of Arimathea in the Vulgate *Estoire del Saint Graal*.

Orcades, see **Orkenay, Iles of**.

Orkenay, Iles of (Orcades, Orcadese, Orchadese, Orkadese): 2.1827, 3.2486m, 3.2493, 3.2780, 3.3193, 3.3981. The Orkney Islands.

Orlience: 3.2668. Orléans.

Orosius: 2.1738m. Orosius.

Osee: 2.1327. Hosea, the prophet.

Ostia: 2.172. Ostia, a harbor city of ancient Rome.

Ostryche: 3.2676. Austria.

Oute Iles: 3.2381m. The name given to the islands in the Scottish loch to which Arthure drives the Scots and Picts in battle.

Ovyde: 2.545. The poet Ovid.

Oysa: 3.2017m, 3.2018, 3.2041, 3.2051, 3.2178, 3.2204. Eosa, son of Octa.

Palestina: 1.176m. Palestine.

Pallas: 2.28. The goddess Pallas Athena.

Pandrase (Pandrasius): 2.358, 2.379. Pandrasus, King of Greece.

Parise (Paryse, Parisse): 3.2640, 3.2653, 3.2689, 3.2731, 3.3513. Paris, France.

Partholoym: 2.1834. Partholoim, leader of the Spanish exiles whom King Gurguyn encounters near the Orkney Islands.

Paryse: 2.124. Paris, son of Priamus.

Passhent (Pascence): 3.1418, 3.1925, 3.1939, 3.1984, 3.1988. Paschent, third son of Vortygere.

Patrike: 2.1070. Saint Patrick.

Paules (Poulys, Poules): 2.766. 2.1193, 3.113. Saint Paul's Cathedral.

Paytow: 3.2659. Poitou.

Peghtes Walle (Peght Wall): 3.1013, 3.2919. Hadrian's Wall.

Pelagiens errysy, see **Errisyes Pelagien**.

Pelles: 3.2565, 3.2957. Pelles, King of North Wales (Venodotia), Knight of the Round Table.

Pendragoun: 3.2222. Pendragon Castle, Cumbria.

Penyssel (Penysselle): 2.2165m, 2.2170. Penessil, King of Britain.

Peredoure: 3.2466. Peredur, Knight of the Round Table. The name derives from Peredur Maheridur in *HRB* §156.

Perse: 2.1749. Persia.

Persyvalle (Percyvalle): 3.2566, 3.3108, 3.3136m, 3.3137, 3.3517. Sir Percival, Knight of the Round Table.

Perydoure (Peridoure): 2.2011m, 2.2011, 2.2025m, 2.2025, 2.2074m, 2.2074. Peredurus, son of Morvyde.

Perte: 3.2584. Perth.

Petir (Petre, Petyre): 2.2571m, 2.2578, 3.613. Saint Peter.

Petro: 3.3483, 3.3492, 3.3512. Petreius Cocta, a Roman senator and captain, who supports Lucius in his battle against Arthure.

Phebus: 2.27. The god Phoebus.

Philistiens: 2.731. The Philistines.

Pli(?): 2.1m. An error for Pompeius Trogus?

Pompey: 2.2436. Pompey the Great.

Porcenna (Persenna, Porsenna): 2.1705, 2.1720, 2.1730. Porsenna, Roman consul who fights against Belyn and Brenny.

Porchestere: 2.2502, 3.744. Porchester. See also **Caerperis**.

Porrex I: 2.1415, 2.1426. Porrex, son of King Gorbodian, brother of Ferrex.

Porrex II: 2.2102m, 2.2102. Porrex II, King of Britain, son of Coyle.

Porte Rupyne: 3.3743. Richborough (Rutupiae).

Portyngale: 3.2673, 3.3360. Portugal.

Poule: 3.613. Saint Paul.

Poules Querfe: 3.105. Saint Paul's Wharf, London.

Priamus (Priam): 2.121, 2.123, 2.131, 2.154, 2.345. Priam, King of Troy.

Protheus: 2.32. Proteus, a sea god.

Puyle: 2.1702. Apulia (Puglia), Italy.

Pynhere (Pynher): 2.1437m, 2.1441, 2.1508. Pinner, King of Loegria during the civil war that follows the death of Porrex.

Pyrame: 3.2416. Piramus, Archbishop of York.

Pyrre: 2.2165m, 2.2170. Pir, King of Britain.

Quyntylian: 3.3463. Quintillian, nephew of Lucius.

Radulphi Cestrensis: 2.801m. Ranulf of Chester, better known as Ranulf Higden, Benedictine monk of St. Werburgh in Chester and author of the *Polychronicon*.

Ragawe: 2.1220, 2.1240, 2.1255. Regan, second daughter of King Leyre.

Redryke (Redrike): 2.2165m, 2.2168. Redechius, King of Britain.

Redyon: 2.2165m, 2.2167. Redon, King of Britain.

Remus: 2.1330. Remus, one of the founders of Rome, brother of Romulus.

Rerecrosse: 2.2680. Rey Cross, Stainmore.

Roberti: 2.1m. Robert, Duke of Gloucester, son of Henry I.

Roderyke (Rodryke): 2.2662m, 2.2669. Roderick (Sodric in *HRB* §70), a Pict who fights against Marius.

Rodes: 3.3175. Rhodes.

Romany: 2.1701. Romagna.

Romayne: 3.1433. Presumably Saint Romanus; Hardyng takes the reference from RMB 1.7641-42.

Rome (Romanye, Romany): 1.1m, 2.75, 2.175, 2.226, 2.227, 2.271, 2.554m, 2.1329, 2.1334, 2.1338, 2.1703, 2.1712, 2.1743, 2.1745, 2.2239, 2.2389m, 2.2414, 2.2429, 2.2447, 2.2460, 2.2465, 2.2569, 2.2573, 2.2579, 2.2599, 2.2666, 2.2698, 3.74, 3.78, 3.141m, 3.143, 3.147, 3.187, 3.309, 3.447, 3.461, 3.463m, 3.466, 3.469, 3.472,

3.477m, 3.526m, 3.526, 3.544, 3.555, 3.569, 3.675, 3.678, 3.737, 3.796, 3.800, 3.813m, 3.827m, 3.914, 3.975m, 3.975, 3.1003, 3.1024m, 3.1024, 3.1077, 3.1973, 3.2634, 3.2726, 3.3185m, 3.3227, 3.3262, 3.3277, 3.3283, 3.3300, 3.3303, 3.3322, 3.3325, 3.3336, 3.3352, 3.3355, 3.3367m, 3.3455, 3.3690, 3.3720. Rome.

Romulus: 2.1330, 2.2243. Romulus, one of the founders of Rome, brother of Remus.

Rounde Table (Table Rounde): 3.2150m, 3.2152, 3.2173, 3.2430m, 3.2437, 3.2444m, 3.2473, 3.2514m, 3.2518, 3.2541m, 3.2555m, 3.2556, 3.2577, 3.2588, 3.2597m, 3.2687, 3.2709m, 3.2713, 3.2767, 3.2947m, 3.2948, 3.2965, 3.3004, 3.3018, 3.3078, 3.3171m, 3.3178, 3.3519, 3.3612, 3.3685, 3.3813, 3.3859, 3.3871m, 3.3908. The Round Table.

Rowen (Rowene): 3.1367, 3.1389, 3.1509, 3.1525, 3.1537, 3.1551. Rowena or Renwein, daughter of Hengest and wife of Vortygere.

Ruddan: 2.1437m, 2.1442, 2.1510. Rudaucus, King of Wales during the civil war that follows the death of Porrex.

Rudhudibrace: 2.1150m, 2.1155. Rud Hud Hudibras, King of Loegria.

Rutupewe: 2.2585. Dover.

Rymo: 2.2074m, 2.2074. Runo, King of Britain, son of Perydoure.

Ryval: 2.1339m, 2.1339. Rivallo, King of Britain.

Saba: 2.1137. The Queen of Sheba.

Sabren: 2.910, 2.927, 2.931. Sabrina (or Habren), daughter of Locryne and Estrilde, drowns in the River Severn, which is named after her.

Seysy: 3.3530. Probably Saussy or Val-Suzon.

Shafftesbyry: 2.1159. Shaftsbury.

Silvy: 2.1075. Silvius, King of Latium.

Sipion: 2.2350. Scipio Africanus.

Sisile: 2.160. Sicily.

Sisilius I: 2.1367m, 2.1367. Sisilius I, King of Britain.

Sisilius III (Sisilyus): 2.2151m, 2.2157. Sisilius III, King of Britain.

Sisilyus II (Sysilius, Sisilius): 2.1864m, 2.1864, 2.1869. Sisilius II, King of Britain, son of Guytelyn and Marcyan.

Socrates: 2.1749. Socrates.

Somersette: 3.2378. Somerset.

Sore: 2.1200, 2.1300. River Soar.

Southamptoun: 2.2520. Southampton.

Spayne: 2.46, 2.487, 2.497, 2.1801m, 2.1835, 3.465, 3.3360. Spain.

Staynemore: 2.2680, 3.752. Stainmore.

Stonehengles: 3.1871m, 3.1915, 3.1956. Stonehenge. See also **Carolle**.

Stryvelyn: 3.2583. Stirling.

Sulwath: 2.1066m. Sulwath, Scotland.

Sychelme: 3.2511. Sichelm, King of Norway.

Sylvestre (Silvestre): 3.615, 3.645m, 3.645, 3.659m, 3.687m. Pope Silvester I.

Sylvyus Julus: 2.248, 2.249, 2.281, 2.730m. Silvius Julius, son of Ascanyus, father of Brute.

Sylvyus Postumus (Silvyus Postumus, Sylvy): 2.241, 2.267, 2.730m, 2.735, 2.947, 2.1082, 2.1105. Silvius Posthumous, son of Eneas, brother of Ascanyus.

Symonde: 3.2157. Simon the Leper.

Syry: 1.176m. Syria

Sythy: 2.2670. Scythia.

Sywarde: 2.1417. Suhard, King of France at the time of Ferrex and Porrex.

Tanguste: 2.1893. Tanguesteaia, mistress of Danyus, mother of Morvyde.

Templers: 3.3171m, 3.3172. The Knights Templar.

Tenette: 3.1474. The Isle of Thanet.

Tenvancyus (Tenvaunce, Tenvancius): 2.2227, 2.2229, 2.2442, 2.2452m, 2.2452. Tenvantius, Duke of Cornwall, King of Britain, youngest son of King Lud.

Thamyse (Themse, Themmys): 2.702, 2.1775, 2.2276, 3.99m, 3.104, 3.367, 3.876. The River Thames.

Thelofyne: 2.2481. A British prophet at the time of Christ, perhaps a corruption of Taliesin?

Thesiphony: 2.29. Tisiphone, one of the Erinyes, or Furies, in Greek mythology.

Thetys: 3.2870. Thetis, a sea nymph in Greek mythology.

Thwongcastre: 3.1318m, 3.1403. Caistor, Lincolnshire. The place where Hengest builds his castle. See also **Castre**.

Tottenes (Totnesse, Totteneys, Totneys, Tottenesse, Toteneys): 2.554m, 2.562, 2.2588, 3.1098, 3.1772, 3.2354. Totnes, Devon.

Toure of Trynovaunt: 2.2015, 2.2034. The Tower of London.

Toures: 2.533, 2.546. Tours, France.

Traherne (Thraerne): 3.561, 3.729m, 3.734, 3.737, 3.743, 3.749, 3.750m, 3.753, 3.770. Trahern, brother of King Coyle, King of Britain.

Trogus Pompeyus (Trogus Pompeius), 1.1m, 1.176m, 2.554m. Pompeius Trogus, author of the *Philippic History*.

Wales: 2.673, 2.794, 2.807, 2.1320, 3.99m, 3.1158, 3.1619m, 3.1662, 3.2464, 3.2565, 3.2777, 3.2815, 3.2817, 3.2842m, 3.2842, 3.2843, 3.2947m, 3.2989m, 3.3038m, 3.3136m, 3.3193. Wales.

Walterum Oxoniensem (Waltier): 2.1m, 2.1189, 3.2947m. Walter of Oxford.

Waltier of Oxenford. See **Walterum Oxoniensem.**

Westmerlond (Westmerlonde): 2.2679, 2.2681, 3.2226. Westmorland.

Whytsonde (Whitesonde): 3.3738m, 3.3743. Wissant, France, where Arthur meets Mordred in battle on his way back to Britain.

Woden: 3.1290m, 3.1290, 3.1372. The Norse god Woden, also associated with Mercury.

Wynchestre (Wynchestere, Wynchester): 2.1158, 2.2526, 3.748, 3.1130, 3.1143m, 3.1144, 3.1629, 3.1994, 3.1997, 3.2591, 3.3752m, 3.3752, 3.3916, 3.3990. Winchester.

Ymeneus: 2.30. Hymen, the goddess of marriage.

Yorke: 2.1032, 3.43m, 3.169m, 3.1626, 3.1839, 3.1920, 3.2025, 3.2289, 3.2409m, 3.2409, 3.2585, 3.2802, 3.3796. The City of York. See also **Ebrauke**.

# BIBLIOGRAPHY

MANUSCRIPTS AND DOCUMENTS

Aberystwyth, National Library of Wales, MS 7006D.
Arundel Castle, John Lydgate's *Lives of Saints Edmund and Fremund*.
Cambridge, Cambridge Trinity College MS R.5.33 (724).
Cambridge, Cambridge University, King's College Archive Centre KCE/11, KCE/20, KCE/106, KCE/110, KCE/136, WIL/34, WIL/47, WIL/48.
Cambridge, Corpus Christi College MS 133.
Cleveland, OH, Cleveland Public Library MS John G. White Collection W Q091.92–C468.
Dublin, Trinity College MS 489.
Edinburgh, National Library of Scotland MS 16500.
Hatfield, Hatfield House, Marquis of Salisbury, Cecil Papers 270.
Leeds, Brotherton Library MS 29.
London, College of Arms MS L6.
London, The British Library MSS Additional 62929; Cotton Augustus A. iv; Cotton Faustina A. ix; Cotton Vespasian A. xii; Egerton 615; Harley 2278; Harley 2885; Harley 3776; Harley 4565; Lansdowne 204; Royal 18 B.xxxi.
London, The National Archives of the UK, Public Record Office: C 1/43/53; C 81/1432/53; C 81/1432/54; C 241/225/6; E 39/2/5; E 39/2/7; E 39/2/9; E 39/2/10; E 39/2/20; E 39/4/3a; E 39/87; E 39/96/3; E 39/96/4; E 39/96/5; E 39/97/4; E 101/69/8/540; E 101/330/9; E 159/217; E 159/221; E 159/234; E 199/23/37; E 199/24/3; E 199/24/4; E 199/32/19; 372/286 to E 372/315; SC 8/304/15182; SC 8/305/15208.
London, Wellcome Library MS 8004.
New York, Columbia University MSS Plimpton 261; Plimpton 263.
New York, Public Library MS Spencer 19.
Norfolk, Holkham Hall MS 669.
Notre Dame, IN, University of Notre Dame MS 67.
Nottingham, Nottingham University Library MS 250.
Oxford, Bodleian Library MSS Arch. Selden B. 10; Ashmole 789; Ashmole 791; Duke Humphrey b. 1; Laud Misc. 740.
Oxford, Corpus Christi College MS 78.
San Marino, CA, Huntingdon Library MS HM55.

BIBLIOGRAPHY

The Abridged English Metrical Brut. Ed. Una O'Farrell-Tate. Heidelberg: C. Winter, 2002.
Abrams, Lesley and James P. Carley, eds. *The Archaeology and History of Glastonbury Abbey: Essays in Honour of the 90th Birthday of C. A. Ralegh Radford*. Woodbridge: Boydell Press, 1991.
Adam of Domerham. *Historia de rebus Glastoniensibus descripsit T. Hearnius, qui et G. Malmesburiensis Librum de antiquitate ecclesiae Glastoniensis et E. Archeri excerpta e registris Wellensibus praemisit*. Ed. T. Hearne. 2 vols. Oxford, 1727.

Allan, Alison. "Yorkist Propaganda: Pedigree, Prophecy and the 'British History' the Reign of Edward
        IV." In *Patronage, Pedigree and Power in Later Medieval England*. Ed. Charles Ross. Gloucester: Alan
        Sutton, 1979. Pp. 171–92.

———. "Political Propaganda Employed by the House of York in England in the Mid-Fifteenth
        Century, 1450–71." Unpublished Ph.D. thesis: University of Wales at Swansea, 1981.

Alliterative Morte Arthure. In Benson. Pp. 129–284.

Alsop, J. D. "Bowyer, William (*d.* 1569/70)." In *Oxford Dictionary of National Biography*, ed. H. C. G.
        Matthew and Brian Harrison. Jan 2008. http://www.oxforddnb.com/view/article/69724.

Anglo-Norman Prose Brut. See *The Oldest Anglo-Norman Prose Brut Chronicle*.

The Anonimalle Chronicle, 1307 to 1334: From Brotherton Collection MS 29. Ed. Wendy R. Childs and
        John Taylor. Leeds: Yorkshire Archaelogical Society, 1991.

The Anonimalle Chronicle, 1333 to 1381: A MS Written at St. Mary's Abbey, York. Ed. V. H. Galbraith.
        Manchester: Manchester University Press, 1927. Rpt. New York: Barnes and Noble, 1970.

An Anonymous Short English Metrical Chronicle. Ed. Ewald Zettl. EETS o.s. 196. London: Oxford
        University Press, 1935, Rpt. 1971.

Arthur: A Short Sketch of his Life and History in English Verse. Ed. Frederick James Furnivall. EETS o.s.
        2. London: Oxford University Press, 1869.

"*Arthur*. A New Critical Edition of the Fifteenth-Century Middle English Verse Chronicle." Ed. Marije
        Pots and Erik Kooper. *The Medieval Chronicle* 7 (2011), 239–66.

Bale, John. *Scriptorum Illustrium Majoris Brytanniae Catalogus*. 2 vols. Basle, 1557–59. Rpt. Westmead,
        Farnborough: Gregg International, 1971.

Barber, Richard. "The *Vera Historia De Morte Arthuri* and its Place in Arthurian Tradition." *Arthurian
        Literature* 1 (1981), 62–77.

———. "The Manuscripts of the *Vera Historia de Morte Arthuri*." *Arthurian Literature* 6 (1986), 163–64.

———. "Addendum on The *Vera Historia De Morte Arthuri*." In Carley, ed. Pp. 143–44.

———. "Was Mordred Buried at Glastonbury? Arthurian Tradition at Glastonbury in the Middle
        Ages." In Carley, ed. Pp. 145–60.

———. *The Holy Grail: Imagination and Belief*. Cambridge, MA: Harvard University Press, 2004.

Barron, W. R. J., ed. *Arthur of the English: The Arthurian Legend in Medieval English Life and Literature*.
        Revised edition. Cardiff: University of Wales Press, 2001.

Bede. *Bede. Ecclesiastical History of the English People*. Trans. Leo Sherley-Price. Harmondsworth:
        Penguin Books, 1990.

Beer, Barrett L. "Stow, John (1524/5–1605)." In *Oxford Dictionary of National Biography*, ed. H. C. G.
        Matthew and Brian Harrison. 2004. http://www.oxforddnb.com/view/article/26611.

Benson, Larry D., ed. *King Arthur's Death: The Middle English Stanziac Morte Arthur and Alliterative Morte
        Arthure*. Revised by Edward E. Foster. Kalamazoo, MI: Medieval Institute Publications, 1994.

The Bodleian Library, Image Collections. Version 6.3.6.2. 2011. http://bodley30.bodley.ox.ac.uk:
        8180/luna/servlet.

Bokenham, Osbern. *Legendys of Hooly Wummen by Osbern Bokenham*. Ed. Mary S. Serjeantson. EETS
        o.s. 206. London: Oxford University Press, 1938.

Brewer, D. S. "The Ideal of Feminine Beauty in Medieval Literature, Especially 'Harley Lyrics,'
        Chaucer, and Some Elizabethans." *The Modern Language Review* 50:3 (1955), 257–269.

The British Library, *Catalogue of Illuminated Manuscripts*. July 2003. http://www.bl.uk/catalogues/
        illuminatedmanuscripts/welcome.htm.

Brown, Michael. *The Wars of Scotland, 1214–1371*. Edinburgh: Edinburgh University Press, 2004.

Bruce, Christopher W. *The Arthurian Name Dictionary*. New York: Garland Publishing, 1999.

The Brut or The Chronicles of England. Ed. Friedrich W. D. Brie. 2 vols. EETS o.s. 131, 136. London:
        Oxford University Press, 1906–08.

Brut y Brenhinedd in the *Black Book of Basingwerk*. Unedited. (Citations taken from Aberystwyth,
        National Library of Wales, MS 7006D.)

Burke, Edmund. *The Annual Register of a view of the History, Politics, and Literature of the Year 1823*. Vol.
        65. London: Baldwin, Cradock, and Joy *et al*, 1824.

Calendar of the Close Rolls Preserved in the Public Record Office: Henry V, 1413–19; 1419–22. London: H. M. S. O., 1929, 1932.

Calendar of the Close Rolls Preserved in the Public Record Office: Henry VI, 1454–61. London: H. M. S. O., 1939.

Calendar of Entries in the Papal Registers Relating to Great Britain and Ireland: Papal Letters, 1427–47. London: H. M. S. O., 1909.

Calendar of the Patent Rolls Preserved in the Public Record Office: Henry VI, 1429–36; 1436–41; 1452–61. London: H. M. S. O., 1907, 1910.

Campbell, L. and F. Steer. *A Catalogue of Manuscripts in the College of Arms Collections.* London: College of Arms, 1988.

Capgrave, John. *Liber de Illustribus Henricis.* Ed. Francis Charles Hingeston. London: Longman, Brown, Green, Longmans & Roberts, 1858.

Carley, James P. and Julia Crick. "Constructing Albion's Past: An Annotated Edition of *De Origine Gigantum.*" *Arthurian Literature* 13 (1995), 41–114.

Carley, James P. "Melkin the Bard and Esoteric Tradition at Glastonbury Abbey." *Downside Review* 99 (1981), 1–17.

———. "A Grave Event: Henry V, Glastonbury Abbey, and Joseph of Arimathea's Bones." In *Culture and the King: The Social Implications of the Arthurian Legend: Essays in Honor of Valerie M. Lagorio.* Ed. Martin B. Shichtman and James P. Carley. Albany, NY: State University of New York Press, 1994. Pp. 129–48.

———, ed. *Glastonbury Abbey and the Arthurian Tradition.* Cambridge: D. S. Brewer, 2001.

Castleford's Chronicle or The Boke of Brut. Ed. Caroline D. Eckhardt. 2 vols, EETS o.s. 305, 306. Oxford: Oxford University Press, 1996.

Chaucer, Geoffrey. *The Riverside Chaucer.* Third ed. Gen. ed. Larry D. Benson. Oxford: Oxford University Press, 1988.

Chrétien de Troyes. *Lancelot, or, The Knight of the Cart (Le Chevalier de la Charrete).* Ed. and trans. William W. Kibler. New York: Garland Publishing, 1981.

———. *The Knight with the Lion or Yvain (Le Chevalier au Lion).* Ed. and trans. William W. Kibler. New York: Garland Publishing, 1985.

———. *Erec and Enide.* Ed. and trans. Carleton W. Carroll, intro. William W. Kibler. New York; London: Garland Publishing, 1987.

———. *The Story of the Grail (Li Contes del Graal), or Perceval.* Ed. Rupert T. Pickens and trans. William W. Kibler. New York; London: Garland Publishing, 1990.

Christine de Pisan. *The Book of Fayttes of Armes and of Chyvalrye.* Ed. by A. T. P. Byles. EETS o.s. 189. London: Oxford University Press, 1932.

Chronicon de Monasterii de Hailes [fragments]. See Fletcher, "Some Arthurian Fragments."

Clark, Andrew. *Lincoln Diocese Documents 1450–1544.* EETS o.s. 149. London: Trubner, 1914.

Cohen, Jeffrey Jerome. *Of Giants: Sex, Monsters, and the Middle Ages.* Minneapolis, MN: University of Minnesota Press, 1999.

Cole, Gavin and Thorlac Turville-Petre. "Sir Thomas Chaworth's Books." In Hanna and Turville-Petre, eds. Pp. 20–29.

Crick, Julia C. *The "Historia Regum Britannie" of Geoffrey of Monmouth: IV. Dissemination and Reception in the Later Middle Ages.* Cambridge: D.S. Brewer, 1991.

Cross, F. L. and E. A. Livingstone, eds. *The Oxford Dictionary of the Christian Church.* Third edition. Oxford: Oxford University Press, 1997.

Davies, R. G. "Kemp, John (1380/81–1454)." In *Oxford Dictionary of National Biography*, ed. H. C. G. Matthew and Brian Harrison. May 2011. http://www.oxforddnb.com/view/article/15328.

The Death of Arthur. Trans. Norris J. Lacy. In *The Lancelot-Grail Cycle. The Old French Arthurian Vulgate and Post-Vulgate in Translation.* Vol. 4. Gen. Ed. Norris J. Lacy.

De Boun, Rauf. *Le Petit Bruit.* Ed. Diana B. Tyson. London: Anglo-Norman Text Society, 1987.

Delano-Smith, Catherine and Roger J. P. Kain. *English Maps: A History.* London: The British Library and Toronto: University of Toronto Press, 1999.

Des Grantz Geanz: An Anglo-Norman Poem. Ed. Georgine E. Brereton. Oxford: Blackwell, 1937.

The Digital Scriptorium. University of California, Berkeley. Bancroft Library. 2011. http://bancroft.berkeley.edu/digitalscriptorium/.

Drijvers, Jan Willem. *Helena Augusta: The Mother of Constantine the Great and the Legend of Her Finding of the True Cross.* Leiden: E. J. Brill, 1992.

Dunphy, R. G., ed. *Encyclopedia of the Medieval Chronicle.* 2 vols. Leiden: Brill, 2010.

The Earliest English Translation of Vegetius' De Re Militari ed. from Oxford MS Bodl. Douce 291. Ed. Geoffrey Lester. Heidelberg: Winter, 1988.

Edwards, A. S. G. "Hardyng's *Chronicle* and *Troilus and Criseyde.*" *Notes and Queries* 229 (1984), 156.

——. "The Manuscripts and Texts of the Second Version of John Hardyng's Chronicle." In *England in the Fifteenth Century: Proceedings of the Harlaxton Symposium.* Ed. Daniel Williams. Woodbridge: Boydell Press, 1987. Pp. 75–84.

——. "Troilus and Criseyde and the First Version of Hardyng's Chronicle." *Notes and Queries* 233 (1988), 12–13.

——. "The Contexts of Notre Dame 67." In *The Text in the Community: Essays on Medieval Works, Manuscripts, Authors, and Readers.* Ed. by Jill Mann and Maura Nolan. Notre Dame, IN: University of Notre Dame Press, 2006. Pp. 107–28.

Ellis, Henry and Francis Douce. *A Catalogue of the Lansdowne Manuscripts in the British Museum.* 2 parts in 1 vol. London: Richard Taylor and Co, 1819.

An English Chronicle 1377–1461: Edited from Aberystwyth, National Library of Wales MS 21068 and Oxford, Bodleian Library MS Lyell 34. Ed. William Marx. Woodbridge: The Boydell Press, 2003.

Estoire del Saint Graal. See *The History of the Holy Grail.*

Eulogium Historiarum sive Temporis. Ed. Frank Scott Haydon. 3 vols. London: Longmans, 1858–65.

Evans, Ruth. "Gigantic Origins: An Annotated Translation of *De Origine Gigantum.*" *Arthurian Literature* 16 (1998), 197–211.

Fleming, John V. "The Round Table in Literature and Legend." In *King Arthur's Round Table: An Archaeological Investigation.* Ed. Martin Biddle. Woodbridge, Suffolk: The Boydell Press, 2000. Pp. 5–30.

Fletcher, Robert H. "Some Arthurian Fragments from Fourteenth-Century Chronicles." *PMLA* 18 (1903), 84–94.

——. *The Arthurian Material in the Chronicles.* Second ed. New York: Burt Franklin, 1973.

Flores Historiarum. Ed. Henry Richards Luard. 3 vols. London: Longmans, 1890.

Gaimar, Geffrei. *L'Estoire des Engleis.* Ed. Alexander Bell. Oxford: Basil Blackwell, 1960.

Gairdner, James and R. H. Brodie. *Letters and Papers, Foreign and Domestic of the Reign of Henry VIII. Preserved in the Public Record Office, The British Museum, and Elsewhere in England.* London: H. M. S. O., 1900.

Geoffrey of Monmouth. *The "Historia Regum Britanniae" of Geoffrey of Monmouth I: Bern, Bürgerbibliothek MS 568 (the "Vulgate" Version).* Ed. Neil Wright. Cambridge: D. S. Brewer, 1984.

——. *The "Historia Regum Britanniae" of Geoffrey of Monmouth II: the First Variant Version.* Ed. Neil Wright. Woodbridge, Suffolk: D. S. Brewer, 1988.

——. *Vita Merlini.* In *The History of the Kings of Britain.* Ed. and trans. Michael A. Faletra. Peterborough, Ontario: Broadview Press, 2008. Pp. 241–76.

Gerald of Wales. *Topographie Hibernica et Expugnatio Hibernica.* Ed. James F. Dimock. Volume 5 of *Giraldi Cambrenis Opera.* Ed. J. S. Brewer, James F. Dimock and George F. Warner. 8 vols. London: Longman, Green, Reader, and Dyer, 1867.

——. *Speculum Ecclesiae.* Ed. J. S. Brewer. Vol. 4 of *Giraldi Cambrensis Opera.* Ed. J. S. Brewer, James F. Dimock and George F. Warner. 8 vols. London: Longman, 1873.

——. *De Principis Instructione Liber.* Ed. George F. Warner. Vol. 8 of *Giraldi Cambrensis Opera.* Ed. J.S. Brewer, James F. Dimock and George F. Warner. 8 vols. London: Eyre and Spottiswoode, 1891.

——. *The Journey Through Wales and Description of Wales.* Trans. Lewis Thorpe. Harmondsworth: Penguin Books, 1978.

The "Gest Hystoriale" of the Destruction of Troy: An Alliterative Romance translated from Guido de Colonna's "Hystoria Troiana"; edited from the unique MS. In the Hunterian Museum, University of Glasgow. Ed. G. A. Panton and David Donaldson. EETS o.s. 39, 56. London: Oxford University Press, 1869–74.

Gloucester, Robert of. *The Metrical Chronicle of Robert of Gloucester.* Ed. William Aldis Wright. 2 vols. London: Eyre and Spottiswoode, 1887.

Gower, John. *Confessio Amantis.* Ed. Russell A. Peck, with Latin translations by Andrew Galloway. 3 vols. Second edition. Kalamazoo, MI: Medieval Institute Press, 2000–13.

Gransden, Antonia. *Historical Writing in England II: c. 1307 to the Early Sixteenth Century.* London: Routledge and Kegan Paul, 1982.

Gray, Sir Thomas. *Scalacronica: A Chronicle of England and Scotland, 1066–1362.* Ed. J. Stevenson. Edinburgh: Maitland Club, 1836.

———. *Scalacronica, 1272–1363.* Ed. and trans. Andy King. Woodbridge: Boydell Press, 2005.

Green, Richard Firth. *Poets and Princepleasers: Literature and the English Court in the Late Middle Ages.* Toronto: University of Toronto Press, 1980.

Griffiths, R. A. *The Reign of Henry VI: The Exercise of Royal Authority, 1422–1461.* Second edition. Stroud: Sutton Publishing, 1998.

Guido delle Colonne. *Guido de Columnis. Historia Destructionis Troiae.* Ed. Nathaniel Edward Griffin. Cambridge, MA: The Medieval Academy of America, 1936.

Hanna, Ralph and Thorlac Turville-Petre. "The Catalogue." In Hanna and Turville-Petre, eds. Pp. 88–130.

———, eds. *The Wollaton Medieval Manuscripts: Texts, Owners and Readers.* York: York Medieval Press, 2010.

Harbus, Antonina. *Helena of Britain in Medieval Legend.* Cambridge: D. S. Brewer, 2002.

Hardyng, John. *The Chronicle of Iohn Hardyng.* Ed. Henry Ellis. London: F. C. and J. Rivington, 1812.

Harker, Christine Marie. "John Hardyng's Arthur: A Critical Edition." Unpublished Ph.D. thesis, University of California, 1996.

Harriss, G. L. *Cardinal Beaufort: A Study of Lancastrian Ascendancy and Decline.* Oxford: Clarendon Press, 1988.

Harvey, P. D. A. *Medieval Maps.* London: British Library; Toronto: University of Toronto Press, 1991.

Henry of Huntingdon. *Henry, Archdeacon of Huntingon. Historia Anglorum: The History of the English People.* Ed. D. Greenway. Oxford: Clarendon Press, 1996.

Hiatt, Alfred. "The Forgeries of John Hardyng: The Evidence of Oxford, Bodleian MS Ashmole 789." *Notes and Queries* 244 (1999), 7–12.

———. "The Use and Reception of Forged Documents in Fifteenth-Century England." Unpublished Ph.D. thesis: University of Cambridge, 1999.

———. "Beyond a Border: The Maps of Scotland in John Hardyngs *Chronicle*." In *The Lancastrian Court: Proceedings of the 2001 Harlaxton Symposium.* Ed. Jenny Stratford. Donington: Shaun Tyas, 2003. Pp. 78–94.

———. *The Making of Medieval Forgeries: False Documents in Fifteenth-Century England.* London: The British Library and University of Toronto Press, 2004.

———. "Stow, Grafton, and Fifteenth-Century Historiography". In *John Stow (1525–1605) and the Making of the English Past.* Ed. Ian Gadd and Alexandra Gillespie. London: British Library, 2004. Pp. 45–56.

Higden, Ranulph. *Polychronicon Ranulphi Higden.* Ed. Churchill Babington and Joseph Lumby. RS 41. 9 vols. London: Longmans, 1865–86.

The History of the Holy Grail. Trans. Carol J. Chase. In *The Lancelot-Grail Cycle. The Old French Arthurian Vulgate and Post-Vulgate in Translation.* Gen. Ed. Norris J. Lacy. Vol. 1.

Hoccleve, Thomas. *Thomas Hoccleve: The Regiment of Princes.* Ed. Charles Blyth. Kalamazoo, MI: Medieval Institute Publications, 1999.

Howatson, M. C., ed. *The Oxford Companion to Classical Literature.* Second ed. Oxford: Oxford University Press, 1989.

Ikas, Wolfgang-Valentin. "Martinus Polonus' Chronicle of the Popes and Emperors: A Medieval Best-Seller and Its Neglected Influence on Medieval English Chroniclers." *The English Historical Review* 116 (2001), 327–41.

Jacobus da Voragine. *Legenda Aurea*. Ed. Theodor Graesse. Third ed. Breslau: Koebner, 1890. Photographic Reprint. Osnabrück: Zeller, 1969.

John of Fordun. *Chronica gentis Scotorum by John of Fordun*. Ed. W. F. Skene. Edinburgh: Edmonston and Douglas, 1871. Rpt. Edinburgh: Paterson, 1981.

John of Glastonbury. *The Chronicle of Glastonbury Abbey: An Edition, Translation and Study of John of Glastonbury's Cronica Sive Antiquitates Glastoniensis Ecclesie*. Ed. James P. Carley. Trans. David Townsend. Woodbridge: Boydell Press, 1985.

Johnson, Lesley. "Robert Mannyng of Brunne and the History of Arthurian Literature." *Church and Chronicle in the Middle Ages: Essays Presented to John Taylor*. Ed. Ian Wood and G. A. Loud. London: Hambledon Press, 1991. Pp. 129–48.

Johnson, P. A. *Duke Richard of York 1411–1460*. Oxford: Clarendon Press, 1988.

Joseph of Arimathie, from the Vernon MS. In *Joseph of Arimathie: Otherwise Called The Romance of the Seint Graal or Holy Grail*. Ed. Walter W. Skeat. Pp. 1–23.

Joseph of Arimathie. In *Joseph of Arimathea: A Critical Edition*. Ed. David A. Lawton. New York: Garland, 1983.

Joseph of Arimathie: Otherwise Called The Romance of the Seint Graal or Holy Grail: An Alliterative Poem Written About AD 1350 and Now First Printed from the Unique Copy in the Vernon MS at Oxford. Ed. Walter W. Skeat. EETS o.s. 44. London: N. Trübner, 1871.

Justin. *Justin, Epitome of the Philippic History of Pompeius Trogus, Volume 1, Books 11–12: Alexander the Great*. Ed. J. C. Yardley and Waldemar Heckel. Oxford: Clarendon Press, 1997, rpt. 2003.

Keen, Maurice. *Chivalry*. New Haven, CT: Yale University Press, 1984. Reprinted 2005.

Keller, Hans E. "Two Toponymical Problems in Geoffrey of Monmouth and Wace: Estrusia and Siesia." *Speculum* 49 (1974), 687–698.

Kennedy, Edward D. "Malory's Use of Hardyng's *Chronicle*." *Notes and Queries* 214 (1969), 167–70.

———. *Chronicles and Other Historical Writing*. Vol. 8 of *A Manual of the Writings in Middle English 1050–1500*. Ed. Albert E. Hartung and J. B. Severs. New Haven, CT: Connecticut Academy of Arts and Sciences, 1989.

———. "John Hardyng and the Holy Grail." *Arthurian Literature* 8 (1989), 185–206.

———. "John of Fordun." In Dunphy, *Encyclopedia of the Medieval Chronicle*. Vol. 2. Pp. 931–32.

King, Andy. "'They Have the Hertes of the People by North': Northumberland, the Percies and Henry IV, 1399–1408." In *Henry IV: The Establishment of the Regime, 1399–1406*. Ed. Gwilym Dodd and Douglas Biggs. York: York Medieval Press, 2003. Pp. 139–59.

Kingsford, Charles L. "Extracts from the First Version of Hardyng's Chronicle." *English Historical Review* 27 (1912), 740–53.

———. "The First Version of Hardyng's Chronicle." *English Historical Review* 27 (1912), 462–82.

Lagorio, Valerie M. "The Evolving Legend of St Joseph of Glastonbury." *Speculum* 46 (1971), 209–31.

Lancelot. In *The Lancelot-Grail Cycle. The Old French Arthurian Vulgate and Post-Vulgate in Translation*. Vols. 2–3. Gen. Ed. Norris J. Lacy. Part I trans. Samuel N. Rosenberg. Part II trans. Carleton W. Carroll. Part III trans. Samuel N. Rosenberg. Part IV trans. Roberta L. Krueger. Part V trans. William W. Kibler. Part VI trans. Carleton W. Carroll.

The Lancelot-Grail Cycle. The Old French Arthurian Vulgate and Post-Vulgate in Translation. Gen. Ed. Norris J. Lacy. New York: Garland Publishing, 1993–95.

Langtoft, Peter. *The Chronicle of Pierre de Langtoft*. Ed. Thomas Wright. 2 vols. London: Longmans, Green Reader, and Dyer, 1866.

Lapidge, Michael. "Additional Manuscript Evidence for the *Vera Historia Arthuri*." *Arthurian Literature* 2 (1982), 163–68.

———, ed. "An Edition of the *Vera Historia de Morte Arthuri*." *Arthurian Literature* 1 (1981). 79–93.

———, ed. "The *Vera Historia de Morte Arthuri*: A New Edition." In Carley, ed. Pp. 115–42.

The Laud Troy Book: A Romance of About 1400 A.D. now First Edited from the unique MS. (Laud Misc. 595) in the Bodleian Library, Oxford. Ed. Johann Ernst Wülfing. EETS o.s. 121–22. London: Kegan Paul, 1902.

Lawton, David. "Dullness and the Fifteenth Century." *English Literary History* 54 (1987), 761–99.

Layamon. *Lawman, Brut.* Trans. Rosamund Allen. New York: St. Martin's, 1992.

———. *Layamon's Arthur: The Arthurian Section of Layamon's Brut (Lines 9229–14297).* Ed. W. R. J. Barron and S. C. Weinberg. Exeter: Exeter University Press, 2001.

Legenda Aurea. See Jacobus da Voragine.

Lestoire de Merlin. See *The Story of Merlin.*

Libelle of Englysche Polycye: A Poem on the Use of Sea-Power, 1436. Ed. George Warner. Oxford: Clarendon Press, 1926.

Liber Monasterii de Hyda. Ed. Edward Edwards. Rolls Series 45. London: Longmans, Green, Reader, and Dyer, 1866.

Lovelich, Henry. *The History of the Holy Grail by Henry Lovelich.* Ed. F. J. Furnivall. 4 vols, EETS e.s. 20, 24, 28, 30 (1874–78). Millwood, NY: Kraus Reprint, 1973.

Lydgate, John. *Lydgate's Troy Book.* Ed. Henry Bergen. 4 vols. EETS e.s. 97, 103, 106, 126. London: Kegan Paul, 1906–35.

———. *Lydgate's Fall of Princes.* Ed. Henry Bergen. 4 vols. EETS e.s. 121, 122, 123, 124. London: Oxford University Press, 1924–27.

———. "Henry VI's Triumphal Entry into London, 21 Feb., 1432." In *The Minor Poems of John Lydgate: Part II.* Ed. Henry Noble MacCracken. 2 vols. EETS o.s. 192. London: Oxford University Press, 1934. Pp. 630–48.

———. *John Lydgate Troy Book: Selections.* Ed. Robert R. Edwards. Kalamazoo, MI: Medieval Institute Publications, 1998.

The Verse "Lyfe of Joseph of Armathia." In *Joseph of Arimathie: Otherwise Called The Romance of the Seint Graal or Holy Grail.* Ed. Walter W. Skeat. Pp. 35–52.

MacDonald, Alastair J. "John Hardyng, Northumbrian Identity and the Scots." In *North-East England in the Later Middle Ages.* Ed. Christian D. Liddy and Richard H. Britnell. Woodbridge: Boydell Press, 2005. Pp. 29–42.

MacPhail, I. M. M. *Dumbarton Castle.* Edinburgh: John Donald Publishers Ltd, 1979.

Mannyng, Robert. *Robert Mannyng of Brunne: The Chronicle.* Ed. Idelle Sullens. Binghampton, NY: Medieval and Renaissance Texts and Studies, 1996.

Martin of Troppau [Martinus Polonus]. *Martini Oppaviensis Chronicon Pontificum et Imperatorum.* Ed. Ludewicus Weiland. *Monumenta Germaniae Historica Scriptores* 22 (1872). Pp. 377–482.

Marvin, Julia. "Albine and Isabelle: Regicidal Queens and the Historical Imagination of the Anglo-Norman Prose *Brut* Chronicles." *Arthurian Literature* 18 (2001), 143–91.

Malory, Sir Thomas. *Sir Thomas Malory, Le Morte Darthur: The Winchester Manuscript.* Ed. Helen Cooper. Oxford: Oxford University Press, 1998.

———. *The Works of Sir Thomas Malory.* Ed. Eugene Vinaver. Revised by P. J. C. Field. 3 vols. Oxford: Oxford University Press, 1990.

Marx, William. "Aberystwyth, National Library of Wales, MS 21608 and the Middle English Prose *Brut.*" *Journal of the Early Book Society for the Study of Manuscripts and Printing History* 1.1 (1997), 1–16.

Matheson, Lister M. *The Prose Brut: The Development of a Middle English Chronicle.* Tempe, AZ: Medieval and Renaissance Texts and Studies, 1998.

Matthews, William. "Where was Siesia-Sessoyne?" *Speculum* 49 (1974), 680–686.

McGerr, Rosemarie Potz, ed. *The Pilgrimage of the Soul: A Critical Edition of the Middle English Dream Vision.* Vol. 1. London: Garland, 1990.

McIntosh, Angus, M. L. Samuels, and Michael Benskin. *A Linguistic Atlas of Late Mediaeval English.* 4 vols. Aberdeen: Aberdeen University Press, 1986.

Meale, Carol. "Manuscripts, Readers and Patrons in Fifteenth-Century England: Sir Thomas Malory and Arthurian Romance." *Arthurian Literature* 4 (1985), 93–126.

———. "Patrons, Buyers and Owners: Book Production and Social Status." In *Book Production and Publishing in Britain 1375–1475*. Ed. Jeremy Griffiths and Derek Pearsall. Cambridge: Cambridge University Press, 1989. Pp. 201–38.

Mercer, Malcolm. *The Medieval Gentry: Power, Leadership and Choice during the Wars of the Roses*. London: Continuum, 2010.

The Middle English Dictionary (MED). April 2013. http://quod.lib.umich.edu/m/med/.

Middle English Prose Brut. See *The Brut or The Chronicles of England*.

Moll, Richard J. "Another Reference to John Hardyng's 'Mewyn'". *Notes and Queries* 245 (2000), 296–98.

———. *Before Malory: Reading Arthur in Later Medieval England*. Toronto: Univerisity of Toronto Press, 2003.

———. "Gower's Cronica Tripertita and the Latin Glosses to Hardyng's Chronicle." *Journal of the Early Book Society* 7 (2004). Pp. 153–158.

———. "Ebrauke and the Politics of Arthurian Geography." *Arthuriana* 15:4 (2005), 65–71.

Morris, Rosemary. *The Character of King Arthur in Medieval Literature*. Cambridge: D. S. Brewer, 1982.

La Mort Artu. See *The Death of Arthur*.

Nennius. *Nennius British History and The Welsh Annals [Historia Brittonum]*. Ed. and trans. John Morris. London: Phillimore and Co., 1980.

Neville, Cynthia J. *Violence, Custom and Law: The Anglo-Scottish Border Lands in the Later Middle Ages*. Edinburgh: Edinburgh University Press, 1998.

Þe New Croniclis Compendiusli Ydrawe of þe Gestis of Kyngis of Ingelond. Unedited. (Citations taken from New York, Columbia University, MS Plimpton 261.)

The New York Public Library Digital Gallery. The New York Public Library. 2005. http://digitalgallery.nypl.org/nypldigital/dgkeysearchresult.cfm?parent_id=185822.

Nicholson, Ranald. *Scotland: The Later Middle Ages*. Edinburgh: Oliver and Boyd, 1974.

Nicolas, N. H, ed. *Proceedings and Ordinances of the Privy Council of England*. 7 vols. London: Record Commission, 1834–37.

———. *History of the Battle of Agincourt and of the Expedition of Henry the Fifth into France in 1415 to which is Added, the Roll of the Men at Arms, in the English Army*. Facsimile edition. New York: Barnes and Noble, 1970.

The Oldest Anglo-Norman Prose Brut Chronicle. Ed. and trans. Julia Marvin. Woodbridge: The Boydell Press, 2006.

De Origine Gigantum. See Carley and Crick.

Orme, Nicholas. *English Schools in the Middle Ages*. London: Methuen, 1973.

———. *From Childhood to Chivalry: The Education of the English Kings and Aristocracy 1066–1530*. London: Methuen, 1984.

———. "Children and Literature in Medieval England." *Medium Aevum* 68 (1999), 218–46.

Otway-Ruthven, J. *The King's Secretary and the Signet Office in the Fifteenth Century*. Cambridge: Cambridge University Press, 1939.

Owst, G. R. *Literature and Pulpit in Medieval England*. Second ed. Oxford: Blackwell, 1961.

Oxford Dictionary of National Biography. Ed. H. C. G. Matthew and Brian Harrison. Oxford: Oxford University Press, 2004. Online ed. 2004–15. http://www.oxforddnb.com/.

Palgrave, Sir Francis. *The Antient Kalendars and Inventories of the Treasury of His Majesty's Exchequer; together with other documents illustrating the history of that repository collected and edited by Sir Francis Palgrave*. 3 vols. London: Commissioners of the Public Records, 1836.

———. *Documents and Records Illustrating the History of Scotland and the Transactions between the crowns of Scotland and England Preserved in the Treasury of Her Majesty's Exchequer*. London: Commissioners of the Public Records, 1837.

Pecock, Reginald. *The Repressor of Over Much Blaming of the Clergy by Reginald Pecock*. Ed. Churchill Babington. 2 vols. London: Longmans, 1860.

Le Petit Bruit. See De Boun, Rauf.

Peverley, Sarah L. "Adapting to Readeption in 1470–1471: The Scribe as Editor in a Unique Copy of John Hardyng's Chronicle of England (Garrett MS. 142)." *The Princeton University Library Chronicle* 66:1 (2004), 140–72.

———. "Dynasty and Division: The Depiction of King and Kingdom in John Hardyng's *Chronicle*." In *Medieval Chronicle* 3 (2004). Pp. 149–70.

———. "'John Hardyng's *Chronicle*: A Study of the Two Versions and a Critical Edition of Both for the Period 1327–1464." Unpublished Ph.D. Thesis, University of Hull, 2004.

———. "'A Good Exampell to Avoide Diane': Reader Responses to John Hardyng's *Chronicle* in the Fifteenth and Sixteenth Centuries." *Poetica* 63 (2005), 19–35.

———. "Genealogy and John Hardyng's Verse *Chronicle*." In *Broken Lines: Genealogy Literature in Late Medieval Britain and France*. Ed. Raluca L. Radulescu and Edward Donald Kennedy. Turnhout: Brepols, 2008. Pp 259–82.

———. "Loke well about, ye that lovers be" (IMEV 1944) and a Sixteenth-Century Reader's Response to John Hardyng's account of Joan of Kent." *Poetica* 69 (2008), 17–25.

———. "Political Consciousness and the Literary Mind in Late Medieval England: Men 'Brought up of Nought' in Vale, Hardyng, *Mankind* and Malory." *Studies in Philology* 105:1 (2008), 1–29.

———. "Hardyng, John." In Dunphy, *Encyclopedia of the Medieval Chronicle*. Vol. 1. Pp. 751–754.

———. "Chronicling the Fortunes of Kings: John Hardyng's use of Walton's *Boethius*, Chaucer's *Troilus and Criseyde*, and Lydgate's 'King Henry VI's Triumphal Entry into London.'" *The Medieval Chronicle* 7 (2011), 167–203.

———. "Anglo-Scottish Relations in John Hardyng's *Chronicle*." In *The Anglo-Scottish Border and the Shaping of Identity, 1300–1600*. Ed. Mark Bruce and Katherine Terrell. New York: Palgrave Macmillan, 2012. Pp. 69–86.

The Physician's Handbook, a digital facsimile of London, Wellcome Library MS 8004. October 2007. http://library.wellcome.ac.uk/physicianshandbook.html.

Porter, Cheryl. "The Meaning of Colour and Why Analyse?" *Care and Conservation of Manuscripts 10: Proceedings of the Tenth International Seminar held at the University of Copenhagen 19th–20th October 2006*. Ed. Gillian Fellows and Peter Springborg. Copenhagen: Museum Tusculanum Press, 2008. Pp. 71–80.

Prestwich, Michael. *Edward I*. Berkeley: University of California Press, 1988.

Putter, Ad. "Finding Time for Romance: Medieval Arthurian Literary History."*Medium Aevum* 63 (1994): 1–16.

La Queste del Saint Graal. See *The Quest for the Holy Grail*.

The Quest for the Holy Grail. Trans. E. Jane Burns. In *The Lancelot-Grail Cycle. The Old French Arthurian Vulgate and Post-Vulgate in Translation*. Gen. Ed. Norris J. Lacy. Vol. 4.

Radulescu, Raluca and Alison Truelove, eds. *Gentry Culture in Late Medieval England*. Manchester: Manchester University Press, 2005.

Ralph of Coggeshall. *Radulphi de Coggeshall Chronicon Anglicanum; De expugnatione terrae sanctae libellus; Thomas Agnellus De morte et sepultura Henrici Regis Angliae junioris; Gesta Fulconis filii Warini; Excerpta ex Otiis imperialibus Gervasii Tileburiensis ex codicibus manuscriptis*. Ed. Joseph Stevenson. London: Longmans, 1875.

Reynolds, Susan. "Medieval *Origines Gentium* and the Community of the Realm." *History: The Journal of the Historical Association* 68 (1983), 375–90.

Riddy, Felicity. "Glastonbury, Joseph of Arimathea and the Grail in John Hardyng's *Chronicle*." In *The Archaeology and History of Glastonbury Abbey: Essays in Honour of the Ninetieth Birthday of C. A. Raleigh Radford*. Ed. Lesley Abrams and James P. Carley. Woodbridge: The Boydell Press, 1991. Pp. 317–31.

———. "John Hardyng in Search of the Grail." In *Arturus Rex*. Ed. Willy Van Hoecke, Gilbert Tournoy, and Werner Verbeke. Vol. 2. Leuven: Leuven University Press, 1991. Pp. 419–29.

———. "John Hardyng's *Chronicle* and the Wars of the Roses."*Arthurian Literature* 12 (1996), 91–108.

———. "Chivalric Nationalism and the Holy Grail in John Hardyng's *Chronicle*." In *The Grail: A Casebook*. Ed. Dhira B. Mahoney. New York: Garland, 2000. Pp. 397–414.

Riley, Henry Thomas, ed. *Registrum Abbatiae Johannis Whethamstede, Abbatis Monasterii Sancti Albani, Iterum Susceptae; Roberto Blakeney, Capellano, Quondam Adscriptum*. 2 vols. RS 28. London: Longman, 1872–73.

Roberts, Julian and Andrew G. Watson. *John Dee's Library Catalogue: Additions and Corrections*. The Bibliographical Society. Nov 2009. http://www.bibsoc.org.uk/sites/www.bibsoc.org.uk/files/John%20Dee%27s%20Library%20Catalogue%204.pdf.

Robinson, J. Armitage. *Two Glastonbury Legends: King Arthur and St. Joseph of Arimathea*. Cambridge: Cambridge University Press, 1926.

Rollason, David and R. B. Dobson. "Cuthbert [St Cuthbert] (c.635–687)." In *Oxford Dictionary of National Biography*, ed. H. C. G. Matthew and Brian Harrison. 2004. http://www.oxforddnb.com/view/article/6976.

Rosenthal, Joel T. "The King's 'Wicked Advisers' and Medieval Baronial Rebellions." *Political Science Quarterly* 82:4 (1967), 595–618.

Roskell, J. S., Linda Clark, and Carole Rawcliffe. *The History of Parliament*. 4 vols. Stroud: Alan Sutton, 1993.

Rotuli Parliamentorum, ut et petitiones, et placita in Parliamento, 6 vols (London: n.p., 1767–77).

Rous, John. *Historia Regum Angliae. Joannis Rossi antiquarii Warwicensis Historia regum Angliae*. Ed. Thomas Hearne. Second Edition. Oxford: J. Fletcher and J. Pote, 1745.

Ruddick, Andrea. "Chronicon de Lanercost." In Dunphy, *Encyclopedia of the Medieval Chronicle*. Vol. 1. Pp. 357–58.

Rymer, Thomas, ed. *Foedera, conventiones, literæ, et cujuscunque generis acta publica, inter reges Angliæ ...* 20 vols. London: A. & J. Churchill, 1704–35.

Seneca, Lucius Annaeus. *De Clementia*. Ed. and trans. Susanna Braund. Oxford: Oxford University Press, 2009.

Scott, Kathleen L. "Lydgate's Lives of Saints Edmund and Fremund: A Newly-Located Manuscript in Arundel Castle." *Viator* 13 (1982), 335–66.

———. *Later Gothic Manuscripts 1390–1490*. 2 vols. London: Harvey Miller, 1996.

———. *Dated and Datable English Manuscript Borders c. 1395–1499*. London: British Library, 2002.

Sharpe, Kevin. *Sir Robert Cotton 1586–1631: History and Politics in Early Modern England*. Oxford: Oxford University Press, 1979.

The Short English Metrical Chronicle. See *The Abridged English Metrical Brut*.

Sir Orfeo. In *The Middle English Breton Lays*. Ed. Anne Laskaya and Eve Salisbury. Kalamazoo, Michigan: Medieval Institute Publications, 1995; Rpt. 2001. Pp. 15–59.

Smith, William. *Dictionary of Greek and Roman Biography and Mythology*. 3 vols. London: James Walton and John Murray, 1869.

Spence, John. "The *Mohun Chronicle*: An Introduction, Edition and Translation." *Nottingham Medieval Studies* 55 (2011), 149–215.

Sprott, Thomas. *Thomae Sprotti Chronica*. Ed. Thomas Hearne. Oxford: Theatro Sheldoniano, 1719. [though attribution to Sprott debated]

———. *Thomas Sprott's Chronicle of Sacred and Profane History*. Trans. W. Bell. Liverpool: D. Marples and Co., 1851 [though attribution to Sprott debated]

Stanziac Morte Arthur. In Benson. Pp. 9–128.

Stones, E. L. G. *Anglo-Scottish Relations 1174–1328: Some Selected Documents*. Oxford: Clarendon Press, 1970.

Stones, E. L. G. and G. Simpson. *Edward I and the Throne of Scotland 1290–1296*. 2 vols. Oxford: Oxford University Press, 1978.

The Story of Merlin. Trans. Rupert T. Pickens. In *The Lancelot-Grail Cycle. The Old French Arthurian Vulgate and Post-Vulgate in Translation*. Gen. Ed. Norris J. Lacy. Vol. 1.

Stratford, Jenny. "John, duke of Bedford (1389–1435)." In *Oxford Dictionary of National Biography*, ed. H. C. G. Matthew and Brian Harrison. Sept. 2011. http://www.oxforddnb.com/view/article/14844.

Summerfield, Thea. "The Arthurian References in Pierre de Langtoft's *Chronicle*." In *Text and Intertext in Medieval Arthurian Literature*. Ed. Norris J. Lacy. New York: Garland, 1996. Pp. 187–208.

———. "The Testimony of Writing: Pierre de Langtoft and the Appeals to History, 1291–1306." In *The Scots and Medieval Arthurian Legend*. Ed. Rhiannon Purdie and Nicola Royan. Cambridge: D. S. Brewer, 2005. Pp. 25–42.

———. "Pierre de Langtoft." In Dunphy, *Encyclopedia of the Medieval Chronicle*. Vol. 2. Pp. 1216–17.

Summerson, Henry. "Hardyng, John (b. 1377/8, d. in or after 1464)." In *Oxford Dictionary of National Biography*, ed. H. C. G. Matthew and Brian Harrison. 2004. http://www.oxforddnb.com/view/article/12296.

———. "Umfraville, Sir Robert (d. 1437)." In *Oxford Dictionary of National Biography*, ed. H. C. G. Matthew and Brian Harrison. Jan 2008. http://www.oxforddnb.com/view/article/27992.

Szarmach, Paul E., M. Teresa Tavormina, and Joel T. Rosenthal, eds. *Medieval England: An Encyclopedia*. New York: Garland, 1998.

Thompson, A. Hamilton, ed. *Visitations in the Diocese of Lincoln*. 3 vols. Hereford: Lincoln Record Society, 1914–29.

Tilley, Morris Palmer. *A Dictionary of Proverbs in England in the Sixteenth and Seventeenth Centuries*. Ann Arbor, MI: University of Michigan Press, 1950.

Tite, Colin G. C. "'Lost or Stolen or Strayed': A Survey of Manuscripts Formerly in the Cotton Library". In *Sir Robert Cotton as Collector: Essays on an Early Stuart Courtier and his Legacy*. Ed. C. J. Wright. London: British Library, 1997. Pp. 262–306.

Trevisa, John. *The Governance of Kings and Princes: John Trevisa's Middle English Translation of the* De Regimine Principum *of Aegidus Romanus*. Ed. David C. Fowler, Charles F. Briggs, and Paul G. Remley. New York: Garland Publishing, 1997.

Vincent, Nicholas. *The Holy Blood: King Henry III and the Westminster Blood Relic*. Cambridge: Cambridge University Press, 2001.

Wace. *Wace's Roman de Brut, A History of The British*. Ed. Judith Weiss. Revised Edition. Exeter: University of Exeter Press, 1999.

Walker, Simon. "Percy, Sir Henry (1364–1403)." In *Oxford Dictionary of National Biography*, ed. H. C. G. Matthew and Brian Harrison. Jan 2008. http://www.oxforddnb.com/view/article/21931.

Walton, John. *Boethius: De Consolatione Philosophiae, translated by John Walton, Canon of Oseney*. Ed. Mark Science. EETS o.s. 170. London: Oxford University Press, 1927.

Watts, John. *Henry VI and the Politics of Kingship*. Cambridge: Cambridge University Press, 1999.

———. "Richard of York, third duke of York (1411–1460)." In *Oxford Dictionary of National Biography*, ed. H. C. G. Matthew and Brian Harrison. May 2011. http://www.oxforddnb.com/view/article/23503.

Waurin, Jean de. *Recueil des Croniques et Anchiennes Istories de la Grant Bretaigne*. Ed. William Hardy and Edward L. C. P. Hardy. 5 vols. London: Longmans, 1864–91.

Whetehamstede, John. *Registrum Abbatiae Johannis Whethamstede, Abbatis Monasterii Sancti Albani, Iterum Susceptae; Roberto Blakeney, Capellano, Quondam Adscriptum*. Ed. Henry Thomas Riley. 2 vols. RS 28. London: Longman, 1872–73.

Whiting, Bartlett Jere. *Proverbs, Sentences, and Proverbial Phrases: From English Writings Mainly Before 1500*. London: Oxford University Press, 1968.

William of Malmesbury. *The Early History of Glastonbury: An Edition, translation and study of William of Malmesbury's De Antiquitate Glastonie Ecclesie*. Ed. and trans. John Scott. Woodbridge: Boydell Press, 1981.

———. *William of Malmesbury, Gesta Regum Anglorum: The History of the English Kings*. Ed. and trans. R. A. B. Mynors, completed by R. M. Thomson and M. Winterbottom. 2 vols. Oxford: Clarendon Press, 1998–99.

Wilson, Robert H. "More Borrowings by Malory from Hardyng's Chronicle." *Notes and Queries* 215 (1970), 208–10.

Withrington, John. "The Arthurian Epitaph in Malory's *Morte Darthur*." *Arthurian Literature* 7 (1987), 103–44.

———. "King Arthur as Emperor." *Notes and Queries* 233 (1988), 13–15.

Wolffe, Bertram. *Henry VI*. New Haven, CT: Yale University Press, 2001.

Wolpe, Berthold. "Florilegium Alphabeticum: Alphabets in Medieval Manuscripts." In *Calligraphy and Palaeography: Essays Presented to Alfred Fairbank on his 70th Birthday*. Ed. A. S. Osley. London: Faber and Faber, 1965. Pp. 69–74.

Worcester, William. *William Worcestre: Itineraries: Edited from the Unique MS. Corpus Christi College Cambridge, 210*. Ed. John H. Harvey. Oxford: Clarendon Press, 1969.

Wright, C. E. *Fontes Harleiani: A Study of the Sources of the Harleian Collection of Manuscripts Preserved in the Department of Manuscripts in the British Museum*. London: British Museum, 1972.

Wylie, James Hamilton and William Templeton Waugh. *The Reign of Henry the Fifth*. 3 vols. Cambridge: Cambridge University Press, 1914–29.

Ynglis Chronicle. In *Short Scottish Prose Chronicles*. Ed. Dan Embree, Edward Donald Kennedy, and Kathleen Daly. Woodbridge: Boydell Press, 2012.

Ywain and Gawain. In *Sir Perceval of Galles and Ywain and Gawain*. Ed. Mary Flowers Braswell. Kalamazoo, MI: Medieval Institute Publications, 1995.

Siege of Jerusalem, edited by Michael Livingston (2004)

The Kingis Quair and Other Prison Poems, edited by Linne R. Mooney and Mary-Jo Arn (2005)

The Chaucerian Apocrypha: A Selection, edited by Kathleen Forni (2005)

John Gower, *The Minor Latin Works*, edited and translated by R. F. Yeager, with *In Praise of Peace*, edited by Michael Livingston (2005)

Sentimental and Humorous Romances: Floris and Blancheflour, Sir Degrevant, The Squire of Low Degree, The Tournament of Tottenham, and The Feast of Tottenham, edited by Erik Kooper (2006)

The Dicts and Sayings of the Philosophers, edited by John William Sutton (2006)

Everyman and Its Dutch Original, Elckerlijc, edited by Clifford Davidson, Martin W. Walsh, and Ton J. Broos (2007)

The N-Town Plays, edited by Douglas Sugano, with assistance by Victor I. Scherb (2007)

The Book of John Mandeville, edited by Tamarah Kohanski and C. David Benson (2007)

John Lydgate, *The Temple of Glas*, edited by J. Allan Mitchell (2007)

The Northern Homily Cycle, edited by Anne B. Thompson (2008)

Codex Ashmole 61: A Compilation of Popular Middle English Verse, edited by George Shuffelton (2008)

Chaucer and the Poems of "Ch," edited by James I. Wimsatt (revised edition 2009)

William Caxton, *The Game and Playe of the Chesse*, edited by Jenny Adams (2009)

John the Blind Audelay, *Poems and Carols*, edited by Susanna Fein (2009)

Two Moral Interludes: The Pride of Life and Wisdom, edited by David Klausner (2009)

John Lydgate, *Mummings and Entertainments*, edited by Claire Sponsler (2010)

Mankind, edited by Kathleen M. Ashley and Gerard NeCastro (2010)

The Castle of Perseverance, edited by David N. Klausner (2010)

Robert Henryson, *The Complete Works*, edited by David J. Parkinson (2010)

John Gower, *The French Balades*, edited and translated by R. F. Yeager (2011)

The Middle English Metrical Paraphrase of the Old Testament, edited by Michael Livingston (2011)

The York Corpus Christi Plays, edited by Clifford Davidson (2011)

Prik of Conscience, edited by James H. Morey (2012)

The Dialogue of Solomon and Marcolf: A Dual-Language Edition from Latin and Middle English Printed Editions, edited by Nancy Mason Bradbury and Scott Bradbury (2012)

Croxton Play of the Sacrament, edited by John T. Sebastian (2012)

Ten Bourdes, edited by Melissa M. Furrow (2013)

Lybeaus Desconus, edited by Eve Salisbury and James Weldon (2013)

The Complete Harley 2253 Manuscript, Vol. 2, edited and translated by Susanna Fein with David Raybin and Jan Ziolkowski (2014); Vol. 3 (2015); Vol. 1 (2015)

Oton de Granson Poems, edited and translated by Peter Nicholson and Joan Grenier-Winther (2015)

The King of Tars, edited by John H. Chandler (2015)

🖋 COMMENTARY SERIES

Haimo of Auxerre, *Commentary on the Book of Jonah*, translated with an introduction and notes by Deborah Everhart (1993)

Medieval Exegesis in Translation: Commentaries on the Book of Ruth, translated with an introduction and notes by Lesley Smith (1996)

Nicholas of Lyra's Apocalypse Commentary, translated with an introduction and notes by Philip D. W. Krey (1997)

Rabbi Ezra Ben Solomon of Gerona, *Commentary on the Song of Songs and Other Kabbalistic Commentaries*, selected, translated, and annotated by Seth Brody (1999)

John Wyclif, *On the Truth of Holy Scripture*, translated with an introduction and notes by Ian Christopher Levy (2001)

Second Thessalonians: Two Early Medieval Apocalyptic Commentaries, introduced and translated by Steven R. Cartwright and Kevin L. Hughes (2001)

The "Glossa Ordinaria" on the Song of Songs, translated with an introduction and notes by Mary Dove (2004)

The Seven Seals of the Apocalypse: Medieval Texts in Translation, translated with an introduction and notes by Francis X. Gumerlock (2009)

The "Glossa Ordinaria" on Romans, translated with an introduction and notes by Michael Scott Woodward (2011)

🖋 DOCUMENTS OF PRACTICE SERIES

Love and Marriage in Late Medieval London, selected, translated, and introduced by Shannon McSheffrey (1995)

Sources for the History of Medicine in Late Medieval England, selected, introduced, and translated by Carole Rawcliffe (1995)

A Slice of Life: Selected Documents of Medieval English Peasant Experience, edited, translated, and with an introduction by Edwin Brezette DeWindt (1996)

Regular Life: Monastic, Canonical, and Mendicant "Rules," selected and introduced by Douglas J. McMillan and Kathryn Smith Fladenmuller (1997); second edition, selected and introduced by Daniel Marcel La Corte and Douglas J. McMillan (2004)

Women and Monasticism in Medieval Europe: Sisters and Patrons of the Cistercian Reform, selected, translated, and with an introduction by Constance H. Berman (2002)

Medieval Notaries and Their Acts: The 1327–1328 Register of Jean Holanie, introduced, edited, and translated by Kathryn L. Reyerson and Debra A. Salata (2004)

John Stone's Chronicle: Christ Church Priory, Canterbury, 1417–1472, selected, translated, and introduced by Meriel Connor (2010)

🖋 MEDIEVAL GERMAN TEXTS IN BILINGUAL EDITIONS SERIES

Sovereignty and Salvation in the Vernacular, 1050–1150, introduction, translations, and notes by James A. Schultz (2000)

Ava's New Testament Narratives: "When the Old Law Passed Away," introduction, translation, and notes by James A. Rushing, Jr. (2003)

History as Literature: German World Chronicles of the Thirteenth Century in Verse, introduction, translation, and notes by R. Graeme Dunphy (2003)

Thomasin von Zirclaria, *Der Welsche Gast (The Italian Guest)*, translated by Marion Gibbs and Winder McConnell (2009)

Ladies, Whores, and Holy Women: A Sourcebook in Courtly, Religious, and Urban Cultures of Late Medieval Germany, introductions, translations, and notes by Ann Marie Rasmussen and Sarah Westphal-Wihl (2010)

🖋 VARIA

The Study of Chivalry: Resources and Approaches, edited by Howell Chickering and Thomas H. Seiler (1988)

Studies in the Harley Manuscript: The Scribes, Contents, and Social Contexts of British Library MS Harley 2253, edited by Susanna Fein (2000)

The Liturgy of the Medieval Church, edited by Thomas J. Heffernan and E. Ann Matter (2001; second edition 2005)

Johannes de Grocheio, *Ars musice*, edited and translated by Constant J. Mews, John N. Crossley, Catherine Jeffreys, Leigh McKinnon, and Carol J. Williams (2011)

🖋 TO ORDER PLEASE CONTACT:

Medieval Institute Publications
Western Michigan University
Kalamazoo, MI 49008-5432
Phone (269) 387-8755
FAX (269) 387-8750
http://www.wmich.edu/medieval/mip/index.html

Typeset in 10/13 New Baskerville
and Golden Cockerel Ornaments display

Medieval Institute Publications
College of Arts and Sciences
Western Michigan University
1903 W. Michigan Avenue
Kalamazoo, MI 49008-5432
http:/ /www.wmich.edu/medieval/mip

Printed and bound by CPI Group (UK) Ltd, Croydon, CR0 4YY

 WESTERN MICHIGAN UNIVERSITY